OXFORD STUDII

OXFORD STUDIES
IN ANCIENT
PHILOSOPHY

EDITOR: DAVID SEDLEY

VOLUME XIX

WINTER 2000

OXFORD
UNIVERSITY PRESS

OXFORD
UNIVERSITY PRESS

Great Clarendon Street, Oxford OX2 6DP

Oxford University Press is a department of the University of Oxford.
It furthers the University's objective of excellence in research, scholarship,
and education by publishing worldwide in

Oxford New York

Athens Auckland Bangkok Bogotá Buenos Aires Calcutta
Cape Town Chennai Dar es Salaam Delhi Florence Hong Kong Istanbul
Karachi Kuala Lumpur Madrid Melbourne Mexico City Mumbai
Nairobi Paris São Paulo Shanghai Singapore Taipei Tokyo Toronto Warsaw
and associated companies in Berlin Ibadan

Oxford is a registered trade mark of Oxford University Press
in the UK and in certain other countries

Published in the United States
by Oxford University Press Inc., New York

British Library Cataloguing in Publication Data
Data available

Library of Congress Cataloging in Publication Data
Oxford studies in ancient philosophy.—
Vol. xix (2000).—Oxford: Clarendon Press;
New York: Oxford University Press, 1983–
v.; 22 cm. Annual.
1. Philosophy, Ancient—Periodicals.
B1.O9   180.'5—dc.19   84–645022
AACR 2   MARC-S

ISBN 0-19-924225-9 (pbk)
ISBN 0-19-924226-7

1 3 5 7 9 10 8 6 4 2

Typeset by John Waś, Oxford
Printed in Great Britain
on acid-free paper by
T. J. International Ltd., Padstow, Cornwall

CONTENTS

NO ONE ERRS WILLINGLY:
THE MEANING OF SOCRATIC
INTELLECTUALISM

HEDA SEGVIC

ἑκὼν ἑκὼν ἥμαρτον, οὐκ ἀρνήσομαι.
(Willingly, willingly I erred; I won't deny it.)
[AESCHYLUS], *Prometheus Bound*, 266

Video meliora proboque, deteriora sequor.
(I see what is better and approve of it, but pursue what is worse.)
OVID, *Metamorphoses*, 7. 20

Concepts, just like individuals, have their history and are no
more able than they to resist the dominion of time, but in and
through it all they nevertheless harbour a kind of homesickness
for the place of their birth.
SØREN KIERKEGAARD, *The Concept of Irony*, 13. 106

I

THE Western philosophical tradition is deeply indebted to the figure of Socrates. The question 'How should one live?' has rightly
been called 'the Socratic question'. Socrates' method of cross-
examining his interlocutors has often been seen as a paradigmatic
form of philosophical enquiry, and his own life as an epitome of the
philosophical life. What philosophers and non-philosophers alike
have often found disappointing in Socrates is his intellectualism. A
prominent complaint about Socratic intellectualism has been memorably recorded by Alexander Nehamas: 'And George Grote both
expressed the consensus of the ages and set the stage for modern

I am grateful to Myles Burnyeat, David Furley, John McDowell, and Julius Moravcsik for their helpful comments on earlier versions of this paper. I also wish to thank
the editor of *Oxford Studies in Ancient Philosophy* for his generous criticisms and
corrections.

attitudes toward Socrates when he attributed to him "the error . . . of dwelling exclusively on the intellectual conditions of human conduct, and omitting to give proper attention to the emotional and volitional".[1]

The complaints against Socratic intellectualism take two main forms. According to some, Socrates ignores or overlooks—or at least vastly underestimates the importance of—the emotional, desiderative, and volitional sides of human nature, being too preoccupied with the intellect. The error attributed to him by Grote belongs here. The second line of criticism does not charge Socrates with ignoring or marginalizing desires, emotions, and volitions, but rather with giving an inadequate, over-intellectualist, account of them. These two lines of criticism have sometimes been combined, and sometimes confused. What they have in common is the thought that the desiderative, the emotional, and the volitional are not given their due by Socrates.

I wish to challenge this understanding of Socrates. He holds that living a good life is a matter of living in accordance with a certain kind of knowledge. Since knowledge is an accomplishment of reason, his view is in some sense intellectualist or, perhaps more appropriately, rationalist. However, I argue that desiderative, emotional, and volitional propensities and attitudes are an integral part of the knowledge in which Socrates locates virtue. This is meant to undermine the more prevalent first line of criticism. Towards the end of the paper I address the second line of criticism and suggest a different overall understanding of Socratic intellectualism, one that centres on the view that every act of the human soul involves an act of reason. I work my way towards this understanding of Socratic intellectualism by looking into the role that volitions, emotions, and desires play in Socratic virtue.

A large part of this paper deals with two Socratic theses. The first, that no one errs willingly, has long been recognized as crucial to Socratic intellectualism; however, the precise meaning of this thesis has remained elusive. I argue that 'willingly' is used here in a highly specific sense. The text which in my view offers the clue to the proper understanding of the No One Errs Willingly thesis is a passage in the *Gorgias* that has been much slandered in the literature

[1] Alexander Nehamas, 'Socratic Intellectualism', in his *Virtues of Authenticity* (Princeton, 1999), 24–58 at 27; the reference is to George Grote, *Plato and the Other Companions of Sokrates*, i (London, 1865), 399–400.

on Socrates. The argument has often been thought confused, and the whole passage has sometimes been treated as a deliberate exaggeration on Socrates' part. I claim that the passage makes perfect sense, that Socrates intends it seriously, and that it plays a central role in the overall philosophical structure of the dialogue. I then turn to the second thesis, that *akrasia*—weakness of the will, as the Greek term is usually rendered—does not exist. I offer an interpretation of the denial of *akrasia* based on my analysis of the No One Errs Willingly thesis. The joint reading of the two theses leads to a perhaps surprising result. Certain kinds of wantings and volitional propensities are constituents of moral knowledge. The same can be shown for desiderative and emotional attitudes and propensities. Far from disregarding the volitional, desiderative, and emotional, Socrates attempts to build them into his account of virtue as knowledge. Furthermore, his remarks on wanting or willing, sketchy and conversational though they are, point—I argue—to a distinct notion of the will. If Socrates does have a concept of the will, this is the first appearance of such a concept in the Western philosophical tradition.[2]

This interpretation shows that it is wrong to assume (as people have done since Aristotle) that Socrates ignores or marginalizes the desiderative and the emotional side of human nature, focusing solely on the intellectual.

II

Socrates claims that no one errs knowingly.[3] Why an intellectualist would make such a claim, we might think, is not so difficult to grasp. The intellectualist believes that when a person does what is

---

[2] We should not conclude from the fact that ancients discuss *akrasia*, which we label 'weakness of the will', that they have a concept of the will. The term *akrasia* indicates only some kind of weakness: the weakness of one who acts against his knowledge or better judgement of what is best. It is not uncommon to find the literature associating a notion of the will with this or that ancient figure, including Socrates. But it is not by dint of translation that we should come to think of the ancients as having a concept, or concepts, of the will, but by dint of interpretation and argument.

[3] See *Prot.* 352 C 2–7: 'Now, do you [Protagoras] too think that that is how things stand with it [sc. knowledge], or do you think that knowledge is fine and such as to rule the person, and if someone recognizes what is good and bad, he would not be overpowered by anything else so as to act otherwise than knowledge dictates, but wisdom is sufficient to help the person?' Protagoras promptly grants that knowledge has this power. See also 358 B 6–C 1.

morally wrong, that moral failure is due to an intellectual error. If only the person exercised his intellect well—if he knew better—he would not do what is wrong. Hence what we have to do in order to make people better, an intellectualist would have us think, is help them see how things really are; in particular, help them see what really is good or bad. I do not dispute that Socrates is a rationalist or intellectualist of some sort, or that a line of thought roughly corresponding to the one just sketched may be linked to his claim that no one errs knowingly. What I wish to emphasize is that in order to determine what *kind* of intellectualist he is, we must see how he conceives of the knowledge the absence of which he takes to be responsible for wrongdoing. I shall argue that Socrates' conception of moral knowledge makes many of the objections traditionally lodged against his intellectualism unwarranted.

In addition to claiming that no one errs knowingly, Socrates also claims that no one errs *willingly*. Why does he make this latter claim? An answer to this question does not leap to one's eye from the pages of Plato's dialogues. One would expect that, if anywhere, an answer is to be found in the *Protagoras*, where Socrates argues at length for the view that *akrasia* does not exist, and where he also briefly formulates, and appears to endorse, the claim that no one errs willingly (*Prot.* 345 C 4–E 6; cf. 352 A 1–358 D 4). But the *Protagoras* is silent on what precisely the dictum 'No one errs willingly' amounts to and how it is related to Socrates' denial of *akrasia*. In view of this silence, it is tempting to think that Socrates himself was in error. He must have thought, mistakenly, that 'No one errs knowingly' implies 'No one errs willingly'. Those who recall Aristotle's discussion of voluntary and involuntary action in the *Nicomachean* and *Eudemian Ethics* may be especially inclined to think that Socrates simply made an error in passing from 'knowingly' to 'willingly'.

Aristotle was the first Greek philosopher, as far as we know, to undertake a systematic analysis of voluntary and involuntary action, and to connect the voluntariness and involuntariness of actions with the agent's knowledge or ignorance. He tried to specify as precisely as he could the kinds of ignorance concerning the circumstances of an action that make it involuntary (see especially *NE* 3. 1 and 3. 4). He stressed that not every kind has this effect: for some sorts of ignorance people are neither forgiven nor pitied—as might be appropriate if their action were due to ignorance. Instead, they are blamed (*NE* 3. 1, $1110^{b}28$–$1111^{a}2$). In Plato, however, we find no comparable attempt at a careful philosophical analysis of voluntariness and involuntariness. So it would be plausible to think that Socrates perceived that knowledge of some kind is connected with voluntariness, but never looked into the thorny issue of voluntariness with proper care. That allowed him to overlook the blunder involved in passing from 'No one errs knowingly' to 'No one errs willingly'.[4] Tempting as this line of thought might be, we should resist it. We should not assume without examination that when Socrates describes someone as acting willingly, the action in question would be of the sort Aristotle classifies as 'voluntary'. (Likewise, we must not assume that those who on Socrates' diagnosis act unwillingly are not to be blamed for their actions.) The intended meaning of 'No one errs willingly' should be gleaned in the first place through careful reading of Plato's dialogues. The relevant passages seem to me to reveal that Socrates was not the least bit confused when he said that no one errs willingly.[5] Rather, I shall argue, he proposed a coherent and interesting, albeit unusual, view.

III

In Plato's *Protagoras* Socrates introduces the thesis that no one errs willingly (at 345 C 4–E 6) while presenting an analysis of a poem by Simonides. That no human being errs willingly is something, Socrates contends, that Simonides as a wise and educated person would surely have known. He proceeds to use this thought to guide his interpretation of Simonides, but he offers no gloss on the thesis itself. Although the *Protagoras* provides us with indispensable material for understanding Socrates' ethical outlook, and hence also for understanding the No One Errs Willingly thesis, a more direct clue to the meaning of this thesis comes from the *Gorgias*.

Our starting-point should be *Gorgias* 466 A 4–468 E 2. In his exchange with Polus Socrates declares that orators and tyrants do

---

[4] John McDowell takes this view in his unpublished piece 'Irwin's Socrates and an Alternative Reading'. The culprit, however, is ultimately Aristotle. See next note.

[5] It is not just our knowledge of the philosophical analysis of voluntary action provided later by Aristotle that might mislead us into thinking that Socrates was confused. The picture of him as confused about voluntariness probably originated with Aristotle himself. Evidence suggests that Aristotle saw Socrates as mistaken on two issues: first, the role of knowledge and ignorance in voluntary and involuntary action (see, in particular, *NE* 3. 1 on τὸ ἑκούσιον and τὸ ἀκούσιον), and second, the issue of the proper object of βούλησις—rational wish or wanting (*NE* 3. 4).

not do what they want to do (467 B 2, 466 D 8–E 1), and that they
have the least power of any in the city. Startled by this, Polus asks if
it is not the case that orators, just like tyrants, kill anyone they want
(ὃν ἂν βούλωνται), and subject anyone they please (ὃν ἂν δοκῇ αὐτοῖς)
to expropriation or exile (466 B 11–C 2). Socrates retorts that Polus
has raised two questions rather than one (466 C 7, 466 D 5–6), and
proceeds to draw a distinction between doing what one pleases, on
the one hand, and doing what one wants, on the other (466 D 5–E 2).
Applying this distinction, he now grants that orators and tyrants
do 'what they please' (ἃ δοκεῖ αὐτοῖς, at 467 A 3 and 467 B 8) or 'what
they take to be best' (ἃ δοκεῖ αὐτοῖς βέλτιστα εἶναι, at 467 B 3–4),[6]
but denies that they do what they want to do (ἃ βούλονται, 467 B 2,
B 6, 467 A 10; cf. 466 D 8–E 1)—presumably when engaged in the
actions mentioned: killing, expropriating, banishing. The passage
makes it fairly clear why Socrates claims that orators and tyrants
do not do what they want to do: what they do is not good, and one
can only want those things that are good (see especially 468 C 2–7).
But why should he construe 'wanting' in such a peculiar way? To
answer this question, we should take a broader look at the matters
discussed at 466–8.

Socrates' claim that neither orators nor tyrants do what they
want to do is meant to be startling. What in common opinion distinguishes a tyrant from others is precisely the enormous power
he has. As Polus had observed at 466 B 11–C 2, the tyrant can put
to death anyone he wants; he can dispossess or exile whomever he
pleases. Thus he can visit what in common opinion are the worst of
evils upon the head of anyone he wants. Another bit of common lore
is that having power consists in being able to do what one wants.
Power is so understood by Socrates' interlocutors in the Gorgias,
and Socrates raises no objection. What Gorgias and Polus add to
the common view is the claim that orators are at least as powerful
as tyrants, and probably more so (see especially 452 E 1–8). This,
of course, is advertising on behalf of oratory by its practitioners or

---

6 See also the variants: ὅτι ἂν αὐτοῖς δόξῃ βέλτιστον εἶναι (466 E 1–2) and ἃ ἂν δοκῇ
αὐτῷ βέλτιστα εἶναι (466 E 9–10). The two expressions 'what they please' (ἃ δοκεῖ
αὐτοῖς) and 'what they take to be best' (ἃ δοκεῖ αὐτοῖς βέλτιστα εἶναι) are treated by
Socrates as equivalent throughout the passage under consideration (466 A 4–468 E
2). A reader with no Greek will observe that the two expressions are rendered quite
differently in English, but actually they look very similar in Greek. To capture the
similarity, one could translate respectively 'what seems to them' (meaning roughly:
as they see fit, or as they please) and 'what seems to them to be the best'.

sympathizers. The advertisement none the less correctly identifies some of the aspirations, and some of the accomplishments, of oratory in the ancient world. Faced with Gorgias' and Polus' claims on behalf of oratory, Socrates does not take the obvious course, to reject as an exaggeration the claim that orators are so powerful. Rather, he takes the entirely non-obvious course of saying, first, that neither orators nor tyrants do what they want to do when they engage in the actions mentioned, and second, that they consequently have no great power in the cities. In making the transition from the first claim to the second, he relies on the above-mentioned assumption about power: to have power is to be able to do what one wants to do; to have a lot of power is to be able to do much of what one wants to do.

There can be no doubt that Socrates wants to shock his interlocutor by his apparently bizarre claim about orators and tyrants. Polus reacts as intended: he describes the claim as 'outrageous' and 'monstrous' (σχέτλια, ὑπερφυῆ, at 467 B 10). It would be a serious error, however, for us to understand the claim as a piece of histrionics, or an exaggeration meant to bring into sharper relief some other views that Socrates seriously holds.[7] He means what he says: orators and tyrants do not do what they want to do. If Polus is shocked by this claim, the shock is meant to prepare him for a more general claim which Socrates wants to be taken quite as seriously.[8]

That doing what one pleases or what one sees fit (ἃ δοκεῖ αὐτῷ) amounts to acting in accordance with one's opinion (δόξα) is suggested in Greek by the very form of the words (δοκεῖν is a verbal counterpart to the noun δόξα). This suggestion is further supported by *Gorg.* 469 C 4–7. There Polus explains to Socrates who, on his understanding, a tyrant is. A tyrant, he says, is someone who is 'in

---

[7] *Pace* Roslyn Weiss, in 'Killing, Confiscating, and Banishing at *Gorgias* 466–468', *Ancient Philosophy*, 12 (1992), 299–315. Her contention that the argument of 466–8 'deliberately . . . exaggerates and distorts' views that the Socrates of Plato's early dialogues 'seriously holds' (p. 299) strikes me as a counsel of despair in the face of the fact that the argument has persistently resisted coherent and plausible interpretation.

[8] The way Socrates proceeds here is not unusual. Something similar goes on during his interpretation of Simonides' poem in the *Protagoras* (338 E 6–347 A 5). In the course of making a peculiar sort of display, he introduces views he seriously holds, including the No One Errs Willingly thesis. A further similarity between his exercise in literary criticism in the *Protagoras* and his handling of Polus in the section of the *Gorgias* we are discussing is that he seriously proposes his thesis while being mockingly playful. Later in the *Gorgias*, as I shall point out below, he subjects Callicles to similar treatment.

a position to do whatever he pleases [ὃ ἂν δοκῇ αὐτῷ] in the city, whether it is killing a person or expelling him from the city, and doing everything [πάντα πράττοντι] in accordance with his opinion [κατὰ τὴν αὐτοῦ δόξαν]'. Polus here treats doing 'whatever he pleases' and doing everything 'in accordance with his opinion' as equivalent. The phrase quoted, πάντα πράττοντι κατὰ τὴν αὐτοῦ δόξαν, which I have rendered 'doing everything in accordance with his opinion', could equally well have been rendered 'doing everything as he pleases'.[9]

If doing what one pleases amounts to acting in accordance with one's *doxa*, opinion or belief,[10] and there is, Socrates suggests, a sharp contrast between doing what one pleases and doing what one wants, it is not unreasonable to suppose that doing what one wants is linked with acting in accordance with one's *epistēmē*, knowledge. I shall defend the view that this is indeed so. In fact, I shall propose that wanting, as understood by Socrates in the present context, is even more intimately connected with knowledge than the phrase 'acting in accordance with knowledge' might suggest. Before I do so, let me make some remarks about the appropriateness of bringing knowledge into the picture.

The contrast between *doxa*, opinion, and *epistēmē*, knowledge, is at the heart of the *Gorgias* as a whole. Socrates recoils from oratory, which he considers dangerous to the human soul. Oratory is dangerous because it enshrines mere *doxa*, opinion, and aims to convert it into πίστις, conviction, without regard for the truth of the opinion, hence *a fortiori* without regard for knowledge. πίστις, conviction, is what persuasion (πειθώ), if successful, leads to, and producing persuasion is the business of the orator. Following Gorgias' descriptions, Socrates characterizes the orator as a πειθοῦς δημιουργός, 'a manufacturer of persuasion' (*Gorg.* 453 A 2). Socrates sees himself, by contrast, as concerned with knowledge, hence he keeps denouncing practices that systematically bypass this concern.

---

[9] In Greek, the difference between acting κατὰ τὴν αὐτοῦ δόξαν and doing ἃ δοκεῖ αὐτῷ lies merely in choosing between a noun-based idiom and a verb-based one. The difference can be illustrated in English by a choice between, say, acting 'as one wishes' and acting 'in accordance with one's wish'.

[10] I use 'opinion' and 'belief' interchangeably. 'Opinion'—a more common rendition of δόξα in Plato—may be too narrow for the passages of the *Protagoras* and *Gorgias* under consideration here. Roughly, one has a δόξα when one takes something to be the case, correctly or incorrectly. This corresponds to 'belief' fairly well, as well as to 'opinion' loosely understood.

The orator and the tyrant, each in his own way, stand accused by Socrates of being mired in such practices. To say that doing as one pleases is to be understood as acting in accordance with one's opinion or belief invites the question: an opinion or belief about what? Likewise for acting in accordance with one's knowledge. As far as opinion or belief is concerned, the very fact that Socrates treats ἃ δοκεῖ αὐτοῖς, what pleases them (467 A 3, B 8), as interchangeable with ἃ δοκεῖ αὐτοῖς βέλτιστα εἶναι, what they think (believe, opine) is best (467 B 3–4), suggests an answer. The opinion is about what is best, or perhaps more generally about what is good, better, or best. Although I think that we can take our cue from the expressions Socrates uses, I do not mean to suggest that his understanding of these matters is determined by the peculiarities of certain Greek idioms. Socrates has philosophical reasons for seeing the matter this way—reasons which will emerge as we proceed. These reasons stand behind the form of words he uses.

My suggestion was that Socrates describes orators and tyrants as not doing what they want to do because in doing what they do they do not act in accordance with knowledge. But what does wanting have to do with knowledge? Why should only those who have knowledge, or perhaps those who have the relevant knowledge, be correctly described as doing what they *want* to do?

I propose the following, preliminary, characterization of the notion of wanting which Socrates relies on in the orators-and-tyrants passage: the agent wants to φ just in case he desires to φ taking φ-ing to be the good or right thing to do (in the circumstances in question), and his φ-ing (in those circumstances) is (or would be) good or right in the way he takes it to be. The point of glossing 'good' as 'right' is that wanting to do something, as wanting is understood here, does not merely involve a desire to φ because φ-ing is seen by the agent as having some goodness in it; the agent wants to φ only if he desires to φ seeing it as the right or correct thing to do.

Now this sort of wanting, which I shall call *Socratic wanting* or *willing*, is presumably still a desiderative state of some sort, in a broad sense of the word 'desiderative'. How can the ascription of a desiderative state to an agent possibly depend on the object of the desiderative state being in fact good? Whether an agent wants something, wishes for it, longs for it, and so on, depends on how he sees, or conceives of, the object of his wanting, wishing, or longing. Must we not leave open the possibility that the agent is wrong in his conception of the object desired, whatever the modality of his desire?

That, I take it, is how many people think of desiderative states; clearly, it is how Polus thinks of them. Socrates, however, is putting forward a different proposal. The issue here is not whether, generally speaking, one can be mistaken about the object of one's desire. Of course Socrates would agree that one can be. The issue is whether every kind of desire or volition that can be ascribed to a person is independent of the correctness of the person's conception of the object desired or wanted. A parallel may be of help here.

In claiming that orators and tyrants do not do what they want to do, Socrates is inviting us to think of *wanting* as a volitional state that is in some ways like perceiving. I do not perceive an object if I have some images; I perceive it only if my sensory impressions derive from the object itself in the right kind of way. Socratic volition is likewise a receptivity of the soul to certain evaluative properties of the object of volition, the properties Socrates designates by the term 'good'. However, wanting is not sheer receptivity; it is mediated by a correct conception of the object of desire as the good or the right thing to do. Just as perception latches on to that aspect of reality that has an impact on our sensory apparatus, so Socratic volition latches on to a certain evaluative aspect of reality. Thus this kind of wanting can be correctly ascribed to the agent only if the object of his volition has the required evaluative properties and the agent recognizes, and responds to, these properties. We should call to mind again the relationship between belief and knowledge. Whereas having a belief consists in taking something to be true,[11] knowing on Socrates' view is the secure grasp of truth. Likewise, he seems to suggest, whereas desire involves believing that the object of desire is good,[12] wanting—the sort of wanting referred to in the *Gorgias* passage—implies knowing that the object of volition is good.

I can now offer a more precise characterization of Socratic wanting: I Socratically want to ϕ just in case I want[13] to ϕ, recognizing

---

[11] If we want to be fastidious, we can say that believing is taking something to be the case, which implies that something—some proposition or statement—is true.

[12] See *Meno* 76 B 6–78 B 2. I shall come to this passage below.

[13] In this occurrence, 'wanting' should be taken in its generic sense, not implying a correct conception of the goodness of the object of the want. I take bitter medicines because I want to be healthy; I try to preserve my health because I want to live well, and so on.

that my ϕ-ing (in the given circumstances) is the good or right thing
to do.[14] Thus I (Socratically) want to ϕ only if my wanting to ϕ is
linked to my recognition of the goodness of ϕ-ing; if it is a mere
coincidence that I believe that ϕ-ing is the right thing to do and
that ϕ-ing in fact is the right thing to do, my wanting to ϕ is not
Socratic wanting.

This characterization is meant to bring Socrates' notion closer to
us, while staying reasonably close to his own idiom. Its drawback is
that it unravels a unitary notion: Socratic wanting is meant to be, I
think, both a volitional and a cognitive state. On the best reading, the
wanting would be a volitional state in virtue of being a certain kind
of cognitive state. Socrates has philosophical reasons for offering us
this notion of wanting. Before turning to them, let me make a few
remarks in defence of my interpretation of the orators-and-tyrants
passage.

IV

I have already pointed to one line of thought that makes it difficult to
understand why orators and tyrants do not do what they want to do.
This is the idea that the claim is a deliberate exaggeration or a piece
of histrionics. Another, more widely shared, line of thought is the
following. To understand the orators-and-tyrants passage one first
has to settle the question whether Socrates uses the verb 'to want'
in a special sense. For, if he does not use it in a special sense, then it
appears that his claim cannot possibly be true; but if he does use it in
a special sense, then he and Polus are not speaking of the same thing;
hence his disagreement with Polus, or with anyone who shares
Polus' point of view, is not genuine.[15] The prevalent interpretation

[14] Compare with this Socrates' formulation of what people take akrasia to be: the
many [who believe that there is such a thing as akrasia] say that 'a lot of people,
recognizing what is best [γιγνώσκοντας τὰ βέλτιστα], do not want to do it [οὐκ ἐθέλειν
πράττειν], when it is possible for them to do so, but do something else instead' (Prot.
352 D 6–7). The relevance of this comparison, which connects Socratic wanting to
his denial of akrasia, will become clear below.

[15] Terry Penner's interpretation of the passage is driven by an attempt to avoid the
second horn of the dilemma. He consequently aims to preserve the ordinary sense
of 'wishing' (his rendition of βούλεσθαι). According to Penner, Socrates' position is
this: orators and tyrants (like everyone else) do what they want to do only if they
get what they want. Whatever they may think they want, it is their real happiness
that they want in everything they do. The only action one ever wants to do (or
desires to do: there is no difference, on this view, between desiring and wanting or
wishing to do something) is the one that in fact leads to the ultimate end, one's own

of the passage seems to be that Socrates does introduce a special sense of 'wanting' in the passage under consideration, but that for this very reason his overall argument is marred by equivocation, and hence flawed.[16]

happiness, through the chains of means and ends that one has correctly envisaged (Terry Penner, 'Desire and Power in Socrates: The Argument of *Gorgias* 466 A–468 E that Orators and Tyrants Have No Power in the City', *Apeiron*, 24/3 (Sept. 1991), 147–202; see esp. pp. 170, 182–97). To use Penner's own example, if the tyrant's killing of his prime minister does not lead to the tyrant's happiness, in the way envisaged by him, we have to conclude that he did not want to kill his prime minister. I cannot offer here a detailed analysis of Penner's rather intricate interpretation. Anticipating the analysis I am about to provide, for Socrates there is indeed a legitimate sense in which we want to do things if the doing of them is good and otherwise we do not want them. This wanting is conditional not, as in Penner, upon what one *gets* from the action in the future, but upon the goodness of what is wanted through the action. The virtue of Penner's interpretation (as of his previous work on Socrates) is that he takes Socrates at his word, refusing to settle for 'charitable' readings of his claims. Thus I think that Penner is right in insisting that for Socrates the object of wanting (in one sense) is what really is good, rather than what one believes to be good. However, Penner in this article attributes to Socrates—and apparently himself subscribes to—an implausible general theory of desire (what we want or desire when we desire to do anything is, without exception, the whole chain of means leading to one's actual happiness, and if we don't obtain happiness by means of an action, then we did not want to do what we did), and an unattractive theory of action (no action is ever undertaken for its own sake). As I am about to argue, the dilemma which motivates Penner's interpretation is not, as he believes, inescapable. In the appendix below I offer an analysis of Socrates' argument at 467 C 5–468 E 5, and show that an instrumentalist account of action cannot be the correct interpretation of this passage.

[16] For a statement of this view see Robin Waterfield's note on *Gorg.* 468 D: 'The problem with the argument is that "want" is ambiguous, in a subtle way. To use the familiar philosophical example, Oedipus wants to marry Jocasta, but he does not want to marry his own mother; one can want and not want the same thing under different descriptions' (Plato's *Gorgias*, translated with explanatory notes by R. Waterfield (Oxford, 1994), 142). Further down, Waterfield accuses Socrates of trading on the ambiguity between 'good' and 'apparent good'. ('Just as importantly, Socrates' argument has not really dented Polus' position because of the ambiguity within "good"', ibid. 143; for this, compare Aristotle's discussion at *NE* 3. 4 on whether the good or the apparent good is the proper object of βούλησις.) Terence Irwin similarly claims that Socrates' question, 'Does A do what he wants?', is misleading, since the answer may be Yes when the action is considered under one description the agent believes true of it, and No when it is considered under another description. Consequently, Irwin takes Socrates' conclusion, that the orator and the tyrant lack power, as 'unjustifiably strong' (Irwin's notes to his translation of the *Gorgias* (Oxford, 1979), 145–6). According to Kevin McTighe, Socrates confuses *de dicto* and *de re* analyses of the verb 'to want'—see McTighe, 'Socrates on the Desire for the Good and the Involuntariness of Wrongdoing', *Phronesis*, 29 (1984), 193–236; repr. in Hugh H. Benson (ed.), *Essays on the Philosophy of Socrates* (Oxford, 1992), 263–97. McTighe provides a useful survey of the received interpretations of the orators-and-tyrants passage, all of which he sees as flawed (see esp. pp. 264–

As Socrates uses the verb 'to want' (βούλεσθαι) in the orators-and-tyrants passage, a sentence saying that someone wants something is false if what the person is said to want is not good. When βούλεσθαι is used in this way, the sentence in question has truth conditions that are different from those that the sentence would have if βούλεσθαι were used as Polus uses it, and as presumably most Greeks of this time would use it. So Socrates does use the verb 'to want' in a special way here. But from this it does not follow that he and Polus are speaking of different things, and hence cannot disagree. The notion of Socratic wanting is meant to express a truth about the underlying structure of human motivation. If we recognized this structure, Socrates appears to think, we would see that the notion is legitimate and useful. Not everyone would agree with his picture of human motivation, and he can disagree with those who reject it.

Socrates is aware that his construal of 'wanting' is not ordinary. When he introduces the distinction between doing what one wants, on the one hand, and doing what one pleases, on the other (*Gorg.* 466 c 9–467 c 4), he deliberately goes against Polus' prior implicit identification of the two. He has quite a bit of explaining to do before it becomes clear what he means by his claim that Polus has raised two questions rather than one (466 c 7–e 2). None the less, he speaks as if Polus is in some way committed to the distinction, whether he realizes this or not. The very fact that Socrates proceeds to produce an argument, at 467 c 5–468 e 5, for the thesis that orators and tyrants do not do what they want to do indicates that he does not take himself to be merely stipulating a new sense for the verb 'to want'. His argument starts from a more or less ordinary sense of 'wanting'. He begins by making claims about wanting that appear acceptable to Polus, as a person with commonsensical views about such matters, but somehow, at the end of the argument, Polus finds himself obliged to agree to the claim he had a little earlier labelled

7). The interpretation that seems to me closest to the truth is that of E. R. Dodds. I cannot agree with him when he says, in his classic commentary on the *Gorgias*, that the concept of wanting employed in the orators-and-tyrants passage—which he construes as the concept of what one really wants as opposed to what one thinks one wants—is 'perhaps only fully intelligible in the light of Plato's later distinction between the "inner man" who is an immortal rational being and the empirical self which is distorted by earthly experience' (Plato's *Gorgias*, edited with a commentary by Dodds (Oxford, 1959), 236). The passage appears to me to be fully intelligible without any such distinction. None the less, Dodds seems to me to be quite right in taking the notion of wanting here as special, and in recognizing that this does not vitiate Socrates' argument.

'outrageous' and 'monstrous'.[17] So it seems that the not exactly ordinary construal of wanting which Socrates proposes to Polus is meant to be connected with what Polus and others normally understand by 'wanting'.

At 468 B 1–4 Socrates formulates the following general claim about human motivation for action: 'Therefore it is because we pursue what is good that we walk whenever we walk—thinking that it is better to walk—and, conversely, whenever we stand still it is for the sake of the same thing that we stand still, [namely, for the sake of] what is good.' Although Socrates does not mention desire (other than wanting) in the *Gorgias* passage, he presumably would not deny that desires move us to act. However, looking at actions in terms of desire, the same principle holds—that we do whatever we do because we pursue what we take to be good—since Socrates believes that people always desire what they take to be good.

For this understanding of desire, we should look at *Meno* 77 B 6–78 B 2. The argument in this passage is meant to bring Meno round to the view that everyone desires good things. Socrates puts the following question to Meno: 'Do you assume that there are people who desire bad things [τῶν κακῶν ἐπιθυμοῦσιν], and others who desire good things [τῶν ἀγαθῶν]? Do you not think, my good man, that everyone desires good things?' (77 B 7–C 2). Further below, the object of desire turns out to be what the person who desires takes to be good, not what as a matter of fact is good. As for those who at first appear to Meno to desire what is bad (77 C 2–3), Socrates argues that they desire what they do thinking (οἰόμενοι) that it is good, and not recognizing (γιγνώσκοντες) that it is bad (77 C 3–E 4). Those who appear to desire what is bad are also described by Socrates as being ignorant about the object of their desire (ἀγνοοῦντες αὐτά [sc. τὰ κακά], 77 E 1 and E 2).

The object of desire according to the *Meno* passage is what people take to be good, whether or not their belief is correct. We should think of this as holding of all desiderative and volitional states: no one desires or wants a thing unless he takes it to be good. The sort of wanting Socrates invokes when he says that orators and tyrants do not do what they want to do is no exception; it fits entirely into the general theory of desire outlined in *Meno* 76–8. One does not Socratically want something without taking it to be good. But the notion of Socratic wanting is stronger, because the agent who

[17] An analysis of Socrates' argument at 467 C 5–468 E 5 is provided in the appendix.

Socratically wants to φ does not merely take φ-ing to be good; he recognizes φ-ing to be good. Thus Socrates does not waver between two different accounts of desiderative and volitional states, unclear whether it is the good or the 'apparent good' (that is to say, what people take to be good) that is the object of such states,[18] as some have suggested. He has a unified view of desire that covers all its modalities, plus a special notion of a volitional or desiderative state that is also a cognitive state. Socrates does think that this sort of wanting in some way underlies all other desiderative and volitional states. This, however, is part of a substantive philosophical position, not the result of an elementary confusion. I shall address this position in Section VII below. In the two sections that follow, I wish to bring out the larger significance of the orators-and-tyrants passage.

V

The ostensible conclusion of the discussion between Socrates and Polus at *Gorg.* 466 A 9–468 E 5 is simply that orators and tyrants— when engaged in killing, expropriating, and banishing—do not do what they want to do (468 E 3–5; see also 468 D 6–7). But Socrates' concern is clearly with anyone who does τὰ κακά, what is bad or wrong. Much later in the dialogue, at 509 E 2–7, he expressly formulates the conclusion of the argument in these wider terms. Talking now to Callicles, he refers back to his discussion with Polus. He says:

Why don't you answer at least this question, Callicles? Do you think that Polus and I were rightly forced to agree in our previous discussion [ἐν τοῖς ἔμπροσθεν λόγοις] that no one does what is unjust (or what is wrong)[19] wanting to [μηδένα βουλόμενον ἀδικεῖν], but that all who do what is unjust (wrong) do so unwillingly [ἄκοντας]? (*Gorg.* 509 E 2–7)

The conclusion of the discussion with Polus is now formulated as follows: no one who does what is wrong does so βουλόμενος, wanting to. βουλόμενος is directly contrasted with ἄκων, unwillingly, suggesting that we should construe βουλόμενος here as equivalent

---

[18] The term 'apparent good' is Aristotle's. It is, however, used by interpreters of Plato, especially to refer to the confusion Socrates is alleged to suffer from. See n. 16 above.

[19] The term ἀδικεῖν, 'to do what is unjust', can be used more broadly to include doing anything that is wrong.

to ἑκών, willingly.[20] If so, the conclusion of the orators-and-tyrants passage turns out to be the claim that no one errs willingly. For a more familiar wording of this claim, see *Prot.* 345 E 1–2: οὐδένα ἀνθρώπων ἑκόντα ἐξαμαρτάνειν, no human being errs willingly. The *Protagoras* passage reads in full:

For [says Socrates] Simonides was not so uneducated [ἀπαίδευτος] as to say that he praised whoever did nothing bad willingly [ὃς ἂν ἑκὼν μηδὲν κακὸν ποιῇ], as if there were anyone who willingly did bad things [κακά]. I am pretty sure that none of the wise men thinks that any human being errs willingly [οὐδένα ἀνθρώπων ἑκόντα ἐξαμαρτάνειν], or willingly does anything shameful or bad [αἰσχρά τε καὶ κακὰ ἑκόντα ἐργάζεσθαι]. They know well that all who do what is shameful or bad [πάντες οἱ τὰ αἰσχρὰ καὶ τὰ κακὰ ποιοῦντες] do so unwillingly [ἄκοντες ποιοῦσιν]. (*Prot.* 345 D 6–E 4)

The Greek verb translated as 'to err', ἐξαμαρτάνειν or ἁμαρτάνειν, ranges over a wide territory. It covers both doing wrong, in a moral sense, and simply going wrong, in the sense of making an error. This suits Socrates' purposes very well. We might try to capture the way in which ἁμαρτάνειν is suitable for his purposes by stating his position this way: no one commits injustice or does what is wrong willingly, but everyone who does wrong goes wrong. When wrongdoing is thought of as involving an error or mistake, it is easy to conclude that this is something one would not want to do. But however felicitous ἁμαρτάνειν may be for Socrates' purposes, he does not rely too heavily on the properties of this particular word.[21] When he suggests that Simonides was not so uneducated as to imply that a human being errs willingly, he may well be ironic, and in more than one way. None the less, he associates a recognition that no one errs willingly with education and wisdom, thus treating it as something that requires insight.

[20] I am not suggesting that Socrates always uses ἑκών as equivalent to βουλόμενος, but only that he does so in this specific context. For that matter, he does not always use βουλόμενος in the sense of Socratic wanting either. He does not do so, for instance, later in the *Gorgias*, at 511 B 4.

[21] A lot has been written about ἁμαρτία, especially in connection with Greek tragedy and Aristotle's *Poetics*. From the point of view of this paper, the most useful discussion is that of T. C. W. Stinton, 'Hamartia in Aristotle and Greek Tragedy', *Classical Quarterly*, NS 25 (1975), 221–54; repr. in Stinton, *Collected Papers on Greek Tragedy* (Oxford, 1990), 143–85.

VI

At *Gorg.* 509 E 2–7 Socrates gets Callicles to agree that no one does what is unjust or wrong wanting to, but that all those who do so do it unwillingly. The larger immediately relevant passage starts at 509 C 6. Socrates has been focusing his and Callicles' attention on two evils—the evil of suffering injustice (ἀδικεῖσθαι) and the evil of doing it (ἀδικεῖν). Now he raises the question of what it would take for us to save ourselves from falling into each of the two evils. In each case, he asks, is it δύναμις, power, or βούλησις, wish—as βούλησις is customarily translated—that enables us to avoid the evil in question?

To avoid being treated unjustly, Socrates and Callicles quickly agree, one needs power (509 D 3–6). But what about doing what is unjust: is it δύναμις or βουλήσις—power or wish—that saves us from this evil? Socrates permits Callicles to say that one needs power in this case as well (510 A 3–5), even though just a moment ago he had secured Callicles' agreement to the conclusion of the previous discussion with Polus, that no one does what is unjust βουλόμενος, wanting to so do (509 E 5–7). He intends Callicles to make the required connection between βούλησις and βουλόμενος. Like Polus before him, Callicles does not quite get Socrates' point. But Callicles is not entirely wrong in his answer, and this may be the reason why Socrates lets him off as he does. βούλησις—as construed by Socrates—is sufficient for a person not to do what is unjust. But this βούλησις, of course, is not merely a *wish*, but rather *wanting* or *willing* in the highly specific sense that Socrates had introduced in his discussion with Polus, and reintroduced here in his discussion with Callicles. This kind of wanting or willing is (in a certain sense) power. Socrates' point is the following. To avoid becoming a victim of an unjust action, one needs power in the straightforward sense; indeed, the power often needed is brute force. To avoid committing injustice, on the other hand, what a person needs is that his will be in a certain condition. When one's will is in this condition, one has all the power one needs, and all the power one can have, not to do what is unjust.

In speaking here of one's will being in a certain condition, I am of course relying on some more current notion of the will. There has been a long-standing dispute over the question whether the ancients had any notion of the will. Presumably, given the large number of widely different conceptions of the will that have emerged in Western philosophical thought since antiquity, the question is whether any of the ancient thinkers had a notion that is in some important way linked to one or more of these later notions. In his claim that orators and tyrants do not do what they want to do, as well as his claim that no one errs willingly, as I have interpreted these claims, Socrates introduces—apparently for the first time in Greek philosophical thought—a certain notion of the will, or something very much like such a concept. This notion of the will is in some ways peculiar. The βούλησις in question—the will, understood as I have suggested—prevents us from doing anything that is wrong. If so, this will—which is essentially the good will—cannot be weak. (This point is linked to Socrates' denial of *akrasia*, which I discuss below.)

We should not fail to notice the playfulness with which Socrates takes up the question whether it is δύναμις or βούλησις that can save us from the evils of suffering and of doing injustice (509 D 2–510 A 5). The playfulness in part depends on the usual meaning of βούλησις—that of a wish. Socrates asks about δύναμις and βούλησις in the course of renewing his argument for the view that the evil of suffering injustice is utterly trivial in comparison with the evil of doing injustice. To acquire things that are much prized by people, a great deal of power is usually needed. What makes the tyrant so enviable to many is the tremendous power he has—power so unrestricted that he can deprive people of what are considered to be their greatest goods: their life, their property, a place in their own city. It now turns out that the evil which it is incomparably more important to avoid—the evil of doing injustice—does not require the usual machinery of power. It would seem, in fact, that nothing could be easier than securing something by means of a wish. Neither the brute force the tyrant employs, nor the skilful manipulation of the soul by words that the orator relies on, is required here. What one needs, Socrates appears to suggest, is hardly anything at all: a mere wish, βούλησις. However, if one follows him to the end of his thought, it transpires that this thing—βούλησις in the sense of Socratic wanting or willing—is something that it is tremendously difficult to have.

Power was also the main ground on which earlier in the dialogue the great orator Gorgias had defended and praised oratory. In arguing that orators are at least as powerful as tyrants, Gorgias had relied on the enormous and nearly universal appeal of power. Polus inherited his argument from Gorgias. Thus in discussing the tyrant's actions of killing, expropriation, and banishing with Polus, Socrates is still addressing Gorgias' defence of oratory. Socrates now in response leaves his three interlocutors, Gorgias, Polus, and Callicles, with the following dilemma: either the power that enables a person to inflict what people consider to be the greatest evils on others is not good, and hence not something to be in the least admired, coveted, or envied; or else if power as such is good, orators and tyrants have none of it.

The notion that power as such is something good—clearly a notion that all three of his interlocutors are eager to push—undergoes a peculiar, deliberate transformation at Socrates' hands. He in effect offers his interlocutors an option of choosing between two concepts of power. In both cases power is the ability to do as one wants. On the first concept, a person is powerful if he can do what he wants or desires, as the words 'wants' or 'desires' are usually understood. On the second concept, a person is powerful if he can do what he wants in the more special sense—in the sense of what I have called Socratic wanting. Socrates is not blind to the fact that this notion is a novelty to his interlocutors. What he wants is to recast the debate in a novel way. Gorgias, Polus, and Callicles may insist as much as they please that power, as they understand it, is good. They are simply wrong about this. Relying now on the second concept of power—the one that Socrates himself is pushing—virtue is power. To express his thought in a different way: a certain kind of knowledge, and a certain kind of will, are power.

VII

Socrates seems to propose his special notion of wanting—that of Socratic wanting—not as a notion we already have at work in our language, but rather as a notion that we occasionally grope for, and a notion that we need. We need it because it enables us to express something that is of relevance to all the willing, wishing, and desiring that we ordinarily do and ordinarily speak of.

The notion of Socratic wanting announces a certain ideal. There is nothing arbitrary, however, about this ideal. Desires and wants of all varieties are, as we would put it, intentional phenomena. They are directed towards something. In Socrates' view, they embody a certain direction of the soul: a striving of the soul for what is good, and a striving of the soul for its own good, or perhaps for the good proper to a human being. The ideal of wanting that he introduces in the orators-and-tyrants passage, and in its follow-up later in the *Gorgias* (509 C 6 ff.), is meant to embody the shape that this striving of the soul takes when the soul has got a grip on what the good that it is after in fact is.

The Socrates of Plato's early dialogues does not often invoke human nature. But here is what we find him saying about it in the *Protagoras*:

Now, no one goes willingly towards things that are bad [ἐπί γε τὰ κακὰ οὐδεὶς ἑκὼν ἔρχεται] or towards those one thinks are bad [οὐδὲ ἐπὶ ἃ οἴεται κακὰ εἶναι], nor is it in human nature [ἐν ἀνθρώπου φύσει], so it seems, to want to go towards what one thinks is bad instead of to what is good [ἐπὶ ἃ οἴεται κακὰ εἶναι ἐθέλειν ἰέναι ἀντὶ τῶν ἀγαθῶν]. And when one is forced to choose between two bad things, no one chooses the greater if he is able to choose the lesser. (*Prot.* 358 C 6–D 4)[22]

We, humans, are hardwired to seek our own good. What we want is, ultimately, to do well for ourselves. The striving for this condition of doing well, which Socrates calls 'the good', is something that every human soul comes equipped with. Striving after the good is as basic to the human soul as is its striving after the truth.

With regard to the considerations that impelled Socrates to introduce his special concept of wanting, it may be useful to quote a passage from outside what we consider Plato's Socratic writings, even if we do not, as we should not, treat it as evidence for the Socratic view:

And isn't this also clear? In the case of just and beautiful things [δίκαια . . . καὶ καλά], many would accept things that are believed (reputed) to be so [τὰ δοκοῦντα], even if they are in fact not so, and they do such things, acquire them, and get a reputation for doing and acquiring them [ὅμως ταῦτα πράττειν καὶ κεκτῆσθαι καὶ δοκεῖν].[23] But when it comes to good things, no

---

[22] I return to this passage in sect. x below.

[23] Older English translations of this passage seem to me greatly preferable to the more recent ones. The first English translator, Spens (1763), is very much on the right track: 'But what, is it also not evident, that with reference to things just and beautiful, the multitude chuse the apparent, even though they be not really so, yet they act, and possess, *and are reputed of accordingly*; but the acquisition of goods . . .' (emphasis added). The best rendition, to my mind, is that of Davies and Vaughan (1852), who clearly take ταῦτα πράττειν καὶ κεκτῆσθαι as the antecedent of

one is content to acquire things that are believed to be so [ἀγαθὰ δὲ οὐδενὶ ἔτι ἀρκεῖ τὰ δοκοῦντα κτᾶσθαι], but everyone seeks things that are in fact good [ἀλλὰ τὰ ὄντα ζητοῦσιν] and spurns mere belief [τὴν δὲ δόξαν ἐνταῦθα ἤδη πᾶς ἀτιμάζει] . . . This, then, [sc. the good] is what every soul pursues [διώκει] and for the sake of which it does everything it does . . . (*Rep.* 505 D 5–E 1)

Whatever special interpretation Plato might be putting in the *Republic* on the distinction between τὰ δοκοῦντα and τὰ ὄντα—things that are reputed (opined, believed) to be good, on the one hand, and things that are good, on the other—there can be no doubt that the Socrates of the early dialogues is interested in a similar distinction: a distinction between what *appears* to be good, and what *is* good. Towards the end of the *Protagoras*, Socrates announces that it is the power of appearance (ἡ τοῦ φαινομένου δύναμις) that makes us wander all over the place and regret our actions and choices (356 D 4–7). We mistakenly take for good things that in fact are not good, but merely appear to us to be so. If we had knowledge about what is good and bad, the appearing (τὸ φάντασμα) would lose its grip over us (become ἄκυρον, 356 D 8); consequently, we would achieve peace of mind (ἡσυχία, 356 E 1) and salvation in life (σωτηρία τοῦ βίου, 356 D 3; see also 356 E 2, E 6, E 8, and 357 A 6–7).

Furthermore, both the Socrates of the *Republic* and the Socrates of the *Protagoras* take goodness to be an evaluative property of a special sort. No other question is of more importance to the business of living than the question 'Is this (what I am about to do, what I contemplate doing, what I am doing) really good?' We might believe that the action we are considering is admirable or useful; or that we shall be envied for it; or perhaps that it is in keeping with our outlook, although we shall be despised for it. But the nagging question always remains whether the action under consideration is really good; whether in acting as we do, we do good for ourselves.[24] This concern is the driving force behind much

---

δοκεῖν: 'Once more: is it not evident, that though many persons would be ready to do *and seem to do*, or to possess *and seem to possess* what seems just and beautiful, without really being so; yet when you come to things good . . .' (quoted from the 4th edn. (1868); emphasis added). καὶ δοκεῖν is misconstrued by Lindsay (1935), Grube (1974), and Grube–Reeve (1992). Until they provide a parallel for their construal of δοκεῖν, the older translations must take precedence. The Grube–Reeve translation reads: 'In the case of just and beautiful things, many people are content with what are believed to be so, even if they aren't really so, and they act, acquire, *and form their own beliefs* on that basis' (emphasis added).

[24] We should set aside the complaint that Socrates wavers between two different

Heda Segvic

:tion. But it is a concern that is operative already at a
є level. What the nagging question brings out is that we
ʲectively no less than reflectively—not at what appears
what is in fact good.

ꞁ nus the special, Socratic wanting is what wanting becomes when we have tracked down what we have been after all along. What we have been after all along—what our desiderative states are always tracking down—is where our well-being in the world lies.

VIII

In saying that no one errs willingly Socrates has in mind, roughly, that no one does what is wrong recognizing it as wrong and wanting it as one wants things one recognizes to be good. We might find it helpful to put the thought this way: no one does what is wrong knowingly and willingly. But Socrates has no need to add 'knowingly' to 'willingly', since his claim that no one does what is wrong willingly implies that no one does it knowingly. If 'willingly' is understood as I have suggested, the claim is clearly not that wrongdoing is involuntary in Aristotle's sense of the word (see *NE* 3. 1). If one thinks that Socrates takes wrongdoing to be involuntary in Aristotle's sense of the word (or in something close enough to this sense), one will feel a need to explain how he came to embrace such a view. This, I think, is what gives rise to the mistaken belief that he infers that no one does what is wrong willingly from the idea that wrongdoing involves ignorance. He fails to realize—unlike Aristotle after him—that only certain kinds of ignorance concerning one's action make that action involuntary (cf. Section II above). On the reading I have proposed, Socrates' claim makes perfect sense; it does not reflect any such gross failure of judgement.

Special as the notion of Socratic wanting or willing is, it is part of a larger disagreement with many of us. Socrates believes, for instance, that all who do what is wrong do so simply because they go wrong. Wrongdoers do not aim at something they recognize as wrong or bad; rather, they are misguided and ignorant about the nature of their action and its goal. Further, the thesis that no one

questions—the question of what is good, and the question of what is good for the agent. The more basic question for him is: what is good? He does also think that everyone seeks his own good. However, since 'what is good for the agent' has little antecedent content, it is left open what the content of the ultimate good will turn out to be. The ultimate good need not be egoistic.

errs willingly, as will transpire shortly, implies that *akrasia* is not possible. This is certainly not what many of us today think about weakness of the will, or what many people thought about *akrasia* in Socrates' own time.[25] We ought to start, however, with the position that Socrates takes himself to be denying when he rejects *akrasia*. At *Prot.* 352 D 4–7 Plato formulates with some care the position that Socrates rejects:

You [says Socrates to Protagoras] know that the many [οἱ πολλοὶ τῶν ἀνθρώπων] are not going to be persuaded by us. They say that a lot of people [πολλούς], recognizing what is best [γιγνώσκοντας τὰ βέλτιστα], do not want to do it [οὐκ ἐθέλειν πράττειν], when it is possible for them to do so [ἐξὸν αὐτοῖς], but do something else instead [ἀλλὰ ἄλλα πράττειν]...[26]

The view that Socrates rejects—imputed to and indeed put into the mouth of 'the many'—is that a lot of people act against their recognition, that is to say, against their knowledge, of what is best. This I take to be Socrates' primary, or official, characterization of *akrasia*.

Nowadays weak-willed action is often characterized as action against one's better judgement—one's judgement of what, under the circumstances, is the better thing to do. When understood in this way, there is no reason why an akratic action could not in principle be a good thing to do, or at any rate better than the action which the agent (incorrectly) takes to be better. However, according to the characterization of *akrasia* which Socrates gives in the passage quoted, akratic action is by assumption wrong: the akratic agent does what is wrong knowing that it is wrong, considering or having considered a different course of action that is open to him,[27] which

[25] To be sure, we should be careful here. We are dealing with more than one party. We are not Socrates' interlocutors: when he discusses *akrasia*, his interlocutors are the 'the many' that he conjures up (see, in particular, *Prot.* 352 B 2–3 and 352 D 5). The notion of *akrasia* that Socrates rejects is somewhat different from the notion (or notions) that we nowadays have of weakness of the will. None the less, as I shall later argue, there is some reason to think that he would not only deny the existence of *akrasia* as (he thinks) his contemporaries conceive of it; he would also deny the existence of *akrasia* as many of us nowadays think of it.

[26] Having formulated what an akratic action is, Socrates goes on to state the cause, τὸ αἴτιον, that the many cite to explain such an action. I shall follow him in keeping the issue of the 'cause' separate.

[27] Davidson argues that Socrates—or, strictly speaking, G. Santas, whose interpretation of Socrates Davidson discusses—fails to realize that an alternative course of action need not in fact be open to the agent, because the agent's *belief* that the course of action is open to him is sufficient. (Donald Davidson, 'How is Weak-

he knows to be better or best. It is because Socrates construes *akrasia* in this way, and not merely as action against one's better judgement, that his denial of *akrasia* follows from his No One Errs Willingly thesis.

One important aspect of the official characterization of *akrasia* at *Prot.* 352 D 4–7 has been generally overlooked. The many, Socrates says, claim that a lot of people, recognizing what is best, do not want to do it (οὐκ ἐθέλειν πράττειν), when it is possible for them to do it, but do something else instead. He invokes wanting here, and builds it into the characterization of *akrasia* offered by the many (see also ἐθέλει at 355 B 2, ἐθέλειν at 358 D 2, and ἐθελήσει at 358 E 3). Thus the thesis he intends to deny is not just that one can fail to do what one recognizes is best, but more fully that an agent may recognize what is best and yet not want, or not be willing, to do it, and consequently, not do it. By contrast, we have to assume, Socrates contends that a person who knows what the right thing to do is, does want to do it and, other things being equal, will do it. (The more neutral word for wanting, ἐθέλειν, that he uses here is appropriate since the position he is denying is that of the many, who would not put their own point in terms of Socrates' special notion of wanting or willing. To express his own position, Socrates could use either the more neutral ἐθέλειν or the more specific βούλεσθαι.)

If Socrates uses 'willingly' in a special way when he claims that no one errs willingly, to designate a volitional act that is also cognitive, does this not make his claim problematic? His concept of willing is not ours. What can we do with such a peculiar concept? In response, I shall match these questions with another one. Socrates' rejection

ness of the Will Possible', in *Essays on Actions and Events* (Oxford, 1980), 21–42 at 22 n. 1; the reference is to Santas's article 'Plato's *Protagoras* and Explanations of Weakness', *Philosophical Review*, 75 (1966), 3–33). Davidson's remark is appropriate given his perspective on weakness of the will. But Socrates is not in error here. His characterization reflects his approach to *akrasia*. Unlike us (and, to some extent, unlike Aristotle), Socrates approaches *akrasia* from outside in. He focuses on putative akratic actions that are in fact cases of wrongdoing, where an alternative course of action is available to the agent and is *recognized* by the agent as available to him. Socrates is interested in (putative) *akrasia* as an ethical problem—primarily an ethical problem of wrongdoing of some kind. One could, of course, restate his views on *akrasia* by taking in an inside-out approach, focusing on the beliefs that the agent has about the action he takes and about the alternative course of action available to him. I shall go on to address this approach (which Socrates to some extent adopts later on in the *Protagoras*: see 358 C 6–D 4), but only after I have looked into what I take to be the primary account of *akrasia*, given in a preliminary fashion at *Prot.* 352 B 5–8, and then, more carefully, in the passage just quoted, 352 D 4–7.

of *akrasia* amounts to the view that one cannot act against one's knowledge of what is best. Now the conception of knowledge that underlies this view should strike us as at least as peculiar as the concept of Socratic wanting. Here is what Socrates has to say about the relevant kind of knowledge:

Now, do you [Protagoras] too think that that is how things stand with it [sc. knowledge], or do you think that knowledge [ἐπιστήμη] is fine and such as to rule the person, and if someone recognizes what is good and bad [ἐάνπερ γιγνώσκῃ τις τἀγαθὰ καὶ τὰ κακά], he would not be overpowered by anything else so as to act otherwise than knowledge dictates, and wisdom [τὴν φρόνησιν] is sufficient to help the person? (*Prot.* 352 C 2–7)

We no more share with Socrates his conception of *knowledge* than we share with him his conception of *wanting* or *willing*. But if this is so, should we regard his claim that no one errs willingly as more suspect than his claim that no one errs knowingly? As I pointed out at the beginning of this paper, the wanting or willing that the expression 'willingly' refers to involves recognition of what is good or bad; it has now turned out that the knowledge of what is good and bad involves wanting that accords with the knowledge in question. Hence, one claim is as problematic or as unproblematic as the other; both claims stand or fall together. They should also be examined together.

IX

Socrates does not want to deny that we have episodes which we incorrectly describe as akratic or weak-willed. We should now take a look at his characterization of the 'cause' of *akrasia*, which is kept separate from the characterization of *akrasia* itself. We have heard what the many believe: that a lot of people, recognizing what is best, do not want to do it, but do something else instead (352 D 4–7). When asked what they think the cause (αἴτιον) of this is (D 7–8), the many—according to Socrates—reply that 'those who act in this way do so being overcome [ἡττωμένους] by pleasure or pain, or being overpowered [κρατουμένους] by one of the things I [Socrates] referred to just now' (352 D 8–E 2). Socrates has in mind the things he referred to at 352 B 5–8, the passage in which he gives his first, informal characterization of *akrasia*. According to this characterization, the many believe that 'often, although knowledge is present in a person, what rules him is not knowledge but something else: sometimes anger [θυμόν], sometimes pleasure [ἡδονήν], sometimes pain [λύπην], at other times love [ἔρωτα], often fear [φόβον] . . .'. So, on the account given by the many, people act akratically—i.e. against their knowledge of what is best—because they are overcome by pleasure or pain, by desire, or by any of a number of passions. At *Prot.*

352 E 5–353 A 2 Socrates says that he and Protagoras should now attempt to persuade and teach the many what the πάθος is which the many describe as being overcome with pleasure, and which in their view is why they don't do what is best when they recognize what it is. He refers to the same thing as a πάθημα a few lines below, at 353 A 4–6: the many, he says, will demand an explanation from him and Protagoras as to what this πάθημα is, if it does not amount to being overcome by pleasure.[28] Thus Socrates grants that a certain πάθος or πάθημα—a particular way of being afflicted—is present. What is presumed to be missing is a correct characterization of this affliction. The two words, πάθος and πάθημα, which are here used interchangeably, refer, I believe, not to the experience associated with putative *akrasia* but to the affliction of the putative akratic—namely, what a person undergoes when he undergoes what the many think of as *akrasia*. The usual translation of πάθος or πάθημα as 'experience' does not seem to me to be accurate. When Socrates draws attention to what is happening with the presumed akratic agent, he may have in mind an experience that the agent has, but he need not. For instance, when he further down declares that the πάθημα in question is in fact ignorance (357 C 7), he is not saying that the *experience* characteristic of putative *akrasia* is ignorance, but rather that the condition of the agent's soul that is wrongly attributed to *akrasia* is in fact ignorance.

Keeping in mind Socrates' preliminary formulation of *akrasia* at 352 B 5–8, and bypassing the hedonistic assumptions from which the discussion of *akrasia* in the *Protagoras* proceeds,[29] the description 'being overcome by pleasure' should be taken as representative of a number of related descriptions that the many had offered to explain *akrasia*. The presumed akratic was described at 352 B 5–8 as

[28] Socrates comes back to this πάθημα at 357 C 7. He is now ready to provide his answer to the question pressed by the many. The πάθημα in question, he now claims, is ignorance (ἀμαθία). See 357 E 2–4.

[29] Here and in what follows I am interested in Socrates' general position on *akrasia*. I thus aim to reconstruct the considerations on which he based his rejection of *akrasia* in a way that should be of interest to hedonists and non-hedonists alike.

being overcome not only by pleasure, but also by pain, desire, fear, love, and so on. In speaking of the condition of being overcome by passion below, I use 'passion' broadly, to refer to any of these states. It would be wrong to assume that Socrates has an easy task here. Once we strip the phenomenon commonly described as *akrasia* of all the descriptions Socrates would find incorrect, it is not quite clear what remains. This, I take it, sets him a task. We speak of our akratic episodes; we know what it feels like to be in the grip of one; we understand what others have in mind when they describe theirs. This presumably is not what Socrates wants to deny. But when the many say, for instance, that people are overcome (ἡττώμενοι or κρατούμενοι) by passion, they seem to have in mind a contest of two forces: one that wins and one that is defeated (being defeated is a usual meaning of ἡττώμενος). Socrates, as we shall see, rejects the picture of contest between two forces as a proper description of what happens in putative *akrasia*. The agent is not really acting against his knowledge; nor is he, as I am about to argue, acting against his better judgement. If this is so, Socrates should be able to tell us how to identify the putative phenomenon of *akrasia* in a way that is independent of all the incorrect descriptions usually given of it. In the *Protagoras* he does not endeavour to do this.

X

Let me now turn briefly to a broader notion of *akrasia*, one that involves acting against one's judgement or belief[30]—not necessarily against one's knowledge—that some course of action is best. The characterization of *akrasia* in the *Protagoras* discussed so far has not included this kind of case. However, in the course of arguing against *akrasia* as officially characterized, Socrates makes observations that amount to grounds for rejecting *akrasia* in a broader sense, viz. *akrasia* thought of as action against one's judgement as to what is best.

The main thought behind this denial can be expressed in the following way. *Akrasia* presupposes an awareness on the part of the agent of alternative courses of action available to him. What

---

[30] One might argue that making an evaluative judgement can fall short of holding an evaluative belief. However, I think that Socrates would not want to make a distinction between belief and judgement. To judge that something is good is to take it as good, and taking something to be such-and-such is on his view a δόξα, opinion or belief.

28   Heda Segvic

supposedly happens here is this: the agent considers two courses
of action; he believes that one of them is correct; none the less, he
does what he believes to be wrong. The main reason why Socrates
thinks this is not possible is that our actions embody our evaluative
beliefs, and that they embody them in a very strong sense. By going
for one of the considered alternative courses of action rather than
the other, the agent shows that he takes the preferred course of
action to be better. Recall again Socrates' statement about human
nature:

Now, no one goes willingly towards things that are bad [ἐπί γε τὰ κακὰ
οὐδεὶς ἑκὼν ἔρχεται] or towards those one thinks are bad [οὐδὲ ἐπὶ ἃ οἴεται
κακὰ εἶναι], nor is it in human nature [ἐν ἀνθρώπου φύσει], so it seems, to
want to go towards what one thinks is bad [ἐπὶ ἃ οἴεται κακὰ εἶναι ἐθέλειν
ἱέναι] instead of to what is good. And when one is forced to choose between
two bad things, no one will choose the greater if he is able to choose the
lesser. (*Prot.* 358 c 6–d 4)[31]

In saying that no one goes willingly towards bad things (ἐπὶ . . .
τὰ κακά), Socrates has in mind that no one goes willingly towards
things that are bad, when it is transparent to the person's mind
that they are bad. (Similarly for choosing between two bad things.)
One reason why one cannot act against one's knowledge of what is
better is that by acting so one would show one has a belief that contradicts the knowledge in question. But Socrates' practice of cross-
examining his interlocutors implies that he thinks that a person who
has a body of knowledge cannot have a belief that contradicts it.

The main intuition behind Socrates' denial of *akrasia* in the
broader sense—the intuition that evaluative beliefs are both embodied and displayed in our actions—seems sound. This intuition
is presumably something that would be understandable and in some
form acceptable to the many. Socrates, however, pushes this thought
much further than the many. He presumably believes that taking
something to be good and going for it are connected far more tightly
than people tend to think.

Now when I φ, where this φ-ing is a presumed akratic action, and
I take myself to be acting against my belief that my φ-ing (here and
now) is wrong, or worse than an alternative action open to me, is
my belief that I have such a belief an illusion? Socrates' views on
doxa, opinion or belief, seem to push him in two different direc-

---

[31] Compare also 358 E 2–6.

tions. On the one hand, having a belief on his view implies having a commitment. Evaluative beliefs in particular involve practical commitments. So he might well argue that the presumed akratic is not committed to his professed evaluative belief to the degree that would be necessary for the ascription of the belief to him to be correct. If he took this line, what Socrates would be telling the presumed akratic is this: you claim to believe that your ϕ-ing (here and now) is wrong, but in fact you don't believe that. What you in fact believe, as your action shows, is that ϕ-ing (here and now) is good or right.

However, Socrates often uses *doxa* in a considerably more relaxed way. For instance, each of his interlocutors is said to have an opinion or belief whenever he sincerely agrees with the view that Socrates proposes for consideration. When we read in our translations of the *Protagoras* that this or that interlocutor 'concurred with' Socrates or 'agreed with' him, the word not infrequently used is συνδοκεῖν. The very word indicates that the interlocutor shares Socrates' *doxa*; that he believes (opines: δοκεῖν) that things are as Socrates says they are. The interlocutors often have a poor grasp of the content of what they agree to, and this (among other things) leads them to contradict themselves. Socrates takes such a contradiction as an indication that the interlocutor does not have knowledge, not that he does not have the relevant opinion or belief.[32]

When *doxa* is understood in this relaxed way, Socrates should say, as before, that the agent believes that his ϕ-ing (here and now) is right or good, since this belief is implied by his action. However, Socrates should now also grant that the presumed akratic agent believes that his ϕ-ing (here and now) is wrong. Now if Socrates

[32] For συνδοκεῖν see 358 B 6, C 3, C 6, and D 4. The four occurrences of συνεδόκει are part of an important global dialectical move Socrates makes at 358 A 1–359 A 1, at the end of his case against *akrasia*. He secures the agreement here not only of Protagoras, but also of Hippias and Prodicus, to the claim that pleasure is the good (358 A 5–B 6); to his denial of *akrasia* and his diagnosis of what in fact happens in putative *akrasia* (B 6–C 3), along with his explanation of what ἀμαθία is (C 3–6), and to the claim that no one willingly goes towards what he thinks is bad (C 6–D 4). In each case, συνεδόκει punctuates the concurrence in belief among the four principal interlocutors. What is at issue at 358 A 1–359 A 1 is what Protagoras, Hippias, and Prodicus believe, or rather have come to believe, having been persuaded by Socrates (see the instances of δοκεῖν at 358 A 3 and A 4, D 7, and E 6). Socrates then moves on to secure the agreement of all three to his definition of fear (358 D 5–359 A 1). Having secured these admissions, Socrates immediately (starting at 359 A 2) moves to show that Protagoras' position on the unity of virtue is incompatible with the admissions he has just made.

takes this line, then on his view an agent can after all act against his belief that his φ-ing (here and now) is wrong. Would this amount to a recognition of *akrasia* on Socrates' part? I have in mind here a recognition of *akrasia* understood in the broader sense, i.e. *akrasia* thought of as action against one's belief about what is better or best. Although it is true that on this analysis the agent acts against his belief, I am inclined to think that this is not what those who hold that *akrasia* exists for the most part have in mind. Being akratic does not consist merely in acting against a belief, in a weak sense of this word, that something is good.[33] Although of course there are many conceptions of what *akrasia* consists in, the agent is usually thought to be acting against something a bit stronger than this sort of belief. I shall come back to this question in a moment.

Let me return to *akrasia* as originally defined—namely, as action against one's knowledge of what is better or best—and look at the diagnosis Socrates would give of the presumed akratic's predicament. It seems reasonable to assume that Socrates sees the putative akratic as himself believing that he acts against his knowledge of what is best. Admittedly, in his official characterization of *akrasia* at *Prot.* 352 D 4–7 Socrates does not explicitly state that the many believe *of themselves* that they often know what is best and yet do something else; his claim is rather that the many (οἱ πολλοί) allege that akratic episodes happen to many (πολλοί). Although this invites us to think that the relevant ascriptions of knowledge involve self-ascriptions, the formulation itself does not settle the question whether such self-ascription of knowledge is constitutive of (what passes for) *akrasia*.

There is some reason to think that it is. What makes it so difficult to deny *akrasia* is precisely the repeatedly insistent first-person claim: 'but—whatever your theory—I knew full well that what I was going to do was bad; yet I did it.' When we find it difficult to go along with philosophical worries concerning the existence of *akrasia*, we do so not because we are confident about third-person ascriptions of knowledge to agents who happen to act against their knowledge. What makes it difficult to deny *akrasia* is rather the first-person experience of going against one's own firm conviction that something is bad, often because of some powerful desire or

---

[33] This, I presume, is why Aristotle comes to think of *akrasia* as action against the agent's προαίρεσις, choice. As he understands it, προαίρεσις involves a firm practical commitment.

impulse. Is the firmly held conviction taken by the akratic himself to be a case of knowledge? In everyday life people often describe their weak-willed episodes this way; they do it when they say, for instance: 'But I *saw* clearly that this was bad; yet I did it.' This conception of *akrasia* is vividly conveyed by Ovid's memorable 'video meliora proboque, deteriora sequor', cited at the head of this paper. Except for being couched as a first-person statement, Ovid's formulation is strikingly close to Socrates' own (at *Prot.* 352 D 4–7): the akratic acts against what he *sees* is better—the Greek γιγνώσκειν, to recognize, has become the even more emphatic Latin *videre*, to see.[34]

If the akratic agent believes, Ovid-style, that he acts against his knowledge of what is better or best, Socrates' case against *akrasia* implies that this belief is false. Socrates would diagnose the Ovid-style akratic as suffering from the affliction he believed it was his task to unmask, and if possible, eradicate (see the *Apology*): ignorance of one's own ignorance. The akratic agent not only lacks knowledge of what is better or best; he also wrongly believes that he possesses this knowledge. When Socrates declares that the πάθος or πάθημα of being overcome by pleasure (or, in general, passion) is in fact ἀμαθία, ignorance[35]—indeed, ἀμαθία ἡ μεγίστη, the greatest ignorance—he might have in mind the ignorance of what is good or bad. However, every wrongdoer is on Socrates' view ignorant of what is good or bad. What is specific to the central type of wrongdoing that the many incorrectly describe as akratic is the specific ignorance of one's own ignorance that this type of wrongdoing involves.

Now what would be Socrates' diagnosis of the putative akratic condition if *akrasia* is construed more broadly, as action against one's better judgement? Here the diagnosis would have to await a more precise description of what *akrasia* is. There is a view ac-

---

[34] One interesting difference is that Socrates does not find it necessary to make separate mention of the approbative attitude that goes along with the recognition of what is better or best. The relevant knowledge or recognition, on his view, implies an approbative attitude.

[35] See *Prot.* 357 E 2–4: 'So this is what being overpowered by pleasure [τὸ ἡδονῆς ἥττω εἶναι] is, the greatest ignorance [ἀμαθία ἡ μεγίστη], which is what Protagoras here and Prodicus and Hippias claim to cure.' What Protagoras professed to teach earlier in the dialogue was (civic) virtue (318 E 5–319 A 2). It is because he claims to teach this (among other reasons) that Socrates, ironically, counts him as being on his side in the argument against the many. Protagoras had better know what putative *akrasia* is, since this issue is at the heart of his professed expertise.

cording to which we can go for something without taking it in any way as good. Values are here seen as being at some remove from the desires or impulses on which we act. So on this view an akratic may, for instance, do something in spite of his judgement that what he is about to do is bad; he does so simply because he 'feels like it', not because he values it in some way. If this is what it means to act against one's better judgement, Socrates would deny that such *akrasia* exists. He would do so because he would reject the view that the agent can act without taking anything to be good or bad. As the *Meno* passage referred to above indicates (as well as the statement in the *Protagoras* about human nature quoted above, 358 C 6–D 4), when an agent acts on a desire, he acts in accordance with the value judgement involved in the desire. This judgement is the one that motivates his action.

But suppose the opponent grants a part of Socrates' point, admitting that our actions are shot through with value judgements, and that value judgements are not motivationally inert; suppose he also agrees that it is not possible to go for something without considering it good in some way. The opponent might none the less think that it is possible to act against one's reflectively considered scheme of values, and he might propose that the 'better judgement' against which the akratic acts be identified with such a reflectively considered judgement. Would Socrates deny this?

Socrates would not be the one to deny that reflective thought can generate values. He could also hardly deny that one's impulses might go against reflectively generated values. However, *akrasia*, as usually understood, is not an affliction that consists merely in holding contradictory evaluative beliefs, and acting sometimes on one such belief and sometimes on another. *Akrasia* is more than confusion about values. A proponent of *akrasia* usually regards the so-called 'better judgement' as something more than a mere judgement that some course of action is better. The 'better judgement' is 'better' because it is reflectively endorsed; or because it has higher epistemic credentials; or because it is the judgement with which the person more fully and directly identifies.

For instance, having considered the evaluative point of view that pushes me into this action, I may form a judgement that the evaluative viewpoint in question is not one that I can ultimately embrace; a more carefully considered judgement, or a judgement that rests on a wider point of view, or a judgement that expresses more directly my will—these are the candidates for that 'better judgement' against which I act when I act akratically. But the more weight we thus put on the notion of better judgement, the less likely it is that Socrates would agree with us. It is likely that he would stick to his basic intuition that our actions reveal more about us and our values than any product of detached reflection might. As he would see it, the mere fact that a desire is a second-order one, or that it is endorsed by some second-order thinking on our part, is neither here nor there. The reflection he is interested in is practical reflection: one that changes preferences, and goes all the way down, to influence the very valuations on which we act. The more we add to the notion of better judgement in terms of one's identification with it, the closer we get to the grounds on which Socrates refused to admit that one can ever act against one's knowledge of what is better.

On his understanding of what knowledge is, in order to know that a course of action is good, it is not sufficient to believe that it is good, and to hold this belief for the right reasons. If one knows something, then on Socrates' view, one cannot have a belief that contradicts that knowledge. Knowledge of what is good precludes false appearances of goodness. This suggests that knowledge—the sort of evaluative and practical knowledge that he has in mind when he speaks of the knowledge of good and bad—cannot be had in bits and pieces. To have the relevant sort of knowledge is to be in possession of a certain regulative and organizing principle that is in control of the overall condition of the soul. Socrates seems to think of knowledge as a condition in which none of one's doxastic commitments ever goes unheeded. One does not concur with a certain opinion, and then proceed to concur with a contradictory opinion a little later; one does not say 'Yes', and fail to recognize what this 'Yes' implies. Hence knowledge could be ascribed only to someone who has thoroughly thought things out. Only someone who grasps what his beliefs imply and how his various beliefs hang together possesses knowledge.

Although the considerations that I have suggested might impel Socrates to reject *akrasia* in the broader sense (thought of as action against one's better judgement) must remain speculative, the considerations he relies on in denying *akrasia* as action against one's knowledge give the impression that he might not be easily persuaded into accepting the existence of *akrasia* by its latter-day proponents. I do not mean to suggest here that he would be likely to reject the possibility of a weak-willed action on most, or even many, present-day conceptions of weakness of the will. For instance, there is no reason why he should reject the notion that a person may act in a way that stands in conflict with some of his second-order desires. In denying *akrasia*, Socrates is denying a certain picture of how human motivation operates. Thus he would be likely to deny weakness of the will as thought of by those who subscribe to the wrong picture of human motivation. In my next section I turn to the issue of what conception of the human soul and its workings he intends to reject when he rejects *akrasia*.

XI

Socrates can deny *akrasia* without ever mentioning desire.[36] Citing the link between actions, on the one hand, and motivating beliefs or opinions, on the other, suffices to bring out the most general grounds on which he denies *akrasia*. However, his view of desires— and also more broadly of passions or feelings (πάθη)—is central to his rejection of what he presents as the cause, αἴτιον, of *akrasia*: the account the many give of how it comes about that one acts against one's knowledge (or belief) of what is better. Socrates' understanding of desires and passions is also central to his own full account of what actually goes on in putative cases of *akrasia*.

The common explanation of *akrasia* that he wants to reject has it that one acts akratically (weakly, as the Greek term indicates) because one is overcome by desire or passion. Recall again the view of the many: 'often, although knowledge is present in the human being, what rules him is not knowledge but something else: sometimes anger, sometimes pleasure, sometimes pain, at other times love, often fear; they [the many] think that his knowledge is dragged around by all of these just like a slave' (*Prot.* 352 B 5–C 1). At *Prot.* 358 D 5–7 Socrates characterizes fear as προσδοκία τις κακοῦ, some kind of expectation of something bad. The word προσ-δοκία, translated usually as 'expectation', means something like 'anticipatory belief'—the component -δοκια is closely related to δόξα, belief or opinion.[37] By adding τίς to προσδοκία (in Greek, *x* τις

---

[36] Indeed, that is what he does. In the *Protagoras* Socrates does not mention desire until his argument against *akrasia* is completed.

[37] The definition of fear as προσδοκία τις κακοῦ is sandwiched between συνεδόκει at

means, roughly, some *x*; a sort (kind) of *x*; *x* of a sort), Socrates apparently wants to indicate that not every sort of expectation of, or anticipatory belief about, something bad qualifies as fear. What sort of expectation of something bad in fact qualifies as fear is at least in part connected with the sort of bad or evil (κακόν) that is the proper object of fear. Socrates intends this as a genuine (even if not fully spelt out) definition of fear. However he would want to spell it out, he appears to take fear as a certain, highly specific, case of taking something to be bad. Other passions would presumably be characterized too in terms of their specific way of taking something to be good or bad. I have already argued that Socrates thinks of desires as involving beliefs that something is good. If we can think of desires as passions of some kind, it would follow that desires too are ways of taking something to be good.

Socrates is sometimes said to reduce desires or feelings to mere beliefs. The assumption seems to be that, in doing so, he is leaving something out. Being in the grip of a passion can be a harrowing, wrenching, or delightful experience. How can having such an experience, people tend to ask, be a matter of holding a mere belief? I suggest that Socrates' characterization of fear need not be thought of as reductive. His view might well be the following: the very motion of the soul that constitutes the passion of fear is what it takes for us to believe that this or that thing is frightful. If this is his view, it need lose nothing from the phenomenological richness of our experiences of fear. What holding a belief amounts to depends on the sort of belief that is being held. Many evaluative beliefs have motivating force; some evaluative beliefs—those that on this view constitute desires and passions—are of such a sort that having them amounts to having experiences of a particular sort.

The belief that being *afraid* cannot consist in *taking* something to be of some sort can perhaps be traced to the view that *taking* or *considering* something is, as such, an act of intellect, and that intellect, again, is something from which the stormy movements of the soul are removed. Contrary to that line of thought, I would suggest that Socrates need not be seen as reducing desires and feelings to something else, with the richness of experience being lost in the process. He can be seen as offering an alternative analysis of what it is to desire something, or what it is to have a certain feeling.

D 4 and ἐδόκει at D 7, in a way that puts emphasis on the -δοκια part of the definition. See n. 32 above.

Similarly, in denying that a host of pleasures and pains, desires and emotions, can drag knowledge around 'like a slave', he need not be seen as denying the heterogeneity of states of the soul (mental states, as we might want to put it) that move us to act. That he does so is a fairly frequent misconception. What he rejects is a picture according to which passions or feelings are psychic states independent of reason. Against this, he believes that in every passion reason is in some way exercised. There is nothing in this view that would commit him to denying that the ways in which reason takes things to be good or bad are many, or even that some of these ways of taking things to be good or bad are irreducibly distinct from others.

What on Socrates' view accounts for wrongdoing—akratic and otherwise—is not the condition of being vanquished by the forces of desire and passion. Rather, wrongdoing is in each case due to an improper functioning of reason. When passion leads us astray, what leads us astray is the incorrect valuation that our reason has adopted. It is perhaps easy to jump from this view to the position that passions as such are nothing but states in which reason has gone off track, and hence to the conclusion that we should get rid of them. (Likewise, it is easy to suppose that Socrates' memorable rejection of the image of knowledge as a slave dragged about by a myriad of passions implies hostility to passions.) But according to the discussion of courage that follows upon Socrates' definition of fear, in the last pages of the *Protagoras*, courage is not a state in which fear is extinguished. Far from it. Courage is a state of the soul which makes one fear those things that ought to be feared, that is to say, things that are genuinely bad. The courageous, as he puts it, do not 'fear disgraceful fears' (*Prot.* 360 A 8–B 2). But they do fear. The courageous person's fear—which is some kind of abhorrence of vice—would admittedly be very different from the sort of fear an ordinary soldier might feel in a battle; none the less, one should not be too quick and on account of this difference deny it the status of fear. Socrates does think that the knowledge that is virtue involves a certain peace of mind—ἡσυχία (*Prot.* 356 E 1). We are given no ground, however, to take this kind of tranquillity to be freedom from passions—ἀπάθεια. On the contrary, Socrates' discussion of courage in the *Protagoras* provides us with a picture of the virtuous person as prone to the right kind of fear.

Virtue is a condition in which one's takings-to-be-good and takings-to-be-bad are not only correct, but are instances of know-

ledge. Those takings-to-be-good or takings-to-be-bad that constitute the passions of a virtuous person are also not just correct
takings, but states of knowledge. The view here is not the more
common one, that a virtuous person's passions are fully appropriate responses to the situations he encounters; rather the view is
that virtue itself (in part) consists in such passions as are correct
takings-to-be-good and takings-to-be-bad.

To put the same point differently: Socrates no doubt believes
that someone who is not sensitive to the aspects of a situation that a
virtuous person would be sensitive to does not know what there is
to know about what is good and bad. However, he goes beyond this
belief. He takes it that such sensitivities are themselves bits of the
knowledge that is virtue. A comparison with Aristotle might make
the point clearer. Socrates is often thought to differ from Aristotle in
not including desiderative and emotional propensities—what Aristotle calls states of character—in virtue, making virtue instead into
a mere excellence of the inert intellect that judges things correctly.
On the interpretation I have offered, Socrates is precisely insisting
that such propensities constitute virtue. I would locate the main
difference between Socrates and Aristotle in the fact that excellent states of character for Socrates are at no remove from moral
knowledge. The excellent states of character simply are states of
knowledge. However close the two might lie for Aristotle (and this
might be closer than some of his formulations suggest), he did
want to make at the very least a notional distinction between the
emotional and desiderative propensities that constitute virtue of
character, on the one hand, and moral knowledge, on the other.

After Socrates gets Polus to agree to the conclusion that orators
and tyrants do not do what they want to do, Polus in effect exclaims:
'As if you, Socrates, do not envy the tyrant!' (468 E 6–9). Olympi-
odorus, who in his commentary on the *Gorgias* judges Polus' inter-
vention to be vulgar (ἰδιωτικόν), entirely misses the point.[38] Polus'
reaction is relevant, and revealing. Envying the tyrant is not a minor
lapse that can be overlooked if the person in question professes the
correct beliefs. Someone who forcefully argues that doing injustice
is one of the greatest evils, yet envies the tyrant, displays a soul that
lacks knowledge and is very much in need of repair. One reason
why so many of Socrates' interlocutors contradict themselves on
the issue of virtue is that they so glaringly lack it. They think, for

---

[38] See Olymp. *In Plat. Gorg.* 95. 22 ff. Westerink, and Dodds ad loc.

instance, that what the tyrant does is disgraceful (αἰσχρόν), but also envy him.

Often, one of the first things Socrates wants his interlocutor to agree to is that virtue is something beautiful or fine (καλόν), and vice something ugly or disgraceful (αἰσχρόν). By concurring with this, the interlocutors commit themselves to more than they had perhaps imagined. They commit themselves, for instance, to not envying the tyrant, and to abhorring the things the tyrant does. The virtuous person's actions express his evaluative knowledge. The evaluative judgements embodied in one's emotions and actions—the values one lives by—are of paramount importance to Socrates. A part of what in his view accounts for putative *akrasia* is precisely the fact that people are mistaken about what values they live by. If putative *akrasia* is so frequent, this is so in part because people are often mistaken about this. In addition to inconsistencies among a person's evaluative beliefs, which testify to a lack of knowledge of what is good and bad, the condition people describe as *akrasia* also involves a certain lack of self-understanding.

XII

The many take it that sometimes, driven by a desire or emotion, we act entirely against what our reason tells us is good, better, or best. Against this, Socrates holds that our actions themselves embody judgements of value. Our reason speaks in the very passion that drives us, even if reason does not speak in a way that is consonant with our remaining opinions or judgements. We take ourselves to be fragmented where we are not. Socrates sees the human soul as one and undivided. In taking the human soul to be unitary and undivided, he is ruling out the possibility that there is an irrational or non-rational part of our souls that is capable of motivating us to act entirely on its own. But the unity of the soul he envisages has a further significance: it ties inextricably together the practical side of our nature—the desiderative, the emotional, and the volitional— with the supposedly non-practical side of us, namely the side that forms judgements and possesses knowledge.

On Socrates' view, it is an inadequate conception of reason that lies at the bottom of the belief that *akrasia* exists. An inadequate and impoverished conception of reason might also lie behind certain misunderstandings of his position. Socratic intellectualism is often criticized as one-sided, on the ground that it does not to do justice to the richness and complexity of our mental life. But on the account given here, the complexity and richness of our mental life, and of our nature, can remain untouched. Rather, Socrates' view might be that more of us goes into every state of our soul than we suspected; in some sense the whole power of the soul goes into every state of the soul. If our reason is at work in more places and in more ways than we might have thought, it should not be too surprising if it turned out to malfunction more often than expected. Specific malfunctionings of reason are also at the bottom of what people call *akrasia*.

One would expect that an intellectualist would propose an intellectual cure for an intellectual ailment. So, for instance, if virtue is knowledge, as Socrates appears to think, it might seem that all we need to do in order to instil virtue in those who lack it is instruct them about what virtue requires. But he never recommends such simple instruction; on the contrary, he insists that becoming virtuous involves much care and therapy of the soul. Reason is quite vulnerable. Susceptible to more maladies than we might have expected, it also requires more extensive and complicated care than expected. If we do not stick to the characterization of *akrasia* given in the *Protagoras*, we could concede that on Socrates' view humans are prone to a condition that might deserve to be labelled *akrasia*. The Greek word simply indicates weakness, and Socrates does take it that weakness of reason is displayed in the episodes usually considered akratic. What he presents as powerful—as not dragged about 'like a slave'—is not reason as such, but knowledge, which is a stable overall condition of a well-functioning reason.

When Socrates describes virtue as knowledge, it is not just any kind of knowledge that he has in mind. Certain desires and feelings are part of the knowledge that is virtue. In addition, Socratic volition as discussed above is part of moral knowledge. This volition is an aspiration; it is part of an ideal of the good life. The virtuous person alone on Socrates' view does entirely what he wants to do. The virtuous person can do what he wants to do because the taking-to-be-good that his willing amounts to is itself a state of knowledge: it is an accurate grasp of what is in fact good. Being instructed on what one ought to want typically does not produce the desired wanting; this holds good for Socratic volition as much as it holds for volition as usually understood. Socrates would certainly agree with those who think that becoming good requires that one's whole soul be turned around. What he might disagree with is what happens in the process of turning the soul around. On his view, any change in the desiderative, volitional, or emotional condition of the soul is itself a change in the condition of reason.

University of Pittsburgh

APPENDIX

Gorgias 467 C 5–468 E 5

Through his argument at *Gorg.* 467 C 5–468 E 5, Socrates gets Polus to agree, even if reluctantly, that orators and tyrants do not do what they want to do. I have argued above that Socrates' position is coherent and does not involve confusions of the sort interpreters have attributed to him. I wish now to show that the argument he uses at 467 C 5–468 E 5 to support his claim that orators and tyrants do not do what they want to do is likewise not flawed. In addition, the argument is worth looking into in its own right for at least two reasons. First, Socrates introduces here important concepts concerning human action, and second, his treatment of Polus is a paradigm of a kind of irony that he often displays in Plato's Socratic dialogues. In fact, one cannot properly assess the philosophical content of the argument at 467 C 5–468 E 5 without paying attention to the way Socrates treats Polus.

Socrates asks Polus if people who take medicines prescribed by their doctors want what they are doing (βούλεσθαι ὅπερ ποιοῦσιν), namely, taking the medicine and being in pain, or that for the sake of which they do this, namely, being healthy (467 C 7–10). Polus agrees that they want to be healthy. Similarly, seafarers do not want sea voyages with all the danger and trouble that these involve; what they want is wealth (467 D 1–5). Socrates then secures Polus' agreement to the claim that this is so in all cases (περὶ πάντων)—when a person does something for the sake of something, he does not want what he is doing (οὐ τοῦτο βούλεται ὃ πράττει), but the thing for the sake of which (ἐκεῖνο οὗ ἕνεκα) he is doing it (467 D 6–E 1).

The troubling clause is 'he does not want what he is doing'. The form of words chosen here might suggest that Socrates intends to assimilate all action to merely instrumental activities like taking bitter medicines. On the strict instrumentalist view ostensibly proposed here, no one ever wants what he does; the agent merely wants the beneficial result which he expects his action to have. Hence, like everyone else, orators and tyrants do not want what they are doing in killing, expropriating, and banishing. Now we know that the conclusion Socrates wants to reach is that orators and tyrants do not do what they want to do. How is the transition made from orators' and tyrants' not wanting what they do to their not doing what they want? The instrumentalist account of action seemingly embraced at the beginning of the argument does not provide means for this transition. But in that case, why did Socrates start by drawing our attention to actions such as the taking of bitter medicine? I suggest that he is not in fact proposing to assimilate all action to merely instrumental activities like this. To see what he is up to, we have to look a bit ahead in the argument. Let me quote an important claim he makes further on:

P_1 Therefore it is because we pursue what is good [τὸ ἀγαθὸν ἄρα δι-
ώκοντες] that we walk whenever we walk—thinking that it is better to walk [οἰόμενοι βέλτιον εἶναι]—and, conversely, whenever we stand still it is for the sake of the same thing [τοῦ αὐτοῦ ἕνεκα] that we stand still, what is good [τοῦ ἀγαθοῦ] . . . And don't we also kill a person, if we do, expel him from the city, or confiscate his property thinking that doing so is better for us than not doing it [οἰόμενοι ἄμεινον εἶναι ἡμῖν ταῦτα ποιεῖν]? . . . Hence it is for the sake of the good [ἕνεκα . . . τοῦ ἀγαθοῦ] that those who do all these things do them. (Gorg. 468 B 1–8)

I propose to view everything that precedes the quoted passage, starting from 467 C 5, not as endorsing an instrumental account of action, but as an attempt to bring Polus to acknowledge the general picture of motivation offered in the lines just quoted. Socrates attempts to do this in two stages.

The first stage is the opening passage at 467 C 5–E 1, where the drinking of bitter medicines and navigation are discussed. Socrates introduces here the notion of an end or goal of an action—that for the sake of which (ἐκεῖνο οὗ ἕνεκα) an action is performed—and connects this notion with the notion of wanting (βούλεσθαι). What we want in whatever we do is that for the sake of which we do it. This point holds regardless of how the goal is related to the activity in question—whether it is separate from it, includes it, or is identical with it. The claim is simply that the proper object of wanting is the goal, whatever this goal might happen to be.

The second stage of his attempt to get Polus to subscribe to the picture of motivation painted in the lines quoted above is found at 467 E 1–468 B 1, the passage immediately following the section on bitter medicines (and immediately preceding the lines quoted). In this passage, Socrates links the goal of an action with something that is good. He gets Polus to accept a division of things into good, bad, and those that are neither good nor bad; he also gets Polus to agree that we do indifferent things for the sake of good things. That we do bad things for the sake of good things is not explicitly stated, but Polus is meant to have in mind examples like the taking of bitter medicines—something that in itself is bad—which he had already agreed we do for the sake of something good, namely health.

Having thus provided the basic concepts of the theory of action he is trying to get Polus to subscribe to, Socrates is now ready to state a central principle of that theory. This is expressed in P_1 above. What we are after—or what we pursue (διώκειν)—in everything we do is the goal (that-for-the-sake-of-which), and this in each case is something we take to be good. Our 'pursuing what is good' (at 468 B 1) is specifically glossed as thinking (note οἰόμενοι at B 2 and B 6) that doing what we do is 'better' (note βέλτιον at B 2 and ἄμεινον at B 6).

It is at this point (at 468 B 8) that Socrates invokes what he takes was agreed upon at the very outset. He says: 'Now didn't we agree that we want not those things that we do for the sake of something, but that for the sake of which we do them?' (468 B 8–C 1; the reference back is to 467 C 5–E 1, especially to 467 C 5–7 and 467 D 6–E 1). I have interpreted the passage which he refers to here as establishing a conceptual connection between wanting and the goal: the goal is the proper object of wanting. If this is the point of 467 C 5–E 1, isn't it distinctly misleading for him to insist that people do *not* want, say, to make troublesome and dangerous journeys at sea? According to my reading of the opening passage, the point Socrates makes there is in a sense trivial: *provided* that making troublesome and dangerous journeys at sea is not the goal, it is not wanted. That making such journeys is not the goal is simply built into his example. (This fits well the statement with which he ends the opening passage: '*If* someone does something for the sake of something, he does not want that which he is doing, but that for the sake of which he is doing it', 467 D 6–E 1.) What he has in mind is clear from what he says immediately after he has reminded Polus of their previous point of agreement. Having received a positive answer (at 468 C 1) to the question 'Now didn't we agree that we want not those things that we do for the sake of something, but that for the sake of which we do them?' (468 B 8–C 1), he goes on to say:

P_2 Hence [ἄρα], we do not simply [ἁπλῶς] want [βουλόμεθα] to slaughter people, expel them from the cities, or confiscate their property, just like that [οὕτως]; we want to do these things if they are beneficial [ἀλλ' ἐὰν μὲν ὠφέλιμα ᾖ ταῦτα, βουλόμεθα πράττειν αὐτά], but if they are harmful, we don't [βλαβερὰ δὲ ὄντα οὐ βουλόμεθα]. (468 C 2–5)

The lines just quoted contain the second central principle of the theory of action Socrates advocates here. The claim now is that we want to do such things as killing, banishing, and confiscating, if they are beneficial; but if they are harmful, then not. So, on the view now expressed, we precisely *do* want to make dangerous journeys at sea—provided, that is, that we shall gain wealth by them. But Socrates cannot have forgotten here the point he had made when bringing up such examples as taking bitter medicines and making dangerous journeys at sea, since at 468 B 8–C 1 he invokes what he takes to be the conclusion of that discussion, and does so precisely in order to establish the point he is now making (in P_2). His current point is that we want to do those things the doing of which is beneficial, and we do not want to do those things the doing of which is harmful. This is a new point, quite different from what we find in P_1, and made expressly for the first time here in the lengthy argument he is presenting to Polus in support of the conclusion that orators and tyrants do not do what they want to do. And it is this new claim that he needs if he is to reach that conclusion.

So what was Socrates up to when he reminded Polus (just before stating P_2) of the opening part of the argument, namely, their agreement concerning actions such as the taking of bitter medicines and the making of troublesome sea voyages? I suggest that he uses these examples to lead up to P_2. Even the things that people generally would not want to do—drink a bitter potion, say, or risk one's life at sea—they will want to do, and will do, if the doing of them is beneficial. The attraction some find in adventures at sea is not a counter-example to the point he is trying to make, just as someone's liking of bitter potions is not such a counter-example. The instances he cites are simply of things that are commonly regarded as highly undesirable. One generally does not want to do them. If this is so, the instrumental reading of the opening passage, 467 C 5–E 1, turns out to be beside the point.

Does Socrates manage to establish his claim that orators and tyrants do not do what they want to do by the argument we find at 467 C 5–468 E 5? The considerations adduced in support of his claim amount to a certain theory of action. Does the argument make it clear what this theory is and how it might be defended? Socrates, I contend, at the very least makes a move in the right direction. Admittedly, he does not say enough within the scope of his exchange with Polus fully to support P_2. In claiming that we want to do things if they are beneficial and otherwise not, he has moved from speaking of things that are merely *taken to be* good (recall οἰόμενοι at 468 B 2 and B 6; see also οἰόμενος at 468 D 3, quoted immediately below) as proper objects of wanting to speaking of things that (as a matter of fact) *are* good as proper objects of wanting. Is his transition from P_1 to P_2 surreptitious? The answer to this depends on whether we should take 'surreptitious' to mean attained by fraud or attained by stealth. Some stealth perhaps, but certainly no fraud, is involved.

Let me observe first that he makes the transition deliberately. He is not himself in a muddle. That the two passages quoted above impose different conditions on wanting is noted clearly, even if implicitly, by Socrates himself at the very end of the argument. He says:

Since we are in agreement about that, then, if someone, whether tyrant

or orator, kills someone or expels him from the city or confiscates his
property because he thinks that [doing] this is better for himself [οἰόμενος
ἄμεινον εἶναι αὐτῷ] when as a matter of fact it is worse [τυγχάνειν δὲ ὂν
κάκιον], this person presumably does what pleases him [οὗτος δήπου ποιεῖ
ἃ δοκεῖ αὐτῷ], doesn't he? . . . And is he also doing what he wants [ἃ
βούλεται] if these things are in fact bad [εἴπερ τυγχάνει ταῦτα κακὰ ὄντα]?
Why don't you answer? [POLUS:] All right, I think that he isn't doing
what he wants. (468 D 1–7).

Socrates here deliberately reserves the term 'wanting' for an attitude
that hits upon what is in fact good, knowing of course that most people do
not use the term in this way. Is he warranted in thus construing the term?
I would like to argue that, dialectically speaking, he is. At 467 E 1–468 B 1
he got Polus to adopt the objective point of view: there Polus accepted the
division of things into those that are good, those that are bad, and those
that are neither good nor bad. The talk there was of things that actually
are good, bad, or neutral, not merely of things that are considered to be so.
Polus further agreed to the claim that people act for the sake of (actually)
good things. It is this agreement that Socrates exploits further down, at
468 C 5–7, while moving towards P_2. He says: 'For we want things that are
good [τὰ γὰρ ἀγαθὰ βουλόμεθα]—as you say [ὡς φῂς σύ]—whereas we don't
want those that are neither good nor bad, nor those that are bad.'

Polus is free to object here; he could interject that he had previously
only meant to say that we go for—and want—things we take to be good,
not things that are in fact good. But he does not object. Not only is he free to
protest; Socrates repeatedly nudges and prods him to do so. When Socrates
says 'For we want the things that are good, *as you say* . . .', he is clearly
warning Polus that the conclusion has been reached using something Polus
himself had previously said or agreed to. This is undoubtedly an invitation
to Polus to reflect on what he had previously agreed to and why. What
is especially intended to serve as a prod is the palpable irony in that 'as
you say'.[39] When Socrates then pointedly asks whether Polus believes that
what Socrates is saying is true, Polus, again, does not stir. Since he makes

[39] Polus has not expressly said this. Since he has gone along with Socrates, Socrates
can count him as having said so, but in that case Polus must be saying something he
does not mean. He clearly does not understand the full force of the view he assents
to, otherwise he would not be granting what in a moment will force him to swallow
what he had not too long ago described as 'outrageous' and 'monstrous'. There is a
hint of irony in the question Socrates will ask immediately after making the assertion
(at 468 C 5–7) that we want things that are good: 'Do you [Polus] think that what I
am saying is true [ἀληθῆ σοι δοκῶ λέγειν])?' (468 C 8). Since 'what I am saying' refers
to Socrates' allegation about what Polus is 'saying' ('For we want the things that are
good, as you [Polus] say, ὡς φῂς σύ . . .', 468 C 5–6), Socrates is in effect confronting
Polus. He is questioning whether Polus has any idea not only what Socrates is saying
and believing, but also what he, Polus, is saying and believing.

no objection, his prior agreements now commit him to saying that we want things that as a matter of fact are good. Is Socrates deliberately confusing Polus? Given that Polus does not quite grasp what he is up to, should he move so nonchalantly from P_1 to P_2? It seems to me that by examining Polus as he does, he precisely intends to bring Polus' confusion into the open. He is suggesting to Polus that he has to rethink the whole issue since he does not understand what he is saying. In thus underscoring the need to think more carefully about the transition from P_1 to P_2, Socrates can hardly be muddling the issue. We must also bear in mind, as we wonder whether he might be confusing Polus, that he really believes what he describes Polus as saying. He decidedly believes that we 'want good things', namely, that we want things that are [as a matter of fact] good. It is therefore reasonable to think that when he says so, he is making a bona fide suggestion to Polus as to what he, Polus, ought to be saying. Finally, the shocking nature of the conclusion, that orators and tyrants do not do what they want to do—the conclusion which, as I have argued, Socrates embraces in all seriousness—is in itself a deterrent against muddles.

Socrates has philosophical reasons for maintaining that we want—in some legitimate sense of this word—what as a matter of fact is good, even if he has not fully set these reasons out in his exchange with Polus at 467 C 5–468 E 5. If in this argument he slips into the guise of the orator and tyrant, forcing what he takes to be true upon the unwilling Polus, we should perhaps be led to suspect that Polus lacks the sort of grasp of the matters discussed that would enable him to follow Socrates willingly.

THE SECRET DOCTRINE:
PLATO'S DEFENCE
OF PROTAGORAS IN
THE *THEAETETUS*

MI-KYOUNG LEE

1. Introduction

WHY does Plato introduce the so-called Secret Doctrine in his examination of Protagorean relativism in the *Theaetetus*? I argue (1) that the relation between Protagoras' claim and the Secret Doctrine is not one of mutual implication, but that the Secret Doctrine has the status of an independent hypothesis which Plato uses to defend Protagoras, (2) that the Secret Doctrine is not simply a doctrine of constant flux, but a collection of loosely related theses, and (3) that it is introduced to explain what it means for things to have properties only relative to perceivers.

Plato's discussion of Protagoras in the *Theaetetus* is the most careful and perceptive examination of relativism in antiquity. It is, however, highly problematic, for in order to explain what Protagoras meant by his claim that 'man is the measure of all things: of what is, that it is, and of what is not, that it is not' (*Theaet.* 152 A 2–4; see also S.E. *M.* 7. 60 = 80 B 1 DK; D.L. 9. 51 = 80 A 1 DK), Plato introduces a theory which is even more contentious and obscure. He calls this theory a 'Secret Doctrine', presumably to acknowledge that Protagoras himself never espoused any such

© Mi-Kyoung Lee 2000

I owe a particular debt of gratitude to Gisela Striker for many helpful and encouraging discussions of this topic over the years and critical comments on previous drafts of this paper. I would also like to thank Gail Fine, Kathrin Koslicki, Susan Sauvé Meyer, Elijah Millgram, Ian Mueller, Hilary Putnam, and Angela Smith for comments on and objections to earlier versions of this paper, and W. D. Hart, Peter Hunt, Constance Meinwald, and Dana Miller for comments on more recent versions. I am very grateful to the Editor for helpful comments and suggestions.

doctrine and that it is of Plato's devising.¹ Its exact relation to
Protagoras' claim is not clear. On the one hand, Protagoras' claim
seems to be a doctrine of relativism, according to which something
is the case for one if and only if it appears so to one. On the other
hand, the Secret Doctrine seems to be a Heraclitean thesis of total flux, which recommends that everything is always changing in
every respect:

ἐγὼ ἐρῶ καὶ μάλ᾽ οὐ φαῦλον λόγον, ὡς ἄρα ἓν μὲν αὐτὸ καθ᾽ αὑτὸ οὐδέν ἐστιν, οὐδ᾽
ἄν τι προσείποις ὀρθῶς οὐδ᾽ ὁποιονοῦν τι, ἀλλ᾽ ἐὰν ὡς μέγα προσαγορεύῃς, καὶ
σμικρὸν φανεῖται, καὶ ἐὰν βαρύ, κοῦφον, σύμπαντά τε οὕτως, ὡς μηδενὸς ὄντος
ἑνὸς μήτε τινὸς μήτε ὁποιουοῦν· ἐκ δὲ δὴ φορᾶς τε καὶ κινήσεως καὶ κράσεως
πρὸς ἄλληλα γίγνεται πάντα ἃ δή φαμεν εἶναι, οὐκ ὀρθῶς προσαγορεύοντες· ἔστι
μὲν γὰρ οὐδέποτ᾽ οὐδέν, ἀεὶ δὲ γίγνεται.

I will tell you, and it is certainly no ordinary theory—I mean the theory
that there is nothing which in itself is just one thing: nothing which you
could rightly call anything or any kind of thing. If you call a thing large
it will reveal itself as small, and if heavy, light, and so on with everything,
because nothing is anything or any kind of thing. The things of which we
naturally say that they 'are' are in process of coming to be, as the result of
movement and change and blending with one another. We are wrong when
we say they 'are', since nothing ever is, but everything is coming to be.
(152 C 8–E 1)²

Anyone familiar with more modern varieties of relativism will be

---

¹ *Theaet.* 152 C 10–D 2: 'Was Protagoras one of those omniscient people? Did he
perhaps put this out as a riddle for the common crowd of us, while he revealed the
truth as a secret doctrine to his own pupils [τοῖς δὲ μαθηταῖς ἐν ἀπορρήτῳ τὴν ἀλήθειαν
ἔλεγεν]? . . . I will tell you; and this, now, is certainly no ordinary theory [ἐγὼ ἐρῶ καὶ
μάλ᾽ οὐ φαῦλον λόγον].' Unless otherwise indicated, translations of Plato's *Theaetetus*
are from the M. J. Levett translation, revised by M. F. Burnyeat, in *The* Theaetetus
of Plato, with an introduction by M. F. Burnyeat [*Introduction*] (Indianapolis, 1990).
The Greek text used in this paper is W. F. Hicken's revised Oxford Classical Text
of the *Theaetetus*, in *Platonis Opera*, i, ed. Duke, Hicken, Nicoll, Robinson, and
Strachan (Oxford, 1995).

² The Levett–Burnyeat translation takes φανεῖται as 'it will reveal itself as', not
as 'will appear' (cf. F. M. Cornford's 'it will be found to be', in *Plato's Theory of Knowledge* (*The* Theaetetus *and the* Sophist *of Plato Translated with a
Commentary*) [*Plato's Theory of Knowledge*] (London, 1935), resulting not in the
fairly weak claim that everything is subject to conflicting appearances, but in the
stronger claim that if one tries to pin something down as being one thing, one
will discover that it is also something opposite or different. Modifications to the
Levett–Burnyeat translation: the second implicit φανεῖται in 152 D 5 is not translated by 'liable to appear', which spoils the translation of the first as 'reveal itself'; the contrasting and emphatic '. . . δὲ δή' in 152 D 7 is left untranslated
to avoid importing 'true' into this sentence, as Levett's 'What is really true, is
this' does.

puzzled about what this has to do with relativism. One might think that it is a doctrine of flux introduced to avoid committing the relativist to contradictions—for example, if Socrates perceives the wind as being hot and Theaetetus perceives it as being cold, then the doctrine of flux tells us that both beliefs are true because the world is constantly changing in such a way that both perceptions turn out to be true. For a relativist, however, the alleged problem is a non-starter. According to a more careful formulation of relativism, if someone believes that some *x* is *F*, then *x* is *F for her*. Once the statements have been suitably relativized, there is no contradiction which results from conflicting beliefs being true, and therefore no apparent role for a doctrine of flux or change to play.[3] (Indeed, the wind is supposed to be hot for one and cold for the other *simultaneously*.) Plato himself seems to have been clear about the importance of specifying qualifications completely in order to avoid the spectre of contradiction (*Rep.* 4, 436 E–437 A). I do not think Plato thought that Protagoras was, at least at this level, entangled in contradictions.[4] But then why did Plato introduce the Secret Doctrine?

During the nineteenth century commentators on the *Theaetetus* from Schleiermacher on tended to assume that Plato had other targets in mind besides Protagoras, and they devoted their efforts to identifying these unnamed opponents (e.g. Antisthenes, Aristippus, Cratylus, the Megarians, Democritus).[5] However, Jackson

[3] So too John M. Cooper, *Plato's* Theaetetus (Harvard dissertations in philosophy, 1967; New York, 1990), 17; R. M. Dancy, 'Theaetetus' First Baby: *Theaetetus* 151 E–160 E' ['Theaetetus' First Baby'], *Philosophical Topics*, 15/2 (Fall 1987), 61–108 at 79; John McDowell, *Plato:* Theaetetus [*Theaetetus*], translated with notes (Oxford, 1973), 125–6; David Bostock, *Plato's* Theaetetus (Oxford, 1988), 45. McDowell speculates that Parmenidean assumptions may have led Plato to view the contradictions as unresolved even when suitable qualifications have been added (*Theaetetus*, 125–6). See Cooper (*Plato's* Theaetetus, 16–58, esp. 39–58) and Dancy ('Theaetetus' First Baby') for the most critically acute discussions of the problems in fitting relativism and flux together.
[4] As I argue elsewhere, the problem with contradiction and self-refutation arises for Protagoras at the level of second-order judgements about beliefs (*Theaet.* 169 E–171 D) (book in preparation; see also *Conflicting Appearances: Protagoras and the Development of Early Greek Epistemology* (Harvard dissertation 1996), 147–77).
[5] See references and discussion in, *inter alia*, Lewis Campbell, *The* Theaetetus *of Plato, with a Revised Text and English Notes*, 2nd edn. (Oxford, 1883), pp. xxix–xlvi; Paul Natorp, 'Aristipp in Platons Theätet' ['Aristipp'], *Archiv für Geschichte der Philosophie*, 3 (1890) 347–62; Annemarie Capelle, 'Zur Frage nach den κομψότεροι in Platons *Theaetet*, P. 156 A', *Hermes*, 90 (1862), 288–94; and Paul Friedländer, *Platon*, iii. *Die Platonischen Schriften, Zweite und Dritte Periode*, 2nd edn. (Berlin,

and Natorp, among others, argued that the Secret Doctrine cannot be conclusively identified with any particular figure and is almost certainly a creative invention of Plato's;[6] commentators then
began to look instead for hints of Plato's own Theory of Ideas in
the *Theaetetus*. In particular, they tended to focus on the striking resemblances between the Secret Doctrine and Plato's own
statements about change and perception in other dialogues. The
problems with this approach were examined in a number of important papers and commentaries, culminating in a brilliant and
influential series of papers by Myles Burnyeat. As he argues, the
question of whether Plato himself endorses the Secret Doctrine is
the wrong question to ask here. For the Secret Doctrine is part of a
complex dialectical construction woven together from three theses:
(T) Theaetetus' definition of knowledge as perception, (P) Protagoras' claim that whatever appears to be the case to one is the
case for one, and (H) the Heraclitean doctrine that everything is
always changing. As Burnyeat argues, Socrates offers an extended
argument that each of the three theses commits one to holding the
others:

$$\text{Theaetetus} \Leftrightarrow \text{Protagoras} \Leftrightarrow \text{Heraclitus.}^7$$

1960), trans. Hans Meyerhoff as *Plato*, iii. *The Dialogues: Second and Third Periods*
(Princeton, 1969), 154–61. They also tended to see *Theaet.* 152–60 as developing not
one 'Secret Doctrine' but several theories; for example, many distinguished the 'Heraclitean' doctrines at 152 D–153 D from those of the 'more subtle type [κομψότεροι]'
at 156 A–157 C.

   [6] H. Jackson, 'Plato's Later Theory of Ideas, IV: The *Theaetetus*', *Journal of
Philology*, 13 (1884), 242–72; Natorp, 'Aristipp'.

   [7] Burnyeat argues that the Secret Doctrine is supposed to provide necessary and
sufficient conditions for the truth of Protagoras' thesis and Theaetetus' definition.
As he puts it, 'It is thought to be reasonably clear that (1) Her ⇒ Prot ⇒ Th. The
work goes into showing (2) Th ⇒ Prot ⇒ Her, and then, that both Protagoras and
Heraclitus engender absurdity. (2) is hammered out step by step through the construction of the Protagorean–Heraclitean theory down to 160 DC' ('Idealism and
Greek Philosophy: What Descartes Saw and Berkeley Missed' ['Idealism'], *Philosophical Review*, 91/1 (Jan. 1982), 3–40 at 6–7 n. 2; see also Burnyeat, *Introduction*,
7–19). Gail Fine endorses Burnyeat's reading here, but cautions the reader not to
suppose that the relations between the three theses are strict implications—rather,
each of the three best supports and is best supported by each of the others ('Protagorean Relativisms' ['Relativisms'], in J. Cleary and W. Wians (eds.), *Proceedings
of the Boston Area Colloquium in Ancient Philosophy*, xix (Lanham, Md., 1996),
211–43 at 214–16, esp. 215 n. 10; 'Conflicting Appearances: *Theaetetus* 153 D–154 B'
['Conflicting Appearances'], in C. Gill and M. M. McCabe (eds.), *Form and Argument in Late Plato* (Oxford, 1996), 105–33 at 108–9, esp. 108 n. 9). She then argues
that we must use a 'connection criterion' in our reading of this part of the *Theaetetus*:

The next step is to demolish them one by one. Socrates is made to give one indirect *reductio* of (T) by offering arguments against (P), a second by arguing against (H), as well as one final direct refutation of (T). Such a strategy, if executed correctly, would provide a thorough and decisive way to investigate, then neatly dispatch, a set of problematic theses.

Burnyeat goes on to offer a compelling answer to the question why Protagoras is committed to the flux doctrine: it offers the metaphysics necessary to guarantee the incorrigibility which Protagoras' measure doctrine claims for human perceivers. Consider the kind of world in which perceivers cannot be mistaken. If all their perceptions are true, then things must change according to their different and changing beliefs. This means that things cannot have continuing identity over time—whether for different perceivers, or for a single perceiver over time. For if there were any kind of stability in an object, this would imply that (1) it is that way independently of how anyone perceives it, and (2) it is possible to be mistaken about how it is. As Burnyeat puts it,

If a thing is stable, or stable in some respect (the qualification makes no odds), that means there is an objective basis for correcting or confirming someone's judgement as to how it is, or how it is in that respect. There is a fact of the matter, independent of the person's judgement. The whole point of eliminating first objectivity between persons and then identity through time was to ensure that there would be no basis in the experience of other times and other people for charging anyone with untruth. . . . Stability, even for a moment, entails objectivity, even if only for that moment. (*Introduction*, 49)

The key idea is that if something remained stably F, this would constitute an objective state of affairs, on the basis of which a judgement about it could be convicted of being false; if then Protagoras' measure doctrine denies objectivity, it is committed to the Secret Doctrine and the doctrine of constant change.[8]

However, there are some problems with this line of interpretation.

'we should aim to interpret each of the three theses in a way that makes it plausible to suggest that each of them is committed to and best supported by the others' ('Relativisms', 217).

[8] Burnyeat's view is more nuanced than I can do justice to here, for he thinks that Plato works out the implications of Protagorean relativism by stages, and it is only at the final stage that this argument (that stability entails objectivity) is introduced ('Idealism', 11–13).

Consider whether a relativist is really committed to the doctrine of flux. Is flux really needed to eliminate objective truth? Is it even successful at eliminating objective truth? Take this cold wind which Theaetetus feels. The proposal is that if it is not constantly changing, then there will be an objective truth about how it is, about which one _could_ be mistaken. But if there is a fact of the matter about the wind's being cold, how does it help to make the wind change? There will also be a fact of the matter about its changing. That is, _if_ stability itself implies that there is an objective truth about an object, then one won't eliminate objectivity by introducing flux. In fact, stability does _not_ by itself imply that there is an objective truth about an object. Stability should be possible even in a Protagorean world where there are no objective, perceiver-independent truths. If it appears to me for all my life that this stone is black, then the relativist ought to say that it will be black for me for that length of time; its remaining black does not, however, make it an 'objective fact', since it is that colour only because it appears so to me, and it may at the same time be different colours for different perceivers. There may be a fact of the matter—that it is black for me now— but this is none the less not an objective, perceiver-independent fact.

If one is persuaded by the thought that relativism does not commit one to the doctrine of constant flux, then one will want to consider two alternatives. (1) Protagoras' measure doctrine in the _Theaetetus_ is not relativism.[9] (2) It _is_ a kind of relativism, but it is not supposed to imply the doctrine of total flux.

I shall argue that option (2) is correct. Plato is not arguing that the three theses provide necessary and sufficient conditions for each other. In particular, he does not argue that $(T) \Rightarrow (P) \Rightarrow (H)$. Rather, once he introduces the Secret Doctrine for consideration, he devotes his efforts to showing that $(H) \Rightarrow (P) \Rightarrow (T)$.[10]

[9] In 'Relativisms' Fine argues that, since Plato is arguing that (P) implies a doctrine of constant flux and since relativism about truth does not in fact imply a doctrine of constant flux, one should interpret (P), on the principle of charity, not as relativism _about truth_, but as infallibilism, the position that all beliefs are true _simpliciter_. I am greatly indebted to her paper, but will not discuss her arguments here, since they raise complex questions about relativism about truth and Plato's self-refutation argument in the _Theaetetus_ which I shall address elsewhere (book in preparation).

[10] Strictly speaking, Socrates only tries to show this in the case of perception and perceptible properties. Accordingly, he focuses on the perceptual case (152 C 1–2, 153 D 8–9, 156 E 7–9, 171 D 9–E 9).

That this is Plato's objective is suggested by Socrates' remarks concerning the relations among the theses.[11] After Socrates has completed the construction of the Secret Doctrine, he announces:

So we find the various theories coincide [lit. 'have converged to the same thing', εἰς ταὐτὸν συμπέπτωκεν]: that of Homer and Heraclitus and all their tribe, that all things flow like streams; of Protagoras, wisest of men, that man is the measure of all things; and of Theaetetus that, *these things being so*, knowledge proves to be perception. (160 D 6–E 2)

This does not mean that the three theses have been shown to be equivalent. Rather, if Protagoras' thesis and the Secret Doctrine are true, then Theaetetus' definition comes out true as well. Again, at *Theaet.* 183 B 7–C 3 Socrates describes the enquiry into the truth of (T) and (P) as proceeding κατά γε τὴν τοῦ πάντα κινεῖσθαι μέθοδον, i.e. on the assumption that everything is in motion.[12]

Why, then, does Plato introduce the Secret Doctrine if it isn't a necessary commitment of (P) and (T)?

Plato introduces the Secret Doctrine in order to develop Protagoras' claim. Developing a philosophical position does not necessarily or even usually consist of working out the implications or necessary commitments of that view; one may fashion a theory out of whatever borrowed materials seem most promising for defending it. Theaetetus' thesis is vague and nebulous—Protagoras' thesis is introduced to firm it up.[13] Similarly, Protagoras' thesis is ambigu-

---

[11] Among the passages Burnyeat lists as containing 'stage directions' for the *Theaetetus*, three appear to indicate that Plato means to be arguing that Th ⇒ Prot ⇒ Her: 152 C–D (Heraclitus gives the 'real truth' behind Protagoras' riddling statements [Prot ⇒ Her]), 160 D–E (Socrates says that the three theses 'come to the same thing' [Prot ⇔ Her]), 183 B (the refutation of Heraclitus demolishes Protagoras [Prot ⇒ Her] and disposes of Theaetetus' definition [Th ⇒ Her]—unless Theaetetus can find some other method than Heraclitus' to work out his equation of knowledge and perception) ('Idealism', 6–7 n. 2). However, Socrates' saying at 152 C–D that the Secret Doctrine gives the 'real truth' behind Protagoras' riddling statements could mean Prot ⇒ Her, or it could mean Her ⇒ Prot; I argue for the latter. The other two passages seem to me to provide little evidence to indicate that Plato means to be arguing that Prot ⇒ Her. None of these passages is absolutely conclusive either way, and the case can only be settled by looking at the arguments themselves.

[12] See Richard Robinson on the puzzling use of μέθοδος here (*Plato's Earlier Dialectic*, 2nd edn. (Oxford, 1953), 68–9).

[13] I argue for this in 'Thinking and Perception in Plato's *Theaetetus*', in Mark McPherran (ed.), *Recognition, Remembrance, and Reality: New Essays on Plato's Epistemology and Metaphysics* (*Apeiron*, 32/4; Dec. 1999), 37–54.

ous and puzzling on its own—the Secret Doctrine is introduced
to amplify and support it. This follows a familiar strategy in Platonic dialogues, where Socrates investigates an initial thesis not by
working out its implications, but by introducing ancillary premises
(see e.g. *Meno* 86 D ff.). Nowhere does Socrates represent the ancillary premises as following from the initial thesis; the interlocutor
must agree to them separately, sometimes with no small amount
of coaxing from Socrates. In the *Theaetetus* Socrates must provide
Theaetetus with reasons to suppose that the Secret Doctrine will in
fact support Protagoras' claim, which in turn will make Theaetetus' definition of knowledge as perception come out true. He must
show that: $(H) \Rightarrow (P) \Rightarrow (T)$.[14]

The Secret Doctrine has the status of an independent hypothesis,
which provides Socrates with substantial metaphysical resources
for developing a Protagorean theory. And the problem which the
Secret Doctrine is meant to address is the following: what does it
mean to say that nothing is anything in itself, but is whatever it is *for*
someone? How is it possible for heat or any other property to exist
for or *in relation to* someone? That it is the function of the Secret
Doctrine to explain what it means to say 'is *F* for *A*', and to show
what the necessary relativization is to consist in, has been proposed
by a number of commentators.[15] However, they generally admit
that it is extremely difficult to see how the flux doctrine provides
this explanation, and have not, in my view, hit upon the correct
account of the role of the flux doctrine in the Secret Doctrine. The
purpose of this paper is to show how to read the Secret Doctrine
in this way.

[14] I do not agree with Burnyeat when he says, 'It is thought to be reasonably clear
that (1) Her $\Rightarrow$ Prot $\Rightarrow$ Th. The work goes into showing (2) Th $\Rightarrow$ Prot $\Rightarrow$ Her . . .'
('Idealism', 7 n. 2). The thesis that everything is changing does *not* obviously im-
ply that all beliefs and perceptions are true for someone, since, after all, things
might change in ways which belie those beliefs and perceptions. (For example, the
weather in Chicago is constantly changing, and I am invariably mistaken about
it.) Showing that the elements of the Secret Doctrine *can* be made to provide a
coherent and consistent defence for Protagoras seems to me difficult, if not impossible.

[15] Cornford, *Plato's Theory of Knowledge*, 33, 39; Cooper, *Plato's* Theaetetus, 35–
6; M. F. Burnyeat, 'Conflicting Appearances', *Proceedings of the British Academy*,
65 (1979), 69–111 at 77; Mohan Matthen, 'Perception, Relativism, and Truth: Reflections on Plato's *Theaetetus* 152–160' ['Perception'], *Dialogue*, 24 (1985) 33–58 at
38; Robert J. Ketchum, 'Plato's "Refutation" of Protagorean Relativism: *Theaetetus*
170–171' ['Refutation'], *Oxford Studies in Ancient Philosophy* [*OSAP*], 10 (1992),
73–105 at 81; Burnyeat, *Introduction*, 13.

First, in Section 2, I restate the problem which Protagoras' thesis poses in the *Theaetetus*. Next, in Section 3, I make some general remarks about the Secret Doctrine. In Section 4 I examine in detail the construction of the Secret Doctrine from 153 to 160, and show how it answers the problem posed by Protagoras' claim. The results are summarized in Section 5.

2. Protagoras: Restatement of the problem

Protagoras' claim—that whatever seems to be the case to one is the case for one[16]—is ambiguous. It can be taken as a simple conditional:

(P1) If *x* seems *F* to *A*, *x* is *F* (for *A*);

or as a biconditional:

(P) *x* is *F* for *A* if and only if *x* seems *F* to *A*.[17]

The conditional tells us that each person is a good measure of what is true and what is false: what one believes is true, what one

[16] τὸ δοκοῦν ἐκάστῳ τοῦτο καὶ εἶναί φησί που ᾧ δοκεῖ (170 A 3–4). Socrates says that he is quoting Protagoras directly from his book (ἐκ τοῦ ἐκείνου λόγου, 169 E 8).

[17] See also Ketchum, 'Refutation', 79–81. Burnyeat argues that Protagoras 'commits himself to the full equivalence [i.e., the biconditional]' ('Protagoras and Self-refutation in Plato's *Theaetetus*', *Philosophical Review*, 85/2 (Apr. 1976), 172–95 at 178). Burnyeat starts with the example given to illustrate Protagoras' claim: the wind seems cold to one person, and does not seem so to the other, and thus it is cold for one, not cold for the other. He stresses that the example is not of two conflicting appearances or beliefs, but of one belief together with the absence of one. In order to infer anything from the absence of a belief, the conditional (P1) 'If *x* seems *F* to *A*, it is *F* for *A*' is not enough. We need in addition (P2) *x* is *F* for *A* only if *x* seems *F* to *A*. Thus Burnyeat concludes that Protagoras' example shows that he is committed to the full biconditional from the beginning. Ketchum argues, persuasively to me, to the contrary: 'Plato makes it abundantly clear that we are to understand the situation as one in which one person feels the wind as chilly and the other feels it to be not chilly. For immediately after pointing out that if we agree with Protagoras we shall have to claim that the wind is cold for the one who feels chilly and not for the one who does not, Socrates asks, "Does it appear thus to each person?" (152 B 9). The anticipated affirmative answer requires us to say that the wind appears some way to the person who does not feel chilly and the only "way" the example makes available to us is "not cold"' ('Refutation', 77). As I argue here and elsewhere, Protagoras' claim and the examples given to support it commit him only to (P1); it requires a second step to introduce (P2). See also G. Fine, 'Relativism and Self-refutation: Plato, Protagoras, and Burnyeat', in Jyl Gentzler (ed.), *Method in Ancient Philosophy* (Oxford, 1998), 138–63 at 140.

doesn't believe is false. The biconditional tells us, in addition, that
only what one believes is true; man is not only a good criterion
of what is true, but the sole determinant of what is true. Nothing
we know Protagoras to have said settles the question of whether
he took himself to be arguing for the full-blooded biconditional,
or for the more modest conditional. That we do not have anything
which would settle the question may be because his own arguments
for this claim do not survive, or because he never gave any arguments in the first place. Protagoras' aim may have been to counter
Parmenides' rejection of human belief and experience as sufficient
for attaining the truth; *contra* Parmenides, human perceptions, experience, and beliefs are a reliable indicator of truth and falsity.[18]
If so, Protagoras' Truth was a moderate empiricism, not radical
relativism.

In any case, Plato pushes Protagoras further. His first concern
upon introducing (P1) in the *Theaetetus* is to secure for Protagoras
the second half of the biconditional, the converse rule of (P1):

(P2) x is F (for A) *only if* x seems F to A.

Because relativism is so familiar to us now, it may seem obvious
that its special punch is delivered by *this* half of the biconditional.
However, this is exactly what Socrates pauses to emphasize when
he asks Theaetetus:

SOCRATES. Well, it's plausible that a wise man wouldn't be saying some-
    thing silly; so let's follow him up. It sometimes happens, doesn't it, that
    when the same wind is blowing one of us feels cold and the other not?
    Or that one feels slightly cold and the other very?
THEAETETUS. Certainly.
SOCRATES. Now on those occasions, shall we say that the wind itself, taken
    by itself, is cold or not cold? Or shall we accept it from Protagoras that
    it's cold for the one who feels cold, and not for the one who doesn't?
THEAETETUS. That seems plausible.   (152 B 1–9)

---

[18] See E. Kapp's review (in two parts) of Hermann Langerbeck's Δόξις ἐπιρυσμίη
in *Gnomon*, 12 (1936), 65–77 and 158–69, at 70–3; endorsed by K. von Fritz,
'*Nous, noein* and their Derivatives in Pre-Socratic Philosophy (Part II)', *Classical
Philology*, 41 (1946), 12–34 at 22; G. Vlastos, 'Introduction', in *Plato*, Protagoras, Jowett's translation revised by Martin Ostwald (Indianapolis and New York,
1956), at xii n. 24; C. Farrar, *The Origins of Democratic Thinking: The Invention
of Politics in Classical Athens* (Cambridge, 1988), 46–9; G. Striker, 'Methods of
Sophistry', *Essays on Hellenistic Epistemology and Ethics* (Cambridge, 1996), 3–21
at 15.

Socrates emphasizes that Protagoras is saying that the wind is not, taken by itself, cold or not cold, but rather is cold for the one who perceives it as such, and is not for the one who doesn't. But this now raises the question: what does it mean to say that the wind is not, in itself, hot or cold, but is only hot or cold for one who perceives it as such? What is being said about the perceived hotness or coldness? And how is it possible for hotness to exist only 'for' someone? By itself, Protagoras' claim (P1) states that human beliefs and perceptions are the measure of what is true, but we still thereby lack an explanation of what it means to say that nothing is anything in itself, but is whatever it is *for* one who is perceiving it. This is what the Secret Doctrine is meant to explain.

3. The Secret Doctrine

Let us now get clear about what the Secret Doctrine is. It is usually thought of as the thesis that everything is changing. For this reason many commentators call it the 'Heraclitean doctrine', a label Plato never uses, in honour of Heraclitus' famous image of a river constantly flowing.[19] It is quite telling that the exact formulation of the Heraclitean flux doctrine tends to differ from one commentator to another: one may select the formulation 'everything is in motion', another may hit upon 'only changes exist', a third will decide on 'nothing is any one thing by itself' as the most precise formulation of the Secret Doctrine. In fact, there is no single, well-formulated statement of the thesis to be found in the *Theaetetus*. What is introduced under the rubric of the Secret Doctrine is a bunch of slogans loosely strung together. Look again at the passage where Socrates introduces the Secret Doctrine, quoted above. In this passage alone I count at least three distinct ideas:

---

[19] Heraclitus B 12, B 91 DK. Whether Plato was right in freely rendering Heraclitus' river statement as πάντα ῥεῖ or πάντα χωρεῖ (*Crat.* 402 A 8–10; cf. Arist. *Phys.* 8. 3, 253^{b}9, *Metaph. A* 6, 987^{a}32), and what influenced him in this interpretation of the historical Heraclitus (Cratylus? 5th-cent. sophists?), is controversial. See G. S. Kirk, J. E. Raven, and M. Schofield, *The Presocratic Philosophers*, 2nd edn. (Cambridge, 1983), 194–7; W. K. C. Guthrie, *History of Greek Philosophy*, i (Cambridge, 1962), 449–54; G. Vlastos, 'On Heraclitus', *American Journal of Philology*, 76/4 (1955), 337–68 at 338–44.

(1) Nothing is any *one* thing by itself—in the sense that where something is qualified by one property, substantial or non-substantial, it will also reveal itself (or appear, φανεῖται) to be qualified by the opposite property. (152 D 2–6)

(2) Nothing is anything *in itself*—in the sense that all things come to be what they are from change, movement, mixture *with respect to one another* (πρὸς ἄλληλα). (152 D 6–E 1)

(3) Nothing *is* anything in itself—in the sense that nothing *is* (anything at all), but everything is always coming to be (i.e. changing). (152 E 1)

These in turn can be construed in different ways. (1), for example, could mean that everything always gives rise to conflicting appearances (if something appears *F* it will also appear not-*F*—either to the same person or to some other perceiver (see 154 A 3–9)). Or it could mean that a thing *can* bear opposite properties, or even that everything *does* always bear opposite properties. (3) could mean that everything is always changing in *some* respect or in *every* respect. The semi-fanciful arguments for these ideas given at 152 E 1–153 D 7 attribute still other theses to the distinguished assembly (including Homer, Heraclitus, Empedocles) gathered by Socrates, e.g.

(4) Being (what passes for such) and becoming are produced by and are the offspring of change or motion, while not-being and passing-away result from a state of rest. (153 A 5–7)

(5) What is good is change, in both mind and body; what is bad is the opposite. (153 C 4–5)

Later Socrates introduces other theses, e.g.

(6) Everything is change. (156 A 5)

There may be others; I simply want to stress that there is a plurality of theses.[20] There is a chaotic variety of ideas sheltering under

---

[20] Others have also noted that the formula 'nothing is one thing by itself [ἓν μὲν αὐτὸ καθ᾽ αὑτὸ οὐδέν ἐστιν]' can be read in several ways, which fact Socrates exploits in the development of the Secret Doctrine (McDowell, *Theaetetus*, 122; Robert Bolton, 'Plato's Distinction between Being and Becoming', *Review of Metaphysics*, 29 (1975), 66–95 at 69–70; Dancy, 'Theaetetus' First Baby', 72; Veda Cobb-Stevens, 'Perception, Appearance and *Kinêsis*: The Secret Doctrine in Plato's *Theaetetus*', in J. P. Anton and G. L. Kustas (eds.), *Essays in Ancient Greek Philosophy*, iii (Albany, 1989), 247–65 at 253; Bostock, *Plato's* Theaetetus, 51). Against this, Fine argues

Protagoras' 'Secret Doctrine'. Plato makes no attempt—at least here at their debut—to show us how they fit together, or to indicate which is the most important. Some of these theses will make another entrance; for others, e.g. (5), this is their single appearance in the show. If there is a core idea and if there is a story to be told about how the other ideas fit together with it, it can only emerge in an interpretation of the Secret Doctrine as a whole— it is not given to us at the outset. For this reason, it is a mistake to label the theory Socrates and his interlocutors develop on behalf of Protagoras 'Heraclitean' and then assume that the entire doctrine can be summed up with the slogan 'everything is changing'. Nowhere does Socrates use the 'Heraclitean' label himself; he usually refers to it as 'the *logos*'.[21] And he attributes this *logos* to Homer just as often as to Heraclitus. This gives it an extravagant genealogy, which suggests that Plato is gesturing towards a way of thinking, a background picture, supposedly shared by the vast majority of Plato's predecessors and contemporaries— not a unified doctrine clearly articulated by any one person.[22] I shall abandon the traditional label 'the Heraclitean doctrine' entirely, and use the more neutral label 'Secret Doctrine' to refer not to a particular thesis among the many listed above, but rather to this collection of theses, and by extension the general strategy of defence Plato develops for Protagoras at *Theaet.* 152 D– 160 D.

The most important element of the Secret Doctrine is not a flux doctrine, but a relativity principle: 'nothing is anything in itself, but

that it is not the case that Plato is only considering a family of loosely related Heraclitean doctrines. Rather, he develops Heracliteanism from a moderate version to a more extreme version as required for Protagoreanism ('Relativisms', 225 n. 28). This again proceeds on the assumption that Plato is trying to show that Th ⇔ Prot ⇔ Her.

[21] It is variously referred to or described in the following ways: οὐ φαῦλον λόγον 152 D 2; περὶ τούτου 152 E 2; τῷ λόγῳ 153 A 5; ὑπόλαβε . . . οὑτωσί 153 D 8; ἐξ ὧν τὸν Πρωταγόραν φαμὲν λέγειν 155 D 6; τὰ μυστήρια 156 A 3; οὗτος ὁ μῦθος 156 C 4; ὁ λόγος 160 C 2; ὁ ὑπὲρ Πρωταγόρου λόγος 179 D 2; τούτου τοῦ λόγου 179 D 8. Sometimes Socrates refers to the entire doctrine he develops for Protagoras; sometimes he refers to individual theses he uses in Protagoras' defence.

[22] References to Homer: *Theaet.* 152 E 5, 153 A 2, 153 C 10, 160 D 7, 179 E 4. References to Heraclitus: 152 E 3, 160 D 7, 179 E 4. The list of people who supposedly subscribed to the Secret Doctrine includes, besides Protagoras, 'virtually every wise man besides Parmenides', including Heraclitus, Empedocles, Homer, thinkers and poets who didn't agree with each other in any meaningful sense on this or any other metaphysical doctrine.

is whatever it is relative to some perceiver'. Since Protagoras' claim is neutral between the simple conditional (P1), that if something seems F to someone, it is F for her, and the full biconditional (P), it is only by bringing in the Secret Doctrine's relativity principle that Plato secures the converse rule (P2), that something is F (for a person) only if it seems so to that person. The flux doctrine, by contrast, plays a subsidiary role in the development of the Secret Doctrine. It describes the generation and behaviour of the main elements in the Protagorean theory of perception which Socrates constructs.

4. Constructing the Secret
Doctrine (*Theaet.* 153–160)

Socrates starts from the tenets of the Secret Doctrine, and fashions them into a defence of Protagorean relativism. The aim of this defence is to explain how it is that perceptual properties and perceptions are relative to perceivers and to objects, respectively. The whiteness of a stone has no independent existence apart from someone's perceiving it; the sweetness of wine exists only for one perceiving it.

Three features of Socrates' construction of the Secret Doctrine require special attention. First, Socrates makes use of high-flown, mysterious language, presumably meant to evoke a secret language of proponents of this doctrine, to describe the participants in each perceptual encounter. The language is so obscure one suspects Plato is hamming it up. Socrates is made to speak of objects and perceivers which are 'parents' giving birth to 'offspring', i.e. perceptual properties and perceptions. He speaks of the offspring quickly zipping around between their parents, while the parents slowly change. Furthermore, his layers of description are not always consistent with each other—for example, he first says objects are constantly changing, later that they are themselves nothing but changes.[23] How all this translates into more sober language is never entirely clear.

Second, the centrepiece of Socrates' construction of the Secret

---

[23] This and other inconsistencies are noted and discussed by Jane M. Day in 'The Theory of Perception in Plato's *Theaetetus* 152–183' ['Theory'], *OSAP* 15 (1997), 51–80. She concludes that there is probably no way to iron them all out.

Doctrine is an analogy with relational properties like 'is taller' or 'is more in number'. This analogy is presented in the form of a puzzle, whose solution, Socrates tells us, lies in the Secret Doctrine. Unfortunately, he never spells the solution out in detail, and most commentators have concluded that the puzzles either involve a confusion on Plato's part about relational properties, or consist of Plato's attempt to show, in an underhanded way, how confused Protagoras is about relational properties. We need to reconsider the presentation of the puzzles and how it relates to the passages which come before and after it.

Third, the construction of the Secret Doctrine is slow going: it starts at 153 and is not pronounced finished until 160. In between, there are four stages of argumentation, each stage revising the result of the previous one. Each step is quite difficult to understand in itself, and how they all fit together is controversial. One should not attempt to read the final result wholesale back into the conclusion of any one of the arguments used to arrive at it. Commentators frequently object that, at the end of a given argument, Socrates does not tell us what the larger conclusion is supposed to be. But each argument refines the results of the previous step, and Socrates only reveals in the final stage how the Secret Doctrine is supposed to support Protagoras' thesis. Our aim is to read these four stages as part of one continuous argument to that end.

(a) Stage I (153 D 8–154 B 6)

Having introduced the basic tenets of the Secret Doctrine (152 D 2–153 D 7), Socrates begins by applying it to the case of colours:

> SOCRATES. Well then, you must think like this. In the case of the eyes, first, you mustn't think of what you call white colour as being some distinct thing outside your eyes, or in your eyes either—in fact you mustn't assign any place to it; because in that case it would, surely, be at its assigned place and in a state of rest, rather than coming to be. (153 D 8–E 2, trans. McDowell)

In accordance with the principle that nothing is but is always coming to be and in a constant state of motion, perceived colours must always 'come to be', and therefore cannot be at rest or be located anywhere, in the eyes or the object. But if one cannot locate the

colour in the eye or in the object, how should one think of it
(153 E 3)?

Socrates recommends that they start with the thesis that nothing
is one thing just by itself and proceed from there:

SOCRATES. Let's follow what we said just now, and lay it down that nothing is one thing just by itself. On those lines, we'll find that black, white,
or any other colour will turn out to have come into being, from the collision of the eyes with the appropriate motion. What we say a given colour
is will be neither the thing which collides, nor the thing it collides with,
but something which has come into being between them; something peculiar [Burnyeat, 'private'] to each one.   (153 E 4–154 A 3)

They will find that the colour is neither the object nor the perceiver,
but something which has come into existence between them, produced by the encounter of the eye with the object, and peculiar
to the two.[24] Socrates will explain this further in Stage III (155 D
5–157 C 3). But first he must show that neither the eye nor the
perceiver is coloured, but rather something in between them is
coloured; or, as he also puts it, the colour should not be located in
the eye or in the perceiver.

One potentially confusing aspect of Socrates' argument is his way
of switching between these two statements. For Socrates, 'Whiteness is not in the stone' and 'The stone is not white' are equivalent. In the first sentence, whiteness is the subject; the gram-
mar suggests that it is an independently existing entity which
has location. In the second, 'white' is the predicate; whiteness
appears to be a property borne by substances. Compare Aristotle's use of the locution '*F* is in *x*' in *Categories* 2 to characterize non-substantial individuals (e.g. individual qualities or quanti-
ties):

Some things are in a subject, but are not said of any subject. By 'in a sub-

---

[24] Socrates repeats this—that colour should not be identified with the perceiver
or the object—three more times: 156 E 4–6, 159 E 4–5, and 182 A 6–8. It might
seem strange for Plato to postulate a third entity in between the eye and the
stone, which will be coloured. What could this be? It must be the colour itself.
The colour comes to be in between the eye and the stone, and *it* is coloured, not
the eye or stone. It may seem peculiar to think that colours and other perceptual
properties can be predicated of themselves, but this is simply another example of
self-predication in Plato (cf. *Prot.* 330 c). That colours are coloured is a premiss
in Socrates' refutation of the Secret Doctrine (182 D 1–5). There, the thesis that
colours are coloured is put in Heraclitean terms: white is flowing white (τὸ λευκὸν
ῥεῖν τὸ ῥέον).

ject' I mean what is in something not as a part and cannot be separated from what it is in. For example, individual grammatical knowledge is in a subject, the soul, but is not said of any subject, and individual white is in a subject, a body (for every colour is in a body), but is not said of any subject. (1^a23–9)

He uses 'F is in x' as a way of characterizing non-substantial individuals, where 'x is [F]' would presumably not yield such a characterization, since all the different kinds of predications superficially share this form. But for Aristotle, 'white is in the stone' is just another way of saying 'the stone is white'. To say, then, that colour is neither in the eye nor in the stone is to say that neither the eye nor the stone is coloured. This is important to keep in mind; the connection for Socrates between the location of a colour and its belonging to a particular object will always be very tight.[25]

Socrates' thesis is that neither the object nor the perceiver is coloured, i.e. that the colour is neither in the object nor in the perceiver, but rather 'something which has come into being between them, something peculiar to each one'. He argues:

. . . Or would you be prepared to insist that every colour appears to a dog, or any other living thing, just the way it appears to you?

THEAETETUS. Certainly not.

SOCRATES. And what about another man? Is the way anything appears to him like the way it appears to you? Can you insist on that? Or wouldn't you much rather say that it doesn't appear the same even to yourself, because you're never in a similar condition to yourself?

THEAETETUS. Yes, I think that's nearer the truth than the first alternative.

(154 A 3–9)

He begins with the assumption (1) that whatever appears F will also appear not-F. Things appear differently to different people— or even to different animals.[26] Since, for Protagoras, whatever seems

---

[25] See also Burnyeat, 'Conflicting Appearances', 77; Matthen, 'Perception', 38, who puts it as follows: 'Plato makes Protagoras correlate *something's coming-to-be-coloured* with the *coming-to-be of a colour* (i.e. of the offspring's whiteness), which, in effect, allows him to reduce attribution and alteration to existence and creation.' Contrast Cornford, who thinks that Socrates is treating properties as things, not as qualities which need some other thing to support them (*Plato's Theory of Knowledge*, 35). Consequently, he thinks that objects for Protagoras are simply collocations of these property-things.

[26] Why does Socrates assume that everything always appears differently to every perceiver, that nothing ever appears the same to different perceivers or to the

to be the case to one is the case for one, this means that anything which is *F* will also be not-*F*. It then follows that colours cannot be located either in perceived objects or in the perceivers themselves. Why? They become different (e.g. are coloured differently), depending on who comes into contact with them, without changing:

ΣΩΚ. οὐκοῦν εἰ μὲν ᾧ παραμετρούμεθα ἢ οὗ ἐφαπτόμεθα μέγα ἢ λευκὸν ἢ θερμὸν ἦν, οὐκ ἄν ποτε ἄλλῳ προσπεσὸν ἄλλο ἂν ἐγεγόνει, αὐτό γε μηδὲν μεταβάλλον· εἰ δὲ αὖ τὸ παραμετρούμενον ἢ ἐφαπτόμενον ἕκαστον ἦν τούτων, οὐκ ἂν αὖ ἄλλου προσελθόντος ἤ τι παθόντος αὐτὸ μηδὲν παθὸν ἄλλο ἂν ἐγένετο.

SOCRATES. Surely then, (1) if what we measure ourselves against or touch had been large, white or hot, it would never have become different by bumping into a different perceiver, at any rate not if it didn't undergo any change itself. (2) And on the other hand, if what does the measuring or touching had been any of those things, then again, it wouldn't have become different when another thing came up against it, or the thing which came up against it had something happen to it: not if it hadn't, itself, had anything happen to it. (154 B 1–6, trans. McDowell, with Burnyeat's modifications in 'Conflicting Appearances', 77 n. 1)

Here are two arguments: first, the perceived object does not have the colour, and second, the perceiver does not have it either. Each contains a counterfactual conditional. (1) If the perceived object were large, white, or hot, then if it did not itself change when something else came up against it, it would not thereby become different, i.e. not large, not white, not hot. But as it is, it *does* become different when something else comes up against it, though it does not

same perceiver at different times (McDowell, *Theaetetus*, 152–3; Bostock, *Plato's Theaetetus*, 49, 60–1)? This is, as Bostock puts it, 'an astounding claim. The suggestion that we cannot have qualitatively similar perceptions for any length of time is flatly contradicted by common sense, and surely not needed by the Protagorean thesis that all judgements of perception are true' (61). Burnyeat thinks it is none the less justified because 'The theory [Socrates] is elaborating is committed to the view that, if this were so, each appearance should still yield knowledge of a real state of affairs. If the theory is to hold good, it must be able to take in its stride the most extreme variation imaginable in the course of appearances. So we had better suppose, for the sake of the argument, that extreme variation actually obtains' ('Conflicting Appearances', 86; see also Fine, 'Conflicting Appearances', 132 n. 48). I think the explanation is simpler: the assumption is not required for Protagoras or Theaetetus. Socrates is entitled to use this assumption because it is already on the table, placed there as part of the Secret Doctrine: (1) whatever appears *F* will also appear not-*F* (152 D 4–6). (He uses it again at 159 E 7–8.)

change. Therefore, the object is not large, white, or hot. And likewise, (2) if the sense-organ were large, white, or hot, then when
another thing approached it and the sense-organ was not affected,
or when something happened to the first thing which approached
it, it would not have become different. But it *does* become different
(without being affected); therefore, the sense-organ is not large,
white, or hot.[27]

One might wonder about the point of (2). Why would anyone
suppose that the *eye* is large, white, or hot? As McDowell puts
it, 'It is not clear what the point of this might be, since it is obscure why anyone might be thought to want to say (except for
obviously irrelevant reasons) that an eye is white; this does not
seem to be quite the same as locating the white colour which one

[27] Burnyeat argues that the aim of this passage (154 B 1–6) is 'to establish on
behalf of Protagoras that sensible qualities like hot and cold, white and black, are
essentially relative to the individual perceiving subject', that 'Neither the object seen
nor the perceiving subject is in itself white (154 B)' ('Conflicting Appearances', 77).
Fine summarizes Burnyeat's construal of the argument, which she calls 'perceptual
relativism', as follows ('Conflicting Appearances', 114):

(A) There are, or at least seem to be, conflicting appearances; for example, the
stone appears white to me, but not to you.
(B) If the stone is really, or in itself white, then (unless it changes) it will appear
white to everyone.
(C) The stone hasn't changed between the different appearances.
(D) Therefore the stone isn't really, or in itself, white; rather, sensible qualities
are relative to perceivers.

She rejects this, on the grounds that Plato's argument does *not* depend on the dubious assumption (B), and furthermore, it does not depend on the conflation of being
really *F* and being *F* in itself. She argues, 'if to be really *F* is to be truly (i.e. in fact) *F*,
and if to be *F* in itself is to be intrinsically (i.e. non-relationally) *F*, then the two are
not the same. For objects can really (in fact) have relational properties' ('Conflicting
Appearances', 115, 118–19; *contra* Burnyeat, 'Conflicting Appearances', 76–81, and
Dancy, 'Theaetetus' First Baby', 66, 78 ff.). When 154 B 1–6 is translated more carefully, it does not contain this conflation. Her objections are sound, but Burnyeat's
basic position can be modified to meet them. First, 'perceptual relativism' should
not depend on assumption (B), that anything which appears *F* and not-*F* cannot
itself be *F* (or not-*F*). Rather, (B) should read as follows: if the stone is in itself
white, then it will not become different (for different people) without changing.
Second, I do not think that Socrates conflates being really *F* with being intrinsically
F. The argument is that things are (really) white and not white, without changing;
the conclusion, drawn in Stage III, is that things are not white in themselves. Third,
the argument begun at 154 B 1–6 is not yet complete; it is premature to say that it
follows from 154 B 1–6 that 'Neither the object seen nor the perceiving subject is
in itself white (154 B)' (Burnyeat, 'Conflicting Appearances', 77, emphasis added).
154 B 1–6 is just the first step in a larger argument leading to the conclusion, reached
in Stage III, that colours and other perceptual properties are relational rather than
intrinsic.

sees in the eyes, which we are told not to do at 153 D 8–E 2.'[28]
It is indeed difficult to make sense of the idea that when the eye
perceives something as white, the eye therefore might be white.
However, as I have already argued, saying that the eye might be
white *is* the same as saying whiteness might be in the eye. The
question is, where should one locate the colour—in the eye, in
the object, or somewhere else (153 D 8–E 1, 153 E 7–154 A 2)? Arguments (1) and (2) eliminate the possibilities: not in the perceiver, not in the perceived object, therefore somewhere else in
between.

If one expected an argument that (P) implies flux, one might
raise, as Fine does, the following objection: why would Socrates
say that the perceiver and the perceived object do not change as
they approach each other, when the Heraclitean doctrine tells us
that everything is always changing?[29] I have interpreted argument
(1) as follows:

(1) If the object were large, white, or hot, then it would not be-
     come different (when it comes into contact with something
     else) without changing. But it does become different when it
     comes into contact with something else, without changing;
     therefore it is not large, white, or hot. (154 B 1–3)

---

[28] *Theaetetus*, 132. Because of this difficulty, McDowell proposes to understand
argument (2) as follows: 'If a perceiver is seeing white and does not himself change,
he does not come to be other than seeing white. But any perceiver of whom one
might be inclined to say that he is seeing white does, without himself changing, come to be other than seeing white, either by coming to perceive a different object or because of a change in the original object. Therefore it cannot
be true of any such perceiver that he is seeing white.' However, this construal of
the Greek is implausible, for the reference of 'each of these' (ἕκαστον τούτων) is
'big or white or hot' (μέγα ἢ λευκὸν ἢ θερμόν); the translation would only be warranted if the text at 154 B 4 read 'But if, in turn, what was measuring or touching
were ⟨perceiving⟩ any of these' (εἰ δὲ αὖ τὸ παραμετρούμενον ἢ ἐφαπτόμενον ἕκαστον ⟨ᾐσθάνετο⟩ τούτων) (see also Burnyeat, 'Conflicting Appearances', 80). Furthermore, the translation severs the connection between this passage and the previous
one: both passages contribute to the argument that neither the object nor the eyes
are white. McDowell thinks that we get a new argument here, that (1) what we
measure ourselves against or touch *is not* but *becomes* large, white, or hot, and
(2) we do not perceive, but *come to* perceive, large, white, or hot. Accordingly,
he inserts a paragraph break between 154 A 9 and 154 B 1. On my interpretation, 154 B 1–6 is meant to confirm a claim that has already been stated twice
before.

[29] Fine, 'Relativisms', 229–30; 'Conflicting Appearances', 115–17.

Shouldn't one rather construe the argument as an argument for
Heraclitean flux?

(1′) If the object is large, white, or hot, it will not become different (when it comes into contact with something else)
unless it changes. But it does become different when it
comes into contact with something else; *therefore, it has
changed.*[30]

The first problem with this construal is to explain what the second
half of the argument is supposed to establish. On my reading, it
goes as follows:

(2) If the sense-organ were large, white, or hot, then when something new approached it or when something happened to the
first thing which approached it and the sense-organ was not
affected, it would not have become different. But it does
become different without being affected; *therefore, the sense-
organ is not large, white, or hot.* (154 B 3–6)

Suppose that this sentence is understood as follows:

(2′) If the sense-organ is large, white, or hot, it will not become
different when something new approaches it or when something happens to the first thing that approaches it, unless
it changes. But it does become different; *therefore, it has
changed.*

Together, (1′) and (2′) tell us that when a stone looks white to
Socrates, the whiteness is *both* in Socrates' eye *and* in the stone,
until they both change. But surely this is the exact opposite of what
Socrates has been arguing so far: that the whiteness is in *neither.*[31]
Secondly, the conditionals are present counterfactuals, with the im-
perfect ἦν in each of the antecedents ('if *X* were true, then *Y* would
be true . . .'), which indicates that neither the consequents nor the
antecedents are true. It is never true at any time that the stone or
Socrates' eye is white—rather, as Socrates has already said twice
before, the colour is somewhere in between the two, so that neither

[30] Fine, 'Conflicting Appearances', 119.
[31] Fine does not discuss argument (2) in 'Conflicting Appearances', but perhaps
to avoid this problem, she would accept McDowell's reading of ἕκαστον τούτων as
'perceiving any of these [i.e. large, white, hot]'. For difficulties with this reading see
n. 28.

the stone nor Socrates' eye can be said to 'have' the colour whiteness.

Arguments (1) and (2) are supposed to show that whiteness should not be located in the perceiver's eye or in the perceived object. In both arguments it is simply asserted that the object of perception and the perceiver become different without changing. But why does the stone become different when different perceivers approach it, without changing? If it becomes different, hasn't it changed? The answer lies in the next stage of the argument. In this notoriously difficult stretch of text, Socrates offers a number of puzzles which will trip one up if one fails to get the point of the Secret Doctrine. Unfortunately, he does not explicitly say how the Secret Doctrine solves the puzzles. I shall argue that we are supposed to see why it would be a mistake to locate the colours—against the dictates of the Secret Doctrine—anywhere but between the object and perceiver. Socrates first illustrates the confusions which would lead one to make that mistake (Stage II), then describes what is required to avoid the mistake (Stage III). The answer: things become different without changing because nothing is white or hot in itself. As we might put it, colours do not belong intrinsically to objects but are relational properties; things take on different perceptual, and relational, properties without undergoing change in themselves.

(b) Stage II (154 B 6–155 D 5)

Having stated that colours should not be located in the object or in the perceiver's eye, since these both become different without changing, Socrates says:

SOCRATES. . . . . As it is, you see, we may easily find ourselves forced into saying the most astonishing and ridiculous things, as Protagoras would point out or anyone who undertook to expound his views.

THEAETETUS. What do you mean? What sort of ridiculous things?

(154 B 6–10)

Socrates offers two examples of the 'ridiculous things' which will follow if one fails to grasp the point of the Secret Doctrine. Place six dice on a table. Put four beside them: the six dice are more than the four. Then put twelve dice beside the six dice. Now the six dice are less than the twelve. The six dice are 'more' when placed next to four dice, and 'less' when placed next to twelve, although they have not themselves changed in number. One can easily become confused by this type of example, as Theaetetus does in trying to answer Socrates' next question:

SOCRATES. Well now, supposing Protagoras or anyone else were to ask you this question: 'Is it possible, Theaetetus, to become bigger or more in number in any other way than by being increased?' What is your answer to that?

THEAETETUS. Well, Socrates, if I answer what seems true in relation to the present question, I shall answer 'No, it is not possible'; but if I consider it in relation to the question that went before, then in order to avoid contradicting myself, I say, 'Yes, it is.'

SOCRATES. That's a good answer, my friend, by Jove it is; you are inspired. But, I think, if you answer 'Yes', it will be like that episode in Euripides— the tongue will be safe from refutation but the mind will not. . . .

(154 C 1–6)

When asked whether it is possible to become bigger or more in number in any other way than by being increased, Theaetetus is initially inclined to say No, that it is not possible to become bigger or more in number (i.e. different) without increasing. However, when he considers the dice, he is inclined to say Yes, that something *can* become more in number (i.e. different) without increasing or changing. Socrates' second example concerns relative size: suppose Socrates is said at one time to be bigger than Theaetetus, but a year later, after Theaetetus has grown, has become smaller than Theaetetus, though he has not changed in height. Though one may be initially inclined to say that it is not possible to become bigger or smaller without changing, it certainly seems that Socrates has become smaller without changing.

How do ordinary, non-Protagorean ways of speaking cause this confusion, and what does the Secret Doctrine recommend to solve the puzzles? McDowell sets out what he takes to be the two main options: 'We can distinguish two possible views as to the identity of the present practice which is said to lead to the puzzles. According to one view, it is the practice of using non-relational forms of statement where we ought to be using relational forms. According to the other, it is the practice of using "be", contrary to the Secret Doctrine' (*Theaetetus*, 133).[32] Both assume that the

[32] For endorsements—some more confident than others—of the first alternative see: Cornford, *Plato's Theory of Knowledge*, 43–5; W. D. Ross, *Plato's Theory of Ideas* (Oxford, 1951), 101–2; R. S. Bluck, 'The Puzzles of Size and Number in

puzzles exhibit apparent contradictions caused by ordinary ways of speaking: the dice are both more and less, Socrates is both taller and shorter. These contradictions are posed when Protagoras says that all beliefs, even contradictory ones, are true, and are supposed to be dissolved by the Secret Doctrine. How? According to the first view, we are supposed to qualify 'the dice are both more and less' by specifying what the dice are more and less *than*. According to the second view, we are supposed to replace the language of being with the language of flux. Socrates *does* change when approached by the taller Theaetetus, and the dice *do* change when approached by twelve dice. But why does Protagoras *need* to appeal to flux, when one can dissolve the contradictions by simply filling in the qualifications? Indeed, introducing flux seems to involve a mistake, since both Socrates and the dice clearly do *not* change while becoming 'shorter' and 'more'.[33] I believe the first solution is essentially correct, but the problem itself has been misdescribed.

The problem with the dice is not that they exhibit contradictions. Cornford, in just a few lines of his commentary, correctly identified both the confusion and the Secret Doctrine solution to the puzzles:

It is clear that the difficulty here exists only for one who thinks of 'large'

Plato's *Theaetetus'*, *Proceedings of the Cambridge Philological Society*, 7 (1961), 7–9 at 8; Burnyeat, *Introduction*, 13. For the second alternative see McDowell, *Theaetetus*, ad loc.; Dancy, 'Theaetetus' First Baby', 82, 87–8; P. L. Gottlieb, *Aristotle and the Measure of All Things* [*Aristotle*] (Ph.D. diss., Cornell, 1988), 21–9; Fine, 'Conflicting Appearances', 122–30.

[33] Some have proposed that Plato has fallen victim to a confusion himself—for example, that he does not know how to distinguish between so-called Cambridge changes (for example, the mug on my right 'changes' when I move to the other side of it) and real changes (McDowell, *Theaetetus*, ad loc., 137; C. Kirwan, 'Plato and Relativity', *Phronesis*, 19 (1974), 112–29 at 127–8; Day, 'Theory', 55). Others think that Plato unfairly attributes such a confusion to Protagoras to make the case against him appear stronger (E. S. Haring, 'Socratic Duplicity: *Theaetetus* 154 B 1–156 A 3' ['Duplicity'], *Review of Metaphysics*, 45 (1992), 525–42). Still others argue that Plato is *right* to charge Protagoras with this confusion. As Fine argues, 'Roughly, his idea seems to be that we can distinguish between genuine and mere Cambridge change only if an object is something in itself; since Protagoras claims that nothing is anything by itself (153 E 4–5), he cannot distinguish between genuine and mere Cambridge change. Plato then commits him to the view that every case of appearing different involves a genuine change in the object that appears different' ('Conflicting Appearances', 130; see also Gottlieb, *Aristotle*, 21–9, and T. H. Irwin, 'Plato's Heracliteanism', *Philosophical Quarterly*, 27 (1977), 1–13 at 5–6).

as a quality residing in the thing which is larger than something else, with 'small' as the answering quality residing in the smaller thing. If that is so, then, when the large thing is compared with something larger instead of something smaller, he will suppose that it has lost its quality 'large' and gained instead the quality 'small'. By suffering this internal change it will have 'become small'. He will then be puzzled when we point out that the thing has not altered in size. (*Plato's Theory of Knowledge*, 43–4)

Those who persist—despite what the Secret Doctrine tells us—in locating largeness and smallness *in* objects will assume that change with respect to these properties constitutes internal change. They will then be unable to understand how something can 'become different'—e.g. larger or smaller—without changing in itself. We find it difficult to understand that things can become different without changing, but the argument at 154 B 1–6 depends on it. Consider again the first part of it:

(1) If whiteness were in the stone, then when something approaches the stone, but the stone isn't affected, the stone wouldn't become different. But the stone *does* become different when something else approaches it (though it is not affected). Thus the whiteness is not in the stone.

The argument turns on seeing that the stone *does* become different without changing. The puzzles are meant to soften up Theaetetus, and the reader, by getting us to see two points.

First, coming to be larger or smaller, more or less, does not necessarily constitute internal change. Socrates' becoming shorter and the dice becoming less are both changes in relational properties produced purely through comparison of Socrates with other objects. Thus, it is possible for something to cease to be the subject of some attribute without undergoing change itself. Second, the reason for this is that things are not intrinsically large, small, more, or less, but only so in relation to something else. One shouldn't locate 'larger', 'smaller', 'more', and 'less' *in* objects themselves—if one does, changes in predicate will appear to constitute changes in the things themselves.

Let me summarize what we have so far. In Stage I Socrates argues that whiteness and other perceptual properties should not be located in the perceiver or in the object itself. For the object is now white, now dark, now hot, now cold, as different per-

ceivers approach it; it becomes different for different perceivers
without changing itself. How is it possible for something to 'become different without changing'? In Stage II Socrates presents
us with two puzzling examples whose solution answers that question. Six dice become more and less, Socrates becomes taller then
shorter, without changing, because these properties do not belong intrinsically, but in relation to other objects. Once one has
grasped this point concerning 'larger', 'smaller', 'more', and 'less',
one can apply it to whiteness and other perceptual properties.
Socrates does this in Stage III. Perceptual properties are neither in perceivers nor in the objects they perceive. Thus, when
we are asked whether something can change with respect to perceptual properties without undergoing change in itself, the correct
answer is Yes; as with relational properties, perceptual properties do not belong to anything intrinsically.[34] The object and the
eye become different—by coming to be coloured and coming to
perceive—without changing just because they do not change in
themselves, but take on qualitative alterations in relation to each
other.

(c) Stage III (155 D 5–157 C 3)

When Theaetetus confesses that he does not see the point of the
puzzles, Socrates *seems* to change the topic. For he simply announces that 'everything is change and nothing else' and then
returns to the perceptual theory which he was describing before
he introduced the puzzles. Has Socrates, as Dancy puts it, simply 'bullie[d] a bewildered Theaetetus into accepting the theory
of perception (157 C–D) without returning to his puzzles to tell
us how to handle them'?[35] On closer examination one can see

[34] Socrates initially discourages Theaetetus from saying Yes not because it is the
wrong answer, but because he does not want Theaetetus to give the right answer
without a proper understanding of it. Otherwise 'it will be like that episode in
Euripides—the tongue will be safe from refutation but the mind will not' (154 D 3–
6). To arrive at a proper understanding, they must examine the three 'apparitions'
(τὰ φάσματα, 155 A 2) battling against one another, causing Theaetetus' confusion. I
cannot discuss them here. But once one sees that the point is that predicates like 'is
larger' are relational, two-place predicates, one can show that the three apparitions,
properly qualified, do not in fact conflict.

[35] Dancy, 'Theaetetus' First Baby', 80. Most commentators take this view, but
Cornford and Ross thought that there were at least *hints* of a solution in the theory
of perception which follows (*Plato's Theory of Knowledge*, 44–5; *Plato's Theory of
Ideas*, 101–2).

that he does spell out the parallels between relational properties (e.g. being taller) and perceptual properties (e.g. being red), although he does not explicitly refer back to the puzzles themselves.

Socrates begins with the principle that 'everything is change, and there is nothing but change' (156 A 5). He tells a genealogical *mythos* on the basis of this principle:

The universe is change and nothing else [τὸ πᾶν κίνησις ἦν καὶ ἄλλο παρὰ τοῦτο οὐδέν]. There are two kinds of change, each unlimited in number, the one having the power of acting and the other the power of being acted on. From their intercourse, and their friction against one another, there come to be offspring, unlimited in number but coming in pairs of twins, of which one is a perceived thing [τὸ αἰσθητόν] and the other a perception, which is on every occasion generated and brought to birth together with the perceived thing. (156 A 5–B 2, trans. McDowell)

There are two kinds of change—active and passive in power—whose intercourse produces a perceptible property (e.g. a colour) and its inseparable twin, the perception of it. For each encounter there are two parents (the sense-organ and the object of perception) plus twin offspring (the perceptible property and the perception).[36] Each encounter between parents issues in twin offspring which cannot exist apart from each other. The offspring are perceivings (e.g. seeings, smellings, hearings) and perceptible properties (e.g. colours, sounds, smells). Despite their apparent reification, the offspring are not objects but properties of the parents.

The key players have been introduced and the stage is set for Socrates' main point, including the solution to the puzzles. He launches into his explanation by saying, 'Well now Theaetetus, what does this story [οὗτος ὁ μῦθος] mean to convey to us? What is its bearing on what came before? Do you see?' (156 C 3–5, trans. McDowell). When Theaetetus replies quite understandably that he does not, Socrates spells out the *mythos* with what I take to be a corresponding *logos* at 156 C 7–157 B 1:

Well, have a look at it, and see if we can get it finished off somehow.

---

[36] Strictly speaking, Socrates does not yet talk of 'perceptible properties', but uses only the more imprecise expression τὸ αἰσθητόν, or 'what is perceived'. Plato coins the more precise expression ἡ ποιότης, 'quality', later when he refutes the Secret Doctrine (182 A 9–B 1).

What it means to say is this. All those things are involved in change, as we were saying; but there's quickness or slowness in their changing. Now anything that is slow keeps its changing in the same place, and in relation to the things which approach it, and that's how it generates. But the things which are generated are quicker; because they move, and their changing naturally consists in motion. (156 C 7–D 3, trans. McDowell)

Here Socrates introduces a new distinction between types of change: slow and fast. The offspring (perceptual property and perception) undergo 'fast' change; they move around between the parents, and do not remain in one place.[37] The parents undergo 'slow' change. We are told that slow change does not consist of change of place, and that it occurs 'in relation to the things which approach it'.

Insufficient attention has been paid to Socrates' distinction between slow and fast changes; I believe it holds the key to the Secret Doctrine. 'Slow change' is Socrates' way of describing relational change, i.e. becoming different without changing intrinsically, which occurs for objects and perceivers in perception. First, we must get clear about what slow changes are. Though everyone agrees that the offspring—the colour and the perception of it—undergo fast changes, that the parents undergo slow changes, and that fast changes consist of local motion, opinions differ as to what slow changes are. One view (A) is that fast and slow changes are both kinds of movement, the former being fast motions from place to place, the latter being slow revolutions in one place. Another (B) is that fast changes are motions, whereas slow changes are qualitative *alterations*. ($\kappa i \nu \eta \sigma \iota s$ can be translated either way.) Most who advocate this reading seem to think that (B1) these slow changes occur *prior* to any encounter between the parents. I will argue, against this, that (B2) slow changes result from encounters between parents.

The principal reasons both for favouring and for rejecting (B) come from Socrates' fuller descriptions of change and its two species at 181 C 2–D 6. There he notes that there are two kinds

---

[37] At 156 D 1–2, where one would expect further explanation of why these are called *fast* changes, there unfortunately seems to be a lacuna, because $o\H{v}\tau\omega$ $\delta\H{\eta}$ at 156 D 2 has no obvious referent. The new OCT edition of the *Theaetetus* prints the passage with a lacuna. Most translators delete $o\H{v}\tau\omega$ $\delta\H{\eta}$ (McDowell, Levett). However, we are also lacking an explanation of what 'slow change' means, with no reason to think that it too has dropped out from the text.

of change: (1) moving from place to place or revolving in the same place (φορά), and (2) remaining in the same place, but growing old, becoming black or hard, i.e. undergoing qualitative alteration (ἀλλοίωσις).[38] Is this distinction the same as the earlier distinction between fast and slow change? Day says No, arguing that 'there is too close a verbal echo between "flux in the same place" characteristic of "slow fluxes" of 156 c and the "turning about in the same place" which is classed at 181 c 7 as a kind of *motion*, i.e., specifically *not* as change'.[39] (Presumably, on this view, parents engender offspring by rotating slowly in the vicinity of each other.) However, remaining in one place is characteristic both of things revolving in one place and of things undergoing qualitative alteration. Thus, going on verbal echoes alone, we can identify either one with slow changes. Since the passages seem to map on to each other, where the latter passage spells out in more prosaic language the distinction made earlier, most opt for (B).[40]

If slow changes are qualitative alterations of the parents, then do these qualitative alterations occur prior to an encounter between parents (B1), or because of them (B2)? According to (B1), parents, i.e. objects and perceivers, undergo slow, gradual qualitative alteration; they become older, paler, healthier, sicker. Depending on their changing qualitative conditions, they produce different sorts of offspring—i.e. different kinds of perceptions. The main attraction of this reading is that it gives us at least a hint of a causal account of how perception takes place. But its main difficulty is precisely that we then have to say that objects have perceptual properties like heat and whiteness prior to and therefore independently of an encounter between parents. We have been repeatedly told not to locate perceptual properties like whiteness or heat in the objects but between the perceiver and the object (154 A 2, 156 D 6). Nothing

---

[38] Plato makes the same distinction much more concisely at *Parm.* 138 B, where he says that there are only two kinds of change: change of quality (or alteration) and change of place (motion).

[39] Day, 'Theory', 64, endorsing Campbell, *The* Theaetetus *of Plato*, 58–9, 147; Matthen, 'Perception', 37.

[40] Cornford, *Plato's Theory of Knowledge*, 49–50; McDowell, *Theaetetus*, 138; Cooper, *Plato's* Theaetetus, 39; George Nakhnikian, 'Plato's Theory of Sensation, I', *Review of Metaphysics*, 9 (Sept. 1955), 129–48 at 135; I. M. Crombie, *An Examination of Plato's Doctrines* (2 vols.; London, 1963), ii. 23.

should be said to be, or become, pale or hot outside of a perceptual encounter.

For this reason, I think that (B2) slow changes must occur in parents not prior to a perceptual encounter, but because of one. Consider Socrates' description of an encounter between parents, which follows on the heels of his introduction of fast and slow changes. We expect Socrates to incorporate these distinctions into his description, and I think he does.

When an eye, then, and something else, one of the things commensurable with it, approach one another and generate the whiteness they do, and a perception cognate with it—things which would never have come into being if either of the former pair had come up against something different—then at that moment, when (A) the seeing, from the eyes, and (B) whiteness, from the thing which joins in giving birth to the colour, are moving in between, (C) *the eye has come to be full of seeing*; it sees at that moment, and has come to be, not by any means seeing, but an eye that sees. (D) *And the thing which joined in generating the colour has been filled all round with whiteness*; it has come to be, again, not whiteness, but white—a white piece of wood, or stone, or whatever it is that happens to have that sort of colour. (156 D 3–E 7, trans. McDowell)

In any given encounter between parents, the parents undergo change along with their offspring. The offspring—seeing and whiteness—change by 'moving in between' (see A and B). These movements are clearly the 'fast changes' Socrates has just described a few lines before. The second set of changes happen to the parents (C, D); the eye 'comes to be full of seeing' and 'becomes an eye that sees', and the object becomes 'filled all round with whiteness', and 'comes to be white'. I think that just as the first set of changes specifies 'fast changes' more fully, so too with this second set of changes—qualitative alterations of the eye and the object—Socrates is specifying 'slow changes' more fully.[41]

Socrates never says so explicitly. But notice that his very next point is that qualitative alterations occur for a parent only when it encounters a partner.[42]

[41] Why are such changes 'slow'? I do not think there is any particular significance to this term other than that 'slow' is the opposite of 'fast', and qualitative changes are to be contrasted with movement. Perhaps the label is in keeping with the strange mystery sect Socrates pretends to be describing. In his refutation of the Secret Doctrine he is free to introduce a more technical and precise term, ἀλλοίωσις, to describe the kind of change he is referring to (181 D 2).

[42] See also 182 A–B, where Socrates summarizes it, stating that the parents 'give

We must think of the other cases, too, in the same way: we must take it that *nothing is hard, hot, or anything, just by itself*—we were actually saying that some time ago—*but that in their intercourse with one another things come to be all things and qualified in all ways as a result of their change*. Because even in the case of those of them which act and those which are acted on, it isn't possible to arrive at a firm conception, as they say, of either of them, taken singly, as being anything. It isn't true that something is a thing which acts before it comes into contact with the thing which is acted on by it; nor that something is a thing which is acted on before it comes into contact with the thing which acts on it. And what acts when it comes into contact with one thing can turn out a thing which is acted on when it bumps into something else. The up-shot of all this is that, as we've been saying since the beginning, noth-ing is one thing just by itself, but things are always coming to be for someone [ὥστε ἐξ ἁπάντων τούτων, ὅπερ ἐξ ἀρχῆς ἐλέγομεν, οὐδὲν εἶναι ἓν αὐτὸ καθ' αὐτό, ἀλλά τινι ἀεὶ γίγνεσθαι]. (156 E 7–157 B 1, trans. McDow-ell)

Here Socrates finally spells out how the *mythos* at 156 A 2–C 3 'bears on what came before', i.e. on the puzzles: nothing is any-thing in itself, but comes to be in relation to something else. Even the active and passive powers of parents, in virtue of which they generate their offspring, must be applied in a given relation, not absolutely. What perceives in one relation may be the object of perception in another. Thus, according to the theory of perception Socrates and Theaetetus have developed for Protagoras, 'seeings' and colours do not exist by themselves: they would not have come into being except for the intercourse between perceiver and ob-ject. They are relational properties: thus, a perceptual property belongs to a thing only in relation to a perceiver, and a perception can be attributed to a perceiver only in relation to the perceived object.

We now have a continuous line of argument from Stage I to

---

birth to perceptions and perceived things, and one lot come to be qualified in cer-tain ways while the others come to be perceiving' (182 B 5–7). Since qualitative alterations are said at 181 C 2–D 6 to include changes like becoming older, one might object that slow changes are meant to cover a wider range of changes than those produced by a perceptual encounter. I think Plato says explicitly that all al-terations and changes are perceiver-dependent, and thus we can infer that even alterations like becoming older must in some way be the product of a percep-tual encounter. For those who think otherwise (and espouse B1), I would argue that one cannot then also claim that Protagoras is *committed* to there being slow changes.

Stage III. In Stage I we are told that whiteness and hotness should not be located in perceivers or objects, but in between, and that objects should not be said to have these properties, lest we fall into the confusions illustrated by the example of the dice in Stage II. The dice show that properties like 'more than' do not belong to objects in themselves, but can be attributed to them because of their interactions with or relations to other objects. In Stage III Socrates applies that lesson to perceptual properties and perceptions: they do not belong to objects in themselves, but can be attributed to them because of their interactions with or relations to other objects.

Perceptual properties and perceptions are similar to relational properties like 'more' and 'bigger' in the following way:[43] like relational properties, perceptual properties and perceivings can only be applied in a given relation. Just as nothing is, or becomes, taller just by itself, so too nothing becomes white, or percipient, just by itself. Perceptual properties and perceptions do not belong intrinsically to anything; they come into being given particular relations, and then go out of existence when those relations no longer obtain. And just as things can take on different relational properties without changing in themselves, so too a stone can become different—white or black—without changing. When a stone comes to be white for someone, it becomes different—since it was not white before—but does not change itself. Rather, it undergoes 'slow change', i.e. quali-

---

[43] The analogy between relational predicates like 'is taller than' and perceptual properties like 'is white' is only meant to go so far. Bostock wonders what the relevance of the puzzles is, since looking white arises as a result of a complex physical interaction, whereas being taller does not. Similarly, McDowell rejects the relational reading of the puzzles because 'comparative adjectives need to be applied to things only in relation to objects of comparison', whereas 'perceptual qualities should be ascribed to things only in relation to perceivers.' And Haring seems to be seriously misled by the fact that being larger and being smaller can be measured and therefore there is a fact of the matter about them, whereas whiteness and hotness do not for Protagoras have inter-subjective existence ('Duplicity', 527). This leads Haring to conclude that Socrates means to confuse Theaetetus and undermine Protagoras with these examples. But Plato is not claiming that the two types of predicates are identical in every respect. One does not need to assume that the logic of relational predicates depends on anyone's beliefs; rather, they are meant as a paradigm for understanding what it means to say that 'nothing is anything in itself'. (George Grote already saw that one should distinguish here between the two senses in which something can be relative; see *Plato, and the Other Companions of Sokrates*, new [4th] edn. (4 vols.; London, 1888), iii. 127–8.)

tative alteration, in relation to something else.[44] That Socrates calls these alterations 'slow changes' may seem peculiar if one assumes that only *intrinsic* changes can be *real* changes. However, it allows him to apply the principle of constant change to the theory of perception while at the same time respecting and accommodating a point which the puzzles demand that we make: when a stone comes to be white for one person, it is not undergoing change in itself, but is none the less coming to have a property which it did not have before.

(d) Stage IV (157 c 4–160 e 5)

In the final stage of the construction of the Secret Doctrine, Socrates shows how the account of perception and perceptual properties developed so far can be used to support and defend Protagoras' claim. He addresses the following objection: what about dreamers and madmen—are their perceptions and beliefs just as true as those of the sane person? Can the Secret Doctrine help Protagoras show

---

[44] These 'slow changes' are the same as Peter Geach's Cambridge changes in the *strict* sense in which he uses that term (*God and the Soul* (New York, 1969)). He defines Cambridge changes as occurring when contradictory properties hold successively of one thing. 'The only sharp criterion for a thing's having changed is what we may call the Cambridge criterion (since it keeps on occurring in Cambridge philosophers of the great days, like Russell and McTaggart): The thing called "x" has changed if we have "F(x) at time t" true and "F(x) at time t1" false, for some interpretation of "F", "t", and "t1". But this account is, intuitively quite unsatisfactory. By this account Socrates would after all change by coming to be shorter than Theaetetus; moreover, Socrates would change posthumously (even if he had no immortal soul) every time a fresh schoolboy came to admire him. . . . The changes I have mentioned, we wish to protest, are not "real" changes. . . . I cannot dismiss from my mind the feeling that there is a difference here. . . . But it would be quite another thing to offer a criterion for selecting, from among propositions that report at least "Cambridge" changes, those that also report "real" change (given that they are true); and I have no idea how I could do that—except that I am certain that there is no "real" change of numbers' (71–2). Slow changes are also coextensive with Irwin's category of 'aspect-changes', which he defines as follows: 'x a-changes iff x is F in one respect, not-F in another, and x is in the same condition where it is F and when it is not-F (e.g., x is big in comparison with y, small in comparison with z).' Irwin distinguishes 'aspect-change' from 'self-change', which he defines as follows: 'x s-changes iff at time t1 x is F and at time t2 x is not-F, and x itself is not in the same condition at t2 as it was at t1' ('Plato's Heracliteanism', 5–6). But I do not agree that '*Theaet*. 155 B–C argues from aspect-change to self-change'; the conclusion at 156 E 8–157 A 2 states explicitly that things change in relation to each other, *not* in themselves.

that all perceptions, even those which we ordinarily think of as false, are in fact true?

Socrates offers two replies. First, he mentions the disputes he imagines Theaetetus has often heard people engaged in: what evidence could one point to, if someone asked at this very moment whether one is asleep and dreaming everything one has in mind, or awake and having a discussion with another (158 B 5–E 4)? These disputes consist of undecidability arguments, according to which there are no non-arbitrary ways of determining which beliefs in a set of beliefs are true and which are false. These arguments undermine Theaetetus' confidence that there is any way to tell which beliefs are true and which are false. However, they give no positive reason to suppose that all beliefs are *true*.

This is the point of Socrates' second reply, in which he uses the Secret Doctrine to argue that all beliefs and perceptions are true (158 E 5–160 E 5).[45] If Socrates ill and Socrates healthy, or Socrates dreaming and Socrates awake, are different, then they must be different in their powers to affect and be affected. It follows, Socrates claims, that the perception and perceptual property generated by a perceiver and object are unique to each episode. The argument depends on some fairly dubious but familiar assumptions taken from the Secret Doctrine: (3) that things are always changing and becoming different, and (1) that things always appear differently and in contrary ways. If Socrates dreaming and Socrates awake are indeed completely different in their powers to affect and be affected, then they will produce different offspring—e.g. sweetness and the perception of sweet—when they encounter the wine on different occasions. Both the perception and the perceived reality will shift from one encounter to another.

Now Socrates can show how the Secret Doctrine supports Protagoras' claim:

---

[45] Burnyeat, Bostock, and others have argued that Socrates is going for a more extreme conclusion: Theaetetus and Protagoras are ultimately committed to the total dissolution of identity of objects and perceiving subjects. The argument has progressed from the initial assumption of public objects to instability, and finally to the dissolution of objects and perceivers into bundles of momentary perceptions. For arguments against this reading see Matthen, 'Perception', and Lesley Brown, 'Understanding the *Theaetetus*: A Discussion of David Bostock, *Plato's* Theaetetus, and Myles Burnyeat, *The* Theaetetus *of Plato*', *OSAP* 11 (1993), 199–224 at 205–9.

SOCRATES. . . . . Whenever I come to be perceiving, I necessarily come to be perceiving something; because it's impossible to come to be perceiving, but not perceiving anything. And whenever it comes to be sweet, bitter, or anything of that kind, it necessarily comes to be so for someone; because it's impossible to come to be sweet, but not sweet for anyone [γλυκὺ γάρ, μηδενὶ δὲ γλυκὺ ἀδύνατον γενέσθαι].

THEAETETUS. That's quite so.

SOCRATES. Then what we're left with, I think, is that it's for each other that we are, if we are, or come to be, if we come to be, since necessity ties our being together, but doesn't tie it to anything else, or indeed to ourselves. So what we're left with is that we're tied to each other. It follows that, whether one uses 'be' or 'come to be' of something, one should speak of it as being, or coming to be, *for* someone or *of* someone or *in relation to* something. As for speaking of a thing as being or coming to be anything just by itself, one shouldn't do that oneself, and one shouldn't accept it from anyone else either. That's what's indicated by the argument we've been setting out. (160 A 8–C 2, trans. McDowell)

Two features of the Secret Doctrine guarantee the truth of each perception. First, perceptions and perceptual properties are necessarily tied together: it is impossible to have a perception without perceiving the property which was generated together with it, and, conversely, nothing is sweet, bitter, etc. without appearing and being sweet for someone. This is a more prosaic way of expressing Socrates' now familiar assertion that perceptual properties and perceptions are twin offspring. Furthermore, there is no room for mismatch between the perception and what it is a perception of: Socrates' perception cannot fail to be true of the object he has perceived. Second, sensible qualities are relative to perceivers, and are perceiver-dependent. At 160 B 8–9 Socrates remarks that it does not really matter whether one says of something that it 'becomes' or 'is'. Nor does it really matter whether one indicates the relations by means of the dative, genitive, or by πρός τι. The important thing is to avoid saying that a thing is *F* in itself. What one perceives is what is for one, i.e. the colour or sweetness which came into being in relation to one. Socrates has now made good on his promise to show how the Secret Doctrine supports Protagoras' thesis, and Theaetetus' claim in turn.

SOCRATES. Now since what acts on me is for me and not someone else, it's also the case that I, and not someone else, perceive it?

THEAETETUS. Certainly.

SOCRATES. So my perception is true for me—because it's always of the being that's mine—and, as Protagoras said, it's for me to decide, of the things which are for me, that they are, and of the things which are not, that they are not.

THEAETETUS. Apparently.

SOCRATES. Well, then, if I'm free from falsehood, and don't trip up in my thinking about the things which are, or come to be, how could I fail to have knowledge of the things I'm a perceiver of?

THEAETETUS. You couldn't.

SOCRATES. So you were quite right to say that knowledge is nothing but perception. The three theories have turned out to coincide [καὶ εἰς ταὐτὸν συμπέπτωκεν]; that all things change, like streams, as Homer and Heraclitus and all that lot say; that a man is the measure of all things, as Protagoras, the wisest of men, says; and that, these things being so [τούτων οὕτως ἐχόντων], knowledge proves to be perception, as Theaetetus says.   (160 C 4–E 2, trans. McDowell, with modifications)

The three theses have converged to the same theory: given the truth of the Secret Doctrine and Protagoras' claim, Theaetetus' definition of knowledge comes out true.

5. Conclusion

The Secret Doctrine is introduced in the *Theaetetus* to develop and provide support for Protagoras' claim that something is the case for one if and only if it appears so to one. It contains a number of metaphysical theses couched in highly metaphorical language, which are vehicles for introducing the components needed to construct a model of perceptual properties and perception for Protagoras. This model recommends a way to think about perceptual properties and perception by analogy with relational properties. A property does not belong to anything intrinsically, but comes into and passes out of existence depending on relations which the object has with other things. Thus, as Burnyeat puts it, the Secret Doctrine offers us 'a perspicuous model for the thoroughgoing relativization which Protagoras' claim recommends' (*Introduction*, 12).

According to this model, the four elements—perceiver, perceived object, perceptual property, and perception—are 'tied together' and inseparable. Because they are generated together in each encounter between perceiver and perceived object, one cannot separate the perception from what it is supposed to be of. Reality is tied to one's perception of it—neither one is prior to the other. Note that even if reality depends on these perceptual encounters, that does not mean it is nothing more than perceptions or ideas. We are not being presented with some kind of thoroughgoing phenomenalism or idealism, where nothing exists but one's thoughts and perceptions. As Burnyeat argues, the *Theaetetus* is remarkable because it never takes the step which modern readers might expect, that of making everything dependent on perceivers and ideas. Throughout the exposition of the Secret Doctrine, perceptions and objects of perception are generated by some independent, uncharacterizable reality.

According to the interpretation I have offered, Plato's Secret Doctrine is exploratory and somewhat unsystematic. It consists of slogans like 'nothing is one thing by itself', 'whatever is *F* will reveal itself as not-*F*', and 'everything is changing', which are used in various ways to construct a theory of perception for Protagoras. Socrates does not even try to show that Protagoras is committed to these doctrines. He uses them instead as starting-points for a defence of Protagoras. As I noted in Section 3, at least five ideas were introduced as part of the Secret Doctrine, and Socrates uses them for different purposes in different contexts. (2) is interpreted as a statement of relativism:

(2) Nothing is anything in itself, but is (or becomes) relative to some (perceiver),

and is central to Socrates' conclusion that the Secret Doctrine confirms the truth of Protagoras' claim. (1) is used at 154A 2–9 to state the fact of conflicting appearances: anything which appears red to one person will appear otherwise to someone else. And the third,

(3) Nothing is, but is coming to be (i.e. is changing),

is used as a principle of generation to introduce and describe the four items involved in any perceptual encounter. Colours and perceivings of colours come into being and literally move around between perceiver and object without coming to rest. Eyes and perceptual objects themselves undergo relational change with respect to each other. Thus, we should avoid saying that anything is white or hot in itself, rather than in relation to some perceiver.

And we should exclude 'be' from everywhere, because it would imply that things have intrinsic properties apart from perceptual encounters. (In both Stage III and Stage IV, though, Socrates emphasizes that it is more important to avoid saying that anything has intrinsic properties like coldness *in itself* than to avoid saying that anything *is*.)

Some may see tighter connections among these theses, and among (T), (P), and the Secret Doctrine, than has been argued for in this paper. For this, further discussion of the rest of the *Theaetetus* is needed, especially of the relations between Socrates' refutations of Theaetetus' thesis, of Protagoras' claim, and of the Secret Doctrine. But even if one is sympathetic to the interpretation offered here, one might still wonder how successful the Secret Doctrine is as a strategy for developing Protagoras' claim.

It seems to me that the Secret Doctrine cannot be the only way to defend or understand Protagorean relativism—and that Plato never says that it is. The Secret Doctrine is an experiment in thinking about relativism; it is not a conclusive proof with far-reaching implications for modern-day versions of Protagoras' claim. It is simply a line of argument which Plato thinks is the most promising one to pursue for a relativist. Plato presumably wanted to undermine any reasons one might have for holding Protagoras' claim, and thought that the metaphysical principles which make up the Secret Doctrine were among a cluster of vague ideas in the air, which form part of the backdrop against which Protagoras' claim seems plausible.

If anything, the direction of implication goes the other way: Plato is not arguing that Protagoras must or ought to have been a secret Heraclitean, but that many philosophers, indeed virtually everyone except Parmenides, think and talk in ways which appear to commit them to some version of Protagorean relativism and to Theaetetus' definition of knowledge. Thus, linking the Protagorean doctrine with those background ideas provides a neat opportunity to examine—and then to demolish—those ideas themselves. If it turns out on independent grounds that Protagorean relativism is insupportable, this provides one more way to undermine these other philosophical views.

Whether Plato's strategy in constructing a defence for Protagoras will succeed is never taken for granted, and is always an open question. In one respect, it is successful, for he uses the elements of the Secret Doctrine to construct a theory of perception which serves as a model for the kind of relativization which would make Protagoras' claim turn out true. We are offered an explanation of what it means to say that nothing is anything in itself, but is whatever it is *for* a perceiver.

However, there *is* something peculiar about the Secret Doctrine, which makes it the last experiment of its kind. Notice that each one of the five ideas presented above as component parts of the Secret Doctrine conflicts in at least two ways with Protagoras' thesis. First, each of them imposes certain linguistic prohibitions: for example, it is incorrect to say that anything is one thing by itself—for example, that the sky is blue as opposed to red. It is also incorrect to say that anything is red, period, as opposed to becoming red. If I think that the sky is *really* blue, that it is blue and *not* any other colour, and that it is blue for everyone—which is, after all, what we usually mean when we make assertions—then doesn't the Secret Doctrine say that I am, strictly speaking, mistaken? If so, then doesn't this contradict Protagoras, who was trying to tell us that we are never mistaken about anything?

Second, each one of the theses in the Secret Doctrine conflicts with Protagoras' thesis in that they make claims about how the world is, absolutely and objectively. They say that things are a certain way for everyone—for example, that everything is changing—and that this is true for all people, regardless of whether they believe it, although Protagoras seems to tell us that there are no such truths. And they are asserted as objective truths, facts about the world which obtain regardless of whether anyone believes them or not. Protagoras' thesis seems to tell us that there is no way the world is in itself, apart from how it appears to one; the Secret Doctrine seems to tell us how the world must be, in itself, for Protagoras' thesis to hold true.[46]

These are very real problems for the Secret Doctrine. The conflicts arise because the Secret Doctrine attempts to describe a world in which Protagoras' thesis holds true. They are nothing less than corollaries of Plato's proof that Protagoras' thesis conflicts with

[46] The second type of inconsistency has been noticed by Dancy, 'Theaetetus' First Baby', 62 and all of sect. 4, 74; R. A. H. Waterfield, *Plato:* Theaetetus, trans. with an essay (Harmondsworth, 1987), 151; Ketchum, 'Refutation', 81; Fine, 'Relativisms', 223 and n. 26.

itself. In his refutation of Protagoras' thesis Plato raises the question 'Does Protagoras' thesis hold whether or not anyone thinks it does?' If Protagoras says that it does, then it will follow that some beliefs are false. If Protagoras says that it does not, then he has taken back his claim that whatever seems to be the case to one is the case for one. A corollary of this problem arises for the Secret Doctrine: is the Secret Doctrine true of the world regardless of whether anyone believes it or not? Plato pointed out and articulated this very problem in his refutation of Protagoras in the *Theaetetus*. And it is the main reason why no attempt at reviving the Secret Doctrine to describe a relativistic world could ever work.

University of Illinois at Chicago

BODY, SOUL, AND TRIPARTITION IN PLATO'S *TIMAEUS*

THOMAS JOHANSEN

FROM the *Phaedo* we are familiar with the view of the body as a
sort of prison for the soul. The body disrupts the proper workings
of the soul, giving rise to irrationality in an essentially rational immortal soul. Embodiment is represented as a punishment for the
soul. As Socrates puts it, 'the philosopher's soul utterly despises
his body and flees from it, seeking to be alone by itself' (65 D).

If this is our only impression of Plato's view of the relationship
between the body and the soul, then reading the *Timaeus* may come
as a surprise. For, as I aim to show, the dialogue offers a more complex and often more constructive view of the role of the body and
the contribution it can make to our rationality and happiness. I hope
to show that readers of Plato who ignore the *Timaeus* risk getting a
seriously incomplete picture of his thought on soul and body. This
applies particularly to our understanding of the origin of the tripartite soul and the nature of soul–body interaction, where it might be
argued that the *Timaeus* offers the most developed account of any
Platonic dialogue.

The argument proceeds as follows. I start by sketching the composition of the world soul according to Timaeus. This is the necessary starting-point since the human soul has its origin in the
world soul. I then discuss the relationship between the human soul
and the human body. The interaction of soul and body is understood in terms of the motions characteristic of each. When the soul

© Thomas Johansen 2000

This paper was written during a fellowship at the Center for Hellenic Studies. I
would like to thank all the staff there for creating such an excellent work environment.
Versions of the paper were delivered at Princeton and Toronto universities, where I
learnt a great deal thanks, in particular, to Sarah Broadie, John Cooper, Eric Csapo,
Brad Inwood, and Christian Wildberg. Elsewhere, I have benefited greatly from
the advice of Myles Burnyeat, Christopher Gill, Dominic Scott, David Sedley, and
Frisbee Sheffield.

is embodied its motions are differentiated into an immortal and a
mortal part. The *tripartite* soul, however, only comes about as the
result of the gods' teleological work. I conclude by bringing out the
distinctive contribution of the *Timaeus* in relation to some comments on the soul–body relationship in other Platonic dialogues.

1. The composition of soul

According to Timaeus, the Demiurge composed the soul of the
kosmos as follows:

In the middle of the being that is without parts and is always the same and
the being that comes to have parts in [περί] bodies he mixed from both a
third kind, and in the same way he also composed a kind of the nature of
the same and a kind of the nature of the other in the middle of the partless
sort and the sort that has parts in [κατά] bodies. And taking the three, he
mixed them all into one character, bringing the nature of the other into
harmony with the same using force because it mixes badly and mixed them
together with being. And having made one thing out of three, he divided
this whole in as many parts as were fitting, each having been mixed from
the same, the different, and being. (*Tim.* 35 A 1–B 3)[1]

On the most common interpretation, that of Grube, Cornford, and
Robinson,[2] the Demiurge composes the world soul as follows. He
takes divided and undivided parts of each of being, sameness, and
difference. He first mixes the divided and the undivided parts of
being together, and then the divided and undivided parts of sameness, and again the divided and undivided parts of difference. Next,
he mixes the three compounds together to form the final soul stuff.
This is the whole he then goes on to divide 'in as many parts as were
fitting'. He divides the soul stuff into intervals according to mathematical ratios and cuts it up into two bands or strips. The strips are
bent into circles, one called the circle of the same, another the circle
of the different. The circle of the different is further subdivided
into seven circles, which move, in accordance with mathematical

---

[1] My translation. However, unless otherwise indicated, all translations of the
Timaeus are from F. M. Cornford, *Plato's Cosmology* (London, 1937).

[2] G. M. A. Grube, 'The Composition of the World-soul in *Timaeus* 35 A–B', *Classical Philology*, 27 (1932), 80–2; Cornford, *Plato's Cosmology*, 60–1; T. M. Robinson,
Plato's Psychology (Toronto, 1970), 70–1. Cf. also now F. Ferrari, 'Platone, Tim.
35 A 1–6 in Plutarco, An. Procr. 101 B–C: Citazione ed esegesi', *Rheinisches Museum
für Philologie*, 142 (1999), 326–39.

proportions, inside the circle of the same in different directions and at different speeds.

What is the point of this elaborate account? Plutarch outlines two different interpretations which were common in antiquity.[3] On the 'kinetic' reading, as one might call it, the composition of the world soul is supposed to explain the soul as a principle of motion. On the 'cognitive' reading, the point of the mixtures is to account for the world soul's ability to make different sorts of judgement. In support of the kinetic reading we may mention that Timaeus later (57 D ff.) says that unlikeness is responsible for motion and likeness for rest. This, presumably, was what Xenocrates had in mind when he said that the soul was a principle of motion and rest because of its elements of difference ('unlikeness') and sameness ('likeness'). The kinetic reading also makes good sense of the claim that the circle of the different was divided into *seven* circles. For it is these seven circles that are later identified with the revolutions of the visible planets.[4] Having described the composition of the soul at 36 E, Timaeus also says that the soul was wrapped around the world body and moved around in a circle and thus became the cause (ἀρχή) of the kosmos' unceasing life. Again this suggests that the soul's circular motions explain the way the kosmos moves. On the other hand, it is clear that the soul is first introduced in order to give the kosmos mind (νοῦς), i.e. the ability to reason (cf. 30 B 1–6). This would make one expect that the composition of the soul first of all should explain how it reasons. *Tim.* 37 A 2–C 5 also makes it clear that the soul's composition is expressed in acts of thinking. Timaeus says that it is because

---

[3] *An. procr.* 1012 E–1013 A: 'The former [sc. Xenocrates *et al.*] believe that nothing but the generation of number is signified by the mixture of the indivisible and divisible being, the one being indivisible and multiplicity divisible and number being the product of these when the one bounds multiplicity . . . but they believe that this number is not yet soul for it lacks motivity and mobility, but that after the commingling of sameness and difference, the latter of which is the principle of motion and change while the former is that of rest, then the product is soul, soul being a faculty of bringing to a stop and being at rest no less than of being in motion and setting in motion. Crantor and his followers, on the other hand, supposing that the soul's peculiar function is above all to form judgments of the intelligible and the perceptible objects and the differences and similarities occurring among these objects both within their own kind and in relation of either kind to the other, say that the soul, in order that it may know all, has been blended together out of all and that these are four, the intelligible nature, which is ever variable and identical, and the passive and mutable nature of bodies, and furthermore that of sameness and of difference because each of the former two also partakes of diversity and identity' (trans. H. Cherniss, Loeb Classical Library).

[4] *Tim.* 38 C 7–8; cf. Arist. *De anima* 406^{b}32–407^{a}2.

the soul already has elements of sameness, difference, and being that it is able to think and make judgements about these things.[5]

There is really no need to choose between the cognitive and the kinetic readings. The point of the composition of the soul is to show how the soul moves when it thinks and thinks when it moves. The question is not whether the soul is composed in a way that explains how it is able to move *or* (exclusive 'or') how it is able to think. At 37 A 2–C 5 Timaeus clearly thinks he has explained both: *since then* (ἅτε οὖν) the soul has been composed in this way 'and *revolves* about itself', then when it touches an object *being moved it speaks*, and 'when the circle *moves aright then true judgment arises*', etc.[6] That, incidentally, is also how Aristotle understands Timaeus: 'the soul having been composed from elements and divided according to harmonious numbers, he bent the straight soul into a circle so that the soul would *both* have cognate perception of harmony *and* move the universe in symphonic motions' (*De anima* 1. 3, 406^{b}28–31).

For Timaeus, then, thinking is a form of circular motion. This position is likely to strike us as odd, to say the least. What does it mean to say that the soul moves around when we think? The position is likely to strike us as even odder when we consider that Timaeus thinks that the soul is immaterial (cf. 36 E 6 with 28 B 8–9). For how can something immaterial undergo spatial motion? At this point it is tempting to say, with many scholars, that the language of cyclical motion is merely an image.[7] Thinking is not literally a circular motion, it is only *like* it in certain respects. However, unless we take the circular motions of the soul literally, we have no way of understanding how the soul moves round with the planets. The circular motions of the planets are also the motions of the thinking world soul. The stars revolve around their own axis when they think about the same thing (40 A 7–B 2). Here there seems no alternative to taking the notion of thinking as circular motion literally. Also in support of a literal interpretation, David Sedley has pointed to the

[5] See D. Frede, 'The Philosophical Economy of Plato's Psychology: Rationality and Common Concepts in the *Timaeus*', in M. Frede and G. Striker (eds.), *Rationality in Greek Thought* (Oxford, 1996), 29–58.

[6] Notice also 43 D–44 A, where a reversal of the psychic motions (in man) issues in a corresponding reversal of the soul's judgements regarding sameness and difference.

[7] Cf. H. Cherniss, *Aristotle's Criticism of Plato and the Academy*, i (Baltimore 1944), 405–6; Aristotle, *De anima*, ed. W. D. Ross (Oxford, 1961), 184; E. N. Lee, 'Reason and Rotation: Circular Movement as the Model of Mind (Nous) in Later Plato', in W. H. Werkmeister (ed.), *Facets of Plato's Thought* (Assen, 1976), 70–102 at 85 with n. 28.

significance of the shape of the head.[8] If the circular motions are going to work as an explanation of the sphericity of the head, they had better be literally round. These points, then, seem to require us to adopt a literal interpretation.

A literal interpretation of the circles of the soul has at least two noteworthy implications. The first is that if we take the circular motions literally it follows that Timaeus cannot use spatial extension to define body in contrast to soul. If the soul literally moves round in the manner of a circle, then it must have spatial extension. But if so, Timaeus' distinction between soul and body cannot be the Cartesian one. How, then, does Timaeus differentiate soul from body? A full answer would require a discussion of the role of the receptacle in which the simple and compound bodies are constructed.[9] However, I would like to make just one observation. At least at an early stage of the dialogue, it seems that it is the perceptibility of body that distinguishes it from soul. Timaeus expresses the contrast between the world body and the world soul as follows at 36 E 5–6: 'the body of the heaven has been created visible; but the soul is invisible'. Perceptibility is the basis of the construction of the world body at 31 B 4–8. Visibility and tangibility are explained in terms of geometrical properties. From the tangibility of the world body Timaeus infers that it is made of solids, i.e. three-dimensional geometrical bodies. This point is confirmed again at 53 C 4–6, where Timaeus begins the geometrical construction of the four simple bodies by saying that every kind of body must have depth ($\beta\acute{\alpha}\theta o\varsigma$). This of course need not be taken to say more than that depth is a necessary condition of body and thus tangibility. It need not imply that depth is also a sufficient condition of tangibility. However, Timaeus' emphasis on depth may also be taken to suggest that depth is a defining

---

[8] D.Sedley, ' "Becoming like god" in the *Timaeus* and Aristotle', in T. Calvo and L. Brisson (eds.), *Interpreting the* Timaeus–Critias*: Proceedings of the IV Symposium Platonicum* (Sankt Augustin, 1997), 327–39 at 329–30; revised version, 'The Ideal of Godlikeness', in G. Fine (ed.), *Oxford Readings in Philosophy: Plato* (Oxford, 1999), ii. 309–28 at 318. M. F. Burnyeat in 'Plato on Why Mathematics is Good for the Soul', in T. Smiley (ed.), *British Academy Symposium on Mathematics and Philosophy in the History of Philosophy* (forthcoming), also argues in favour of a literal interpretation, mentioning the way the world body is extended within the world soul at 36 D–E. Like these authors, I would like to acknowledge my debt to Sarah Broadie's ground-breaking contribution to the 1993 Cambridge May Week seminar on the *Timaeus*.

[9] 51 A 4–6 suggests that the role of the receptacle is limited to what is corporeal: 'the mother and receptacle of what has come to be visible and otherwise sensible must not be called earth or air or fire or water, nor any of their compounds or components.'

characteristic of body and in that sense sufficient to distinguish body from soul. In contrast, there is no indication that the circular strips of soul *themselves* have depth even if they are made to move in three dimensions. The difference between soul and body seems, then, to lie primarily in geometry. If so¦ body is differentiated from soul by its specific spatial attributes, i.e. depth and solidity, rather than by having spatial attributes as such.

Another implication (which is central to this paper) is that if we take the motions literally we can understand why Timaeus seems to see no ontological problem in soul–body interaction. Both soul and body are spatially extended and move in space. Because both body and soul move in space we can see how the motions of the soul may affect the motions of the body and vice versa. Body and soul may have different spatial properties, as I suggested in the previous paragraph, but there is no fundamental ontological difference between the two. G. Ryle, in his famous critique of Cartesian dualism, argued that the origin of the category mistake of thinking that the mind was another 'thing' next to the body lay in thinking of mental processes as 'para-mechanical' processes:

> since mental-conduct words are not to be construed as signifying the oc-
> currence of mechanical processes, they must be construed as signifying
> the occurrence of non-mechanical processes; since mechanical laws ex-
> plain movements in space, other laws must explain some of the non-spatial
> workings of minds as the effects of other non-spatial workings of minds . . .
> Somewhat as the foreigner expected the University to be an extra edifice,
> rather like a college but also considerably different, so the repudiators of
> mechanism represented minds as extra centres of causal processes rather
> like machines but also considerably different from them. Their theory was
> a para-mechanical hypothesis.[10]

In contrast, it should be clear now (on the literal interpretation at least) that for Timaeus the motions of body and mind both fall under a general mechanics explaining the motions of extended figures (whether two- or three-dimensional) in space. The motions of the soul are not 'like machines but also considerably different from them'. The soul literally moves in space according to the same sort of mathematical regularities that govern the motions of bodies. If we find this proposal so difficult to imagine (let alone accept), it

---

[10] G. Ryle, *The Concept of Mind* (London, 1949; Penguin edn., Harmondsworth, 1963), 20–1.

may be because of another Cartesian influence, the association of spatial extension with body to the exclusion of mind.

2. Embodiment and tripartition

From the general account of soul I turn now to the body–soul relationship in human beings. The human soul is composed of the same 'stuff' (if slightly less pure) as the world soul and mixed in the same manner (41 D 4–7). The human soul therefore has the same sorts of motions as the world soul. It has a circle of the same and a circle of the different. The difference between the world soul and the human soul arises when the soul is embodied. By being put in a human body, the soul comes to experience not just the circular rational motions but also the six rectilinear motions: up and down, left and right, forwards and backwards. The world body was so composed by the Demiurge as to participate only in circular self-motion (34 A 1–7). In contrast, the lesser gods now construct the human body in a way that exposes it to all seven sorts of motion:

they confined the circuits of the immortal soul within the flowing and ebbing tide of the body. These circuits, being thus confined in a strong river, neither controlled it nor were controlled, but caused and suffered violent motions; so that the whole creature moved, but advanced at hazard without order or method, having all the six motions. For strong as was the tide that brought them nourishment, flooding them and ebbing away, a yet greater tumult was caused by the qualities of the things that assailed them, when some creature's body chanced to encounter alien fire from outside, or solid concretion of earth and softly gliding waters, or was overtaken by the blast of airborne winds, and the motions caused by all these things passed through the body to the soul and assailed it. For this reason these motions were later called by the name they still bear—'sensations' [αἰσθήσεις]. And so at the moment we speak of, causing for the time being a strong and widespread commotion and joining with that perpetually streaming current in stirring and violently shaking the circuits of the soul, they completely hampered the revolution of the same by flowing counter to it and stopped it from going on its way and governing; and they violently shook the revolution of the different. Accordingly, the intervals of the double and the triple, three of each sort, and the connecting means of the ratios, 3/2 and 4/3 and 9/8, since they could not be completely dissolved save by him who bound them together, were twisted by them in all manner of ways, and all possible deflections [κλάσεις] and deformations were caused; so they barely held together with each other, and though they moved, their motion was irrational [ἀλόγως], now reversed, now sidelong, now inverted. (*Tim.* 43 A 4–E 4, trans. Cornford with alterations)

The circles of the soul are exposed to linear motions through the bodily processes of nutrition and perception. At 43 A 6 Timaeus employs the image of a river to illustrate the impact of the body's motions on those of the soul. We can elaborate the image as follows. Imagine dropping a stone into a torrid river. The stone makes rings in the water, which, however, are soon disturbed by the motions of the running water. In the same manner, the circles of the soul lose their circular shape under the impact of the motions that flow through the body.[11]

The exposure to the motions of the body has different effects on the two circles of the soul. On the one hand, the motions of the circle of the same stop in their tracks altogether. Meanwhile, the intervals of the circle of the different are 'twisted'. As a consequence, this circle suffers 'deflections' (κλάσεις) in its motions. For 'deflection' Timaeus uses κλάσις, the only occurrence of the term in Plato. The mathematical context (cf. the circles and the mathematical intervals) suggests that the term is used in its technical geometrical sense of a deflection of a line against another line or surface.[12] In other words, we should think of the deflection of the circle of the different as the result of a change of direction in its motions. Affected by linear motions from all directions, the circle of the different moves, as Timaeus says, 'now reversed, now sidelong, now inverted' (43 E 3–4).

The interplay between rationality and irrationality is thus understood in terms of the interaction of circular and rectilinear motions. The extent to which the soul has become irrational through embodiment can be measured by the extent to which the motions of the soul have changed from circular towards rectilinear. This notion receives a rather comic exemplification in the reincarnation story at the end of the dialogue. We are told here that humans who failed to regain their rationality were reborn as animals with elon-

---

[11] Notice the similarity to Aristotle's use of the image to illustrate the distorting influence of the blood on our sense impressions in dreams: *De somniis*, 3, 461ᵃ8–18. Like Timaeus, Aristotle uses the image as an illustration of an account that works entirely in terms of the interaction of κινήσεις.

[12] Cf. Arist. *Phys.* 228ᵇ24. The term is also used in optics for the refraction of light, cf. Arist. *Meteor.* 343ᵃ14, 373ᵃ5.

gated heads that 'took any sort of shape, in which their circles were crushed together through inactivity' (91 E 6–92 A 2).

Already in this account of the effects of embodiment on the soul one can discern a differentiation of two parts within the soul. On the one hand, there is the circle of the different, whose motions lose their circularity under the influence of rectilinear bodily motions. On the other hand, there is circle of the same, which, at least temporarily (cf. τότε ἐν τῷ παρόντι, 43 C 7), is put out of action. The circle of the same is stopped in its track, losing control over the circle of the different (ἐπέσχον ἄρχουσαν καὶ ἰοῦσαν, 43 D 3). The result is a loss of co-ordination between the motions of the circles of the different. As Timaeus put it, the circles of the different *'barely held together with each other*, and though they moved, their motion was irrational, now reversed, now sidelong, now inverted' (43 E 2–3).[13] Earlier, we saw that an ingredient of the composition of the soul was 'the being that becomes divided around bodies' (35 A 2–3). The circle of the different was particularly related to this divisible being in so far as it was divided into seven subcircles that moved in different directions. The circle of the same, in contrast, remained undifferentiated. In one sense, then, the pre-embodied soul was divided, in that it consisted of several circles. However, though the soul was internally differentiated in this sense, all of its motions seemed to be perfectly circular prior to human embodiment.[14] With embodiment the circles of the different seem to lose their degree of rational cohesion because the circle of the same is no longer able to co-ordinate them.[15] The lack of co-ordination might be said to exploit the fact that the circle of the different requires the regulating influence of the circle of the same to ensure its rationality. Without the further controlling power of the circle of the same, the circle of the different does not itself have the power to maintain its rational motions when confronted with irrational influences. The soul has a potential for irrationality since it is internally structured in a way that allows some of its motions to lose their circular shape in certain

---

[13] ὥστε μετ' ἀλλήλων μόγις συνεχομένας φέρεσθαι μέν, ἀλόγως δὲ φέρεσθαι, τοτὲ μὲν ἀντίας, ἄλλοτε δὲ πλαγίας, τοτὲ δὲ ὑπτίας . . .

[14] Cf. the emphasis on the mathematical regularity of the planetary circuits at 38 E–39 E. We are given no indication of how or why the circle of the different would not be ὀρθὸς ἰών at 37 B 7 or the circle of the same εὔτροχος (37 C 2) until the soul is confined to a human body.

[15] Cf. 44 A 4–5 οὐδεμία τε ἐν αὐταῖς τότε περίοδος ἄρχουσα οὐδ' ἡγεμών ἐστιν, contrasting with 36 C 7–D 1 κράτος δ' ἔδωκεν τῇ ταὐτοῦ καὶ ὁμοίου περιφορᾷ.

circumstances. One might say that the irrational motions caused in
the soul by embodiment bring out a potentiality that the soul itself
has in so far as the motions of the circle of the different are not *necessarily* co-ordinated by the circle of the same. If, in contrast, the
soul had been a rigorous 'Parmenidean' unity with no internal differentiation of different circles with different compositions, then it
would not have had the potential to react to embodiment in this way.
The distinction between the circles of the same and the different
constitutes, to use a seismic metaphor (cf. σείουσαι, 43 D 1), a fault
line in the soul which is activated by the tremors of the human body.

So far I have simply referred to the irrational experiences of
the embodied soul as 'perceptions', in accordance with the use of
αἰσθήσεις at 43 C 6 as a generic term for the affections caused by the
human body. However, in an earlier passage (42 A 3–B 1), where the
Demiurge predicts to the human souls what will happen to them
when embodied, αἴσθησις is used specifically for one of *three* sorts of
affection. This passage is especially important because it introduces
the central notion of 'necessity' into the account of the irrational
affections:

Whensoever, therefore, they [the immortal souls] should of *necessity* have
been implanted in bodies, and of their bodies some part should always
be coming in and some part passing out, it is *necessary* that there arise,
first, perception [αἴσθησιν], one for all,[16] arising from violent impressions
[βιαίων παθημάτων] and kindred to them [σύμφυτον];[17] second, desire [ἔρωτα]
blended with pleasure [ἡδονῇ] and pain [λύπη], and besides fear and anger
[φόβον καὶ θυμόν] and all the feelings that accompany these and all that are
of a contrary nature. (42 A 3–B 1)

The passage underlines the necessary and enforced character of
what the soul experiences when embodied. However, there seem
to be two notions of necessity in play. The notions roughly correspond to the notions of hypothetical and simple or 'material'
necessity developed later by Aristotle.[18] The first is the necessity
of embodiment. It is necessary that the souls be embodied *if* the

[16] Timaeus has just said that the first genesis is μία πᾶσιν in order that no one feel
slighted (41 E 3–4), so it makes sense to take αἴσθησιν . . . μίαν πᾶσιν as stressing again
that everyone had the same obstacles before him.

[17] That is, kindred to the violent affections, not innate, as Cornford translates; cf.
Aristotle's understanding of Timaeus' use of σύμφυτον at *De anima* 406ᵇ30.

[18] Cf. Arist. *Phys.* 2. 9. I am not saying here that Timaeus actually makes the
distinction but rather that he uses the notion of necessity in ways that it is helpful
for us to articulate in terms of Aristotle's distinction.

universe is to be complete. For unless the souls are embodied, there will be no mortal living beings (cf. 41 B 7–D 3).[19] In this instance, it is only hypothetically necessary that the soul be embodied *given the end*, a complete kosmos, which the Demiurge wants to bring about. The second necessity, in contrast, relates to the necessity with which perception, pleasure, desire, etc. arise in the soul when it is embodied. This is the necessity by which the soul is moved through the body because it is affected by external forces. It is necessary that the soul be so moved by the four simple bodies, given their natures. For given their natures, the simple bodies will necessarily move in rectilinear ways and therefore they will necessarily deflect the circular motions which they encounter. It is necessary that once the soul has been put in a human body it will be affected by water, air, etc., simply because of the motions that these bodies have in and of themselves. The simple nature of this necessity is indicated here by βιαίων at 42 A 5 and by βίᾳ again at 43 A 7.[20] It is this sort of necessity that is described in the second part of the dialogue (47 E–69 A, sometimes referred to as 'the works of necessity') and which has to be persuaded by reason to work for good ends.

So far I have argued that the affections that cause the circle of the different to undergo irrational motions arise by simple necessity. I now want to show the way in which these affections form the basis for the tripartition of the soul. At 69 C 3 Timaeus resumes his account of the creation of man. He begins with what seems to be a recapitulation of 42 A 1–B 1:

Of the divine he himself [i.e. the Demiurge] undertook to be the maker; the task of making the generation of mortals, he laid upon his own offspring. They, imitating him, when they had taken over an immortal principle of soul, went on to fashion for it a mortal body englobing it round about. For a vehicle they gave it the body as a whole, and therein they built on another form of soul, the mortal, having in itself dread and necessary affections: first pleasure, the strongest lure of evil; next, pains that take flight from good; daring [θάρρος] moreover and fear, a pair of unwise counsellors; anger hard to entreat, and hope too easily led astray. These they combined with irrational perception [αἰσθήσει] and desire that shrinks from no venture,

---

[19] The other animals are to be explained as reincarnated human beings (42 B–C, 90 E–92 C). The contrast between mortal living beings and immortal ones such as the planets has to be qualified in the light of 41 A 7–B 6.

[20] αἱ δ' εἰς ποταμὸν ἐνδεθεῖσαι πολὺν οὔτ' ἐκράτουν οὔτ' ἐκρατοῦντο, βίᾳ δὲ ἐφέροντο καὶ ἔφερον . . .

and so in the manner necessary compounded the mortal element. (*Tim.* 69 C 3–D 6)

As the commentators note,[21] there is a close correspondence between 42 A–B and this passage. The necessary and terrible affections are here listed as (in order) pleasure, pain, daring, fear, anger ($\theta\upsilon\mu\acute{o}s$), hope, and perception mixed with desire ($\check{\epsilon}\rho\omega s$), where in the earlier passage we had (in order) perception ($\alpha\check{\iota}\sigma\theta\eta\sigma\iota s$), desire ($\check{\epsilon}\rho\omega s$) blended with pleasure ($\dot{\eta}\delta o\nu\acute{\eta}$) and pain ($\lambda\acute{\upsilon}\pi\eta$), fear and anger ($\phi\acute{o}\beta os\ \kappa\alpha\grave{\iota}\ \theta\upsilon\mu\acute{o}s$), and, finally, 'all the feelings that accompany these and all that are of a contrary nature'. The later passage explicitly mentions hope and fear in addition to those mentioned in the earlier passage, but this addition can be seen as covered by the reference in the earlier passage to 'all the feelings that accompany these and all that are of a contrary nature'. The two passages also operate with slightly different mixtures: in the earlier passage desire was mixed with pleasure and pain, in the other all the affections are mixed with perception and desire. These differences may be stylistic, but they may also be substantive, indicating that the lesser gods have to some extent altered the combination of affections.

The important difference between the two passages may indeed seem to be that whereas the first makes the affections seem to arise necessarily from the insertion of the immortal soul in the body, the second seems to make the creation of the mortal soul a deliberate act of the lesser gods. The lesser gods 'built on [$\pi\rho o\sigma\omega\kappa o\delta\acute{o}\mu o\upsilon\nu$, 69 C 8] another form of soul' and 'they composed [$\sigma\upsilon\nu\acute{\epsilon}\theta\epsilon\sigma\alpha\nu$, D 6] the mortal kind [of soul]' by 'mixing [$\sigma\upsilon\gamma\kappa\epsilon\rho\alpha\sigma\acute{\alpha}\mu\epsilon\nu o\iota$, D 5]' the affections. This seems to challenge the idea that the affections arise by simple necessity. For if they are the result of the lesser gods' work, surely they are the product of rational design rather than mere simple necessity. Let us investigate further.

Like the earlier passage at 42 A, 69 C–D makes two crucial references to necessity: the mortal soul is described as having dread and necessary affections ($\delta\epsilon\iota\nu\grave{\alpha}\ \kappa\alpha\grave{\iota}\ \dot{\alpha}\nu\alpha\gamma\kappa\alpha\hat{\iota}\alpha$) and the lesser gods are said to have composed the mortal soul, in the manner described, by necessity ($\dot{\alpha}\nu\alpha\gamma\kappa\alpha\acute{\iota}\omega s$). Cornford sees these references to necessity as referring back to the necessity at 42 A, which he took exclusively to be (what I have called) hypothetical. These affections are neces-

---

[21] Cf. R. D. Archer-Hind, *The* Timaeus *of Plato* (London, 1888), 256; Cornford, *Plato's Cosmology*, 281 n. 3.

sary, according to Cornford, because they are indispensable tools
for man if he is to survive on earth. However, this makes little
sense of the connection between βία and necessity in the earlier
passage and the juxtaposition of δεινὰ καὶ ἀναγκαῖα in the present
passage. Surely, if the affections were introduced as necessary for
our survival at this point, they should be described as welcome and
beneficial rather than as violent and dreadful. The negative epithets
of the affections, I think, clinch the point against Cornford: 'first,
pleasure, *the strongest lure of evil*; next, pains that *take flight from
good*; daring moreover and fear, *a pair of unwise counsellors*; passion
hard to entreat, and hope *too easily led astray*. These he combined
with *irrational* sense and desire *that shrinks from no venture*.' This
is no way to describe affections that are necessary from the point of
view of our *good*.

However, the fact that these affections are not for our good does
not yet give us the conclusion that they are not hypothetically necessary. For it is possible that the lesser gods gave us these affections
exactly *in order* to trip us up. By giving us irrational affections, the
lesser gods would ensure that some of us will remain irrational and
be reincarnated as lower animals. So the irrational affections would
be hypothetically necessary in order to ensure that lower animals
would be created. However, this puts a *very* negative interpretation on the work of the lesser gods: not only would they not be
helping us become rational by embodying our immortal soul, they
would deliberately act so as to make us irrational. This interpretation, I think, is inconsistent with the explicit claim that the lesser
gods were imitating (μιμούμενοι, 69 c 5) the Demiurge, since the
Demiurge's intentions in creating the immortal soul were entirely
benign.[22]

The necessity of the affections is therefore best taken as simple,
not hypothetical. The necessity attaches to the disordered processes
before they have been persuaded to co-operate with reason. This is
what we would expect, given the larger argument of the third part
of the dialogue. Having discussed the processes of simple necessity
in the second part of the dialogue, Timaeus now goes on to show
how this necessity is made to co-operate with reason in the creation of human beings. So we would expect to find a distinction in
the passage between, on the one hand, the necessary materials that

---

[22] Cf. 71 D 5–7: 'those who composed us remembered the command of their father
when he bade that the mortal genus should be made as good as possible . . .'.

the gods have to work with and, on the other. the order or rational design that they impose on these materials.[23] Our expectation is
fulfilled if we read the passage as distinguishing between the simple
necessity of the affections and the work the lesser gods perform to
make these affections co-operate for our good.

We can detect, then, two stages in the creation of the human soul.
At the first stage the lesser gods create the necessary affections by
embodying the immortal soul. The next stage of the account occurs
at 69 D 6, when Timaeus goes on to describe the way in which the
necessary affections are put to good use for us:

Fearing lest because of this they pollute the divine [part of the soul], unless
it was absolutely necessary [ὅτι μὴ πᾶσα ἦν ἀνάγκη], they housed the mortal
apart from it in a different dwelling-place in the body, building between
head and breast, as an isthmus and boundary, the neck, which they placed
between in order to keep the two apart [ἵν᾽ εἴη χωρίς]. In the breast, then,
and the trunk (as it was called) they confined the mortal kind of soul. And
since part of it has a nobler nature, part a baser, they built another partition
across the hollow of the trunk, as if dividing the men's apartment from the
women's, and set the midriff as a fence between them. (*Tim.* 69 D 6–70 A 2)

The shift in grammatical mood in this passage is significant.
Whereas up until 69 D 6 Timaeus had been describing the necessary
results of the soul's embodiment in the indicative mood, from D 6
on he describes the actions of the lesser gods using ἵνα clauses with
the optative.[24] The change indicates a shift in the explanatory status
of the account. The organization of the soul is no longer to be explained as a necessary result but as the result of purposeful action.
This part of the account then describes the way in which the lesser
gods persuade the processes of necessity to co-operate for the best.
The passage acknowledges that some pollution of the divine part
might be necessary. Again the necessity is clearly not of the hypothetical sort, in so far as it is an obstacle, not an aid, to the goal that
the lesser gods are trying to bring about, the purity of our divine
part. The necessity is thus best taken to refer back to the necessity
of the previous lines, i.e. the simple necessity by which the soul
suffers irrational affections in the body. The lesser gods proceed to

---

[23] This is the distinction drawn at 47 E 3–48 E 1, where he says that the kosmos
arose by necessity (i.e. simple necessity) being persuaded to co-operate with reason
for a good end.

[24] Cf. 70 A 4 (ἵνα τοῦ λόγου κατήκοον . . .), B 3 (ἵνα, ὅτε . . .), C 7 (ἵνα τό τε πνεῦμα . . .),
D 3 (ἵν᾽ ὁ θυμός . . .).

construct the body in such a way that the divine part may be as unaffected by the mortal part as possible and control it as much as possible. The body is divided into three sections, the head containing the immortal part, the chest holding the spirited part, and the section beneath the midriff being the seat of the appetitive part. The physiology is largely cognitive—that is, it explains the composition of the body from the point of view of aiding (or at least not hampering) the motions of the intellect. The spirited part is set between the head and the midriff so that 'it might be within hearing of the discourse of reason and join with it in restraining by force the desires, whenever these should not willingly consent to obey the word of command from the acropolis' (70 A 4–7). The heart is the source of blood that runs throughout the body so that it can communicate between the intellect and the entire body, ensuring that the intellect is in command of the entire body. The lungs cool the heart, so that being in less distress it may be better able to help the spirited part in the service of reason (70 D 2–6). The liver is smooth and bright so that 'the influence proceeding from reason should make impressions of its thoughts upon the liver, which would receive them like a mirror and give back visible images' (71 B 3–5). The spleen serves to keep the liver clean, like a napkin, so that it is always ready to receive the messages from reason (72 C–D 3). The basic outline of the body, then, shows how the body is so constructed as to aid the intellect in maintaining control over itself and the mortal soul.

We saw that the affections of perception, desire, fear and courage, etc. are a necessary result of embodying the soul. However, these affections are at first only placed together in one sort of soul, called 'the mortal'. The division of the mortal part into two main parts, the spirited and the appetitive, is a further step. Though desire and fear, courage, etc. seem already to display different degrees of rationality before they are located in different parts of the body (that, after all, is why the spirited part is located nearer to reason than the appetitive part), what allows these to maintain their separate motions and distinctive degrees of rationality is that they are located in separate parts of the body. The body is so composed as to ensure that the different parts of the soul are able to do their proper job without interference from the other parts. The impression is that without a tripartite physiology to go with the tripartite psychology the soul would be the forum of a disorganized and motley set of more or less irrational affections. It would not have the functional differentiation or hierarchical structure that we associate with the tripartite soul. The tripartite psychology, to this extent, depends on a bodily constitution that allows the soul to main its order.

   The distinction between circular and rectilinear motions continues to play a role within the tripartite psychology. When composing the human body the lesser gods seem to negotiate our need to preserve our rational circular motions with our need also to experience and control rectilinear motions. These two considerations are reflected in the composition of the marrow. God created the frame of the body, beginning with the marrow. As the place where the soul and the body are tied together, the marrow is crucial to our understanding of soul–body interaction. God created the marrow by mixing the four elements in proportion. Next, Timaeus says,

> he implanted and made fast therein the several kinds of soul; and also from the first, in his original distribution, he divided the marrow into shapes corresponding in number and fashion to the several kinds of soul that the marrow was going to hold. And he moulded into spherical shape the ploughland, as it were, that was to contain the divine seed; and this part of the marrow he named 'brain', signifying that, when each living creature was completed, the vessel containing this should be the head. That part, on the other hand, which was to retain the remaining, mortal kind of soul he divided into shapes at once round and elongated, naming them all 'marrow'. From these, as if from anchors, he put forth bonds to fasten all the soul. (*Tim.* 73 C 3–D 6, trans. Cornford, with alterations)

Talk of a place where soul meets body may conjure up worrying associations with the Cartesian pineal gland, the place where *res cogitans* and *res extensa* supposedly could interact. However, we have already seen that no such problem need arise for Timaeus. Soul and body are both spatially extended, so the idea of locating both in a part of the body need not in itself be conceptually objectionable. Rather the challenge that faces Timaeus is to present a physiology that plausibly shows how the marrow caters for the various motions of the soul. One problem, which scholars have noted here, is how the location of the soul in marrow can be seen to accommodate the tripartite psychology. I translated, with Taylor and Archer-Hind, 'he divided the marrow into shapes corresponding in number and fashion to the several kinds of soul that the marrow was going to hold'. In contrast, Cornford takes the several kinds to refer to other future living species. He does so even though the context clearly requires that the marrow is worked out in relation to the three sorts of soul and there is no other mention in this part of the dialogue of the living beings that will later be generated out of man until 90 E. However, he sees the following difficulty as overriding these concerns:

It is difficult to understand that the two shapes (spherical and columnar) which are described in the following sentence can correspond to the three parts of the soul, or that the two mortal parts, seated in heart and belly, can be said to wear (σχήσειν) the columnar shape of the marrow in the bones, to which they are merely rooted or anchored.[25]

Once we consider the fundamental role of circular and rectilinear motions in distinguishing the immortal from the mortal soul, Cornford's problem disappears. The brain is spherical because it carries the circular motions of the intellect. The rest of the marrow is both circular and rectilinear because it carries the parts of the soul that are produced by the influence of rectilinear motions on the soul's natural circular motions. Both the spirited and the appetitive part belong to this category. Once we understand how the opposition between circular and rectilinear motions underlies the distinction between the rational and the more or less irrational parts of the soul, we can also see how the physiological distinction between a spherical brain, on the one hand, and a circular and rectilinear marrow, on the other, is consistent with, and appropriate to, the tripartite psychology. The marrow is appropriately round and elongated in order to allow both for it to be connected to and controlled by the circular motions in the head and for the rest of the body to participate in rectilinear motions. Compare in this respect the description of the creation of the human body earlier at 44 D ff. The gods made the head round as an appropriately spherical seat of the rational circular motions but created the rest of the body with flexible limbs because man is also going to participate in the six other, rectilinear, forms of motion. The circular–rectilinear opposition is fundamental to Timaeus' physiology because it reflects the two sorts of motion that living beings undergo as, on the one hand, immortal and rational and, on the other, embodied and subject to the forces of simple necessity.

Given the good works of the gods, many of the rectilinear motions that human beings undergo are not imposed from without and disruptive of rational order. Rather, they are made part of the

---

[25] Cornford, *Plato's Cosmology*, 294 n. 4.

body's own rational order.[26] When the soul was first embodied, all
rectilinear motion was imposed on it, but given the teleological ordering of some of the rectilinear motions that we experience, the
focus is now rather on eliminating those motions of external origin
which are not in accordance with this order. Once the body has been
fashioned in our best interest, the fundamental opposition between
bad and good motions is no longer primarily to be understood in
terms of 'rectilinear' vs. 'circular' motion but rather in terms of
imposed motions vs. self-motion. Even the disturbing appetitive
motions are given a purpose (i.e. the body's nourishment, 70 D 7–E
5) and made subject (through the agency of the liver, cf. 71 A 3–72 B
5) to the rule of reason.

The result of the lesser gods' work is, then, to create the human
being as a teleologically ordered system in which motions that arise
by simple necessity and rational motions are combined. Motions
that were initially disruptive and chaotic are harnessed to serve a
rational end. The result is the creation of a tripartite psychology.

Each of the three parts of the soul thus has its own motions,
which should be tended to (89 E 3–90 A 2). Our aim should not be
to eradicate the motions of the mortal parts of the soul but to reg-
ulate each part so that its proper motion neither overwhelms nor is
overwhelmed by the motions of other parts. The rational order of
the soul, after embodiment, is not one in which *only* the motions
of the intellect thrive but a complex order in which other psychic
motions operate alongside those of the intellect in common pursuit
of the human good.

3. The *Timaeus* in context

It is time now to bring the message of the *Timaeus* further into focus
by comparing it with some other Platonic dialogues. I would suggest that Timaeus' account of the tripartite soul is, generally speak-

---

[26] An emphasis on circular motion remains in the workings of the lower parts
of the soul, such as the respiratory and nutritive systems in which the elements
are circulated around the body. But a motion such as vision remains essentially
rectilinear (cf. 45 C 5 κατὰ τὴν τῶν ὀμμάτων εὐθυωρίαν) even though the planetary
motions that we are supposed to observe are circular. As just mentioned, we are also
equipped with a body that enables us to move in a rectilinear manner. The human
body and its functions thus represent a compromise between rectilinear and circular
motions.

ing, different in *emphasis* from that of the *Republic*.[27] In the *Republic* the three parts of the soul are clearly distinguished in terms of the different objects that they desire: the intellect has a proper desire for truth, the spirited part for esteem, and the appetitive for bodily gratification.[28] Similarly, Timaeus makes reference to the spirited part's being a lover of victory (φιλόνικον, 70 A 3) and he describes the appetitive part as desiring 'food and drink and such things as the soul requires because of the nature of the body' (70 D 7–8). However, Timaeus presents these parts not so much as having desires that contrast with the desire of reason for truth and wisdom but rather as desires that themselves serve a rational end. The spirited part listens to reason and carries out its orders, while we feel desire for food and drink in order that we may survive. Even the appetitive part has a perception of rational commands which is mediated through the images projected by the intellect on to the liver. The marrow's circular shape ensures its continuity with circular motions in the head. The vascular system is constructed so as to allow messages to pass from the intellect to all parts of the body, while all parts of the body in turn have perception (αἴσθησις) so that they can understand the messages received. The cognitive physiology emphasizes the extent to which the lower parts of the soul are geared to co-operating with reason. This point goes some way towards explaining why we are later told that 'human beings by nature [φύσει] have two sorts of desire, the desire for nourishment [τροφῆς] because of the body and the desire for wisdom [φρονήσεως] because of the most divine part in us' (88 A 9–B 2). These are both rational desires in the sense that they are desires for our real good. Since Timaeus takes the other parts of the soul to have been fashioned by the lesser gods so as to ensure as much rational order as possible while embodied, the workings of all of the soul might be said to express our rational desires. In *Republic* 4 (438 D–441 C), in contrast, the tripartite soul explains how we may have desires that are opposed to our rational desires. In books 8–9 (543 A–576 B) the tripartite soul

---

[27] I deliberately refer to differences in emphasis or outlook between the two dialogues. I do not claim to have identified any disagreements or inconsistencies in doctrine between them.

[28] Cf. J. M. Cooper, 'Plato's Theory of Human Motivation', *History of Philosophy Quarterly*, 1 (1984), 3–21, repr. in his *Reason and Emotion: Essays on Ancient Moral Psychology and Ethical Theory* (Princeton, 1999), 118–37. Note, however, that *Rep.* 4, 436 A ff., seems, initially at least, to distinguish parts of soul by function (knowledge, anger, etc.) rather than by desires for specific objects. For a helpful summary of the complexities cf. C. Gill, *The Self as Structure* (forthcoming).

explains the non-philosophical sorts of character in terms of their nurturing desires of parts of the soul other than the intellect.

The contrast between the two dialogues can be lessened in several ways. First, Timaeus allows for a similar explanation of conflict between the intellect and the lower parts, though in accordance with his brief as a natural philosopher he recasts the explanation in terms of the disproportionate strength of the *motions* of the appetitive and spirited parts. Second, it should be pointed out that the *Republic* by no means always presents the lower parts of the soul as being in conflict with the intellect. The case in which the parts of the soul are in conflict with each other is a useful way of introducing the distinction between the three parts, but that does not mean that we should take this case to be representative of the general, let alone the natural, state of the soul. The argument to show that the individual will be happy only if all the parts of the soul are harmonized under the rule of reason surely presupposes that the lower parts of the soul are fundamentally able to co-operate with ends that have been determined by reason.

Nevertheless, the general difference in emphasis between the *Timaeus* and the *Republic* remains. While the *Timaeus* emphasizes that the lower parts of the soul and their bodily organs are organized by the lesser gods so as to aid the aims of reason, the emphasis in the *Republic* is more often on showing how the non-rational parts have desires which may oppose what reason tells us to be good. Thus Timaeus does not use the desires of the lower parts to demarcate these parts as non-rational and as opposed to the desires of the intellect. Rather, he attempts to show how an essentially rational soul works within the body by using those motions that the body necessarily gives rise to in order to further our rationality while embodied. The spirited and appetitive parts for Timaeus thus appear as a sort of 'devolved rationality' in our embodied state,[29] by which I mean that the lower parts, as we saw, have assumed rational functions in the body.[30] The tripartite soul is the lesser gods' way of furthering our rationality given that we have to be embodied.

It might seem preferable to describe the result of embodiment as a devolution of *irrationality* to the lower parts of the soul in the

---

[29] I owe the expression to John Cooper.

[30] In other words, I do not use 'devolved' to mean 'evolved from' or 'developed from', though it is no doubt relevant to the fact that the lower parts can now execute rational functions that they have their origin in a fully rational soul.

sense that the irrational motions that necessarily arise in the rational soul when embodied are set apart from the intellect.[31] Thereby the intellect is allowed as far as possible to maintain its circular rational motions while the irrational motions are passed on to the lower parts. The purpose of such a devolution of irrationality would be to ensure that at least this part of our soul, the intellect, retained its circular motions. As separate the intellect can then continue exercising rational control over the rest of the soul and the body. My reason for preferring to talk of devolved *rationality* lies in the distinction I drew earlier between two stages in the creation of the human soul. At the first stage embodiment brought about a range of irrational affections in the soul, particularly, it seemed, in the circle of the different. At the second stage the lesser gods organized those affections so as to serve rationality within the entire living being. The lower parts of the soul are not just set apart from the intellect (though that happens too); they also work together with the intellect in bringing about the ends that the intellect prescribes. I talk, therefore, of devolved rationality to emphasize the positive point that the lower parts of the soul co-operate with the intellect in maintaining rational order in the entire living being.

The implications of this view of the lower parts of the soul for the concept of the self are far-reaching.[32] To the extent that rationality is devolved to the lower parts of the soul, our rational self extends to those other parts while we are embodied. In contrast, one often has the impression in other Platonic dialogues, particularly the *Phaedo*, that, even while we are embodied, the intellect alone remains our true self, whereas those aspects of the soul which are associated with the workings of the body appear extraneous to the self. The *Timaeus* emphasizes that the intellect should remain in control over the other parts (90 A 2–D 7). However, the other parts of the soul have their own distinctive motions that contribute to our greater rationality and well-being while we are embodied. Consequently, our rationality is not exhibited simply in rational contemplation in disregard of the influence of the body, but in the pursuit of a composite life of soul and body. Caring for the self, as we saw, extends to caring for the entire tripartite soul, not just the intellect.

Caring for the self also involves caring for the body. I argued

[31] I owe this suggestion to David Sedley.
[32] Independently, C. Gill has recently argued for a similar conclusion: cf. *The Self as Structure*. I am grateful to him for showing me parts of this work in draft.

earlier that the body was organized in a way that allowed the soul to maintain its hierarchical tripartite structure with the intellect in command. The body is in this sense part of a psycho-somatic whole which allows us to pursue a good life under the rule of the intellect. Again the point is explained in terms of proportionality of motions. Good proportion, Timaeus claims, is a necessary condition of beauty and goodness. But living creatures are composites of soul and body. Therefore, if they are to function well, they have to maintain good proportion between soul and body. Lack of proportion between the motions of the two is the main cause of disease:

Just as a body that is out of proportion because the legs or some other members are too big is not only ugly, but in the working of one part with another brings countless troubles upon itself with much fatigue and frequent falls due to awkward convulsive movement, so is it, we must suppose, with the composite creature we call an animal. When the soul in it is too strong for the body and of ardent temperament, she dislocates the whole frame and fills it with ailments from within; she wastes it away, when she throws herself into study and research . . . On the other hand, when a large body, too big for the soul, is conjoined with a small and feeble mind . . . the motions of the stronger part prevail and, by augmenting their own power while they make the powers of the soul dull and slow to learn and forgetful, they produce in her the worst of maladies, stupidity. (*Tim.* 87 E 1–88 B 5)

The ailments are prevented by exercising the motions of body and soul proportionately:

Now against both these dangers there is one safeguard: not to exercise the soul without the body, nor yet the body without the soul, in order that both may hold their own and prove equally balanced and sound. So the mathematician or one who is intensely occupied with any other intellectual discipline must give his body its due meed of exercise by taking part in athletic training; while he who is industrious in moulding his body must compensate his soul with her proper exercise in the cultivation of the mind and all higher education; so one may deserve to be called in the true sense a man of noble breeding. (*Tim.* 88 B 5–C 6)

Notice that the passage is not simply making the point familiar from *Republic* 411 E that the guardians should take physical exercise (γυμναστική) along with the education of the soul (μουσική). There the point was that γυμναστική was a way of developing the spirited part of the soul—that is, it was a way of working on the soul through the body. But here the aim is not to affect the soul through the body, at least not directly, but to keep a proportion between the motions of the soul and those of the body independently of each other. This assumes a degree of interest in bodily processes independently of their relation to the soul.

In comparison with the *Phaedo* the passage suggests that the motions of the body are not seen simply as a hindrance to a good life but as a part of a more positive view of embodied life. Timaeus shows in detail how the affections that necessarily arose with embodiment and which initially simply disrupted the soul can contribute to our greater rationality and well-being within a rationally ordered body. Although a purely rational and disembodied life (at least in the sense of having no *human* body) seems to remain the ultimate ideal of happiness for Timaeus (βίον εὐδαίμονα, 42 B 4), the human body appears less like a prison for the rational soul and more, as one might put it, like a rather comfortable hotel with quite a few research facilities inbuilt. There are suggestions in the *Phaedo* that perception (and by implication the body) is necessary in some sense for recollection (cf. *Phaedo* 75 A) and might in such a sense be instrumental to our happiness.[33] However, the *Timaeus* gives a much more assertive and explicit account of how the body is designed with a view to increasing our rationality.

One might make a similar point with respect to the famous image in *Republic* 10 (611 B 9–D 8). The embodied soul is like Glaucus, the sea deity, who has been deformed by the battering of waves and the encrustation of shells and seaweed. Cleared of these, however, he appears not like a monster but like the god he is. There is a debate (which I shall not enter here) about whether this image implies that the immortal soul is unitary or in some sense tripartite. However that may be, we can see how the passage could be read from the point of view of the *Timaeus*. Timaeus would agree with Socrates that our 'original' nature, as they both say,[34] is our rational soul. He would also concur in attaching greater value, and immortality (at least of the sort available to created beings), to the intellectual part of the tripartite soul. However, for Timaeus the human physiology is not so much presented as an obstacle to our happiness as a way of promoting it given that we have to be embodied. In the same way, the tripartite soul is not simply to be considered as an obstacle to

---

[33] Such a suggestion, however, has to be squared also with *Phaedo* 65 A–C.

[34] *Rep.* 611 D 2 τὴν ἀρχαίαν φύσιν; *Tim.* 90 D 5 τὴν ἀρχαίαν φύσιν; cf. *Tim.* 42 D 2 τῆς πρώτης καὶ ἀρίστης . . . ἕξεως.

rationality but rather as a way of aiding the intellect in pursuing a good life for us while we are embodied. Timaeus would therefore resist the implications of the image *if* it is taken to mean that embodiment is necessarily *only* to be viewed as a monstrous accretion to the soul. For Timaeus the tripartite soul is established in the context of a physiology that allows the parts to perform their proper tasks without interference from each other. Each of the three parts of the soul is housed in organs whose shape and location in the body allow it to maintain its proper motions. Individual parts of the body seem to have been composed as the necessary instruments for individual parts of the soul in performing their proper tasks. We are in this respect closer to an Aristotelian teleological conception of the relationship between the psychic parts and their proper organs than we are to anything that is explicitly offered in Plato's other dialogues.

This conclusion should come as no surprise to us given the general nature of Timaeus' project, namely, to show how the whole kosmos, body and soul, is arranged for the greatest possible good.[35] One might say that the change in emphasis between the *Republic* and the *Timaeus* reflects the fact that the *Timaeus* explicitly sets out to integrate the entire living being, body and soul, into a teleological account. The *Republic*, in its concern with setting out a programme of rigorous intellectual education and the negative consequences of ignoring this education, naturally downplays the positive contributions that the lower parts of the soul and the body may make to the overall happiness of the individual and the city. Therefore we need not say that Plato changed his mind between the *Republic* and the *Timaeus,* only that in the *Timaeus* he re-examined the tripartite soul and its relationship to the body from the point of view of a cosmic teleology.

The most significant contribution that the *Timaeus* makes to our understanding of Platonic psychology may lie in its distinctive account of the origin of the tripartite soul. This point can be brought out by comparing the *Timaeus* with standard, here oversimplified, readings of the *Phaedo* and *Phaedrus*. In the *Phaedo* the soul seems to be essentially unitary and rational, as we see, for example, in the argument from its kinship with Forms (78 B–80 C). In contrast, the image of the chariot in the *Phaedrus* presents the soul as having three parts already prior to embodiment (246 A–B). In comparison

---

[35] I explore the terms of this project in greater detail in *Plato's Natural Philosophy* (Cambridge, forthcoming).

with these claims, the *Timaeus* occupies a more developed halfway house.[36] The soul is not tripartite before it is embodied. Tripartition arises only when the irrational and rational motions of the soul are organized by the lesser gods within the human body. However, the soul in its pre-embodied state is not, strictly speaking, a unity either. For not only did different ingredients reluctantly have to be mixed in order to create the soul; but once the soul 'stuff' had been mixed it was also divided into the circles of the same and the different, each of which was put in charge of grasping different sorts of entity. There was thus already a certain structural and functional differentiation within the soul even if the different circles moved in perfect mutual harmony. I have argued that this internal differentiation of the soul provided the template for the division within the embodied soul between more and less rational parts. This division could be attributed to the tendency of the circles of the different to lose their proper ratios ('rationality') unless regulated by the circle of the same. Embodiment in this sense brought out a potential for irrationality already inherent in the soul's original composition. The *Timaeus* thus explains in a way the *Phaedo* does not why a soul which is essentially rational can nevertheless be susceptible to irrationality. Yet the *Timaeus* explains this without attributing a fully articulated tripartition to the immortal soul in the manner of the *Phaedrus*. In this way the *Timaeus* might favourably be seen to avoid potentially problematic questions raised by the *Phaedrus* about what exactly an appetitive or a spirited part would be doing when the soul is separated from a body.

In conclusion, I hope to have shown that the *Timaeus* deserves more than a mention in the history of philosophical psychology. Not only does the dialogue have original things to say about the nature of soul–body interaction and the origin of the tripartite soul; it also presents a detailed teleological picture of living beings as psycho-somatic wholes. The dialogue forces us to rethink the image of Plato as enemy of the body.

University of Bristol

---

[36] Cf. G. Reydams-Schils, *Demiurge and Providence* (Turnhout, 1999), 64, who argues on different grounds that in bringing together 42 A–B and 69 C–D 'Plato has reconciled "the Socratic" model known best from the *Phaedo* (as in 81 C and in 83 D) with his tripartite psychology.'

SOME LOGICAL PROBLEMS
IN *METAPHYSICS* GAMMA

MICHAEL V. WEDIN

Metaphysics Γ 4 opens with a reference to persons who (*a*) say (φασι) that it is possible for the same thing to be and not to be and (*b*) hold things to be the case in just this way (ὑπολαμβάνειν οὕτως).[1] Certain of the writers on nature are said to 'make use of this thesis' (χρῶνται τῷ λόγῳ). The thesis in question is presumably (*a*), and so (*b*) probably adverts to specific claims that violate the principle of non-contradiction, claims of the sort Heraclitus and others are alleged to have made. Aristotle will have none of this, of course, and in Γ 4 he proceeds to hammer such views. So it might seem that the sole object of Aristotle's attention is defence of the principle of non-contradiction (PNC) itself. This would be hardly surprising in the light of its vaunted status in the corpus as a whole. But in *Metaphysics* Γ he is, I believe, chiefly concerned

© Michael V. Wedin 2000

I wish to express thanks to the participants in my Aristotle seminars in the falls of 1997 and 1998. Their questions and worries about my views on *Metaphysics* Gamma greatly improved the paper. The paper achieved further improvement as a result of friendly fire at the 1999 Princeton Classical Philosophy Colloquium. I am particularly indebted to Alan Code and, above all, to the comments of my commentator, David Charles, and to remarks of John Cooper, who graciously introduced the paper in my absence. A number of their points have been incorporated into the paper or are addressed in notes. In the final stage I was helped by David Sedley, who provided a number of astute observations and pertinent criticisms. To him also I owe a debt of gratitude.

[1] Usually, Γ 4 is taken to open by addressing an opponent who asserts (*a**) that it is possible for something to be and not to be and (*b**) that it is possible to believe this. On this reading, the opponent first asserts an ontological thesis, the denial of PNC itself, and then asserts a doxastic thesis having the ontological thesis as its object. But Aristotle says only that certain people, who say it is possible for something to be and not to be, also ὑπολμβάνειν οὕτως. That is, they also hold things to be the case *in this way* (οὕτως). Here nothing need refer back to the general denial of PNC in (*a**) but only to holding things to be the case in accordance with it. This reading, suggested by John Cooper and, independently, by David Charles, is discussed at greater length in sect. 9.

with the proposal that it is possible to believe the negation of PNC. For he immediately adds that in the previous chapter, Γ 3, he had *accepted* that it is impossible for something to be and not to be simultaneously and *shown*, on the basis of this, that PNC is the firmest principle of all. For this is just to say that it is impossible to believe the negation of PNC.[2] Γ 4 further counsels that only the under-trained would seek to prove so fundamental a principle. So the chapter's extended defence of the principle itself is arguably motivated by a desire to secure PNC's status as a premiss in the argument that proves its firmness.[3]

Aristotle's focus on the *firmness* of PNC is a function of the fact that *Metaphysics* Γ promotes a discipline, sometimes dubbed the general science of metaphysics, that studies things that are in so far as they are and what holds of things in so far as they are. Every science is charged with studying the firmest principles within its proper domain, and so the general science of metaphysics should study the firmest principles of everything. For Aristotle a principle with respect to which error is impossible will be such a principle, for it will be the firmest of all. And a principle whose negation cannot be believed will be a principle with respect to which error is impossible. So Γ 3's proof that it is impossible to believe the denial of PNC establishes its credentials as the firmest principle of the general science of metaphysics. For convenience, I shall sometimes refer to this as the Indubitability Proof.

In this paper I wish to discuss a number of logical problems arising from reflection on Aristotle's arguments in *Metaphysics* Γ 3 and 4, including the Indubitability Proof. By a logical problem I here understand problems of the sort that have led commentators to question Aristotle's logical acumen—errors in reasoning, mistakes about what the reasoning shows, and so on. It is not my intention to discuss all so-called logical problems or even all of the most important of them. Nor, concerning those I discuss, do I promise

[2] Or, perhaps, that it is impossible to believe something that PNC declares to be impossible. This touches on an issue raised in sect. 2 and revisited in sect. 8, namely, whether PNC itself is the object of Γ 3's proof or whether the proof applies only to instances of PNC.

[3] *Pace* J. Lear, *Aristotle and Logical Theory* (Cambridge, 1980), 98–114, and A. Code, 'Metaphysics and Logic', in M. Matthen (ed.), *Aristotle Today: Essays on Aristotle's Ideal of Science* (Edmonton, 1987) 127–49, this does not mean that Γ 4's *object of proof* is a doxastic claim to the effect that no one can disbelieve PNC. Its focus, rather, is PNC proper even though the cause of the attention is PNC's role as a premiss in the argument for Γ 3's doxastic claim *about* it.

to exonerate Aristotle on all counts. But there is something useful to be said on a few problems that have vexed commentators, and it is hoped that this will serve to deliver Aristotle from some of the harsher judgements he has received for his performance in *Metaphysics Γ*. I begin with two problems from *Γ* 3 and then turn to *Γ* 4.

1. PNC as the ultimate principle of demonstration

At *Metaphysics Γ* 3, 1005^{b}18–20, Aristotle states the firmest principle: 'It is impossible for the same thing to belong and not to belong to the same thing at the same time and in the same respect.' For present purposes we may represent this as

(1) $\neg \Diamond (\exists x)(Fx \wedge \neg Fx)$,

which may be taken as the canonical formulation of PNC as an ontological principle, i.e. a principle governing things and their attributes.[4] To show that (1) is the firmest principle of all is, for Aristotle, to show that it is impossible to believe the negation of (1). So it requires showing something like

(2) $\neg \Diamond (\exists y)(y \textbf{ bel } \Diamond (\exists x)(Fx \wedge \neg Fx))$.

The proof of (2) makes use of (1).[5] So Aristotle proves the impossibility of believing the negation of PNC by appeal to PNC itself. Roughly, (2) is taken to deny the possibility that *y* has two beliefs,

---

[4] A propositional or 'logical' version of PNC is also attested in *Metaphysics Γ*. This we might formulate as $(p)\neg \Diamond (p \wedge \neg p)$ or, perhaps, as $\neg \Diamond (\exists p)(p \wedge \neg p)$.

[5] Because they express appropriately different propositions, no circularity is involved in proving (2) by using (1). So I do not understand Lear's complaint (*Aristotle and Logical Theory*, 10) that Kirwan believes the argument depends on PNC as a premiss (C. Kirwan, *Aristotle's* Metaphysics, *Books Γ, Δ, E*, trans. with notes [*Aristotle's* Metaphysics] (Oxford, 1971)). Indeed, Lear, *Aristotle: The Desire to Understand* (Cambridge, 1988), 252, finds that the Indubitability Proof *does* beg the question if (1) is false, but not if (1) is true. It is not clear what to make of this. For one thing, the falsity of (1) would make the argument unsound and so the issue of begging the question need even be raised by the opponent of PNC. For a second thing, what *Metaphysics Γ* says about begging the question makes Lear's line of doubtful expository use. As we shall see shortly, when Aristotle gets down to the actual 'proof' of PNC, the refutative or elenctic proof of *Γ* 4, he maintains that the question is begged if the proponent of PNC, who is mounting the argument, issues the crucial premiss, but not if the opponent issues it. Here the truth of the premisse(s) is not in question, only who is responsible for entering it (them) into the argument.

the belief that Fx and the belief that $\neg Fx$. The latter belief is then taken as the *contrary* of the former, and this amounts to the disbelief that Fx. Thus, to deny (2) is to hold that y could have a property corresponding to the belief that Fx and a contrary property corresponding to the disbelief that Fx. This, in turn, entails that y could both have and not have the property corresponding to the belief that Fx. But this violates PNC. This is what Aristotle is recalling at the outset of Γ 4, in effectively reporting that (2) is proved by using (1).[6]

Commentators have raised a number of worries about the reasoning used in this proof, specifically about some of the principles it employs, e.g. the principle that believing the contradictory of Fx is the contrary of believing Fx. I shall not press these issues here, in part because they have received adequate attention elsewhere.[7] Rather I shall focus on two different problems. The first concerns the 'ultimacy' claim Aristotle makes on behalf of PNC once it has been shown to be the firmest principle. The second is a problem concerning exactly what he has shown to be impossible to believe.

The ultimacy claim, as I am calling it, closes *Metaphysics* Γ 3. Taking himself to have established (2), Aristotle adds expansively:

That is why all those who demonstrate go back to this doctrine [δόξα] in the end; it is in the nature of things the principle of all the other axioms also [φύσει γὰρ ἀρχὴ καὶ τῶν ἄλλων ἀξιωμάτων αὕτη πάντων]. (1005ᵇ32–4)

Lukasiewicz ('Aristotle on the Principle of Contradiction') is particularly disparaging of this closing flourish to Γ 3 and urges his readers to resist the false but widely distributed belief that PNC is the highest principle of all demonstrations. Although this holds for

---

[6] Again, lurking here is an issue that is addressed explicitly in the next section, namely, whether the Indubitability Proof secures the principle itself or instances of the principle. ((2) favours the former, but the course of proof might suggest only the latter.)

[7] For some assessment of the proof itself see J. Lukasiewicz, *Über den Satz des Widerspruchs bei Aristoteles* (Zur modernen Deutung der Aristotelischen Logik, 5; 1993) [trans. by J. Barski of *O zasadzie sprzeczności u Arystotelesa* (Cracow, 1910), and 'Aristotle on the Principle of Contradiction', *Review of Metaphysics*, 24 (1971), 485–509 [trans. by M. V. Wedin of 'Über den Satz des Widerspruchs bei Aristoteles', *Bull. intern. de l'Académie des Sciences de Cracovie*]. References will be to this authorized translation. Also now as 'Aristotle on the Law of Contradiction', trans. J. Barnes, in J. Barnes, M. Schofield, and R. Sorabji (eds.), *Articles on Aristotle* (London, 1979), iii. 50–62. See also J. Barnes, 'The Law of Contradiction', *Philosophical Quarterly*, 10 (1969), 302–9; R. Dancy, *Sense and Contradiction: A Study in Aristotle* (Dordrecht, 1975); and J. Stevenson, 'Aristotle and the Principle of Contradiction as a Law of Thought', *The Personalist*, 56 (1975) 403–13.

indirect proofs, it is false for direct proofs, and in general any number of logical principles are independent of PNC. This opinion of Lukasiewicz may lie behind Kirwan's complaint (*Aristotle's Metaphysics*, 90), that immunity to disbelief does not establish that every argument relies on PNC but only that no argument questions it.

So it appears that Aristotle fails badly in assessing the logical station of his firmest principle. We can sharpen the issue by following Lukasiewicz's account of Aristotle's woes. While indirect proofs presuppose PNC, direct proofs do not. In a direct proof we may have, for example, something to the effect that, given $p \supset q$, and p, we are to infer q. The idea is that this is one of 'innumerable deductions . . . which proceed only by affirmative propositions; consequently, the principle of contradiction finds no application to these because it always joins an affirmative proposition and its contradictory negative.'[8] This sounds plausible but will it stand scrutiny?

Well, it is quite correct that direct inferences do not typically use PNC as part of the inferential reasoning. But this may not establish that such inferences are independent of PNC because what is presupposed by a pattern of inferential reasoning need not be a part of that reasoning itself. Let us, then, take Aristotle at his word when he says that in the end all demonstrating goes back to PNC. Moreover, let us suppose, plausibly, that the reasoning is deductive. Then he is claiming that all deductive reasoning somehow goes back to PNC. We may, then, represent the above pattern of reasoning as depending on

(3) $((p \supset q) \wedge p) \supset q$,

in particular as depending on its validity. We may say that the parenthesized schema implies q. If so, then the conjunction of the antecedent with the negation of the consequent should lead to an inconsistency.[9] In the case of (3), we would have on the left: $\neg(p \wedge \neg q) \wedge p$; and on the right: $\neg q$. But the left side is equivalent to $(\neg p \vee q) \wedge p$ and, hence, to q. So, we are left with q and $\neg q$. Thus, we may conclude that (3) is valid. More to the point, however, we conclude this by appeal to the principle of non-contradiction. Hence, one

---

[8] Lukasiewicz , 'Aristotle on the Principle of Contradiction', 504.

[9] To follow W. V. O. Quine, *Methods of Logic* (New York, 1966), 100: 'One schema implies another if and only if the one in conjunction with the other's negation is inconsistent.'

can conclude that the validity of (3) depends on the principle of non-contradiction, even if no application of (3) or instances of (3) *uses* the principle.

It should be obvious that the same result is forthcoming from consideration of any pattern of reasoning that is deductively valid. Thus, simplification depends on the validity of

(4) $(p \wedge q) \supset p$,

for conjoining $p \wedge q$ with $\neg p$ leaves us with $p \wedge \neg p$, which again violates the principle of non-contradiction. Yet, Lukasiewicz ('Aristotle on the Principle of Contradiction', 504) claims that simplification is independent of PNC.

So why does Lukasiewicz insist that only indirect arguments presuppose PNC? We are already familiar with his claim that because (3) and (4) contain only affirmative propositions there could be no dependence on PNC. But, as we have just seen, this does not detract from the fact that their *validity* can be seen to rest on the principle. Perhaps, however, Lukasiewicz has something else in mind. If so, it should be evident from his account of how indirect proofs *do* depend on PNC. Here is what he says:

> The *ad impossibile* mode of inference turns namely on the principle of contraposition which—as symbolic logic has shown—presupposes the principle of contradiction. This can also be put into words: The *ad impossibile* mode of inference runs: If *a* is, then *b* must be; now *b* is not; thus, *a* also cannot be. Reason: Were *a* to be, then a contradiction would ensue, for *b* must be, which it is not. ('Aristotle on the Principle of Contradiction', 499)

In more customary terms, given $p \supset q$, and $\neg q$, we are to infer $\neg p$ *because* were we to have p, we would have q and so we would have q and $\neg q$. But this violates PNC and so PNC is presupposed by indirect proofs.

Notice that Lukasiewicz arrives at this result by asking, in effect, what would be the case were the mode of inference not deductively valid. Thus, were

(5) $((p \supset q) \wedge \neg q) \supset \neg p$

not valid, we would have on the left $(\neg p \vee q) \wedge \neg q$, which simplifies to $\neg p$, and on the right we would have p. Once again, the principle of non-contradiction is violated, and so we may conclude that (5) is valid. This, Lukasiewicz avers, shows that indirect proofs depend on PNC. For some reason he thinks this case is different from cases (3) and (4) and from direct patterns of inference generally. But it is hard to see the force of this. No more than those cases do applications of (5) or instances of (5) *use* PNC. (5)'s dependence on PNC is secured by asking why the inference goes through and answering that, were it not to go through, a contradiction would result. This is precisely the procedure we followed in assessing (3) and (4)—*modus ponens* and simplification. So whatever sense of 'presupposition' Lukasiewicz has in mind when he claims that (5) presupposes PNC, in that same sense (3) and (4) presuppose the principle.[10]

So there appears to be a sense in which PNC is the doctrine that everyone who demonstrates goes back to in the end. It is not the principle *from which* all deductions start because then it would be used in all deductions; but it is not. It does, however, appear to be a presupposition of the *validity* of principles of valid reasoning, in the sense suggested above. In this way PNC's claim to ultimacy holds despite the fact that it is not *used* in all cases of valid reasoning. The importance of this fact will emerge in Section 5 below, in connection with Aristotle's explanation of how elenctic proofs avoid begging the question.

Still, there is a worry, for if PNC is such a presupposition, then it might yet parade as a principle that is somehow 'deeper' than other logical principles. This, of course, might be doubted on the grounds that the validity of principles such as $p \wedge q \rightarrow p$ or $p \rightarrow p$ is hardly less transparent than that of $\neg(p \wedge \neg p)$. While this rings true, there is a reason why Aristotle gives pride of place to PNC. Recall his claim that it is *because* it is the firmest of principles that PNC is the principle every demonstration goes back to. From this point of view, we might take the principle not as *establishing* the validity of principles of deduction but rather as *displaying* their deductive firmness. Someone might suppose it possible to grant their deductive utility, even validity, but still insist that they are not immune to error, that is, that someone might be mistaken about them. So Aristotle points out that for this to be the case it must be possible for principles of demonstration not to hold; but this amounts to the possibility that PNC may fail to hold. Not only is this impossible, by Γ 3's Indubitability Proof it cannot even be believed. Hence,

---

[10] So I am not denying that there may be another sense of presupposition according to which indirect, but not direct, proofs presuppose PNC.

the firmness attaching to PNC is inherited by all principles whose denials flout the principle of non-contradiction.[11] Because these principles inherit their firmness from PNC and because PNC establishes its own firmness, he declares that it is the principle of all other principles.[12] In this way its claim to ultimacy holds up.

2. What is proved by the Indubitability Proof?

What I am calling the Indubitability Proof takes up the final section of Γ 3, 1005^{b}22–32, and leads into the claim which we have just discussed. The proof concerns the principle of non-contradiction as stated at 1005^{b}18–22. This principle, which I formulated above as (1), is the firmest of all principles and, therefore, the Indubitability Proof ought to focus on *its* firmness. That is, it ought to establish the impossibility of anyone's believing the negation of the *principle itself*. And this is just how I have represented the proof's conclusion in (2) above.

Unfortunately, it is not clear that the argument Aristotle gives is sufficient to establish (2). Here I am not referring to problems with the proof itself, a topic that has rightly exercised a number of scholars, but rather to a problem about what is proven. For this purpose, we may assume that the proof is sound as it stands.

The difficulty is that the Indubitability Proof appears to establish only that it is not possible to believe *instances* of '$p \wedge \neg p$' or of '$Fx \wedge \neg Fx$'. That is, for anything you believe, you can't believe it and

---

[11] To take a case we have discussed, (4) is not demonstratively firm if it is possible that some x believes $\neg[(p \wedge q) \rightarrow p]$. But this requires that it be possible that x believe $(p \wedge \neg p)$, something the Γ 3 Indubitability Proof shows to be impossible. So (4) is also immune to error, and hence is demonstratively firm.

[12] I have concentrated mainly on Aristotle's claim that PNC is the doctrine all demonstration goes back to, but he finishes the chapter with the further claim that it is the principle of all other axioms, and this implies either that PNC is itself an axiom or that it is the principle of axioms other than those figuring in demonstration. In either case, our story will have to apply to principles that are not standard principles of inference, i.e. those that do not govern relations between propositions. One of Aristotle's favourites is the so-called 'equals axiom': where $A = B$, $(A + C = D) \rightarrow (B + C = D)$. Here, if x thinks the axiom does not hold, then x thinks it is possible to have $(A + C \wedge D) \wedge (B + C \wedge \neg D)$, and thus that it is possible to have $D \wedge \neg D$. That is, given $A = B$, it must be possible for the same thing to sum to D and not to sum to D. But this appears to violate PNC. So, again, x can deny the equals axiom only on pain of contradiction. Although only analogous to the proposition-friendly principles (3), (4), and (5), the analogy is close enough, I think, to explain why Aristotle might have taken PNC as presupposed by this sort of axiom as well.

believe its negation. What is troublesome here emerges clearly when we formalize this, either as a result about propositions,

(6a) $\neg\Diamond(\exists x)(\exists p)(x$ **bel** $p \wedge \neg p)$,

or as a result about properties holding of subjects,

(6b) $\neg\Diamond(\exists x)(\exists z)(x$ **bel** $Fz \wedge \neg Fz)$.

Proposition (6a) says that it is not possible that there be someone such that there is some proposition he believes along with its negation. (6b) says that it is not possible that there be someone such that, for some thing and some property, he believes the thing has the property and does not have the property. In short, there will be no one who believes any instance of the negation of PNC, whether it governs propositions, as in (6a), or things and their properties, as in (6b).[13]

Unfortunately, it is not obvious that either (6a) or (6b) establishes that PNC is the firmest principle of all. For neither obviously establishes that it is not possible to believe its negation. In fact, the principle *itself* is not the target of *x*'s belief in either. What is required are parallel formulations to (6a) and (6b) that make the negation of PNC itself the object of doxastic interest. So we need something like

(7a) $\neg\Diamond(\exists x)(x$ **bel** $\Diamond(\exists p)(p \wedge \neg p))$,

and its ontological counterpart,

(7b) $\neg\Diamond(\exists x)(x$ **bel** $\Diamond(\exists z)(Fz \wedge \neg Fz))$,

which is just an algebraic variation of (2). By most accounts, the Indubitability Proof establishes (6a) and (6b) only, namely, that no instance of the negation of PNC can be believed.[14] It does not establish that the negation of the principle itself cannot be believed. Someone might agree that every proposition he happens to believe is such that he cannot believe it and its negation but none the

---

[13] That is, alternatively, everyone and every proposition is such that it is not possible for that person to believe the proposition and its negation. Similarly, every person, every property, and every thing is such that it is not possible for the person to believe that the thing has the property and does not have it. The first is equivalent to (6a): $(x)(p)\neg\Diamond(x$ **bel** $p \wedge \neg p)$; and the second is equivalent to (6b): $(x)(z)(F)\neg\Diamond(x$ **bel** $Fz \wedge \neg Fz)$.

[14] e.g. S. M. Cohen, 'Aristotle on the Principle of Non-contradiction', *Canadian Journal of Philosophy*, 16 (1986), 359–70 at 367, and Code, 'Metaphysics and Logic', 141.

less insist that there might be *some* proposition such that it and its negation can be believed. He is, of course, under no obligation to produce this proposition, for his insistence rests on the general point that claims such as (6a) are not sufficient to establish claims such as (7a). To take an analogue from standard belief cases, it is plausible that every proposition I believe, I believe to be true, and also that I do not believe that all of my beliefs are true. Here there is no temptation to find me holding contradictory beliefs. Similarly, I can hold (6a) and also hold it possible that someone believes that it is possible that there is *some* proposition such that it and its negation are true. But this last belief is just the negation of (7a). Hence, to establish (6a) is not to establish (7a).[15]

This fact may be of some strategic importance, for Aristotle has promised to establish that PNC is the firmest *principle* of all and to do so by showing that its negation cannot be believed. Rather than this, he delivers the firmness of *instances* of PNC, not the firmness of PNC itself. Now it may be that this is the best Aristotle can do and that he takes it to be good enough. Here the idea would be that to establish PNC as the firmest principle it is sufficient to demonstrate the impossibility of believing an instance of its negation. But the worry remains that Aristotle may not have proven what he claims to have proven. This point, not included in Lukasiewicz's laundry list of fallacies, was, so far as I know, first noted by Cohen[16] in commenting on Code's account of the role of the principle of non-contradiction as a chief object of investigation for the general science of metaphysics.[17] As part of this general investigative enterprise, it may be important that Γ 3 prove something about the principle itself. Code seems to be of this opinion ('Metaphysics and Logic') and proposes a remedy for the problem, one that views Γ 3

---

[15] Although I have appealed to the notion of belief in arguing for the consistency of holding (6a) and denying (7a), Aristotle's reasoning may be related to a more purely logical point. Rather than the quantified sentence, (6a), suppose he is claiming, for indefinite individual propositions, $p_1 \ldots p_n \ldots$, that a certain property fails to hold of each, namely, the property P (=can be believed jointly with its negation). Then we would have Aristotle proving $\neg Pp_1 \wedge \ldots \wedge \neg Pp_n \wedge \ldots$, and this is not inconsistent with holding also that $(\exists p)(Pp)$. Although not inconsistency in the ordinary sense, this looks like what we now call ω-inconsistency. But ω-inconsistency, unappealing though it might be, does not entail ordinary inconsistency, and the latter, as governed by the principle of non-contradiction, is what preoccupies Aristotle in *Metaphysics* Γ 3.   [16] 'Aristotle on the Principle of Non-contradiction'.
[17] A. Code, 'Aristotle's Investigation of a Basic Logical Principle: Which Science Investigates the Principle of Non-contradiction', *Canadian Journal of Philosophy*, 16 (1986), 341–58.

as producing an incomplete argument that is to be completed by the so-called elenctic proof in *Metaphysics* Γ 4. I shall look at this proposal before moving at greater length to Γ 4 proper.

3. Does Γ 4's elenctic proof complete the Indubitability Proof of Γ 3?

The Indubitability Proof, which takes up the last section of Γ 3, establishes the impossibility of believing that something can have a property and not have it and, hence, that error is impossible regarding this. It is this impossibility, the impossibility of error, that entails the firmness of PNC. But the entailment itself rests on a more general principle, which I shall write as

(8) (a) Error is impossible regarding principle $P \rightarrow$ (b) P is the firmest of all principles.

Aristotle feels the need to support this principle, and at $1005^b 11$–18 an argument is provided for (8). A key, and unstated,[18] assumption of the argument is

(9) (a) Error is impossible regarding principle $P \rightarrow$ (c) P is understood by anyone who understands anything.[19]

Although Aristotle's text does not contain (9) itself, it does contain the entailment's constituent propositions; and, of course, PNC turns out to be an instance, if not the sole instance, of each. So it is not unreasonable to assume that Aristotle holds

(10) (c) $\rightarrow$ (d) PNC is believed by anyone who believes anything.

It is (d) that is pressed into service by Code to get beyond the 'instantial' reading, as I shall call it, of the conclusion of the Indubitability Proof.[20] That is, so far from applying just to instances, (d) excludes belief in the negation of the principle, *itself*, of non-contradiction. The idea is that (d) entails

---

[18] So, correctly, Kirwan, *Aristotle's* Metaphysics, 88.
[19] Of course, more is required to get (8). Aristotle's actual argument is rather involved. Our immediate aim is to isolate an assumption from Γ 3 that could play a role in answering the charge that Aristotle proves only indubitability for *instances* of PNC. For this it is enough to highlight (9). See Kirwan, *Aristotle's* Metaphysics, 87–8, for help on the argument itself.   [20] 'Metaphysics and Logic'.

(11) $\neg \Diamond (\exists x)(x$ **bel** $\neg$PNC$)$

because by (d) anyone holding the belief that $\neg$PNC is bound to believe PNC and, hence, it would have to be the case that

(12) $\Diamond (\exists x)(x$ **bel** PNC$\wedge \neg$PNC$)$.

But, by the Indubitability Proof, (12) violates PNC itself. Thus, (11) must be true and so we appear to get indubitability, not just of instances of PNC, but of the *principle itself*.

Unhappily, as Code points out,[21] this defence of the 'principled' reading, as it might be called, has the drawback that Γ 3 nowhere provides support for (d). So its argument appears to remain critically incomplete. For this reason I shall occasionally refer to (d) as Code's lemma. To remedy this defect, he considers the idea that the purpose of the elenctic argument of Γ 4 is to provide the missing support for (d). This is an extremely interesting proposal and its acceptability depends on what demands it places on the elenctic proof. So let us see what these are and then turn to the elenctic proof to determine whether it is up to the task.

Roughly, the idea is that the elenctic proof, which dominates the discussion of Γ 4,[22] establishes that all significant thought and language presupposes conformity with PNC. So we may begin with an assumption, common to all parties, that what is believed is significant:

(13) $(x)(p)(x$ **bel** $p \rightarrow p$ is significant$)$.

Then Γ 4's elenctic proof can be used to establish the crucial condition on significance:

(14) $(p)(p$ is significant$\rightarrow p$ conforms to PNC$)$.

According to Code, (14), along with (13), 'provides Aristotle with a reason for accepting the claim that everyone must believe of the principle [PNC] that it is true'.[23] Even if Aristotle's, it is not clear that this is a good reason. For it requires that (13) and (14) are sufficient for

(15) $(x)(p)(x$ **bel** $p \rightarrow x$ **bel** p conforms to PNC$)$,

---

[21] 'Metaphysics and Logic', 143.
[22] And which I turn to in detail in sect. 6 below.
[23] 'Metaphysics and Logic', 144.

but why should we suppose this? All (13) and (14) warrant is the weaker claim

(15a) $(x)(p)(x$ **bel** $p \rightarrow p$ conforms to PNC).

This, however, falls short of the task Code has set, for (15a) means something like

(15b) $(x)(p)(x$ **bel** $p \rightarrow \neg \Diamond (p \wedge \neg p))$,

and, even when p is taken as $\neg$PNC itself, we get nothing more than

(15c) $(x)(p)(x$ **bel** $\neg$PNC $\rightarrow \neg \Diamond (\neg$PNC$\wedge$PNC$))$,

and here we have nothing that supports (d) because such support requires that x *believe* that his belief—even if $\neg$PNC—be in conformity with PNC. Conform it must, but he need not believe that it conforms.[24]

So it is not at all clear that Γ 4's elenctic proof can provide the sort of support that Code seeks.[25] Nor, I think, is it any clearer that Aristotle thought it could. This, of course, depends on a certain reading of the proof, in particular one that yields nothing stronger than the sort of conformity registered in (14). So we need to take a closer look at Γ 4.

---

[24] Code, 'Metaphysics and Logic', 145, puts his point also as follows: if x believes p and x does not believe that p conforms to PNC, then p is not significant. But x may have no belief at all about PNC, so perhaps we need: if x believes p and x believes that p does not conform to PNC, then p is not significant. But again, why should we suppose that all believers have such a sophisticated meta-belief about their beliefs? What is probably acceptable is this: if x believes p and p does not conform to PNC, then p is not significant. Although the latter may support the claim that PNC has the *per se* attribute of being necessary for significance, nothing is forthcoming from it about belief in PNC itself. So it is not clear how we get here any support for (d), the claim that anyone who believes anything believes PNC.

[25] In Code's words, '. . . an independent argument for the claim that everybody must believe the PNC' ('Metaphysics and Logic', 146). This is just (15). According to Code, in the end the elenctic proof fails to establish the fully general result registered in (15). Still, this views the Γ 4 proof as attempting, unsuccessfully, to complete Γ 3's Indubitability Proof. On the view to be defended here, the elenctic proof could not be party to such an attempt in the first place.

4. The organization of Γ 4

It will be useful to begin with organization. The introductory section of Γ 4 ($1005^b35–1006^a11$) begins, as we have seen, by reminding us that Γ 3 uses PNC to prove the indubitability and, hence, firmness of PNC and chides those who insist that PNC itself be demonstrated. Owing to a lack of training in analytics, they fail to grasp that there cannot be demonstration of everything. So there are some things whose demonstration ought not to be sought, and chief among these is PNC. Immediately, and somewhat surprisingly, Aristotle qualifies his prohibition with the remark that even PNC can be demonstrated, so long as this is elenctic demonstration or demonstration 'in the manner of a refutation'. So in the chapter's second section ($1006^a11–28$) Aristotle explains, or tries to explain, how elenctic proofs differ from proofs proper and prepares the reader for the upcoming elenctic proof by pinning the difference on the fact that in elenctic proof the opponent says something significant and so is responsible for his own dialectical downfall.

Then come the actual arguments of Γ 4. Commentators divide them differently, and the Appendix displays three such divisions—those of Lukasiewicz, Ross, and Kirwan—in addition to my own. For the most part I agree with Ross on the points of division but not, I think, on their import. Here is the way I see matters. *Metaphysics* Γ 4 does contain an argument, the conclusion of which is PNC, but it contains *only one* such argument. This is the long elenctic argument running from 1006^a28 to 1007^b18 (marked W1 in the Appendix). Granted, there follow no fewer than six arguments in the balance of the chapter. But none of these has PNC as its conclusion. So, at least, I shall argue. They are what I call 'shriek' arguments, designed to impress on the opponent exactly what he is committed to by denying PNC. None of these arguments actually draws the conclusion that *therefore* PNC is true, and so none are classic *reductio* arguments against the supposition that PNC is false. This means, *contra* Lukasiewicz, 'Aristotle on the Principle of Contradiction', and others, that none is guilty of the fallacy of begging the question. I shall say more about this in Section 10 below. First, however, something needs to be said about the general strategy of elenctic proofs and then about the elenctic proof of PNC.

5. The strategy of elenctic proof

I do not intend to go fully into the nature of elenctic proofs, even as delineated in *Γ* 4, but shall adopt for the purpose of discussion Lukasiewicz's understanding.[26] First, it is important to remember that they are not indirect proofs and so do not use (5) above, the rule of contraposition. They are, rather, direct proofs, typically relying on principles such as (3) above. Second, there is no formal difference between elenctic proof and proof proper. Both may be represented as instances of *modus ponens*:

$$p \supset q$$
$$\underline{p}$$
$$\therefore \quad q$$

By proof proper Aristotle means proof as understood in the *Analytics*, i.e. proofs where one sets down premises and draws as the conclusion what follows necessarily from the premises. The premisses are truths, not suppositions to be rejected as in the case of indirect proofs. This point holds for elenctic proofs as well. Third, elenctic proof and proof proper differ pragmatically. How? Well, recall that an elenctic proof purports to establish something directly, say *q*, and it does so by finding something else, *p*, such that *p* is the case and *p* entails *q*. But the proof is aimed at an opponent of *q*, and so it is critical that the opponent accept the truth of *p*. Aristotle puts this by requiring that the opponent assert *p*. Otherwise, he says, one might be open to the charge of begging the question. And this is the situation with proper direct proofs. This is avoided in elenctic proofs because the opponent is responsible for the assertion that commits him to the truth of a proposition that conflicts with what he holds.[27]

---

[26] This will be sufficient for the purposes of essaying the 'logical' problem at hand. See Dancy, *Sense and Contradiction*, and R. Bolton, 'Metaphysics as a Science', in T. Scaltsas, D. Charles, and M. L. Gill (eds.), *Unity, Identity, and Explanation in Aristotle's* Metaphysics (Oxford, 1994), 321–54, for more extended discussions.

[27] Code, 'Metaphysics and Logic', 144, calls attention to another difference between a proof of PNC and analytics-style demonstrations. The latter explain *why* the state of affairs represented in the conclusion obtains, and they do so in part because the premises of the demonstration are prior and more knowable than the conclusion. But no principle is prior to or more knowable than PNC. So no proof of it could explain it. This emerges quite clearly in sect. 6 below.

Lukasiewicz complains: 'I cannot grasp what is being said here.'[28] Although he does not explain himself, the nature of his complaint can be discerned from the fact that he regards the fallacy of *petitio principii* as a formal fallacy. On this view, begging the question ought to be a feature of the formal structure of an argument. While the form and meaning of its constituent propositions may be relevant to determining the structure, it is unclear why it should matter who enters them into the argument. The opponent might decide not to accept *p* when I offer it to him. But if, when I proceed anyway, my argument begs the question, surely it would do so were he to have asserted *p* on his own initiative. In the first case *I* beg the question against the opponent; in the second case *he* begs the question against himself. As a formal fallacy, it should not matter who is responsible for constructing the *petitio*, nor should it matter were I to gain a certain forensic advantage from getting my opponent to beg the question against himself. Rather, because begging the question is a formal mistake, both must be guilty of it or both innocent. Little wonder, then, that Lukasiewicz could not make sense of Aristotle's asseveration that his argument is protected against begging the question by the mere fact that the opponent asserts the crucial premisse(s).[29]

The trouble with this, of course, is that begging the question is not a formal fallacy at all, but a mistake typically involving pragmatic considerations. So *who* believes *what* may be relevant to the charge of *petitio principii*. Indeed, on some accounts begging the question depends on belief. Sanford, for example, thinks it is inconceivable without appeal to actual belief and builds this into his account.[30] On his view, the fallacy occurs whenever one must believe that the conclusion of an argument is true, in order to believe of a premiss, or a conjunct of a premiss, that it is true. Intuitively,

---

[28] 'Aristotle on the Principle of Contradiction', 495.

[29] C. W. A. Whitaker, *Aristotle's De Interpretatione: Contradiction and Dialectic* (Oxford, 1996), 187–8, wants to spare Aristotle Lukasiewicz's judgement. But his proposal, that the proof proper and elenctic proof differ on the point that the latter starts from the *opponent's* asserting *p*, does not address Lukasiewicz's worry. For, on Whitaker's line, it is only if the opponent puts forward something that cannot be advanced by the proponent of PNC that the argument manages to avoid begging the question. But this makes the charge turn on the *content* of the opponent's 'saying' and not on the simple fact that it is *he* who does the 'saying'. Yet only the latter is said to be relevant to the charge of begging the question.

[30] D. Sanford, 'Begging the Question as Involving Actual Belief and Inconceivable without it', *Metaphilosophy*, 19 (1988), 32–7.

the charge may be fairly levelled against me when my *reason* for believing in the truth of a premiss is my belief that the conclusion is true. Consider, for example, Sanford's sample argument:[31]

> All the members of the club attended the University of Texas. Twardowski is a member of the club.
>
> ∴   Twardowski attended the University of Texas.

Suppose Orcutt offers this as a proof. If Orcutt's reason for believing the first premiss is the fact that he knows the club's six members, one of whom is Twardowski, and knows that each attended the University of Texas, then his argument begs the question. For he believes the premiss true only because he believes the conclusion true. If, on the other hand, he believes the premise true on independent grounds, perhaps because it is a by-law of the club, then Orcutt does not beg the question. Thus, begging of the question is relative to beliefs and believers. This might appear to hold out promise for making sense of Aristotle's strategy, for on his view whether an argument is a *petitio* depends on who puts forward the premisse(s). So let us see if this works for the general form of the elenctic proof of PNC, as Aristotle spells it out.

The elenctic proof is directed against an opponent who maintains that it is possible for something to be the case and not to be the case at the same time and in the same respect. We can take him simply to deny PNC. What Aristotle says is that if the opponent will only assert something significant, say 'σ', then PNC can be established, and thus in some sense the opponent is refuted. We may represent the broad outlines of the argument's strategy, first entering the opponent's position:

> (16) ¬PNC   [opponent's view],

and then the elenctic argument itself:

> (16a) 'σ' is significant   ['σ' asserted by opponent]
> (16b) 'σ' is significant→PNC
>
> ∴ (16c) PNC.

Now if Aristotle has in mind Sanford's notion of begging the

---

[31] Ibid. 33. See M. Degnan, 'Does Aristotle Beg the Question in his Defense of the Principle of Non-contradiction?', *Proceedings of the American Catholic Philosophical Association*, 63 (1990), 146–59, on the connection between Aristotle's account and recent theories of begging the question.

question, then it ought to be the case that the proponent of the proof believes that (16a) or (16b) is true only because he believes that (16c) is true. One might seize on (16b), for it is true just in case 'σ' is not significant or PNC is true—and, of course, the proponent believes the latter. The opponent, on the other hand, does not accept PNC and so this could not be the reason for his acceptance of (16b). Thus, the argument begs the question relative to the *proponent*, but not relative to the *opponent*. However, this cannot be right, if only because the 'swing' premiss is explicitly said to be (16a) alone.[32] All that Aristotle requires is that the opponent say *something* significant, and surely it tests credulity to take this 'something' to be (16b).

Aristotle has in mind, I think, something simpler. The argument leads from (16a) to (16c), which conflicts with the opponent's thesis, (16). So a choice must be made between (16), the negation of PNC, and (16a), the proposition that 'σ' is significant. Aristotle will insist on (16a). To this, however, the opponent can reply that Aristotle simply begs the question. Rather than withdraw his denial of PNC, the opponent boldly reserves the right to reject the claim that 'σ' is significant. If, however, *right from the start* the opponent grants (16a), the charge of begging the question can no longer be levelled against the proof. This is the point of Aristotle's remark that there will be a refutation, 'if only the opponent says something' (1006^a12–13). For with this, he is exposed to the underlying argument of (16b), and, so, appropriately, this becomes the heart of the matter.

It is important to be clear on the point that only (16a)–(16c) contain the elenctic proof proper, and thus that it has the general structure of a *modus ponens* inference. So Aristotle holds, not that he has a *reductio* argument against the supposition that ¬PNC, but that he has an elenctic argument *for* PNC.[33] That is, he claims to have a direct argument for PNC but the argument will have elenctic or refutative *effect* because he who espouses ¬PNC (in (16)) is responsible for the premiss that yields PNC (namely (16a)) by asserting significant 'σ'. It is in this way that Aristotle promises to avoid begging the question.

Now, however, another worry surfaces. The ultimacy claim advanced at the close of Γ 3 is plainly stated: PNC is presupposed

---

[32] Not to mention the fact that the opponent in this case can, at the start, hardly be imagined to entertain (16b) at all.

[33] Lear, *Aristotle: The Desire to Understand*, 255, takes Aristotle to be offering a negative, indirect proof of PNC. But it is not clear whether this is meant to characterize the proof proper or only its elenctic effect. I would resist the first.

by all other 'logical' principles and axioms. Its final acceptability aside, we at least need to provide the claim with a coherent reading. Section 1 did this by proposing that PNC is a presupposition of the validity of the principles and rules that underlie deductive inferences. Since such patterns of inference include *modus ponens* and since one instance of this pattern is the elenctic proof of PNC, it appears that the elenctic proof of PNC presupposes, by the ultimacy claim, the truth of PNC. It thus appears guilty of circular reasoning, and so, after all, threatens to beg the question.

Here it is useful to return to the promissory note issued at the end of Section 1. According to Section 1, the rule underlying *modus ponens* presupposes PNC despite the fact that actual *modus ponens* inferences do not *use* PNC in the reasoning. Thus, Aristotle might reply that the elenctic proof begs no questions because it does not *use* PNC, even though PNC is presupposed as a condition of the validity of the rule that the proof does use. Although some may find this an acceptable response, it will strike many as over-subtle. So Aristotle stakes out another line of defence.

The opponent of PNC is represented not as an opponent of all reasoning, not even of all deductive reasoning. Indeed, he demands that he be *proven* wrong. So he is in principle open to deductive proof. In particular, we can take him to be open to any proof that does not *use* PNC in the reasoning. Thus, there is no reason to suppose that he would baulk at the use of *modus ponens* in deductive argumentation. Grant, then, that the opponent approves of the structure of elenctic proof. Now, of course, having exacted this much, Aristotle could go on to explain how *modus ponens* presupposes PNC as a condition of its validity, i.e. of its use in deductive proof. But he wisely resists this manœuvre. Rather, he grants the opponent *modus ponens*, without insisting on the 'validating' presupposition (after all, the opponent is demanding that he be *proven* wrong),[34] and then proceeds to use *modus ponens* in a direct proof of PNC. In this way, ultimacy is preserved but not at the cost of rendering the elenctic argument a *petitio*.

In committing the opponent to (16a), Aristotle does not say that everything the opponent says must be significant but that he must

---

[34] *Contra* Lear, *Aristotle and Logical Theory*, 104, and *Aristotle: The Desire to Understand*, 256 and 262, the latter of which represents the opponent as arguing 'in a reasoned way against the principle of non-contradiction'. On the contrary, Aristotle's opponent demands only to be refuted by reasoned argument.

say *something* significant. Moreover, (16b) must mean that, if something is significant, then it must conform to PNC. So it will look like

(16b′) 'σ' is significant→¬◊(Φ[σ]∧¬Φ[σ]),

where Φ[ ] is any 'propositional' context containing σ. Two preliminary points arise here. The first addresses the fact that (16b′) allows us to establish PNC relative to σ only, and so one could still maintain ¬PNC. For surely I can admit ¬◊(Fa∧¬Fa) and still hold ◊(∃x)(Fx∧¬Fx). But 'σ' is arbitrary, and so what holds for it will hold for any like thing. Whether this is enough to establish a fully general PNC depends on our second point, which concerns the unit of significance. Is 'σ' a sentence, a phrase, or a word? This is not decided by (16b′). If Φ[ ] just is σ itself, then 'σ' will be an assertion; if not, 'σ' may be a phrase or word. When we look at the details of Aristotle's account of signification, there will be some reason to favour the latter. Moreover, this account suggests that Φ[ ] is an essentialist context, in that its completion yields a proposition in which one thing is essentially tied to another.[35] But then the elenctic proof will establish PNC for essential predications only, and hence cannot serve as a deterrent to the opponent's denial of PNC. This was the opinion of Lukasiewicz.[36]

Although virtually all commentators join Lukasiewicz in holding that the elenctic proof establishes, if anything, only a restricted version of PNC, there is a way to extend its results to a fully general version of the principle. I do this in Section 7. But we first need to see how Aristotle carries out in detail the elenctic strategy I have just sketched. This will also help us to assess, finally, Code's suggestion that the elenctic proof is designed to show that anyone who believes anything believes PNC and so that it is a candidate for completing the argument of Γ 3.

[35] Note that 'Φ[σ]' marks a propositional context in the broadest sense, and so we should not assume that *Fa* is a straightforward instance of it. Thus, σ might be '*F*' and Φ 'belongs to *a*'.

[36] 'Aristotle on the Principle of Contradiction', 497.

6. The elenctic proof of PNC

There is some dispute about the boundaries of the elenctic proof. Ross, whom I follow, takes it to consume the entire first stretch of argument (his R1 and our W1), while Kirwan finds that it begins only after a brief opening argument (his K1). On my view, K1 belongs with the elenctic proof because it describes what is to be proved by direct argument:

(17) If (a) a name signifies being or not being something ($\epsilon\hat{\iota}\nu\alpha\iota\ \hat{\eta}$ $\mu\hat{\eta}\ \epsilon\hat{\iota}\nu\alpha\iota\ \tau o\delta\acute{\iota}$), then (b) it could not be the case that something was and was not so and so.[37]

Since it is already given that the opponent says something significant, we may think of (17) as proposing to use this fact to prove PNC by considering two kinds of cases.[38] If the name signifies *being* something, then it can be shown that PNC holds, and likewise if the name signifies *not being* something. This, in fact, is precisely what Aristotle proceeds to do. Thus, 1006ª31–ᵇ34, our W1.1, proves the case for names signifying being something; 1006ᵇ34–1007ª20, W1.II, proves it for names signifying not being something; and W1.III, 1007ª20–ᵇ18, considers a special consequence for language if PNC is denied.[39]

[37] There is a textual reason for taking K1 as a separate argument, namely, that Aristotle wrote 'everything' rather than 'something': '. . . it could not be the case that everything [$\pi\hat{\alpha}\nu$] was so and not so'. For this represents the opponent as holding the strong denial of PNC, namely, that everything is such that it is so and not so, but the elenctic proof claims to rebut not this but the weak denial that there is something such that it is so and not so. This is surely what is announced at the end of Stage 1 of the elenctic proof, at 1006ᵇ33–4. However, there is a countervailing textual ground in favour of taking K1 as part of the elenctic proof (see the following paragraph, and especially n. 40). So I shall stay with (17) as written.

[38] *Contra* C. Rapp, 'Aristoteles über die Rechtfertigung des Satzes vom Widerspruch', *Zeitschrift für philosophische Forschung*, 47 (1993), 521–41 at 531, who takes Aristotle to require, in (17), that the opponent grants that the sample expression signifies something that is or something that is not. Indeed, he takes this to commit the opponent immediately to honouring an instance of PNC: 'It is true that the expression X signifies this definite thing [dieses-da] and does not at the same time not signify it' (535). This moves too quickly and makes far too much of the opponent's contribution. On my view, the opponent has completed his work once he has issued a significant expression, period.

[39] Actually, W1.III is more of a support argument for the elenctic proof as a whole. As we shall see below, Stage 3 offers a proof of PNC that makes use of modal notions and of Aristotle's standard notion of an essence. So it might be vulnerable to attack by the opponent on just this point. In W1.III Aristotle argues that if one

I shall consider the first part of the proof only, W1.1, and from here on it is this I shall be referring to as the elenctic proof. The elenctic proof itself has three stages. First, Aristotle argues at 1006ᵃ31–ᵇ13 that a name signifies one thing (σημαίνει ἕν). If (17)'s signifying something (τοδί) is signifying one something, then Aristotle's strategy is to argue first for the truth of the antecedent of (17). This is plausible in the light of the fact that Aristotle concludes this first stage of the elenctic proof, at 1006ᵇ11–13, on the following note: 'Let the name, then, as was said originally, signify something [σημαῖνόν τι] and signify one thing [σημαῖνον ἕν]'.⁴⁰ In the second stage of the elenctic proof, at 1006ᵇ13–28, Aristotle uses this result to establish a further constraint on signification, namely, that a name and its negate, 'man' and 'not-man', cannot signify the same thing. This result, in turn, is used in the final stage of the elenctic argument, at 1006ᵇ28–34, to prove PNC.⁴¹ I shall consider each stage in turn.

(a) Stage 1: that a name signifies one thing

Aristotle begins by stating what he understands by a name signifying one thing and then argues, against the supposition that it signifies more than one thing, that this is a condition on its meaningful use in thought and language. The reasoning proceeds by example:

does away with essences (and so substances), then one is forced into an intolerable situation: either there will be no subjects for predication or predication will continue *ad infinitum*. I shall not pursue this argument here.

⁴⁰ At the beginning of W1.1 Aristotle says *only* that the name 'man' is to mean one thing. So when he reports at 1006ᵇ11–13 that at the beginning he said that the name was to signify something, he can only mean at 1006ᵃ30 in Kirwan's K1. This suggests, *pace* Kirwan, that K1 is not a separate argument but introduces K2 and is part of the long elenctic proof in the way I have specified.

⁴¹ This differs from Code's way of organizing the elenctic proof in 'Metaphysics and Logic'. First, he takes Stages 1 and 2 already to establish the main result; second, he takes this to be, not PNC, but the proposition that if someone understands something, then that person believes PNC. Third, he takes Stage 3 to be a meta-elenctic proof that reflects on the elenctic proof (Stages 1 and 2), essentially by drawing modal consequences from essentialist claims. The trouble with this is that Stages 1 and 2 do not mention PNC at all, and so it is hard to see how they could reach any conclusions about PNC or about the necessity of believing it. Only in Stage 3 is something like this forthcoming, and there Aristotle appears to be drawing a conclusion from what has been established in the earlier stages of the argument, namely, that 'σ' signifies in such a way that any context containing it must conform to PNC.

. . . if 'man' signifies one thing, let it be *two-footed animal*. By signifying one thing I mean this: if that thing (that is signified) is man, then if anything is a man, then that thing (that is signified) will be what it is to be a man (1006ᵃ31–4).[42]

Now, it is a bit unclear what to make of this. Aristotle might mean no more than

(18) 'M' signifies one thing, $T \equiv (x)(x$ is $M \rightarrow x$ is $T)$,

which says just that *two-footed animal*, for example, must apply to everything that *man* applies to because 'man' signifies *two-footed animal*. On the other hand, his remark that the signified thing will be *what it is to be a man* (τὸ ἀνθρώπῳ εἶναι) indicates that he may have in mind the stronger claim[43]

(18a) 'M' signifies one thing, $T \equiv (x)(x$ is $M \rightarrow T$ is what it is to be x).

On (18a), signification is modally laden. It is not just that *being a two-footed animal* gives the essence of *man* or that *being penetrative colour* gives the essence of *white*, but also that it gives the essence of anything that is a man, i.e. of individual men. This requires that '*x* is *M*' itself expresses an essential tie. For only if *x* is essentially *M* can we say that *x* is essentially *T*. This works for *M* as *white* and *T* as *penetrative colour* as well as for *M* as *man* and *T* as *two-footed animal*. On (18), on the other hand, it appears that we can say that *M* applies to *x* and *T* applies to *x*, even where *x* is not essentially *T*. Only the relation between *M* and *T* is modally laden, and so (18) appears to give us a notion of signification that supports a completely general account of predication. Since Stage 1 is developing a notion of signification that is put to use in Stage 3 in the final proof of PNC, (18) does not foreclose the possibility that the proof is offered for a fully general PNC. So many will prefer it.

Unfortunately, it is hard to square the text with this preference.

---

[42] . . . ἔτι εἰ τὸ ἄνθρωπος σημαίνει ἕν, ἔστω τοῦτο τὸ ζῷον δίπουν. λέγω δὲ τὸ ἓν σημαίνειν τοῦτο· εἰ τοῦτ' ἔστιν ἄνθρωπος, ἂν ᾖ τι ἄνθρωπος, τοῦτ' ἔσται τὸ ἀνθρώπῳ εἶναι.

[43] D. Charles, 'Aristotle on Names and their Signification', in S. Everson (ed.), *Companions to Ancient Thought*, iii. *Language* (Cambridge, 1994), 37–73 at 66–8, understands the notion of *signifying one thing* in a slightly different way. Rather than signifying one essence, for 'man' to signify one thing is for it to signify one thing that *has* an essence. Decision on this has no effect on our argument, and so I shall not press the point here.

For it is clear that Aristotle requires that x be essentially T. And this is violated where x is a person, *white* applies to x, and 'white' signifies *penetrative colour*. For Socrates may be white and *white* may be, essentially, *penetrative colour*, but Socrates is surely not penetrative colour, essentially or otherwise.[44] So we seem stuck with (18a). This means that right from the start, Aristotle appears to tailor the elenctic proof for a restricted version of PNC. Despite this, in Section 7 below I show how this result can be used to extend the range of PNC.

Does Stage 1 establish Code's lemma? Well, it does claim to establish that if 'σ' does not signify *one* thing, then it cannot be used meaningfully in thought and language. The strategy of Stage 1 is to declare what counts as signifying one thing and then to argue, by consideration of cases, that every word must signify one thing. Either a word signifies one thing or a definite number of things or an infinite number of things. The last supposition entails that the word does not signify at all and so can play no role in language and thought, and the second reduces to the first. What Code's lemma requires, however, is that 'σ' conform to PNC and that anyone who has a belief involving σ believe that σ, or perhaps 'σ', conforms to PNC. Nothing like this is forthcoming from the argument of Stage 1. The most it could show is that if PNC itself is taken as the significant 'σ', it must signify one thing. This does not establish even that PNC must be believed to signify one thing. And even if it did, this would not be enough.[45]

(*b*) *Stage 2: that 'man' and 'not-man' cannot signify the same thing*

Stage 1 of the elenctic proof places constraints on what it means for a word or term to signify one thing. Stage 2 adds, apparently as a consequence:

Then it is not possible that 'what it is to be a man' [τὸ ἀνθρώπῳ εἶναι] signifies precisely what is signified by 'what it is not to be a man' [μὴ εἶναι

---

[44] Of course, Socrates is penetrative*ly* colour*ed* but he is not *essentially* penetratively coloured. So it would not help to insist that 'white' signifies 'penetratively coloured'. Indeed, properly speaking, this is probably nothing 'white' would signify.

[45] Compare Whitaker, *Aristotle's* De Interpretatione, 193, who finds in Stage 1 'a very compressed argument to the effect that nothing which can be referred to in words is both so and not so'. But the stuff of compression contains nothing that yields this on expansion.

ἀνθρώπῳ], if 'man' [τὸ ἄνθρωπος] signifies not only about one thing but also signifies one thing [μὴ μόνον καθ' ἑνὸς ἀλλὰ καὶ ἕν]. (1006ᵇ13–15)

If Aristotle wants signification to play a role in the elenctic proof of PNC, then it must be able to accommodate contexts involving negation. This is precisely what he appears to do in Stage 2. But his opening remark is odd in two ways. First, it embraces talk, awkward even for Aristotle, about the *expression* 'what it is to be a man' signifying something different from what is signified by the *expression* 'what it is not to be a man'. These are hardly standard referring expressions. But the talk probably amounts to holding that *what it is to be a man* is essentially different from *what it is not to be a man*, and this is a less strange idea.[46] Second, it is not exactly clear how the remark, which I shall represent as

(19) (e) 'N' signifies one thing→(f) ¬◊('what it is to be N' and 'what it is not to be N' signify the same thing),

works in the passage as a whole. This is because midway through the passage, after giving examples that illustrate (19), he appears to consider, as an entirely fresh point, whether 'man' and 'not-man' signify the same or not.

Thus, at 1006ᵇ20–2 he confesses that it would be surprising, not if something is called 'man' and 'not-man', but if in fact something *were* both (i.e. if both really signified the same thing). His argument against this begins with an entailment,

(20) (g) 'N' and 'not-N' signify the same→(h) 'what it is to be N' and 'what it is not to be N' signify the same thing,

which he proceeds to argue for. Quickly, we get

(21) (g)→(i) 'what it is to be N' and 'what it is not to be N' will have the same definition,

(22) (i)→(j) *what it is to be N* and *what it is to be not-N* will be the same thing,

and

(23) (j)→(h).

(23), along with (20), (21), and (22), gives us the entailment, (20).

[46] Save for the possible suggestion that something like 'what it is not to be a man' signifies an essence. But in the present context we can, I think, waive Aristotle's usual scruples against inviting talk of negative essences.

At this point Aristotle remarks 'But it had been shown that they signify something different' (1006^b28), and he means by this that (h) has been shown false. But where was (h) shown false? The only possibility is (19). Since Aristotle takes (19) to follow from Stage 1's argument that every name signifies one thing, there is at least an attenuated sense in which (h) has been shown false. But it is an attenuated sense at best, especially in the light of the fact that in expressly rejecting (h) Aristotle appears to regard (g) as the prime target at this point in the argument. That is, he is chiefly concerned to establish that 'man' and 'not-man' signify different things. There can be little doubt about this. The fact that Aristotle has gone to such considerable lengths to support (20) suggests that he takes it to express a truth. This, of course, is required for it to be of use in establishing the negation of (g) by rejecting (h). And the negation of (g) is something he wants to establish, for he needs a constraint that will apply to standard predicates and their negates, since these are the predicates that figure in standard formulations of PNC. So it is apparent that his chief concern is securing the proposition that 'man' and 'not-man' do not signify the same thing. Unfortunately, it is not clear that we can make much sense of (19) without assuming something like this. To this extent, it is not clear that (19) can provide independent support for the proposition that is his chief concern.

To reflect again on Code's lemma, does Stage 2 of the elenctic proof establish that anyone who believes anything must believe PNC? Apparently not, for it concerns only the *significations* of expressions and so would at most establish that anyone who believed 'σ' would believe something that had a signification that was different from the signification of 'not-σ', whatever 'σ' turns out to be. This does not entail that anyone *believe* that the signification of 'σ' is different from that of 'not-σ', only that they be different, if discourse about σ is to be possible. And, in any case, it is not clear that we should allow Aristotle to count PNC *itself* as having a signification in the sense deployed in Stage 2 of the argument. For this would require that the expression '$\neg \Diamond (\exists x)(Fx \wedge \neg Fx)$' have a signification and, moreover, a signification that is something like an essence. But what sort of thing is *what it is to be PNC*?

Better, I suggest, to take Stage 2 as focusing on words or expressions used in standard assertions. This, of course, threatens to restrict the range of PNC in so far as the elenctic proof is concerned.

Indeed, (21) embraces the view that expressions having the same signification will have the same definition, and so appears to treat signification as an essentially modal notion. The effects of this are evident in the final stage of the elenctic proof.

(c) *Stage 3: the proof of PNC*

On my view, Stages 1 and 2 of the argument impose constraints on the notion of signification that is put to use in the final stage. It is only here, in Stage 3 of the elenctic proof, that PNC itself makes an appearance. Thus, Aristotle says by way of concluding the elenctic proof:

> It is accordingly necessary, (α) if it is true of anything to say that it is a man, that it be a two-footed animal (for that was what 'man' signified); and (β) if that is necessary, it is not possible that the same thing should not be, at that time, a two-footed animal . . . Consequently, (γ) it is not possible that it should be simultaneously true to say that the same thing is a man and is not a man. (1006^{b}28–34)[47]

The argument proceeds by example but is meant to be general in effect. Just how general will depend on exactly what is proved, and this requires a careful look at the argument's form. Aristotle begins in (α) with a premiss that has been taken in two ways by commentators. Depending on whether necessity is given wide or narrow scope, we have

(24a) 'M' signifies $T \rightarrow \Box(x)(Mx \rightarrow Tx)$,

or

(24a$'$) 'M' signifies $T \rightarrow (x)(Mx \rightarrow \Box Tx)$.

Choice of (24a) or (24a$'$) will yield slightly different versions of the argument. With (24a) the argument continues:

(24b) $\Box(x)(Mx \rightarrow Tx) \rightarrow \neg \Diamond (\exists x)(Mx \wedge \neg Tx)$,
(24c) $\neg \Diamond (\exists x)(Mx \wedge \neg Tx) \rightarrow \neg \Diamond (\exists x)(Mx \wedge \neg Mx)$,

and thus, given that 'M' signifies T, we may conclude

(24d) $\neg \Diamond (\exists x)(Mx \wedge \neg Mx)$,

which is just the ontological version of PNC. So here, finally, we appear to have our proof. Because it gives wide scope to the necessity operator, I shall refer to (24a)–(24d) as the 'wide-scope' version of the proof.

The 'narrow-scope' version of the proof, so called because it begins in (24a′) with a narrow-scope reading of the necessity operator, begins in parallel with the first version:

$(24b′)$ $(x)(Mx{\rightarrow}\Box Tx){\rightarrow}\neg(\exists x)(Mx{\wedge}\Diamond\neg Tx)$.

But in order to get the crucial counterpart to (24c), it requires two additional assumptions:

$(24b″)$ $\neg(\exists x)(Mx{\wedge}\Diamond\neg Tx){\rightarrow}\neg(\exists x)(Mx{\wedge}\Diamond\neg Mx)$,

and

$(24b‴)$ $\neg(\exists x)(Mx{\wedge}\Diamond\neg Mx){\rightarrow}\neg\Diamond(\exists x)(Mx{\wedge}\neg Mx)$.

With these two assumptions we get, parallel to the first version,

$(24c′)$ $\neg(\exists x)(Mx{\wedge}\Diamond\neg Tx){\rightarrow}\neg\Diamond(\exists x)(Mx{\wedge}\neg Mx)$,

and, again on the assumption that 'M' signifies T, we conclude as before

$(24d′)$ $\neg\Diamond(\exists x)(Mx{\wedge}\neg Mx)$.

Now both versions of the argument make use of a notion of signification, in (24a) and (24a′), and it is clearly the notion that is at work in Stage 1 of the elenctic proof. A few pages back I argued that Aristotle's preference is for the modally laden notion registered in (18a), rather than the weaker formulation found in (18). We now see why: the notion of signification in (24a)/(24a′) must support an explicit modal claim, and (18a) seems tailor-made for this purpose. Moreover, Stage 2 gets a role in the story. On the assumption that 'not-M' signifies *not-T*, the second stage shows that one could not hold that an x that is M could also be T and *not-T*. This figures as something like a deep assumption behind, for example, (24b). Thus, we may fairly paraphrase Aristotle's remark in (β): '. . . if that is necessary, it is not possible that the same thing should not be, at that time, a two-footed animal (otherwise, "man" and "not-man" would have the same signification, which they cannot).'

If these considerations confirm that the elenctic argument is governed by a unified strategy, it is confirmation at a cost. For just as the notion of signification in (18a) is suited for essential predication, so the final proof appears to hold for 'Mx' as an essential predication.

If so, the elenctic proof as a whole may prove at most that PNC holds for things and their *essential* properties. This is troubling because a chief effect of the elenctic proof is to confirm the *firmness* of PNC by supporting, albeit 'elenctically', the principle that was used in *Γ* 3's Indubitability Proof to prove its own firmness, and this must be an unrestricted version of PNC because it must be a principle that is immune to *all* error.

7. How to extend the range of PNC

We can get clearer on what is at issue here by considering Kirwan's view of Stage 3 of the argument. The narrow-scope version requires additional premisses, (24b″) and (24b‴). This plus Aristotle's wording in (*a*) of the text, cited above, favour the wide-scope reading. But Kirwan has a more serious objection to the narrow-scope version, namely, that '*Mx*' can imply '□*Tx*' only if the first arrow in (24b′) is read as strict implication and, hence, only if '*Mx*' is an essential predication. In short, (24b′) is satisfied only by essential predications and so also for the conclusion, (24d′). According to Kirwan, however, (24b) is not so restricted and so the wide-scope version of the argument holds out hope for proving an unrestricted version of PNC.

But even if its '→' is not read as strict implication, surely (24b)'s modal formula, $□(x)(Mx → Tx)$, is satisfied only by Aristotelian essential predications. For interpretation of the formula is governed by (18a), which requires that T be the essence of x. This is clear from instantiating the formula with non-essential T. So far from being even contingently true, it is plainly false that if Callias is white than he is a colour, while it is true, and necessarily so, that if he is a man he is a two-footed animal. So the truth of (24b)'s antecedent also depends on construing '*Mx*' as a schema for essential predication.[48]

In either version, then, the elenctic argument would prove PNC for a restricted class of predications. Lukasiewicz[49] and Anscombe[50]

[48] On this paragraph, recall n. 44 above.
[49] *Über den Satz des Widerspruchs bei Aristoteles* and 'Aristotle on the Principle of Contradiction'.
[50] G. E. M. Anscombe, 'Aristotle', in P. T. Geach and G. E. M. Anscombe, *Three Philosophers* (Oxford, 1963).

reduce these to essential predications about substances.[51] By thus construing the range of values for the universal quantifiers of (24b) and (24b′) to be substance individuals, they preclude any interpretation relating Stage 3 to a general defence of PNC. But notice that even were Lukasiewicz, Anscombe, and their followers correct about the force of the elenctic proof, it would not follow that Aristotle affirms PNC as a restricted principle.[52] Lukasiewicz is tempted to do this when he declares that PNC is not a general ontological law but rather a metaphysical one holding primarily for substances but not, at least not obviously, for appearances as well.[53] However, there simply is no evidence that Aristotle would entertain such a restriction. Indeed, *De interpretatione* features just such predicates in offering, as standard *contradictory* assertions, 'Socrates is white' and 'Socrates is not white'. Moreover, a good deal of the argument of *Γ* 5 aims to establish that the perceptible domain does not fall outside the scope of PNC.

Even taking the elenctic proof as it stands, there is no reason to restrict its conclusion to substance individuals only. Allowing accident individuals to count as values does not vitiate the argument and, more importantly, opens the way to a fully general PNC. That the argument's validity is unaffected by allowing '$\Box(x)(Mx \to Tx)$' to range over non-substantial individuals is clear from example. Let 'a' be the name of a colour individual. Then it is a necessary truth that if a is white then a is a colour. Likewise for the narrow-scope formula, $(x)(Mx \to \Box Tx)$. If a is white, then a is necessarily a colour. Moreover, because it is a *colour* individual, a is essentially white and so the constraint on essential predication is satisfied on both versions of the argument.[54]

---

[51] They appear to be followed by M. Furth, 'A Note on Aristotle's Principle of Non-contradiction', *Canadian Journal of Philosophy*, 16 (1986), 371–82; D. S. Hutchison, 'L'Épistémologie du principe de contradiction chez Aristote', *Revue de philosophie ancienne*, 6 (1988), 213–27, and M. Cresswell, 'Non-contradiction and Substantial Predication in Aristotle', in M. Braghramian and P. Simons (eds.), *Proceedings of the Conference Lukasiewicz in Dublin* (forthcoming).

[52] *Were* the argument to establish PNC for substances only, one would rather seek to explain this restriction in a way that related it to Aristotle's programme in *Metaphysics Γ*. Thus, Cresswell, 'Non-contradiction and Substantial Predication in Aristotle', suggests that the argument's focus on substances reflects the fact that *Γ* installs them at the centre of the science of being *qua* being. But this just gives an additional reason *not* to take Aristotle to have held, in general, that PNC is a restricted principle.

[53] 'Aristotle on the Principle of Contradiction', 502.

[54] Compare this paragraph with Furth, 'A Note on Aristotle's Principle of Non-

How does this enable us to extend the range of PNC? Begin by explicitly registering the restriction on the conclusion with subscript '$_E$': $\neg\Diamond(\exists x)(Mx_E \wedge \neg Mx_E)$. Here we may read 'M' as standing for any standard predicate because, for Aristotle, any such predicate is essentially predicated of something.[55] The trick now is to use this fact to extend the elenctic proof of PNC to accidental predications.

Consider, then, a standard accidental predication, e.g. 'Socrates is white'. For Aristotle the truth conditions for such a predication are not just that Socrates exist and be white. There must also obtain what I shall call a fine ontological configuration of the following sort: $(\exists x)(\exists y)(x$ is a substance particular $\wedge x = $ Socrates $\wedge y$ is a colour individual $\wedge y$ is in $x \wedge Wy_E)$. That is, in addition to Socrates there exists a second individual, a colour individual, that is present in Socrates and that is essentially white.[56] Suppose now we consider what sort of fine configuration would have to obtain were it possible that Socrates be simultaneously white and not white. Aristotle, I suggest, requires that the following hold: $(\exists x)(\exists y)(x$ is a substance particular $\wedge x = $ Socrates $\wedge y$ is a colour individual $\wedge y$ is in $x \wedge Wy_E \wedge \neg Wy_E)$. But since the restricted conclusion of the elenctic argument, $\neg\Diamond(\exists x)(Mx_E \wedge \neg Mx_E)$, holds for any predicates whatever, it is impossible that there be a y such that $Wy_E \wedge \neg Wy_E$. Therefore, the ontological configuration that would have to obtain were it possible that Socrates be white and not white is, by the elenctic proof, an impossible ontological configuration.

The rough principle, then, that extends the elenctic proof to a fully general PNC is this:

contradiction', n. 3, who offers a more sanguine opinion of Anscombe's view as 'an interesting and . . . too-little-attended case for the thesis that the argument *requires* that the "one thing" be the essence of a substantial kind'. No such requirement is at hand. Although it is not clear that he recognizes the fact, Lear (*Aristotle and Logical Theory*, 108–9) also appears committed to restricting the proof to essential predications about substances. For this is a consequence of his explanation of the modal-ladenness of (18a): 'It is the notion of substance, not signifying, which enables Aristotle to make the distinction between signifying one thing and signifying about one thing.' But this simply assumes that the pair 'man' and *two-footed animal* cannot serve to exemplify the general relation between a thing and its essence.

[55] By a standard predicate I mean a categorial predicate, i.e. a predicate from any category. For more on this see M. V. Wedin, 'The Strategy of Aristotle's *Categories*', *Archiv für Geschichte der Philosophie*, 79 (1977), 1–26, and *Aristotle's Theory of Substance: The* Categories *and* Metaphysics Zeta (Oxford, 2000).

[56] These are the items demarcated in the *Categories* as present in, but not said of, a subject. On the claim that such items are non-recurrent particulars see M. V. Wedin, 'Nonsubstantial Individuals', *Phronesis*, 38 (1993), 137–65.

(25) $\Diamond(\exists x)(Fx \wedge \neg Fx) \rightarrow \Diamond(\exists x)(\exists y)(y = x \vee y \in x \wedge Fy_{E} \wedge \neg Fy_{E})$,

where ' $\in$ ' may be read as the *Categories*' 'in but not as a part'.[57] But given the elenctic argument's prohibition against joint predication of any essential predicate and its negate, we may conclude

(26) $\neg \Diamond(\exists x)(\exists y)(y = x \vee y \in x \wedge Fy_{E} \wedge \neg Fy_{E})$,

and so

(27) $\neg \Diamond(\exists x)(Fx \wedge \neg Fx)$.

In (27) we are free to read Fx as a general predicative schema accommodating accidental as well as essential predication. Thus, if Aristotle implicitly supposes something like (25), restriction of the conclusion of Stage 3 of the elenctic proof does not show him to regard PNC as a restricted principle. Indeed, it is part of proving the fully general version registered in (27).

This proposal has been resisted by Cresswell on the grounds that 'it seems to depend on analyzing Socrates' not being white as his having in him something which is not a whiteness. But Socrates can have many such things in him and still be white.'[58] Such reluctance would be well placed and it does appear to be invited by (25). But (25) is only a rough principle. Once it is explained how (25) is to be interpreted, the grounds for Cresswell's reluctance are removed.

I say that (25) is a rough principle because, where $y \in x$, what can serve as the value of y depends on the predicate, F. Thus, where F is white, y will be a colour individual; where F is sweet, y will be a taste individual. So understood, (25) demands, at most, that Socrates has in him a *colour individual* that is not a *whiteness*. The existence of a *colour* individual that is not white is incompatible with Socrates' being white. So the account does not welcome, as values of y, items that fail to exhibit the required incompatibility with Socrates' *whiteness*.[59]

---

[57] Some might object that this is an unjustified intrusion of *Categories* doctrine into the exegesis of *Metaphysics* Γ. But the reading is a convenience, not a requirement. Any reading that accommodates an accidental as well as an essential predicative tie will do. And this distinction is clearly attested in *Metaphysics* Γ: witness Γ 2, 1004^{b}1–3, where the philosopher is charged with deciding whether Socrates and Socrates sitting are the same or different.

[58] Cresswell, 'Non-contradiction and Substantial Predication in Aristotle'. The proposal was first advanced in M. V. Wedin, 'Aristotle on the Range of the Principle of Non-contradiction', *Logique et analyse*, 97 (1982), 87–92.

[59] Somewhat more fully, the idea behind (25) is that, where $x = y$, y will be a

A second objection to extending the result of the elenctic proof to a fully general PNC is that the possibility of Socrates' simultaneously being white and not white could as well be explained by the possibility that an essentially white colour individual exist and not exist.[60] Rather than (25), we would have

(25a) $\Diamond(\exists x)(Fx \wedge \neg Fx) \rightarrow \Diamond((\exists x)(\exists y)(y = x \vee y \in x \wedge Fy_{E}) \wedge \neg(\exists x)(\exists y)$
       $(y = x \vee y \in x \wedge Fy_{E}))$.

While the consequent of (25a) is false, and so would imply $\neg\Diamond(\exists x)$ $(Fx \wedge \neg Fx)$, its falsity is due to straightforward infringement of PNC. Here it is not obvious how the elenctic proof can be brought to bear on a general version of PNC.

Now, one response to this situation would be simply to insist that we *do* have an interpretation that extends the result of the elenctic proof, and hence we need not follow Lukasiewicz and others in saddling Aristotle with the thesis that PNC holds only for essential predications—*even if* the conclusion of Stage 3 is so restricted. But we want something stronger, something that reflects Aristotle's settled view that PNC *must* not be so restricted.

Suppose we begin with an instance of the general formula that starts (25a), say, the proposition *that Socrates is white and not white*. Representing subject and predicate in the standard way, we replace (25a), which is shorthand anyway, with the more fine-grained formulation

(25a′) $\Diamond(Fa \wedge \neg Fa) \rightarrow \Diamond((\exists x)(\exists y)(x$ is a substance individual $\wedge x = a \wedge y$ is a colour individual $\wedge y \in x \wedge Fy_{E}) \wedge \neg(\exists x)(\exists y)(x$ is a substance individual $\wedge x = a \wedge y$ is a colour individual $\wedge y \in x \wedge Fy_{E}))$.

(25a′) just combines the Aristotelian truth conditions for '*Fa*' and '*¬Fa*'. So it would be unreasonable to challenge it on this basis.

substance individual and F will be a species or genus that holds of it essentially; and, where $y \in x$, y will be a non-substantial individual of a certain kind, say a bit of white, and F will be a universal such as *white* or *colour* that holds of it essentially. So y will always be an individual from a determinate range, in the case at hand, a *colour individual*. Cases where x is a non-individual with F holding of it essentially could be handled by adding a proviso corresponding to the *Categories'* *said-of* relation.

   [60] Of course, Socrates might have in him two colour individuals, one (essentially) white and one (essentially) not. But this will correspond, not to the proposition *that Socrates is white and not white* but to the proposition *that Socrates is white in one respect and not white in another*. So it does not give us a way the world would have to be should the contradiction hold.

What is at issue is the way to understand the truth conditions for '$\neg Fa$', when this is paired with its contradictory opposite. Contained in the second main conjunct of the consequent of (25a'), these truth conditions can be expanded further. Thus, *that Socrates is not white* is the case, if (i) there exists no substance individual identical with Socrates, or if (ii) there exists no colour individual, or if (iii) both exist but the colour individual is not in Socrates, or if (iv) both exist and the color individual is in Socrates but is not essentially white. For convenience, represent these disjunctive alternatives as follows:

(25b) (i) $\neg(\exists x)(x$ is a substance individual$\wedge x=a)$;
       (ii) $\neg(\exists y)(y$ is a colour individual$)$;
       (iii) $(\exists x)(\exists y)(x$ is a substance individual$\wedge x=a\wedge y$ is a colour individual$\wedge y\notin x)$;
       (iv) $(\exists x)(\exists y)(x$ is a substance individual$\wedge x=a\wedge y$ is a colour individual$\wedge y\in x\wedge\neg Fy_{\text{E}})$.

The task now is to determine which of these conditions is relevant to the case at hand. That is, which of the four disjuncts can contribute to a description of what the world would have to be like were it possible that Socrates be white and not white. It is important to bear in mind that Aristotle requires, fairly, that this possibility hold for *one and the same thing*. For his version of PNC denies that there could exist something, some one and the same thing, that was white and not white. This excludes the first disjunct. For according to (25b(i)), there will be no one and the same thing that is the putative subject of the contradictory assertions Fa and $\neg Fa$. The second and third disjuncts are now seen to be hardly more plausible. For this one and the same thing, whose existence is required, will be the subject of contradictory assertions either because there exist no colour individuals at all, as in (25b(ii)), or because colour individuals exist, but not in the subject in question, as in (25b(iii)). However, these are proposals that Aristotle can hardly accept, for they fall foul of a favoured principle governing the relation between basic subjects and their accidents.

The principle is a certain globalization of propositions like

(25c) $(x)(\exists y)(x$ is a substance individual of type $T\rightarrow y$ is a colour individual$\wedge y\in x)$,

where to be of type T is to be capable of being coloured. According to (25c), any such substance individual must have in it some colour individual or other. Proposition (25c) allows that a substance individual could be, say, pale at one moment and green at another; what it rules out is that there could be a moment when it has no particular colour at all. In effect, this was the point made five paragraphs back, in responding to Cresswell. Because every colour individual falls into the category of quality,[61] every such substance individual must be of some quality. Analogues of (25c) hold for items from the accidental categories generally. So, any substance individual must be at some place or other, of some size or other, in relation to some thing or other, etc.[62] Indeed, this generalization arguably lies at the heart of the theory of primary substance developed in the *Categories*.[63] So the second and third disjuncts, (25b(ii)) and (25b(iii)), are not plausible.

We are thus left with the fourth alternative, (25b(iv)). This alone could play a role in specifying what the world would have to be like were it possible that Socrates be white and not white. Such a world would have to satisfy

(25a″) $\Diamond(Fa \wedge \neg Fa) \rightarrow \Diamond(\exists x)(\exists y)(x$ is a substance individual $\wedge x = a \wedge y$ is a colour individual $\wedge y \in x \wedge Fy_E \wedge \neg Fy_E)$;

but this way of the world is precisely what the elenctic proof declares impossible, when it proscribes joint ascription of an essential predicate and its negate. So we are, after all, able to extend this result to a fully general PNC in precisely the manner prescribed by our principle (25). Of course (25c), and its underlying generalization, introduces additional, non-logical, considerations, but these are entirely neutral with respect to the immediate question. For (25c) is part of an ontological scheme that is proposed quite independently of PNC and of worries about the range of the principle.

---

[61] For an account of how this works see Wedin, 'The Strategy of Aristotle's *Categories*'.

[62] Here I am restricting the domain of discourse to sensible substances. So I do not wish to claim that Aristotle's unmoved mover has in it a colour individual or is at a place. But for such a transcendent entity the question of extending the scope of PNC is not relevant in the first place. For it will have no accidental properties at all—unless one includes under this title Cambridge properties such as *being thought of by Sedley at high noon*. But by no stretch of the imagination is this an Aristotelian accident, let alone an accident of the unmoved mover.

[63] See Wedin, 'The Strategy of Aristotle's *Categories*', and J. M. E. Moravcsik, 'Aristotle's Theory of Categories', in Moravcsik (ed.), *Aristotle: A Collection of Critical Essays* (Notre Dame, 1967), 125–45.

At the very least, the principle enhances the Aristotelian credentials of (25a″).[64]

8. Revisiting the Indubitability Proof: a strategy for completion

Stage 3 carries through the strategy Aristotle proposed for an elenctic proof of PNC. For he can at least *claim* to have shown, finally, that the significance of a linguistic item requires its conformity with PNC, just as (16b) recommends. On my reconstruction of the argument, (16a), the assumption that 'σ' be significant, is very weak. Although Aristotle carries out the proof for the term 'man', we are free to take 'σ' to be any categorial term—'man', 'red', 'colour', and the like. This gives us something that the opponent will be hard pressed to deny. For at the outset we are asking him to count significant, not even a simple assertion, but a mere word.[65] From this first foothold, Aristotle argues that for any propositional context, $\Phi[\ ]$, containing the word 'σ', it is not possible that $(\Phi[\sigma] \wedge \neg \Phi[\sigma])$. So even if the unit of significance is the word, Aristotle's proof holds for propositions or the matters of fact that are their truth-makers.

The third stage of the elenctic proof proceeds without aid of doxastic idioms, and so it cannot establish, by itself, the proposition that he who believes anything must believe PNC. It thus leaves

---

[64] Cresswell, 'Non-contradiction and Substantial Predication in Aristotle', takes the point of restricting the proof to be the establishing of PNC as a metaphysical principle, rather than as a logical law. But surely my (27) can be read as a metaphysical principle and it is completely general. Likewise, we now see, for (25). Proponents of the restricted reading also run up against a textual and an interpretative consideration. Textually, as Cresswell is aware, the canonical formulation of PNC at 1005^{b}18–20 shows no hint of restriction; and, when Aristotle finishes the elenctic proof, his formulation again appears to be fully general. On the interpretative side, it often goes unnoticed, and so bears repeating, that Γ 4 aims to establish PNC *because* it enters as a premiss in the proof of its own firmness—Γ 3's Indubitability Proof. Since this concerned a principle that was immune to *all* error, it would be odd, indeed, were Aristotle to admit that certain instances of $\neg(p \wedge \neg p)$ do not enjoy such immunity.

[65] This is confirmed in the final chapter, at 1012^{b}5–7, when Aristotle approves of the strategy deployed in the elenctic proof because it requests 'not that something is or is not, but that something signifies'. Contrast Bolton, 'Metaphysics as a Science', 331, who takes the opponent's initial significant saying to be a saying of, or assent to, ¬PNC itself: 'It is possible for the same thing at the same time to be a man and not to be a man.' Lear, *Aristotle: The Desire to Understand*, 104, also appears to take the opponent to assert that the principle of non-contradiction is false. Rapp, 'Aristoteles über die Rechtfertigung des Satzes vom Widerspruch', 529, on the other hand, appears to agree with my estimate of the opponent's 'saying'.

Code's lemma unsupported. At most, Stage 3 says that any significant term must conform to PNC. And even were this made to require that the opponent believe that the term is significant, he is not thereby committed to believing that the term *conforms* to PNC, let alone to believing the subtler proposition that his believing that 'σ' is significant *entails* that it conforms to PNC.[66] On this score, Stage 3 adds nothing to Stages 1 and 2 and so *Γ* 4's elenctic proof cannot complete the Indubitability Proof of *Γ* 3. So it appears, after all, that the most Aristotle can claim to have *established* is that PNC is the firmest of principles because it is impossible to believe any instance of its negation (the instantial reading, as we have called this). None the less, this is arguably one way to understand what it means for a *principle* to be the firmest, and it may also be that this is sufficient to guarantee PNC's position in the general science of metaphysics. In addition, the instantial reading may actually enjoy sufficient strength to secure the indubitability of the *principle itself*. To see the latter, we need to revisit a key feature of the Indubitability Proof.

Here is how our problem arose. Because the Indubitability Proof established (6a) only and because (6a) does not entail (7a), it seemed that one could grant (*a*) that it is not possible to believe *instances* of ¬PNC and yet insist (*b*) that it is possible that someone believe the negation of the *principle itself*. So long as this 'splitting hypothesis', as I shall call it, is in play, it appears that Aristotle fails to deliver on his promise to establish PNC as the firmest *principle*. One worry about this line of reasoning, however, is the very coherence of the splitting hypothesis. Can we really hold the belief entertained in (*b*), once we have granted (*a*)? In response to this, Section 2 attempted to improve the credentials of the splitting hypothesis by appealing to standard cases of belief. I now wish to suggest that this appeal fails, and in a way that undercuts the splitting hypothesis itself.

Standard cases of belief I took to be governed by two theses: (*c*) for any proposition I believe, I believe it to be true; and (*d*) I believe that some of my beliefs are not true. None will doubt the consistency of holding (*c*) and (*d*), and hence none would suppose that (*c*) could establish a proposition to the effect that I believe that all of my beliefs are true. So, by analogy, none should expect to

---

[66] This may be applied against Lear, *Aristotle: The Desire to Understand*, 256, who also takes the elenctic proof to establish that everyone must believe the principle of non-contradiction.

move from the claim that every proposition I believe is such that I cannot believe it along with believing its negation to the claim that I believe every proposition is such that it cannot be believed along with believing its negation. That is, one should not expect to move from (6a) to (7a), to revert to earlier formulations.

In effect, the analogy with standard cases of belief uses the fact that one can hold

    (28a) $(x)(p)(x$ **bel** $p \rightarrow x$ **bel** $p\text{-}is\text{-}true)$,

and, also, hold

    (28b) $(\exists x)(x$ **bel** that $(\exists p)(x$ **bel** $p \wedge \neg(p$ is true$)))$,

to shore up the splitting hypothesis and so block chances for giving a principled reading to the conclusion of the Indubitability Proof.

Rather than standard belief, however, suppose I believe something on grounds that assure knowledge. Call this basis 'C' and replace (28a) with

    (28a*) $(x)(p)(x$ **bel** p on the basis of $C \rightarrow x$ **kn** $p)$.

This changes the situation dramatically, for anyone holding (28a*) would, I suggest, automatically deny

    (28b*) $\lozenge(\exists x)(x$ **bel** that $(\exists p)(x$ **bel** p on the basis of $C \wedge \neg(p$ is true$)))$,

and affirm

    (28c) $\neg\lozenge(\exists x)(x$ **bel** that $(\exists p)(x$ **bel** p on the basis of $C \wedge \neg(p$ is true$)))$.

For if, of each of my C-based beliefs, I believe it to be something known *on that basis*, then surely I would deny that any of them could be false. In short, beliefs that allow no space for error to enter are beliefs that assure knowledge.[67] According to Aristotle,

---

[67] Here I pass lightly over treacherous ground by simply neglecting questions bearing on the evidential basis of belief and knowledge claims. But their resolution has no bearing on the simple point I am making. A point pressed by David Charles at the Princeton Colloquium, however, bears comment. Grant that believing p on the basis of C guarantees knowledge of p, and grant further that this undermines the use of the splitting hypothesis to block the move from (6a) to (7a). Still, one can ask, for what exactly is C the knowledge-assuring basis? For example, is it the basis (*a*) just for p (e.g. *that the orange is round*), (*b*) for all propositions of the same type as p (i.e. any perceptual belief), or (*c*) for any proposition whatsoever? Option (*a*) is too weak because the claim of interest states that there is no *possible* proposition

beliefs that are instances of PNC are just such beliefs. Because error is impossible regarding them, belief in such a proposition assures knowledge of it, and it is impossible even to believe their negations.

This suggests that standard belief is not the appropriate notion for illuminating the relation between the instantial and the principled readings of the conclusion of the Indubitabilty Proof. *C*-based or knowledge-assuring belief is. But we have just seen that *instantial C*-based belief (28a*) secures *principled C*-based belief (28c). This is not deductive security but a kind of epistemic sanction: we are simply at a loss to account for someone who affirms (28a*) and denies (28c). So far from enhancing the splitting hypothesis, then, the parallel with belief impugns its coherence, and thus gives principled *force* to the conclusion of the Indubitability Proof. For the parallel now suggests that we are, after all, at a loss to explain someone who affirms the impossibility of anyone's believing a given contradiction but holds that there might be some such instance that someone believed. That is, we are at a loss to explain how anyone satisfying (6a) or (6b) could fail to satisfy (7a) or (7b). Hence, the former may be said to secure the latter, not deductively, of course, but as a kind of sanction on epistemic credibility.[68] So the parallel with belief, now adjusted to knowledge-assuring belief, may actually give the instantial reading sufficient strength to account for Aristotle's confidence that the Indubitability Proof secures the firmness of the *principle itself* of non-contradiction. In this light, it is of little consequence that the elenctic proof is unable to complete the Indubitability Proof.

that can be believed along with its negation. So at least (*b*) must be meant. This would mean, perhaps, that for different types of propositions, different bases would have to be spelt out. Of course, I have not tried to do that here. Option (*c*) will be the choice for unitarians, among whom may be counted Cartesians who regard the criterion of clear and distinct perception as yielding a kind of certainty. Holding that one could not err in believing $\neg(p \wedge \neg p)$ is probably not a function of which (type of) proposition p is. So option (*c*) may be the most likely way to read basis *C*. But, again, this is not the place to work out a detailed response to Charles's query. After all, my aim is merely to upset the splitting hypothesis as applied to those beliefs that are instances of PNC, and these are probably held to with certainty.

[68] Thus, to be clear, I am not claiming that, after all, the Indubitability Proof *deductively* establishes (7a) but only that the *force* of establishing (6a) is to secure (7a). This is possible only because of special features about the objects that (6a) ranges over and so goes beyond mere deductive procedures.

9. Retargeting the Indubitability Proof

The strategy of the above section operated under the assumption that Aristotle's aim in Γ 3 is to prove something about PNC itself, namely, that it is the firmest of principles, and that this is to be accomplished by establishing

(7b) $\neg\lozenge(\exists x)(x\ \textbf{bel}\ \lozenge(\exists z)(Fz\wedge\neg Fz))$.

Virtually all commentators take this to be the target of the Indubitability Proof, and, as we have suggested, most of these would agree that the argument is sufficient only for

(6b) $\neg\lozenge(\exists x)(\exists z)(x\ \textbf{bel}\ Fz\wedge\neg Fz)$.

The fact that (6b) is not formally sufficient for (7b) motivated the strategy proposed in the above section. But might not this fact also suggest that (7b) is not the target of the Γ 3 proof in the first place? Indeed, just such a proposal was broached at the beginning of Section 8. It deserves further comment.

Begin with the observation that *Metaphysics* Γ 4 appears to continue the discussion of Γ 3. On the traditional reading, Γ 4's opening lines address persons who assert that it is possible for something to be and not to be at the same time and that it is possible for someone to believe this.[69] Here the 'opponent' is represented as holding the negation of (7b), and so the traditional reading contributes to the impression that this is a shared theme of the two chapters. In particular, it suggests that (7b) is the target of the Indubitability Proof. But the traditional reading is not unassailable. John Cooper and, independently, David Charles have suggested an alternative reading of 1005^b35–1006^a2, the opening lines of Γ 4. They note that Aristotle states only that certain people say (*a*) it is possible for something to be and not to be and also (*b*) ὑπολαμβάνειν οὕτως. That

⁶⁹ Thus, Ross, *Metaphysica*, vol. iii (*The Works of Aristotle*, ed. W. D. Ross; Oxford, 1928), renders the opening lines, 1005^b35–1006^a2, 'There are some who, as we said, both themselves assert that it is possible for the same thing to be and not to be, and say that people can judge this to be the case.' He appears to be followed by Kirwan, *Aristotle's* Metaphysics: 'There are those who, as we said, both themselves assert that it is possible for the same thing to be and not to be, and [assert that it is possible] to believe so.' So also J. Warrington, *Aristotle's* Metaphysics, ed. and trans. (London, 1961), who glosses the lines: 'i.e., they maintain the possibility of contradiction both in fact and in belief', and J. Tricot, *Aristote, La Métaphysique* (Paris, 1974).

is, they also hold things to be the case *in this way* (οὕτως), namely, in violation of PNC. But here there is nothing that plausibly refers back to the general denial of PNC itself in (*a*); for this τοῦτο rather than οὕτως would probably be required. So (*b*) refers only to the fact that the theoreticians in question hold something to be the case in agreement with their denial of PNC in (*a*). On this reading, the context containing ὑπολαμβάνειν οὕτως is not governed by ἐνδέχεται εἶναι καὶ μὴ εἶναι, but only by εἶναι καὶ μὴ εἶναι. So, rather than believing the negation of (7b), an admittedly abstract item in any case, Aristotle has in mind specific statements of the sort allegedly made by Heraclitus and company. And these are just statements that assert states of affairs that PNC declares impossible. If this is correct, then the opening of *Γ* 4 does not focus on deniers of (7b) and so, if *Γ* 4 is tracking the themes of *Γ* 3, it is not so obvious that *Γ* 3's Indubitability Proof targets (7b) in the first place. This is not to deny that *Γ* 3 holds fast to (7b) but only to shift its role in the chapter. It is not the target of *proof*.

There now appear to be at least three ways to regard the Indubitability Proof: (i) The object of proof is (7b) but what is established is only that no instance of the negation of PNC can be believed; (ii) the object of proof is (7b) and (7b) is established by proving that no instance of the negation of PNC can be believed; (iii) the object of proof is not firmness of PNC itself and so not (7b), rather PNC is taken to be the firmest principle from the start and a mark of this is the fact, established by the Indubitability Proof, that no instance of its negation can be believed. On (i), the Indubitability Proof simply fails. This was highlighted above by pressing the point that (6b) is not sufficient for (7b). Option (ii) tries to make a virtue of failure by urging that one respectable way to establish something about PNC itself is to prove something about its instances. I have shown some sympathy with this option in Section 8 of the paper. Option (iii), on the other hand, simply denies that *Γ* 3 is concerned to prove anything about the principle itself of non-contradiction. Rather, we might imagine, it assumes what the other options would prove, namely, that PNC is the firmest of principles, and proceeds to illustrate this by arguing that no instance of the principle's negation can be believed. Hence, we are to think of the Indubitability Proof as focusing on specific, concrete beliefs that appear to fall foul of PNC. Firmness of PNC *itself* is not the object of proof. As Cooper put it, 'So maybe Aristotle's intention in laying down his criterion of maximum firmness for the principle . . . was not to say that the firmest principle is the one that, if true, no one can disbelieve—but only that it is the one such that, if true, no one can actually believe any of the things that it rules out.' This spares Aristotle the embarrassment of a failed argument and makes for an easy transition to Γ 4 because, on the Cooper–Charles reading, Γ 4 does not attribute to the opponent the claim that it is possible to believe the negation of PNC itself. Rather than this meta-belief, he is held to assert specific propositions that violate the principle.

This suggestion does agree rather nicely with my account of the argument of Γ 4. For on my account, the elenctic proof is not attempting to establish that everyone must believe PNC, if they believe anything, and so it could not be completing the Indubitability Proof. On the Cooper–Charles reading, no such completion is required. Still, there is a lingering worry, for at Γ 4, 1006^{a}4–5, Aristotle does appear to be speaking of the principle itself when he says that it was 'shown to be the firmest of all principles'. He can only mean that this was shown in the Indubitability Proof of Γ 3. So some will remain convinced that this proof ought to be establishing something about PNC itself. For them option (ii) may remain attractive.

10. Final thoughts on the elenctic proof

Let us turn, now, to a worry voiced by Lukasiewicz about the elenctic proof. Emphatic in claiming that the strategy of elenctic proof does not involve the fallacy of begging the question,[70] he is less

---

[70] Lukasiewicz, 'Aristotle on the Principle of Contradiction', 496, remarks: '. . . Aristotle commits no contradiction when, on the one hand, he declares the principle of contradiction to be nondemonstrable and, on the other hand, attempts to demonstrate the same principle elenctically and *ad impossibile*.' The claim about the first of these is based on Lukasiewicz's opinion that elenctic proofs are a kind of direct proof and so do not presuppose the principle of non-contradiction. But it might seem odd to find him exonerating proofs *ad impossibile*, since he takes these to rest on PNC and explicitly says that for this reason the *ad impossibile* proofs of PNC beg the question. Possibly Lukasiewicz meant that, in general, proofs proper are direct demonstrations differing from both elenctic and *ad impossibile* demonstrations. So, in general, one could hold, consistently, that q is not demonstrable by a proper proof but is demonstrable in either of the other two ways. The fact that *ad impossibile* proofs of PNC are question-begging would then be a function of the particular object of proof, namely, PNC. But if this is what Lukasiewicz meant, his remark is misleading in a non-trivial way.

sanguine about Aristotle's execution of the strategy. Although he thinks Stage 3 is unproblematic,[71] he worries that Stage 2 commits the fallacy. Recall that the crucial move in this stage is to reject the claim that 'what it is to be N' and 'what it is to be not-N' signify the same thing, i.e. to reject (h) above. This is done by appealing to (19), which says that if 'N' signifies one thing, then it is impossible that the expressions 'what it is to be N' and 'what it is to be not-N' signify the same thing. Lukasiewicz explains that this is so because 'otherwise' N would not be unified in its essence and this would *contradict* the fact that it is so unified. In effect, this takes (19) itself to rest on a further round of justificatory reasoning and one that appeals to PNC itself. But, as I have pointed out, Aristotle simply enters (19) as a truth,[72] and so, as far as (19) is concerned, it is a principle fit for use in a direct proof. On the other hand, (g), which is the target of Stage 2's argumentation, is rejected by a *modus tollens* argument, and so by Lukasiewicz's standards Stage 2 contains a piece of question-begging argumentation, albeit not where Lukasiewicz found it. Thus, even if the overall strategy of elenctic proof is insulated against the fallacy, it may emerge in the details.[73]

Do we have such a case here? Well, this depends on how we describe Aristotle's project. If he is intent on establishing PNC as an *ontological* principle, then he is free to make certain assumptions about the signification of terms. For example, even the opponent will grant that, in asserting that *a is F* and *a is not-F*, he means to be asserting of *a* the very thing he also denies of it. This presumes not only that 'F' has the same significance throughout but also that 'not-F' means something different. Were he to insist that 'F' and 'not-F' signify the same thing, his original assertion would lose interest. Seen in this light, the argument for rejecting (g) begs no questions because what the elenctic proof aims to establish is

---

[71] That is, unproblematic in the sense of not begging the question. But Lukasiewicz, 'Aristotle on the Principle of Contradiction', 498, does think that it proves only the principle of double negation. However, his reconstruction of the proof differs from mine, in addition to omitting some of the details of Aristotle's text, and it is hard to see why one would take my version, in sect. 6 above, to prove only the principle of double negation.

[72] Or, perhaps, as following from Stage 1's result that every (categorial) name signifies *one* thing.

[73] Although in assessing this we should bear in mind my remark in sect. 5 that the opponent is open to reasoned argument. For this will include any arguments that do not use PNC in the reasoning, and *modus tollens* arguments are of this type.

an ontological version of the principle, whether formulated objec-
tually, for objects and their attributes, or propositionally, for states
of affairs.[74] This introduces a restriction on PNC. But it is not a
restriction commentators have typically insisted on, for these have
been restrictions on the principle *as an ontological principle*. Nor
does this appear to be a restriction that compromises the principle's
status as the firmest principle of the general science of metaphysics.

Finally, return to my decision to follow Ross, rather than Kirwan,
in including K1 (1006^a28–31) as part of the elenctic proof. The difficulty that led Kirwan (*Aristotle's* Metaphysics) to count it as a
separate argument was that it promises to defeat, not the negation
of PNC, but the *contrary* of it. This was sidestepped in (17) above
by providing a formulation of what Aristotle *ought* to have said in
K1. More precisely, Aristotle was made to propose

(29a) 'N' signifies being or not being something $\rightarrow \neg \Diamond (\exists x)(Fx \wedge \neg Fx)$,

rather than

(29b) 'N' signifies being or not being something $\rightarrow \neg \Diamond (x)(Fx \wedge \neg Fx)$,

despite the fact that the text calls for (29b). I did this because K1
appears to propose an outline of the argument to follow and, when
this argument gets down to details, what is proved is the consequent
of (29a). Holding fast to the strict textual reading gives us (29b),
and this does not promise to prove PNC.

We may, however, be able to keep the strict textual reading without relinquishing our view that K1 is part of the elenctic proof or
flouting the fact that the elenctic proof expressly claims to estab-
lish $\neg \Diamond (\exists x)(Fx \wedge \neg Fx)$, rather than its weaker relative, $\neg \Diamond (x)(Fx \wedge \neg Fx)$. Thus, suppose we take Aristotle to suggest, in league with
(29b), that if a given name satisfies certain significance conditions,
then it cannot be the case that every x is such that $Fx \wedge \neg Fx$. It
will, for example, not be true of propositional contexts containing
the sample name. This, of course, is just what (29b) says. Now reflect on the fact that the elenctic proof proceeds by example—the

---

[74] This is less benign than I am making it sound. While none would quarrel
with the requirement that all parties grant that the *meaning* of terms remains fixed,
Aristotle uses a modally rich notion of signification, and this is certainly a more
contentious assumption.

sample name being 'man'. Because this is meant to be an arbitrary instance, what holds for it will hold for any name. Thus, throughout the argument, Aristotle proceeds on the assumption that its results are generalizable. So, because 'N' is arbitrary, (29a) is effectively equivalent to

(29a′1) $(y)(y$ is a name $\wedge y$ signifies being or not being something $\rightarrow$
      $\neg \Diamond (\exists x)(Fx \wedge \neg Fx))$.

That is, because every name must satisfy a certain condition on significance, no propositional context in which a name occurs can fail to conform to PNC. Seen this way, K1 nicely describes the course of the elenctic proof that follows.

11. *Γ* 4's remaining proofs: *reductio* or 'shriek' arguments?

Metaphysics Γ 4's long elenctic argument purports to establish PNC. In fact, it purports to establish the principle three times. The first part of that argument, W1.1, which we have been tracking, ends with a proper version of PNC, and the second part, W1.II, begins with the promise to deploy the same argument for terms that signify *not being something*, e.g. *not being a man*. And in the third part, W1.III, the entire stretch of elenctic argumentation is concluded with finality: '. . . it has been shown that it is impossible to predicate contradictories simultaneously'.

The balance of the chapter contains at least five (Kirwan) and possibly six (Ross) arguments. These have been uniformly regarded as *reductio* or *ad impossibile* arguments for PNC.[75] So they have been taken to have the following form:

$$\neg PNC \supset q$$
$$\underline{\neg q} \qquad \qquad [q \text{ being awkward, absurd, or impossible}]$$
$$\therefore \ PNC$$

The opponent denies PNC but this denial entails something awkward, absurd, or impossible, q. So q is rejected, and so also is the supposition that led to it. This was just $\neg$PNC. Hence, we are to conclude that PNC is true.

---

[75] So Łukasiewicz, *Über den Satz des Widerspruchs bei Aristoteles* and 'Aristotle on the Principle of Contradiction', as well as Lear, *Aristotle and Logical Theory*, 114, and Whitaker, *Aristotle's* De Interpretatione, 200.

These arguments have not fared well with commentators. Lukasiewicz sounds a common, and now familiar, chord: 'All the proofs *ad impossibile* are inadequate because they contain the following formal mistake(s): A *petitio principii* is contained in each. The *ad impossibile* mode of inference turns namely on the principle of contraposition, which . . . presupposes the principle of (non)contradiction.'[76] This depicts an Aristotle who completes Γ 4 by producing fallacious argument after fallacious argument. It is not a pretty picture.

But is this a correct picture? I think not. For if the elenctic argument thrice argues to PNC as a conclusion, *none* of the so-called *ad impossibile* arguments does so. Indeed, with one exception, they do not even mention the principle. So it is hardly clear that they are indirect arguments for PNC, nor, thus, that they are fallacious as charged.

Rather than indirect, *reductio* arguments, W2 through W7 (my division follows Ross) are what I call 'shriek' arguments. They grant the opponent's claim that ¬PNC and proceed to extract from it an embarrassing or awkward consequence. That is all they do. In particular, they do not take the further step of declaring that the claim of the opponent is false. So they have the following 'form':

$$\neg PNC \supset q$$
$$\underline{!q} \qquad \text{[q being awkward, absurd, or impossible]}$$
$$\therefore \quad !\neg PNC.$$

The fact that the negation of PNC entails an awkward consequence is marked by the shriek sign, '!'. This may justify attaching the shriek sign to ¬PNC, but this simply amounts to transferring awkwardness from what is entailed to the proposition that entails it. This, of course, leaves truth values unaffected; in particular, it does not give us the negation of ¬PNC. In effect, Aristotle says to his opponent, perhaps more for the benefit of his friendly auditors, 'See what embarrassments you have brought upon your house by this brazen denial of the principle of principles!' Aristotle may

---

[76] 'Aristotle on the Principle of Contradiction'; also Lear, *Aristotle and Logical Theory*, 113. As already indicated, it is customary nowadays to treat the fallacy of *petitio principii* or begging the question as an informal fallacy. So it is slightly odd to find Lukasiewicz classifying it as a formal mistake. He may have in mind just that, in the immediate case, there is a kind of formally circular reasoning.

hope that this has persuasive effect but he does *not* suggest that the embarrassments are grounds for denying the negation of PNC.[77]

The awkward consequences extracted from the opponent of PNC can be characterized, roughly, as follows:[78]

W2: That everything will be one,
W3: That the law of excluded middle will fail,
W4: That it will be impossible to truly assert anything,
W5: That the argument may be self-refuting,
W6: That the denier's beliefs and actions contravene his denial,
W7: That nothing is nearer to or further from the truth, or more or less the case.

Cumulatively, these shriek arguments aim to impress on the opponent, and Aristotle's audience, that one can deny PNC only at considerable cost to overall coherence. Piling up the score does not amount to refutation but it does make the opponent's position appear increasingly less attractive. Of course, for me the important point is that, persuasive effects aside, none of the arguments is a Lukasiewicz-style *petitio* because none of them is a *reductio* in the first place. In short, Aristotle has been unfairly represented and too hastily chastened by Lukasiewicz and company.

The reader can easily check these arguments for himself. But something should be said about W4 and W5, for each contains wording that might lead some to classify them as *reductio* arguments after all. In the course of W4, for example, Aristotle takes up the idea that one who asserts p and q jointly is entitled to assert them separately. In particular, if the joint assertion is true, then so are the separate assertions of each conjunct. This, in turn, is taken to imply that he who asserts, say, '$Fa \wedge \neg Fa$' would 'have the truth and . . . be in error, and be in error by his own admission' ($1008^a 28$–30). This might suggest that Aristotle envisages a *reductio* that begins with assertion of $\neg$PNC, or an instance thereof, and ends with the claim

[77] As Lukasiewicz ('Aristotle on the Principle of Contradiction') and others have observed, the shriek arguments appear to address, at least sometimes, an opponent who strongly denies PNC, i.e. an opponent who espouses not just its negation, $\Diamond(\exists x)(Fx \wedge \neg Fx)$, but its contrary, $\Diamond(x)(Fx \wedge \neg Fx)$. This shift in the point of proof, as Lukasiewicz called it, continues on into the next chapter, Γ 5. Although it calls for an accounting, it does not bear on the question immediately at hand and so I shall not address it. I say more about this in M. V. Wedin, 'The Curious Case of *Metaphysics Gamma*: Protagoras and Strong Denial of the Principle of Non-contradiction' (in progress).

[78] Again, numbered lettering refers to divisions of the text given in the Appendix.

that this is in error. Hence, ¬PNC is false and so PNC is true, and proven true by a *reductio* argument.

This, however, misrepresents Aristotle's reasoning in W4. Rather than mounting a *reductio*, he relies on the general point that the conjoint assertion of several propositions licenses the separate assertion of each conjunct. So, in the case at hand, joint assertion of '*Fa*∧ ¬*Fa*' licenses the assertion, separately, of '*Fa*' and of '¬*Fa*'. Since at least one of these (say *Fa*) must be true, the opponent is guaranteed to have the truth; yet, if he is correct, the other conjunct (¬*Fa*) must also be true; but then he must be in error with regard to the first, *Fa*—and this by his own admission. Such a result calls for our shriek operator, '!', but nothing more. Note, in particular, that Aristotle refrains from declaring that this result is false, and so he quite deliberately avoids the move that would invite the charge of begging the question.

That the fallacy of *petitio principii* is on Aristotle's mind is clear from the immediately following argument, W5:

Again, if whenever an assertion is true, its denial is false and whenever the latter is true its affirmation is false, there can be no such thing as simultaneously asserting and denying the same thing truly. However, they would no doubt assert that this is the question originally posed.[79]

Whatever else one makes of this argument,[80] it alone of W2–W7 displays PNC in the position of the conclusion. So it is clear why one might take it as a *reductio* rather than a shriek argument. There is some temptation to think that Aristotle takes the argument this way, for he seems to be suggesting that the move from

(30) $(p)(p \text{ is true} \equiv \neg p \text{ is false})$

to

(31) $\neg \Diamond (\exists p)(p \wedge \neg p)$

works because (30) is equivalent to

(30a) $(p)(p \text{ is true} \equiv \neg (p \text{ is not true}))$.

For (30a) licenses '$p \rightarrow \neg(\neg p)$', which seems enough to establish

---

[79] 1008ª34–ᵇ 2, following Kirwan (*Aristotle's* Metaphysics).
[80] For example, it saddles the opponent with strong denial of PNC, and indeed may represent him as holding the strong principle: $(p)(p \equiv \neg p)$.

(31).[81] And some will urge that using (30a) to get (31) comes close, indeed, to begging the original question.

However, so far from tarnishing Aristotle's logical shield, W5 testifies to his awareness of the probative risks involved in attempting an indirect proof of PNC. For it is precisely because of worries about begging the question that he backs away from the inference from (30) to (31).[82] Presumably, the denier of PNC would be committed to denial of (30). To this last denial Aristotle can attach the shriek operator; in fact, given his characterization of the opponent as *strongly* denying PNC, the opponent is held committed to the strong denial of (30) as well. And this, the claim that *all* propositions are true and false, surely calls for 'shrieking'. But Aristotle appears to be quite aware that he can do no more, in particular, that he cannot deliver a *reductio* argument whose conclusion is PNC. This is clearly the force of the final line of W5. Thus, PNC's only appearance in *Γ* 4, outside of the elenctic proof, is in a text that recommends against attempting a *reductio* proof of the principle. I conclude that none of the shriek arguments is guilty of the fallacy of begging the question.

University of California at Davis

APPENDIX
The Arguments of *Metaphysics Γ* 4

K = Kirwan; R = Ross; L = Lukasiewicz; W = Wedin

K1	(1006^{a}28–31)	R1 = K1 & K2	L1 (1006^{b}28–34)
K2	I (1006^{a}31–^{b}34)	R2 (1007^{b}18–1008^{a}2)	L2 (1006^{b}11–22)
	II (1006^{b}34–1007^{a}20)		
	III (1007^{a}20–^{b}18)		
K3	(1007^{b}18–1008^{a}7)	R3 (1008^{a}2–7)	L3 (1007^{b}18–21)

---

[81] By knocking out its negation, $\lozenge(\exists p)(p \wedge \neg p)$.

[82] Kirwan, *Aristotle's Metaphysics*, 104, takes Aristotle's 'However, they would doubtless assert that this is the question originally posed' to signal a quite different sort of hesitation, namely, Aristotle's hesitation: 'Here, but not at *Γ*.7, 1011^{b}25, and *Γ*.8, 1012^{b}7–8, . . . to appeal to the definition of "true" and "false".' But precisely because neither *Γ* 7 nor *Γ* 8 betrays the slightest hesitation, it is implausible to find *Γ* 4 concerned about using the definitions of truth and falsity. Rather, Aristotle is concerned about precisely what he says he is concerned about, namely, that appeal to PNC, implicit in the preceding line, invites the charge of *petitio*.

Michael V. Wedin

K4	(1008^a7-34)	R4 = K4		L4 (1008^a28-30)
K5	$(1008^a34-{}^b2)$	R5 = K5		L5 (1008^a12-19)
K6	(1008^b2-31)	R6 = K6		
K7	$(1008^b31-1009^a5)$	R7 = K7		

W1 $(1006^a28-1007^b18)$: The Elenctic Proof of PNC

         (1006^a28-31): Outline of the Proof (Two Cases)

     I $(1006^a31-{}^b34)$: Case One: Where a Name Signifies Being

       Stage 1 $(1006^a31-{}^b13)$: That a Name Signifies One Thing

       Stage 2 (1006^b13-28): That 'Man' and 'Not-man' Cannot Signify the Same Thing

       Stage 3 (1006^b28-34): The Proof of PNC

    II $(1006^b34-1007^a20)$: Case Two: Where a Name Signifies Not Being

   III $(1007^a20-{}^b18)$: Support Argument: the Ineliminability of Essence

W2 $(1007^b18-1008^a2)$: That Everything Will Be One

W3 (1008^a2-7): That the Law of Excluded Middle Will Fail

W4 (1008^a7-34): That It Will be Impossible to Truly Assert Anything

W5 $(1008^a34-{}^b2)$: That the Argument May be Self-Defeating

W6 (1008^b2-31): That the Denier's Beliefs and Actions Contravene His Denial

W7 $(1008^b31-1009^a5)$: That Nothing is Nearer to or Further from the Truth, or More or Less the Case

LEXICAL ANOMALIES IN THE INTRODUCTION TO THE *POSTERIOR ANALYTICS*, PART 1

MARK GIFFORD

THE opening chapter to the *Posterior Analytics* is troublesome, far more so than scholars have realized; so troublesome is it, in fact, that close inspection will reveal a text which unquestionably underwent considerable alteration early on in the course of its transmission. So numerous and severe are the problems confronting us in *Posterior Analytics* 1. 1—particularly in its central section, 71^a17–30, which boasts, among other things, the only explicit attempt in the corpus to solve the notorious 'paradox of enquiry' from Plato's *Meno*—that the text which has reached us simply cannot have come from Aristotle without having suffered significant editorial modification at some point early in its career. On its first announcement, this novel and radical contention is bound to induce a most assured state of disbelief; and unfortunately, that initial condition in the reader is one that can only be ameliorated but not completely relieved within the limits of the present undertaking. Nevertheless, no matter what sort of immediate reaction it may provoke, the claim that for the past two millennia students of Aristotle have unwittingly been reading a badly tainted version of the introduction to the *Posterior Analytics* represents a conclusion we shall eventually be driven to acknowledge by the cumulative force of the many disturbing philosophical and linguistic aberrations to be found in the received text.

As for its philosophical woes, the transmitted text of 1. 1 not only advances embarrassingly wrong-headed solutions to elementary epistemological problems, in the course of doing so it manages to contradict standard Aristotelian doctrines, including fundamental epistemological theses which Aristotle carefully expounds in adjoining passages. Yet these philosophical blunders and inconsistencies, manifest and distressing though they are, can perhaps be handled in ways that stop short of impugning the soundness of the received text. Even when presented with a complete catalogue of the several unaccountable doctrinal flaws in the text we possess, readers of Aristotle will still have at their disposal the facile remedy of loose interpretation ('Aristotle here is neither saying what he means nor meaning what he says'); or, should textual infidelity begin to disquiet the scholarly conscience, commentators can always resign themselves to the idea that even Aristotle, after all, must on occasion be granted an intellectual holiday. Disagreeable as this thought may be, and shocking as it would be to discover Aristotle's intellect taking a vacation on its first day of employment in the *Posterior Analytics*, scholarly prudence might seem to counsel surrendering even weak versions of the principle of charity (such as those which prohibit our allowing Aristotle to contradict himself repeatedly in the course of a single discussion) when their acceptance would force the displeasing dilemma of either reading the received text irresponsibly or attempting to emend by 'conjecture' the time-honoured bequest of a unanimous manuscript tradition.

Now, if the text of I. I were guilty of doctrinal lapses alone (and if we were also deprived of abundant and compelling documentary evidence, both inside and outside I. I, that could readily account for the changes to the original text and then reliably guide the work of emendation), resigned acceptance of the received text with all its philosophical faults might indeed be upheld, at least in conservative quarters, as the only sober course. But, beyond its philosophical defects, the opening chapter of the *Posterior Analytics* also presents us with a number of inexplicable oddities in Aristotle's language; and in the face of these linguistic challenges to the integrity of the transmitted text, the attitude of pious acquiescence is far less comfortably maintained. Not only does the text house words and phrases that defy all attempts to give them sense, but—what is the surest sign of alteration to the original text, and the thesis of the present paper—the short stretch at 71^a17–30 is also home to several egregious misuses of key Aristotelian *termini technici*, including self-coined epistemological expressions which lie at the heart of the *Posterior Analytics* and which, in addition, are expressly defined in the immediate context. When the grave philosophical failings of I. I are compounded by these stunning lexical irregularities, continued acceptance of the traditional text will no longer be a course that is open to us, conservative or no; for while it has to be admitted that even Aristotle can sometimes nod—and while, though scandalous, it is at least conceivable that he could have done so in laying the groundwork for a major treatise, when we would normally expect him to be displaying the utmost vigilance—what lies wholly beyond the sufferance of thought is that, in the midst of these untimely philosophical slumbers, he could also flagrantly violate the explicit and habituated rules of his own technical vocabulary.

Once unveiled for viewing, the many startling incongruities of thought and expression in the transmitted text of 1. 1 should have a deep and disconcerting effect on serious readers of Aristotle. But there is an inconvenience facing the expositor of these bewildering aberrations: their sheer number precludes a proper exhibition of the entire collection within the space of a single paper. In the following study, accordingly, I confine my attention to the lexical anomalies in 1. 1, deferring discussion of its other linguistic difficulties, as well as its philosophical problems, to another occasion. My principal aim here will be to establish that, if the text we have is accepted in its present condition as representing unadulterated Aristotle, then the important technical expressions ἐπίστασθαι ἁπλῶς, ἐπάγειν, and λαμβάνειν (appearing as it does in 1. 1, with συλλογισμός as its object) must be taken in ways for which there are no good parallels and which, moreover, directly and needlessly contradict the central and explicit rules governing their standard usage.

My discussion of these lexical anomalies will be divided into four sections. In the first I describe the context within which the perverse passage at 71ᵃ17–30 appears and sketch the traditional reading of the passage, specifying the meanings we must assign to the three problematic expressions on this, the only even faintly plausible way of understanding the text as it stands. In the remaining three sections (Sections 3 and 4 of which will appear in Part 2) I take up each expression in turn and show why Aristotle himself could not possibly have employed these items from his technical vocabulary in the ways he would have to be using them were the received text sound.

At a minimum, the lexical investigation that follows will afford a more precise appreciation of fundamental concepts in Aristotle's logic and epistemology, as well as a more accurate understanding of several key passages in the corpus that depend on those concepts. But, beyond that, this paper should also expand and sharpen

awareness of some of the grievous philological difficulties that beset
the traditional reading of *Posterior Analytics* 1. 1. And finally, by
fixing the actual meanings of several crucial expressions that occur
in the chapter, this study will perform the further service, I believe,
of helping us to attain a vantage-point from which we can easily
identify the corruptions in the text that has been passed on to us
(by obscure early editors) and then securely reclaim, to the great advantage of our understanding of Aristotelian epistemology, a more
authentic version of the introduction to the *Posterior Analytics*.

1. The received view

In its transmitted form the *Posterior Analytics* begins with a dis-
jointed chapter whose precise purpose in the treatise is not easy to
discern. What we can say at least is that, as it has come down to
us, the introductory chapter to the treatise does eventually lead up
to, if it fails actually to motivate, the pivotal passage at the start
of the second chapter (71^{b}9–12) where Aristotle defines the central
concept in the work as a whole: ἐπίστασθαι ἁπλῶς, or 'knowing in
the unqualified sense'.

Chapter 1. 1 itself opens with a sententious announcement of
the universal epistemological principle that every act of inferential
knowledge acquisition is based on some knowledge or other that
is already possessed (71^{a}1–2). After an inductive defence of this
basic thesis on the general preconditions for any sort of inferential
learning (71^{a}2–11), Aristotle effectively blocks an epistemological
regress which his initial principle threatens to generate (71^{a}11–
17). We then meet up with the problematic text at 71^{a}17–30 (with
unmarked occurrences of 'know' rendering the verb εἰδέναι and 'has
2R' abbreviating the predicate expression 'has angles equal to the
sum of two right angles' in the translation that follows):

A (**1**) But it is possible to come to know [γνωρίζειν] by coming to know
[γνωρίζοντα] some things beforehand and acquiring knowledge [γνῶσιν]
of other things at the very same time, namely, all those things which
fall in actual fact under a universal truth of which[1] you have knowledge
[γνῶσιν]. (**2**) For you knew beforehand that every triangle has 2R, but
you came to know [ἐγνώρισεν] that this thing here in the semicircle is

---

[1] At this point in the translation I follow Ross's OCT and its emendation of the
manuscripts' reading ὧν to οὗ; but see n. 39 below.

a triangle at the same time as you were <u>led to perform the induction</u> [ἐπαγόμενος]. (3) For the learning of certain things occurs in this way—that is, the final item comes to be known [γνωρίζεται] without using the middle term—namely, all those things which at that time fall in actual fact among the particulars (i.e. things not ⟨predicated⟩ of an underlying subject).

B (1) But before you are <u>led to perform the induction</u> [ἐπαχθῆναι], or before you <u>acquire a syllogism</u> [λαβεῖν συλλογισμόν], we should presumably say [ἴσως φατέον] that you know [ἐπίστασθαι] in one sense but not in another. (2) For if you didn't know whether ⟨the triangle in the semicircle⟩ exists,[2] how did you know [ᾔδει] *in the unqualified sense* [ἁπλῶς] that it has 2R? (3) Still, it's clear that you do know [ἐπίσταται] in this sense: the fact that ⟨this particular triangle has 2R⟩ you do know in a universal way [καθόλου ἐπίσταται], but you don't <u>know in the unqualified sense</u> [ἁπλῶς ἐπίσταται]. (4) Otherwise, the puzzle in the *Meno* will result: you will learn either nothing or what you ⟨already⟩ know.

The remainder of the chapter ($71^a30–^b8$) is taken up with the presentation and subsequent criticism of an alternative solution to Meno's Paradox (or, if we judge from philosophical substance rather than from linguistic signposts, to the puzzle about knowing universal truths that Aristotle is supposed to be addressing, along with Meno's Paradox, in the second half of our passage); and the foundational definition of ἐπίστασθαι ἁπλῶς at the start of 1. 2 then abruptly follows, apparently with little if any preparation from what has gone before.

So much for the text and context of $71^a17–30$. When we turn to the extensive commentary tradition for assistance with this curious stretch of 1. 1, what we find there, despite discrepancies on lesser points of detail and on the larger question of overall philosophical import, is widespread agreement on a basic outline for understanding the passage. This fundamental unanimity among interpreters is hardly surprising; for the received text will have it no other way. Conveniently, then, we can assemble the common products of multitudinous commentaries under a single head and refer to the compulsory framework for understanding the transmitted text of $71^a17–30$ as representing the 'received view' of the passage.[3]

---

[2] My translation shuns the problematic occurrence of ἁπλῶς in this first clause of **B2**; I doubt it will be missed (see further n. 41 below).

[3] The essential interpretative scheme that I am calling the 'received view' can be found in all of the major commentaries of recent times: J. Barnes, *Aristotle:* Posterior Analytics, 2nd edn. (Oxford, 1994); W. Detel, *Aristoteles: Analytica Posteriora*

The shared interpretative theses that make up the received view
of 71ª17–30 can be set out as follows. Having solved the regress
problem that imperilled his initial principle on the epistemic prerequisites for inferential learning, Aristotle now offers further clarification of this general principle by bringing forward two apparently
contrary cases of knowledge acquisition for special consideration,
treating them separately in the sections marked '**A**' and '**B**' above.
Both of these cases pertain to syllogistic knowledge acquisition,
and throughout the two sections that comprise our passage Aristotle operates with the following illustrative syllogism (where 'T'
names the particular triangle drawn in the semicircle which gets
introduced in **A2**):

> Every triangle has 2R.
> T is a triangle.
> _____
> T has 2R

In section **A** Aristotle treats the situation in which we apprehend the singular statement in the conclusion of this syllogism by
(as most commentators think) performing the syllogistic inference
from our prior knowledge of the universal major, while in section **B**
he addresses the epistemic situation we find ourselves in when we

(Berlin, 1993); M. Mignucci, *L'argomentazione dimostrativa in Aristotele* (Padua,
1975); and W. D. Ross, *Aristotle's* Prior *and* Posterior Analytics (Oxford, 1949).
The same view is represented from antiquity by the compendium of Themistius,
In Posteriora Analytica paraphrasis, ed. M. Wallies (Commentaria in Aristotelem
Graeca, 5.1; Berlin, 1900), and the commentary of J. Philoponus, *In Aristotelis Analytica Posteriora commentaria*, ed. M. Wallies (Commentaria in Aristotelem Graeca,
13.3; Berlin, 1909), as well as in the interim by the works of, among other notables, J.
Zabarella, *In duos Aristotelis libros Posteriorum Analyticorum commentaria* (Venice,
1582), and J. Pacius, *In Aristotelis Organon commentarius analyticus* (Frankfurt,
1597). Although the focus of this paper will be on the lexical anomalies generated by
the shared claims that comprise the received view, I shall also speak to the idiosyncratic suggestions of individual commentators when they bear on our issues. (The
well-known commentaries listed above will hereafter be cited by author's name.)
   Perhaps unsurprisingly, given the philosophically disappointing character of the
received text (and despite the explicit solution it proposes to the much-discussed
'paradox of enquiry' from the *Meno*), other than the official commentators on the
Posterior Analytics, whose duties forbid them from skipping over 71ª17–30 altogether, students of Aristotle have evinced very little interest in our passage—save to
speculate on his allegedly distinctive conception of 'induction' (ἐπαγωγή) under the
guidance of the apparently unorthodox use of the verb ἐπαγεῖν that is found there (see
sect. 3 in Part 2). Nevertheless, the more significant scholarly contributions from
outside the tradition of commentaries proper will be introduced when relevant. (See
the 'Bibliographische Anmerkungen' in Detel's commentary on 1. 1 for a helpful
overview of the scholarship on the chapter.)

know the universal major without knowing that T exists. Why the elementary case of syllogistic knowledge acquisition supposedly examined in **A** should seem to Aristotle to merit any particular attention at this point in the chapter is not immediately obvious; but the epistemic situation described in **B** furnishes the premisses for the following logical puzzle (developed more fully at 71ᵃ30–3), which we might call the 'Paradox of Knowing Universals'.[4] Since we know the universal major that *every* triangle has 2R, and since T is in fact a triangle, it seems we must also know the singular statement that T has 2R; but since, on the other hand, we lack knowledge that T exists, it seems we can know neither the singular minor that T is a triangle nor, in consequence, the singular conclusion that T has 2R. Thus, if we know a universal truth without knowing of the existence of some instantiation of that statement, it apparently follows that we shall both know and not know the same thing at the same time. In order to eliminate this contradiction and solve the Paradox of Knowing Universals, Aristotle goes on in **B** to draw a distinction between potential and explicit knowledge, maintaining that the possession of *potential* knowledge of singular statements, which is all that knowledge of a universal truth by itself can yield, is not incompatible with the simultaneous absence of *explicit* knowledge of those same statements. And, at the close of our passage, he then puts this same epistemological distinction back to work in proffering a solution to Meno's Paradox—thereby killing with commendable thrift, it seems, two birds of paradox with a single philosophical stone.

At any rate, having furnished this brief summary of the received view, I can now specify the ways in which the three expressions ἐπίστασθαι ἁπλῶς, ἐπάγειν, and λαμβάνειν συλλογισμόν must be construed on this required way of reading the transmitted text.

First, in **A2**, where Aristotle is generally supposed to be describing the syllogistic process by which we acquire knowledge of the singular conclusion that T has 2R, we learn that in such cases of syllogistic knowledge acquisition, while we do know the universal major beforehand (in keeping with the opening thesis of 1. 1), we

---

[4] Aristotle also handles this puzzle at *Pr. An.* 2. 21, 67ᵃ8–30, a text which plainly echoes our passage at key points and thus provides in those places a most fortunate and decisive touchstone for readings of 1. 1 (see further sect. 2.3 below and esp. sect. 3 in Part 2). For close analysis of Aristotle's solution to the paradox in 2. 21, see my 'Aristotle on Platonic Recollection and the Paradox of Knowing Universals: *Prior Analytics B*. 21 67a8–30', *Phronesis*, 44 (1999), 1–29.

gain knowledge of the singular minor at precisely the moment we are 'led to perform the induction' (ἐπαγόμενος). Although largely agreed that Aristotle is describing a case of knowledge acquisition via syllogistic inference in **A2** as a whole, and although united on the point that ἐπαγόμενος serves to indicate the process by which we come to know one of the statements in Aristotle's exemplary syllogism *other than its universal major* (which is apparently said to be known 'beforehand', i.e. before the 'induction', or before the process of grasping the minor, which is itself supposed to be simultaneous with the 'induction', if not identical to it), commentators divide over the precise construal to be given the term ἐπάγειν in this occurrence: some take it to indicate the actual process of drawing the syllogistic inference to the singular conclusion that T has 2R, while others have it indicating the non-inferential process by which we apprehend the singular minor that T is a triangle. Showing the extreme implausibility of each of these two readings of ἐπάγειν will be the burden of Section 3 in Part 2.

Turning to **B**, we find an identical use of ἐπάγειν in **B1**, where Aristotle supposedly introduces the problematic epistemic situation that arises when we know the universal major that every triangle has 2R but have yet to learn of the existence of the particular triangle T, and hence before we have been 'led to perform the induction' (ἐπαχθῆναι) or before we have 'acquired a syllogism' (λαβεῖν συλλογισμόν). Commentators again part ways over the use of the term ἐπάγειν, as above, but all agree that with λαμβάνειν συλλογισμόν Aristotle is signalling the process of 'acquiring' the simple syllogism under discussion and hence the process of performing the syllogistic inference itself. Section 4 in Part 2 will reveal the forbidding but hitherto unsuspected obstacles that confront this construal of λαμβάνειν συλλογισμόν—a combination of (technical) terms which, what might seem surprising at first blush, scarcely appears in the corpus and which, tellingly, would bear the suggested sense only here in 1. 1.

Our final lexical irregularity occurs in **B3**, where Aristotle purportedly solves the Paradox of Knowing Universals by invoking the distinction between potential and explicit knowledge. The subject of the proposition that is known potentially but not explicitly before being syllogistically inferred is not itself expressly stated in **B**; nevertheless, context demands that we supply from **A2** the particular triangle drawn in the semicircle. On the received view, accordingly, the point made in **B3** is this: simply in virtue of knowing the universal truth that every triangle has 2R, we possess *potential* knowledge of the singular statement that T has 2R (we know it 'in a universal way': καθόλου ἐπίσταται); but, since we lack knowledge that T exists, we fail to have *explicit* knowledge of that same statement (we don't know it 'in the unqualified sense': ἐπίσταται ἁπλῶς). Commentators are therefore of one mind on the point that in this occurrence the expression ἐπίστασθαι ἁπλῶς indicates the sort of knowledge we would have of the singular conclusion that T has 2R were we to perform the syllogistic inference to that statement, namely, explicit knowledge of a singular truth. The next section exposes the indefensibility of this construal.

2. ἐπίστασθαι ἁπλῶς

In this section I furnish the textual evidence and accompanying argumentation needed to appreciate the severity of the lexical anomaly that would be involved in Aristotle's use of ἐπίστασθαι ἁπλῶς in 1. 1, given the assumption that the text we are dealing with is sound. In Section 2.1 I elucidate Aristotle's official definition of 'knowing in the unqualified sense' at the start of *Post. An.* 1. 2; in Section 2.2 I survey his use of the expression ἐπίστασθαι ἁπλῶς elsewhere in the corpus outside of *Post. An.* 1. 1; and in Section 2.3 I demonstrate how its use in *Post. An.* 1. 1, at least as it must be understood on the received view, inexplicably violates both Aristotle's formal definition and his otherwise uniform usage of this crucial technical term.

2.1. *Aristotle's official definition of* ἐπίστασθαι ἁπλῶς

The expression ἐπίστασθαι ἁπλῶς[5] is evidently a technical coinage from Aristotle's own, highly productive mint. Although a stray occurrence of the locution can be found in Plato (*Rep.* 438 E 7), evidently no one before Aristotle had employed the compound expression as a unitary technical term, or attached to it the specific meaning that he does. We are therefore entitled to speak of

---

[5] Unless otherwise indicated, my remarks about Aristotle's use of ἐπίστασθαι ἁπλῶς, as well as the other technical expressions treated in this paper, should be understood to embrace their respective cognate forms as well.

ἐπίστασθαι ἁπλῶς as an Aristotelian coinage, since that is effectively what it proves to be.

We encounter a mere eight occurrences of this uncommon expression in the Aristotelian corpus. Significantly, all of them fall within the confines of a single work, the *Posterior Analytics*, a treatise comprising various studies aimed at clarifying the nature and defending the possibility of the epistemic state Aristotle calls 'demonstrative knowledge' (ἀποδεικτικὴ ἐπιστήμη)—a state which for him represents the perfection of human cognition and which we may best think of as the state of *scientific understanding*.[6] As a matter of fact, the eight occurrences of ἐπίστασθαι ἁπλῶς in Aristotle all congregate within the first eight chapters of the *Posterior Analytics*,[7] which constitute the bulk of an uninterrupted discussion devoted to specifying the core properties of this consummate cognitive condition.

The most illuminating, and indeed the most illustrious, occurrence of ἐπίστασθαι ἁπλῶς is found at the very start of the second chapter of the work, where Aristotle chooses to employ the locution in order to introduce the two basic requirements he will be placing on the ideal state of demonstrative knowledge:

EH1 We think we <u>know in the unqualified sense</u> [ἐπίστασθαι ἁπλῶς]—and not merely in the sophistical, accidental sense—when we think we know [γινώσκειν] the cause of a fact as the cause of that fact and that this ⟨fact⟩ cannot be otherwise.

Aristotle here sets out two requirements on the state of *true ἐπιστήμη* (*perfect* or *indefective ἐπιστήμη* might answer even better to Aristotle's actual definiendum), and his use of the unusual compound expression ἐπίστασθαι ἁπλῶς is evidently intended to signal his specific concern with ἐπιστήμη in this more precise and restricted

---

[6] The idea that the epistemological theory of the *Posterior Analytics* is focused upon an epistemic state that is more informatively and less misleadingly characterized as a form of *understanding* rather than as a form of *knowledge* is defended in M. Burnyeat, 'Aristotle on Understanding Knowledge' ['Understanding Knowledge'], in E. Berti (ed.), *Aristotle on Science* (Padua, 1981), 97–139—an influential paper which, despite serious flaws (see e.g. n. 28 and appendix B below), has little trouble carrying its incontrovertible main thesis, which was proposed earlier in L. A. Kosman, 'Understanding, Explanation, and Insight in the *Posterior Analytics*', in E. N. Lee, A. P. D. Mourelatos, and R. M. Rorty (eds.), *Exegesis and Argument* (Assen, 1973), 374–92.

[7] It might seem that there is a ninth occurrence of the expression at I. 22, 84ᵃ5–6, but see n. 42 below.

sense.[8] When he presents the parallel and equally restrictive definition of ἐπιστήμη at *NE* 6. 3, Aristotle effects the same narrowing of semantic focus by signalling through his use of ἀκριβολογεῖσθαι (1139ᵇ18) that he is going to be dealing with the term ἐπιστήμη in a sense more precise than that sanctioned by the liberal usage of ordinary language (for light on the practice of 'precise speaking' and its relationship with common speech see *Rep.* 1, 340 D 1 ff., esp. 341 C 4–7, where we learn that a physician in precise speech is one who, by virtue of perfectly satisfying the abstract requirements of physicianhood, is *truly* (τῷ ὄντι) a physician; cf. *H.Ma.* 284 E 1–2). In our passage ('**EH1**') the use of ἁπλῶς to modify ἐπίστασθαι cannot be put down solely to a need on Aristotle's part to distance his formal definiendum, regarded as plain ἐπίστασθαι, from 'knowledge in the sophistical, accidental sense', the qualified or defective type of knowledge that appears immediately afterwards; for, besides the fact that sophistical knowledge seems to come in here as something of an aside (albeit a significant one), Aristotle will also use the expression ἐπίστασθαι ἁπλῶς even in contexts where there is no mention of any specific second-rate or qualified form of cognition that needs to be banished from consideration—see especially the passages **EH3**, **EH4**, and **EH7** below; cf. the similarly 'absolute' usages in book 1 of both its official synonym εἰδέναι ἁπλῶς (**EH8** and **EH9** in Appendix A) and its thematic twin ἀποδεικνύναι ἁπλῶς (at 72ᵇ25, 31, and (with n. 42) 83ᵇ38 and 84ᵃ5–6, but most clearly at 75ᵇ23–4 (in **EH5**) and 76ᵃ14; cf. *Metaph.* 1015ᵇ7).[9] Thus, as will become even more evident as we proceed, ἐπίστασθαι ἁπλῶς is for Aristotle a unitary technical locution with a determinate sense and a context-independent reference of its own;[10] and he evidently de-

---

[8] For this effect of ἁπλῶς cf. e.g. the function this modifier performs in the locution ὁ ἁπλῶς πολίτης at *Pol.*1274ᵇ38–1275ᵃ23, where the expression carries absolute reference to a person who fully meets Aristotle's theoretical conditions for citizenship and hence can be characterized as a 'citizen' without *any* debilitating qualification appended—see esp. 1275ᵃ19–20.

[9] In all of these occurrences ἀπόδειξις ἁπλῶς plainly denotes the form of argument which is defined in Aristotle's official account of what a demonstration is at 1. 2, 71ᵇ17 ff. (and which he also refers to as an ἐπιστημονικὴ ἀπόδειξις at 75ᵃ3). The expression carries a different sense only in its three other appearances in the corpus, all of which occur, suspiciously enough, within the dubious epitome of *Metaph. Γ* 4 found in *K* 5 (1062ᵃ2–3, 5, and 30–1), where ἀπόδειξις ἁπλῶς serves to indicate merely a non-dialectical proof (as opposed to a proof πρὸς τόνδε), the kind of argument which Aristotle had indicated in the source passage by a bare use of ἀπόδειξις (in contrast to a proof proceeding ἐλεγκτικῶς)—see 1006ᵃ8–18.

[10] The absolute use of εἰδέναι ἁπλῶς in **EH8** (1. 3, 72ᵇ30), which refers us directly

vised the expression for performing a single, definite, and leading
role within the elaborate system of epistemic terminology on display in the *Posterior Analytics*, namely, that of marking off *true*
ἐπιστήμη from any and all forms of cognition, whether mentioned
in context or not, which he for one reason or another regarded as
falling short of this impeccant state.[11]

back to the definition in **EH1**, is most instructive on the point that Aristotle intends the locution ἐπίστασθαι ἁπλῶς to be a self-sufficient vehicle of meaning whose
denotation is determined independently of any context-relative contrast; for the definite article τό that there introduces the words εἰδέναι ἁπλῶς evidently does duty for
quotation-marks—note ὡρισμένον at 72ᵇ30–1 (cf. e.g. 72ᵃ25–7) and διττόν at 72ᵇ31 (cf.
e.g. 77ᵇ28). Thus, since the compound expression εἰδέναι ἁπλῶς in 1. 3 is clearly intended to be a synonymous surrogate for the locution defined at the start of 1. 2, **EH8**
shows conclusively that the formal definiendum in **EH1** is not merely ἐπίστασθαι, a
term with pre-existing usages in both ordinary and Academic speech, but the special
and self-reliant technical term ἐπίστασθαι ἁπλῶς.

Because **EH1** is not exactly attempting to define ἐπίστασθαι, we need not fault
Aristotle for incompetence in the analysis of ordinary usage; but nor, on the other
hand, should we think that he is altogether abandoning the intuitions that steer the
common use of ἐπίστασθαι and merely either stipulating a technical meaning for
the term or reporting a technical usage already current among philosophers. The
simple categories of reportive, analytic, and stipulative definitions furnish snares
that are too crude to capture Aristotle's subtle approach to defining *true* ἐπιστήμη:
as against simple stipulation, Aristotle does want to garner at least some evidence
for his definition from everyday intuitions governing the use of ἐπίστασθαι in the
general sense of *knowledge* (and not merely from an established philosophical use of
the term for expressing some narrower concept of *scientific cognition*, pace e.g. Detel
ad 71ᵇ12—see n. 18); yet, as against reporting or ordinary analysis, he considers
himself to be under no obligation to respect all of the norms comprising an already
established concept. One should compare the approach to defining *true* ἐπιστήμη
here in 1. 2 with the manner in which (true) σοφία gets defined in *Metaph. A* 1–2,
where Aristotle likewise appeals to ordinary-language intuitions in the course of justifying an extraordinary definition of a key epistemic term. The rationale behind the
seemingly curious practice of definition exhibited in both of these cases is basically
this: Aristotle thinks that the ideas embedded in the linguistic practice of layfolk,
along with those articulated by his philosophical predecessors, disclose something
of the truth about these ideal and desirable epistemic states, for he thinks that everyone has caught at least a glimpse of *what it is that human beings by nature really
want and aspire to in the way of cognition* (cf. *Metaph.* 980ᵃ21 ff.), and it is precisely
this that he is trying to define in each case. For this reason, then, Aristotle justifies
his definitions by drawing on ideas that lie behind the popular and philosophical
usages of the corresponding terms, but without meekly submitting himself to those
usages: they furnish him with endoxa that can certainly guide and support, but need
not wholly determine, his answer to a substantive philosophical question—such as
the partly psychological, partly epistemological, and partly metaphysical question
of what the ideal form of ἐπιστήμη, or ἐπιστήμη ἁπλῶς, really is.

[11] *Pace* Themistius (5. 13–16) and Barnes ad 71ᵇ16 (see also ad 71ᵇ9), the expression ἐπίστασθαι ἁπλῶς also serves to distinguish the explanatory form of scientific
cognition defined in **EH1** from the special type of *non-explanatory* scientific cogni-

Aristotle's decision to engage the particular expression ἐπίστασθαι ἁπλῶς for carrying out this vital technical mission in the treatise was no doubt driven by the desire to have a wieldy locution that also fulfilled two further desiderata: first, that it serve as a distinctive sign of the special concept of ἐπιστήμη which, as we shall see presently, constitutes the very heart of the *Posterior Analytics*; and second, that it maintain some linguistic contact with the everyday and philosophical endoxa about ἐπιστήμη (which are endoxa neither about ἐπιστήμη ἁπλῶς nor about ἀποδεικτικὴ ἐπιστήμη, at least not *de dicto*) by which he motivates his account of true ἐπιστήμη in **EH1**[12]—for the passage is actually governed by the phrase 'we think', which shows that Aristotle there is simply reporting two endoxic beliefs that he finds to have some bearing on the epistemic state whose nature he is concerned to clarify.[13] But since he goes on

tion which Aristotle officially baptizes νοῦς ('scientific insight')—the state in which one grasps the brute facts in the Aristotelian universe (particularly essences, or the explanatorily basic properties of natural and mathematical kinds), along with the indemonstrable first principles of Aristotelian science which limn these ultimate and inexplicable states of affairs (particularly real definitions). Consider the issue raised at 71^{b}16–17 about whether there is another form of ἐπίστασθαι, i.e. a form other than ἐπίστασθαι ἁπλῶς or scientific understanding. Owing to an ambiguity inherent in the use of the unmodified term ἐπίστασθαι, which in philosophical usage can refer generally to scientific cognition (as it does here) or specifically to the explanatory state of scientific understanding (see n. 17), this question actually turns out to be a double one, and Aristotle gives it a twofold response: in 1. 3 he informs us that the non-demonstrative grasp of first principles is another form of *scientific cognition* (i.e. ἐπιστήμη in a more generic sense—see 72^{b}18–25), while in 2. 19 he tells us that it is not another form of *scientific understanding* (i.e. ἐπιστήμη in its most specific and precise technical sense, the sense carried in book 1 by, among other expressions (see again n. 17), the special coinage ἐπιστήμη ἁπλῶς—see 100^{b}5–17). (For ἐπιστήμη in the more generic sense of 'scientific cognition' see also e.g. 71^{b}27–9, 72^{b}5, 19–20, 21, 76^{a}18, 79^{a}24, and 88^{b}36; for the distinction between ἐπιστήμη, precisely conceived, and νοῦς see also e.g. 72^{b}23–5, 85^{a}1, and 88^{b}33–6; cf. 89^{b}7–9 and *NE* 6. 6.)

[12] It is this desire to tie his account of *true* ἐπιστήμη to existing usages of ἐπιστήμη and ἐπίστασθαι that ultimately explains why Aristotle bothers to introduce the language of ἐπιστήμη ἁπλῶς into the *Posterior Analytics* at all; for, without that desire, since he immediately proceeds to identify ἐπιστήμη ἁπλῶς with ἀποδεικτικὴ ἐπιστήμη (71^{b}17 ff.), he could have begun 1. 2 simply by defining 'demonstrative knowledge' in terms of explanation and necessity, noting that this is the sort of knowledge which the sciences aim at (cf. e.g. 74^{b}18–21), and thus dispensed with the novel and otherwise superfluous technical term ἐπιστήμη ἁπλῶς altogether.

[13] These two endoxa about true knowledge make several appearances in the corpus: for the endoxon on explanation see e.g. *Post. An.* 71^{b}30–1, 94^{a}20, *Phys.* 184^{a}12–14, 194^{b}18–20, *Metaph.* 983^{a}25–6, and 994^{b}29–30 (cf. *Meno* 97 E 6–A 8, which is no doubt Aristotle's ultimate source for this specifically philosophical endoxon); and for the more widespread intuition on necessity, see n. 18.

in his next breath to endorse these endoxa (71ᵇ12–13, in **EH2**), the passage in **EH1** does effectively yield two conditions that Aristotle himself believes the state of true or unqualified ἐπιστήμη must satisfy, and hence two conditions that he will be requiring of the ideal state of demonstrative knowledge as well.

As for the two conditions themselves, while there is room for some debate over their precise formulation and force, even on the weakest construction of the passage Aristotle is placing the following two independent and necessary conditions on the state of unqualified knowledge:[14]

> If S possesses unqualified knowledge of the fact that p, then
> (1) S knows that the fact that q is the cause of the fact that p, and
> (2) the fact that p is necessary.[15]

Thus, in this, his official account of true or unqualified ἐπιστήμη, Aristotle places what I shall call an 'explanation condition' (to avoid the more cumbrous but more accurate 'knowledge-of-the-explanation condition') on any cognitive state worthy of the title ἐπιστήμη ἁπλῶς and a 'necessity condition' on any statement that might form the content of that state.[16]

---

[14] That the two conditions are independent is shown not only by the fact that Aristotle introduces them co-ordinately, but also by that fact that non-explicable first principles are necessary and non-necessary singular truths are explicable (see e.g. 2. 11, 93ᵃ36 ff.).

[15] The two conditions could be taken as *jointly sufficient* for unqualified knowledge (as the direction of the conditional statement underlying **EH1** would itself suggest); and they could also be read more strongly as requiring both or merely the second of the following: (1*) knowledge of the explanation why p is *necessary* and (2*) *knowledge* of the fact that p is necessary (which I shall call the 'epistemic reading' of the necessity condition). Fortunately, attempting to settle the involved questions concerning the exact formulation and strength of the conditions Aristotle places on unqualified knowledge would be largely beside the point here, since the anomalous character of ἐπίστασθαι ἁπλῶς in 1. 1 will become manifest even on the most timorous construal of **EH1**. (We shall, however, see reasons for favouring the epistemic reading of the necessity requirement in the discussion of **EH6** in sect. 2.2.)

[16] For the purposes of the present study we need not delve much further into the conception of necessity that Aristotle is working with in **EH1** than to note that **EH5** informs us that necessity entails omnitemporality (but see also appendix B). Further articulation of the explanation condition at this point, however, will prove serviceable later on. From (1) Aristotle plainly invites us to infer the following obvious consequences:

> (1.1) S knows that p (see e.g. 93ᵃ18–19).
> (1.2) S knows that q (see e.g. 71ᵇ20 ff.).

In an Aristotelian demonstration, the explanans q will typically represent the ex-

With this (at least partial) definition of unqualified knowledge in place, Aristotle then exploits a further endoxon (71ᵇ17 ff.), this one concerning the relationship between knowledge and demonstration (φαμὲν καὶ δι᾿ ἀποδείξεως εἰδέναι), in order to unveil the items advertised as the *telos* of both *Analytics* (see *Pr. An.* 24ᵃ10; cf. *Post. An.* 99ᵇ15–17): demonstration (ἀπόδειξις), or the explanatory syllogism, and demonstrative knowledge (ἀποδεικτικὴ ἐπιστήμη), or scientific understanding. Although the point is generally under-appreciated, what is crucial to observe about the introduction of these banner concepts of the *Posterior Analytics* is that Aristotle expressly defines them, not by invoking established philosophical usage or current mathematical practice, but instead by reference to the special concept of unqualified knowledge which he has just explicated in **EH1** (see further n. 21): demonstrative knowledge is knowledge gained through a demonstration (cf. 73ᵃ23), while a demonstration just is a deductive argument that issues in unqualified knowledge (71ᵇ17–22). In this way, then, the three endoxa about true knowledge (i.e. that it involves explanation, necessity, and 'demonstration') are led to converge on one and the same epistemic state, and Aristotle thereby effectively identifies the state of unqualified knowledge with that of demonstrative knowledge. And (to anticipate the argument of Section 2.2 here), with this object attained, he thereafter employs the two locutions ἐπιστήμη ἁπλῶς and ἀποδεικτικὴ ἐπιστήμη virtually interchangeably (see esp. **EH3**, **EH5**, and **EH7**), allowing either expression to flag the ideal state of scientific understanding.[17]

planatory first principles relevant to the explanandum *p*; thus, given the equivalence we are about to see between 'unqualified knowledge' and 'demonstrative knowledge', the requirement in (1.2) amounts to the demand that one know the appropriate first principles which explain why a given demonstrative conclusion is true. The requirement in (1.1), on the other hand, makes explicit the simple idea that *knowing why* a certain fact obtains entails *knowing that* it does.

[17] For ἀποδεικτικὴ ἐπιστήμη (outside of its use to indicate a scientific *discipline*) and related expressions see also 72ᵃ37–8, ᵇ19, 73ᵃ22–3 (in **EH3**), 23, 74ᵃ5, 75ᵃ12, 19, 87ᵇ19, 88ᵃ10–11, and 99ᵇ20 (cf. εἰδέναι δι᾿ ἀποδείξεως at e.g. 84ᵃ4). Although the two expressions clearly carry the same reference, Aristotle seems to favour ἐπιστήμη ἁπλῶς over ἀποδεικτικὴ ἐπιστήμη when he wants either to recall its priority in the order of presentation or to make direct reference back to the foundational definition in **EH1** (see **EH3**, **EH7**, and **EH8**). And, no doubt owing to the ungainliness of both of these modified locutions (as well as the phrase ἐπίστασθαι τὸ διότι—see e.g. 75ᵃ35 and 78ᵃ25–6), Aristotle will also indicate the state of scientific understanding by a bare use of ἐπιστήμη when context makes his intentions clear, as e.g. at 71ᵇ13 (in **EH2**), 19–20, 72ᵇ23, 74ᵇ6, 75ᵇ33, 39, 99ᵇ23–4, and 100ᵇ14; for the use of plain εἰδέναι in this

Thus, since the declared focal points of the *Posterior Analytics*, demonstration and demonstrative knowledge, are actually defined in terms of 'knowing in the unqualified sense', the concept of knowledge heralded by the coinage ἐπίστασθαι ἁπλῶς at the start of 1. 2 emerges as the fundamental epistemic idea in Aristotle's reflections on human cognition, and the text cited above as **EH1** is thereby revealed as the centre of gravity for the epistemological theorizing in the work as a whole. Small wonder, then, that Aristotle would resort to his technical mint on this occasion in order to strike a special expression for the precise and unequivocal communication of a concept so basic to the entire enterprise of the treatise.

2.2 *Aristotle's use of* ἐπίστασθαι ἁπλῶς *outside of* Post. An. *1. 1*

Since Aristotle elected to give the core idea in his epistemology its formal introduction under the escort of the technical coinage ἐπίστασθαι ἁπλῶς, we would naturally expect that when this uncommon and privileged expression appears elsewhere in book 1 it would likewise carry the sense specified in **EH1** and refer to a cognitive state that satisfies the two conditions explicitly placed on unqualified knowledge in its official definition at the start of 1. 2, and thus, in view of 71^{b}16 ff., to a cognitive state identical to demonstrative knowledge or scientific understanding. And, if we put aside the problematic occurrence of ἐπίστασθαι ἁπλῶς in 1. 1 for the time being, this is exactly what we find.

In the following four passages the necessity condition on unqualified knowledge is plainly at work in Aristotle's use of the expression:

EH2 It's clear, then, that knowing [τὸ ἐπίστασθαι] is a state of this sort [i.e. as characterized in **EH1**]; for those who know and those who don't both think they occupy such a state, while those who know actually

---

sense, see most clearly 76^{a}26–8. It is true that, undecorated, ἐπιστήμη and εἰδέναι can also be used to indicate epistemic states that fail to satisfy fully the explanation and necessity conditions on unqualified knowledge (see nn. 11 and 37), as is also true of plain ἀπόδειξις in connection with knowledge-producing arguments (see n. 21); nevertheless—as we shall see for ἐπιστήμη ἁπλῶς in sect. 2.2 and for εἰδέναι ἁπλῶς in appendix A, and as the reader can satisfy herself regarding ἀποδεικτικὴ ἐπιστήμη by consulting the passages cited at the start of this note—at least outside of 1. 1, when Aristotle goes to the trouble of attaching the modifying expressions ἁπλῶς and ἀποδεικτική to ἐπιστήμη or εἰδέναι, as when he attaches ἁπλῶς or ἐπιστημονικός to ἀπόδειξις (see n. 9), he invariably has in mind the special sort of epistemic state whose nature is characterized in the official definition of **EH1**.

do occupy it. Thus the object of <u>knowledge in the unqualified sense</u> [ἐπιστήμη ἁπλῶς] cannot be otherwise. (1. 2, 71ᵇ12–16)

EH3 Given that the object of <u>knowledge in the unqualified sense</u> [ἐπιστήμη ἁπλῶς] cannot be otherwise, the object known by demonstrative knowledge [τὸ ἐπιστητὸν τὸ κατὰ ἀποδεικτικὴν ἐπιστήμην] will have to be necessary. (1. 4, 73ᵃ21–3)

EH4 In connection with <u>the objects of knowledge in the unqualified sense</u> [τῶν ἐπιστητῶν ἁπλῶς] , then, properties said ⟨to belong to their subjects⟩ *per se*—i.e. in the sense that they are constituents in the essence of their subjects or their subjects are constituents in their essence— are true ⟨of their subjects⟩ in virtue of the subjects themselves and by necessity. (1. 4, 73ᵇ16–18)

EH5 It's clear also that, if the premises of the ⟨demonstrative⟩ deduction are universally true [in the strong sense of 'universality', entailing necessity, that is defined in 1. 4], then the conclusion of this sort of demonstration, i.e. 'demonstration' intended in the unqualified sense [τῆς ἁπλῶς εἰπεῖν ἀποδείξεως], must also be true at all times [ἀΐδιον]. Of impermanent facts [τῶν φθαρτῶν], therefore, there is no demonstration, nor is there <u>knowledge in the unqualified sense</u> [ἐπιστήμη ἁπλῶς], but only in a sense like that of accidental knowledge, since they do not hold universally, but only at a certain time and in a certain way. (1. 8, 75ᵇ21–6)

In **EH2**, which immediately follows the introduction of the two requirements on unqualified knowledge in **EH1**, Aristotle appeals to common intuitions in order to support at least the necessity condition on ἐπιστήμη ἁπλῶς.[18] In **EH3**, which opens 1. 4 and launches an extended investigation focused on the necessity condition, Aristotle reaches back to the definition of unqualified knowledge in **EH1** and then transfers the necessity demanded of the objects of ἐπιστήμη ἁπλῶς to the objects of the identical state of demonstrative knowledge, and thereby also to the conclusions of demonstrations. In **EH4**, which comes later in 1. 4, the necessity condition remains to the fore in his thought: returning from a brief digression in which

---

[18] The explicit conclusion at 71ᵇ15–16 points to the fact that the endoxic argument in **EH2** is intended to serve primarily if not exclusively as a defence of the necessity condition. That Aristotle is here appealing to the entire linguistic community and not just to its philosophical sophisticates is borne out by two other appearances of the endoxon on knowledge and necessity, at *Post. An.* 89ᵃ6–9 (note οὐδείς) and *NE* 1139ᵇ19–21 (note πάντες). (Exactly how Aristotle thinks he can get his uncommon necessity condition out of a demotic conception of knowledge which lacks that precise requirement cannot be further entered into here, but see n. 10 above for the general strategy involved.)

he noted a third and fourth sense in which things can be characterized as holding *per se* (73ᵇ5–16), Aristotle identifies his first two types of *per se* predications (73ᵃ34–ᵇ5) as those that are relevant to his study of unqualified or demonstrative knowledge; and his reason for doing so (73ᵃ24–5; cf. 74ᵇ5–11 and 75ᵃ28–31) is that these statements will carry the necessity required of demonstrative premisses if they are to generate the necessary truths that will serve as both the conclusions of demonstrations and the contents of the state of ἐπιστήμη ἁπλῶς.[19] Finally, in **EH5** Aristotle infers from the fact that the premisses of demonstrations are 'universally true' (in the strong sense defined at 73ᵇ26–7), and hence are necessary truths (27–8), the further condition that the necessary demonstrative conclusions derived from those premisses, and hence the objects of unqualified knowledge, must themselves be omnitemporally true (cf. 74ᵇ32–9 and *NE* 1139ᵇ22–4); impermanent facts in the universe— or statements susceptible to change in truth value (see e.g. *Cat.* 4ᵃ22–ᵇ19 and *Metaph.* 1051ᵇ13–17), including, most notably, singular statements whose subjects are mundane sensible particulars (see e.g. *Metaph.* 1039ᵇ27–1040ᵃ7; cf. *Post. An.* 85ᵇ15–18)—are here expressly disqualified as objects of ἐπιστήμη ἁπλῶς.

In all four of the above passages, then, the necessity condition on unqualified knowledge is either explicitly stated or at least operative in what Aristotle does say in connection with the cognitive state designated by ἐπίστασθαι ἁπλῶς; and, while the explanation condition may fail to make its presence immediately felt in these passages, it is clear at least that nothing said about the state of ἐπίστασθαι ἁπλῶς

---

[19] In **EH4** Aristotle is not saying that the *statements* representing the first of these two types of *per se* predication, i.e. primitive propositions predicating essential properties of their subjects, can form the content of a state designated by ἐπιστήμη ἁπλῶς; thus he is not allowing, in violation of the explanation condition, that there can be ἐπιστήμη ἁπλῶς of indemonstrable first principles. Rather, talk of the 'objects' of knowledge in Aristotle is often host to 'subject–statement' ambiguity, referring either to the statements known or to the subjects of those statements (cf. 1. 33, 89ᵃ23–37, where Aristotle explicitly calls attention to this ambiguity); and it is clearly the latter that are being described in **EH4** as 'the objects of knowledge in the unqualified sense': Aristotle is here contrasting the universal *subjects* of scientific statements—and hence the bearers of '*per se* properties' (τὰ λεγόμενα καθ' αὑτά) in the first two senses introduced in 1. 4—with the individual substances and events which he introduced in connection with the two non-scientific forms of *per se* predication treated in the excursus preceding **EH4**, since those singular entities are obviously unsuitable subjects of the universal and necessary truths apprehended by ἐπιστήμη ἁπλῶς. (Given this reading of **EH4**, we can happily sidestep here the vexed question of whether Aristotle's second form of scientific *per se* predication will furnish demonstrations with premisses, conclusions, or both.)

in **EH2–5** is incompatible with that second requirement from the formal definition of unqualified knowledge in **EH1**.

In the following passage from 1. 3 Aristotle is drawing the conclusion of the second limb of a sceptical regress argument against the possibility of knowledge which would, if sound, plainly render unattainable the ideal form of cognition whose nature he has just been analysing in 1. 2, i.e. unqualified knowledge or scientific understanding; and although the necessity condition on unqualified knowledge may not directly determine Aristotle's use of ἐπίστασθαι ἁπλῶς in this occurrence (which is not to deny, however, that it acts as a strong background constraint—see Appendix B and n. 24), the explanation condition, as we shall see, turns out to provide the principle that licenses the inference drawn concerning unqualified knowledge:

> **EH6** And ⟨the skeptics conclude that⟩ if you cannot know [εἰδέναι] the primary truths [as has just been argued], then the statements which follow from them cannot be <u>known in the unqualified sense [ἐπίστασθαι ἁπλῶς]</u>, nor [οὐδέ] ⟨known⟩ properly speaking [κυρίως], but only hypothetically [ἐξ ὑποθέσεως]: ⟨you could know merely the conditional statement that⟩ *if* those ⟨primary⟩ statements are true, ⟨then their consequences must be true as well⟩. (1. 3, 72^{b}13–14)

Now, it has generally been taken for granted that the modifying expressions ἁπλῶς and κυρίως on ἐπίστασθαι in the apodosis of **EH6** function as synonymous alternatives for signalling precisely the same sort of epistemic state, with κυρίως being merely epexegetic on ἁπλῶς (see e.g. Philoponus and Mignucci, each ad 71^{b}9). But, as I shall show here, perforce by extended argument, the implication in **EH6** should instead be read as leading to the denial of two (at least conceptually) distinct forms of cognition: the explanatory form of cognition which is defined in **EH1** ('scientific understanding') as well as a form of cognition that can be viewed in isolation from the explanation condition on unqualified knowledge (and which I shall often refer to simply as 'knowledge'). In other words, Aristotle is best understood here to be reworking the conclusion of the sceptics' original regress argument against knowledge in a more common, non-explanatory sense, indicated here by ⟨ἐπίστασθαι⟩ κυρίως, so that it also expressly applies to his own explanatory conception of scientific understanding, indicated here, as in **EH1**, by ἐπίστασθαι ἁπλῶς.[20]

Let me begin my defence of this unconventional reading of the regress, and hence this construal of the expression ἐπίστασθαι ἁπλῶς here in 1. 3, by delineating the three possible constructions (unmarked in the commentary tradition) that can be placed on the conclusion of the argument in **EH6**. First, as a strictly linguistic matter, the two expressions ἐπίστασθαι ἁπλῶς and ἐπίστασθαι κυρίως could serve here as synonymous alternatives for indicating the same epistemic state, as most commentators assume, or they could be indicating two distinct forms of cognition. If (1) they are interchangeable alternatives, then we face two possibilities: either (*a*) the two expressions indicate knowledge in a non-explanatory form, in which case the modifying expression ἁπλῶς attached to ἐπίστασθαι, instead of serving to signal the special epistemic state defined in **EH1**, would function here in 1. 3 (much as it does in 1. 1 according to some commentators, as we shall see in Section 2.3) simply to expunge the deprecatory qualification ἐξ ὑποθέσεως, leaving behind a form of ἐπιστήμη which, while non-hypothetical, need not also fulfil the explanation condition on scientific understanding; or (*b*) they are both being used to indicate the specific state of scientific understanding, in which case ἐπίστασθαι ἁπλῶς here in 1. 3 would carry the sense given the expression in its official definition at the start of 1. 2. If, on the other hand, (2) the two epistemic expressions in the apodosis of **EH6** are being used to indicate different states (or different aspects of the same state), then, most naturally, ἐπίστασθαι ἁπλῶς would still indicate scientific understanding, while ἐπίστασθαι κυρίως would indicate the non-explanatory state of knowledge.

The preceding three linguistic possibilities match up with three possible ways of reading Aristotle's explicit presentation of the regress argument that leads to the conclusion in **EH6**. To see this, it should be noted first that the text of 1. 3 will not permit a regress argument designed to undermine only the possibility of scientific

---

[20] That Aristotle can insinuate his own epistemological thoughts into his presentation of the sceptics' argument is strongly suggested by **EH6** itself; for if Aristotle were not filtering the sceptics' argument through his own epistemological vocabulary and concepts, then we would be obliged to think that the sceptics had themselves couched their conclusion in terms of ἐπίστασθαι ἁπλῶς and ἐπίστασθαι κυρίως, which is highly unlikely. This point will suffice as a necessary reminder that in our initial approach to Aristotle's formulation of the sceptical regress argument in 1. 3 we should be prepared to meet with anything from duplication of the sceptics' actual wording to an adaptation of their argument for his own philosophical ends.

understanding; rather, for reasons given below (see esp. n. 25), a regress in 1. 3 directed against scientific understanding would have to depend in part on premises that are sufficient by themselves to generate a regress against the possibility of knowledge as well. Now, one way to get a conclusion against scientific understanding from a regress against knowledge would be to make use of the obvious epistemological principle that knowing why a statement is true entails knowing that it is true (see n. 16). As it turns out, however, the text bears no trace of an inference from the impossibility of knowing a certain statement to the impossibility of having scientific understanding of that same statement: **EH6** is the only place in 1. 3 where such an inference might occur, but Aristotle there neither derives a conclusion about ἐπίστασθαι ἁπλῶς from a conclusion about ἐπίστασθαι κυρίως nor vice versa; instead, each of the two (perhaps identical) conclusions in the apodosis descends directly from the premiss in the protasis of **EH6**. So, although Aristotle's explicit presentation of the regress might take any of the three possible forms to be introduced presently, the argument at work in the text will take one of only two possible forms: either it will rely exclusively on premises directed against the possibility of knowledge, yielding (1*a*) above, or it will draw on additional premises about scientific understanding other than the principle that knowing why entails knowing that, yielding either (1*b*) or (2).

Now, the first possibility for understanding Aristotle's handling of the regress in 1. 3 is this: in presenting his formulation of the regress, Aristotle is concerned solely with the crucial point about the impossibility of knowledge, and he leaves it to his audience to draw for themselves the simple consequence for the state of scientific understanding that would follow from this conclusion in conjunction with the principle that knowing why entails knowing that. In that case, since the conclusion against scientific understanding would fall outside the text, our two expressions ἐπίστασθαι ἁπλῶς and ἐπίστασθαι κυρίως would both be indicating the state of knowledge (= 1*a*).

Alternatively, Aristotle could be concerned to make explicit the specific consequences that the regress argument has for the explanatory form of cognition which he has just been treating at length in 1. 2. In that case, since, as was mentioned, he could not be relying on the simple inference from the impossibility of knowledge to the impossibility of scientific understanding, he would have to be introducing into his formulation of the regress certain additional premisses concerning scientific understanding that are necessary to derive a co-ordinate conclusion against this epistemic state from the sceptical rejection of the possibility of knowing first principles in the protasis of **EH6**. And, on this interpretation of the regress in 1. 3, we would still be left with two possibilities for understanding the apodosis of **EH6**: either Aristotle focuses there exclusively on his conclusion against scientific understanding, leaving the coordinate conclusion against knowledge to be drawn by his audience, in which case the two expressions ἐπίστασθαι ἁπλῶς and ἐπίστασθαι κυρίως would both indicate scientific understanding (= 1*b*); or, what would be far more likely, he explicitly draws the collateral conclusions against each of the two states of knowledge and scientific understanding, in which case, again, ἐπίστασθαι ἁπλῶς would naturally indicate scientific understanding and ἐπίστασθαι κυρίως the state of knowledge (= 2).

Thus, in view of this preliminary survey of the territory, if I am to establish that the occurrence of ἐπίστασθαι ἁπλῶς in **EH6** conforms to the official definition of the expression in **EH1**, I must show that in his formulation of the argument in 1. 3 Aristotle does in fact supplement the premisses necessary for a regress against knowledge with the additional principles needed to derive an explicit and collateral conclusion against the explanatory state of scientific understanding. And, while I need not show here that ἐπίστασθαι ἁπλῶς and ἐπίστασθαι κυρίως indicate distinct forms of cognition in **EH6** (i.e. decide whether (1*b*) or, as I believe, (2) answers to what explicitly occurs in the text), treatment of this issue will serve to clinch an already strong case.

So let us turn now to consider the principles about demonstration and cognition that are needed to generate a regress argument that exclusively targets non-explanatory knowledge, as well as the more inclusive set of premisses that is required for collateral conclusions against both knowledge and scientific understanding, and then try to ascertain which set of premisses is most in keeping with **EH6** and its argumentative context.

First of all, whether its explicit target is knowledge, understanding, or both, the regress argument in 1. 3 depends on the following general conception of what a demonstration is:

D A demonstration is an argument that derives its conclusion from premisses that are prior in a linear ordering.

This definitional premiss in the regress argument presupposes that the statements which can appear in demonstrations form sets that are linearly ordered in terms of priority and posteriority (see esp. $72^{b}9$–10), a point evidently shared by Aristotle and the sceptics, though not with the advocates of circular demonstration whose position he takes up in the second part of 1. 3 ($72^{b}25$–$73^{a}20$). Yet the principle in **D**, reflecting the lack of specificity in Aristotle's brisk presentation of the regress, leaves open the question whether priority here is to be understood merely in terms of *justificatory priority* ('J-priority') or in terms of both J-priority and *explanatory priority* ('E-priority'). We can define these two notions as follows:

p has J-priority over q iff knowledge that p is required for knowledge that q, but not vice versa.

p has E-priority over q iff p explains why q is true, but not vice versa.

Now, if the explicit formulation of regress in 1. 3 sets its sights exclusively on knowledge in some non-explanatory sense, then the principle in **D** should require only J-priority from demonstrative premisses, whereas if the argument at work in the text is also meant to encompass the explanatory state of scientific understanding, along with the Aristotelian ἀποδείξεις which are meant to generate that state, then **D** must obviously embrace the notion of E-priority as well.

Let us begin by taking up the considerations that favour reading **D** as carrying the idea of E-priority. First, the initial objection against circular demonstration that Aristotle advances shortly afterwards in 1. 3 (at $72^{b}25$–32) specifically turns on the idea of an explanatory ordering of demonstrative statements (see the discussion of **EH8** in Appendix A for defence of this point and for corroboration of the two that follow). Moreover, the occurrence in that context of the expression εἰδέναι ἁπλῶς ($72^{b}30$, in **EH8**), whose sense should naturally be given to our earlier occurrence of ἐπίστασθαι ἁπλῶς in **EH6**, plainly serves to indicate the specific and explanatory form of cognition that is defined in **EH1** (see n. 10). Likewise, in that same context, the occurrences of ἀποδεικνύναι ἁπλῶς at $72^{b}25$ and 31 clearly betoken the presence of Aristotle's proprietary and

explanatory conception of demonstration (see n. 9). Finally, since
explanatoriness furnishes the standard of priority that Aristotle invoked in his formal account of what a demonstration is at 1. 2,
71^{b}19–32 (see esp. 71^{b}31), we would naturally expect this same
standard to lie behind the talk of demonstrative priority in his presentation of the regress argument in 1. 3, as well—or at least this
would be the expectation if we could assume, as might seem reasonable, that in his presentation of the regress, as in both 1. 2 and
his first criticism of circular demonstrations in 1. 3, Aristotle is
working with his own explanatory conception of demonstrations.

But against that assumption, and as a first consideration in favour
of taking **D** to be bearing or at least utilizing only a notion of J-
priority, it must be observed that at this stage in 1. 3 Aristotle
purports to be rehearsing, not his own views, but the argument
of certain unnamed (and to us unknown) sceptics; and we cannot simply assume that these anonymous thinkers, even though
they too evidently committed themselves to the abstract principle
in **D**, employed the term ἀπόδειξις in precisely Aristotle's sense.
On the contrary, from a historical point of view, we should find it
more plausible to think that the regress argument, as it was originally developed and as Aristotle found it, was being put to the
use to which sceptics have regularly put it, namely, to undermine
arguments designed merely to justify belief in the truth of their
conclusions (i.e. ἀποδείξεις in the larger and more common sense of
'proofs', whether explanatory or not, and perhaps even embracing
non-deductive forms of argument) rather than those designed to explain, or designed also to explain, why their conclusions themselves
are true.[21] In that case, then, the original regress would have relied

---

[21] In support of the idea that there are these two conceptions of demonstrations
behind the discussion in 1. 3, note that the endoxon which broaches the concept
of ἀπόδειξις in 1. 2 is introduced by the collectivizing 'we say' (φαμέν: 71^{b}17), while
Aristotle's official definition is introduced by the privatizing 'I say' (λέγω: 71^{b}18 and
19). This is a powerful indication that Aristotle there is taking over a common view
about the relationship between demonstration and knowledge in some pre-existing
and looser senses (note the generic εἰδέναι at 71^{b}17) and appropriating it for his own
very special and precise concepts of demonstration and unqualified knowledge (note
the return to ἐπίστασθαι at 71^{b}18–25), just as he had done earlier with the common
intuition about the relationship between knowledge and necessity when formulating
his special necessity condition on unqualified knowledge at the start of 1. 2 (see n. 18).
Indeed, it is precisely because both ἐπιστήμη and ἀπόδειξις were already circulating in
more relaxed senses that Aristotle attaches the modifier ἁπλῶς to these terms when he
feels the need to send an unambiguous signal that he is giving them the precise and
technical values they were assigned by their formal definitions in 1. 2. Moreover,

on a version of **D** that required only J-priority from demonstrative premises; and, if Aristotle is faithfully recording the sceptics' argument, as might also seem reasonable, then the regress as it appears in 1. 3 would likewise be working only with a justificatory conception of demonstrations. Second, even if the first limb of the regress (72^{b}7–11) is thought to be neutral on our question (see n. 25; but cf. the remarks on **K$_d$**→**K$_p$** below), Aristotle's second and third objections to circular demonstrations (72^{b}32–73^{a}20) have little to do with explanatory considerations; indeed, in the case of the second objection at least (72^{b}32–73^{a}6), it is manifest that Aristotle focuses his attack specifically on the idea that circular demonstrations can justify claims to know their several conclusions, regardless of the explanatory status of their premises (see n. 43). Finally, at 1. 2 71^{b}33–72^{a}5 Aristotle himself alerted us to an ambiguity in talk of 'priority', remarking that it can refer not only to E-priority ('what is prior without qualification') but also to at least a certain kind of J-priority ('what is prior and better known to us'), where these two types of priority are thought of, paradigmatically at any rate, as inversely correlated, with scientific first principles being primary in the order of explanation and simple perceptual truths claiming primacy in the order of justification (72^{a}1–5). And, having distinguished these two types of priority, Aristotle went on at the end of 1. 2 (72^{a}25–^{b}4) to require that the premises of his own demonstrations be prior to their conclusions, not only in the explanatory sense noted in his initial account of demonstrations at 71^{b}20–33, but also in at least some sort of justificatory sense as well (a sense which he can express through the phrase 'what is better known

and what is most significant, within 1. 3 itself (72^{b}27–32) Aristotle clears up the epistemological confusion that could arise from failing to keep his technical sense of 'demonstration' (marked by ἀπόδειξις ἁπλῶς) separate from a less stringent use of the expression; this looser usage, unencumbered by the requirement of E-priority, is evidently that which is observed by the advocates of circular demonstration, and certainly that which is implied by the objection which Aristotle tries to forestall at 72^{b}28–32 (see the discussion of **EH8** in appendix A). (For other lax uses of ἀπόδειξις in the *Posterior Analytics* see e.g. 78^{a}29–30, 35–6, 87^{b}5, and 98^{b}20, where in each case the explanatory requirement on Aristotelian demonstrations is waived.) Finally, it should also be observed that there is no hint in the sceptical regresses alluded to at *Metaph.* 1011^{a}3–13 (cf. 1006^{a}5–11) that the 'demonstrations' called for by those sceptics are supposed to meet explanatory requirements; on the contrary, the basic statements there at issue (e.g. 'this wine is sweet' and 'I am awake') obviously do have explanations—what such statements are thought to lack are more evident facts that could serve as premises in arguments designed to justify claims to know them.

without qualification').[22] On pain of contradiction, however, the special sort of J-priority that Aristotle demands for his demonstrative premises at the end of 1. 2 (let us call it 'top-down' J-priority), unlike the 'bottom-up' form of J-priority mentioned at 71^b33-72^a5 (in opposition not only to E-priority ($\pi\rho\acute{o}\tau\epsilon\rho\sigma\nu$ $\acute{a}\pi\lambda\hat{\omega}s$) but also to top-down J-priority ($\gamma\nu\omega\rho\iota\mu\acute{\omega}\tau\epsilon\rho\sigma\nu$ $\acute{a}\pi\lambda\hat{\omega}s$), as the occurrence of $\gamma\nu$-$\omega\rho\iota\mu\acute{\omega}\tau\epsilon\rho\sigma\nu$ at 72^b1 subsequently makes clear), must be directly correlated with E-priority.[23] It turns out, then, that the premises of an Aristotelian demonstration are going to be prior to their conclusions not only in terms of explanation and understanding but also in terms of (at least some form of) justification and knowledge, with these two forms of priority understood as entailing one another.

[22] The switch in Aristotle's use of epistemic verbs from $\dot{\epsilon}\pi\acute{\iota}\sigma\tau\alpha\sigma\theta\alpha\iota$ at 71^b9-25 to the more generic $\epsilon\dot{\iota}\delta\acute{\epsilon}\nu\alpha\iota$ at 72^a25-37 is indicative of the turn in his attention away from considerations of explanation and towards those of justification. Moreover, the 'unpersuadability' condition at 72^b1-4 (in **EH7**) plainly bespeaks an interest in the justification of knowledge claims. But the most telling sign of the shift in Aristotle's focus at the end of 1. 2 to this justificatory requirement on demonstrations (cf. *NE* 1139^b31-5) is furnished by the emergence there of the verb $\pi\iota\sigma\tau\epsilon\acute{\upsilon}\epsilon\iota\nu$ ('to be rationally convinced'), as well as by the newly announced demand that the premises of demonstrations be known 'more' ($\mu\hat{\alpha}\lambda\lambda\sigma\nu$) than their conclusions.

It should be noted here that this last demand represents only one of (at least) two (and perhaps three) epistemological requirements carried by the $\gamma\nu\omega\rho\iota\mu\acute{\omega}\tau\epsilon\rho\sigma\nu$ ($\acute{a}\pi\lambda\hat{\omega}s$) condition at 71^b21, which was cashed out at 71^b31-3 in terms of *fore*knowledge (cf. 72^a27-8) rather than *more* knowledge (cf. 72^b1). And it should also be observed that the requirement of 'foreknowledge' at 72^a27-8, unlike that of 'more knowledge' which immediately follows it, need not entail that demonstrative premises have J-priority over their conclusions; the requirement could instead be read—less plausibly here (cf. 72^a32-7), but more plausibly at 71^b31-3—simply as a consequence of the explanation condition on scientific understanding (see (1.2) in n. 16), in which case (fore)knowledge of demonstrative premises would be necessary, not for knowing *that* their conclusions are true, as J-priority requires, but only for knowing *why* they are true. Yet, since Aristotle does also demand that demonstrative premises have at least a certain form of J-priority over their conclusions, his talk of 'foreknowledge' can be used to express this additional, justificatory requirement as well, as it clearly does at 72^a32-7. It turns out, then, that the epistemic $\gamma\nu\omega\rho\iota\mu\acute{\omega}\tau\epsilon\rho\sigma\nu$ condition that Aristotle places on knowledge of demonstrative premises at 71^b21 could be carrying three at least conceptually distinct requirements, namely, the 'more knowledge' condition and two different 'foreknowledge' requirements: one for (some form of) knowing *that* and one for knowing *why* demonstrable conclusions are true (cf. $\mathbf{K}_d\rightarrow\mathbf{K}_p$ or $\mathbf{U}_d\rightarrow\mathbf{K}_p$ below). But, although conceptually distinct, these three conditions are treated by Aristotle, at least paradigmatically, as extensionally equivalent—see appendix B.

[23] For further discussion of the relationship between Aristotle's two accounts of J-priority see appendix B below. As I argue there, bottom-up J-priority should be understood as priority in the order of justifying claims to know that a certain statement *is true*, while top-down J-priority should be understood as priority in the order of justifying claims to know that a certain statement *is necessarily true*.

Thus, even if Aristotle is operating with the proprietary conception of demonstration that he developed in 1. 2, and hence is taking the principle in **D** to be imposing the dual demand of E-priority and top-down J-priority on demonstrative premisses, the regress argument which he formulates in 1. 3 could still hinge only on the notion of J-priority. And this possibility might be thought most probable since, as was noted, it is the requirement of J-priority rather than the demand of E-priority that is more likely to have been common to the respective conceptions of demonstration held by Aristotle and the sceptics whose regress argument he purports to be developing.[24]

We see, then, that consideration of the principle in **D** must ultimately leave us reluctant to declare that the regress in 1. 3 takes

[24] This is not to suggest that the original regress would have relied on Aristotle's top-down conception of J-priority, and thus, like Aristotle's formulation, would have targeted claims to know *necessary truths*. Rather, what seems most likely is that Aristotle was confronted by a simple sceptical regress argument that operated with an undifferentiated notion of J-priority, and, in bringing this argument to bear on the special form of cognition of interest to him in the *Posterior Analytics*, he simply ignores the differences between the ideas about J-priority that inform his and the sceptics' respective conceptions of what a demonstration is (as I too shall do in the body of this paper); for what is most significant about the regress argument for him here in 1. 3 is that it constitutes a challenge to the basic and general idea of *linear justification*, regardless of both the metaphysical direction in which the assumed linearity tends and the modal status of the statements known through this non-looping manner of justification.

That in his own presentation of the regress Aristotle restricts his focus to top-down J-priority, thereby limiting his concern to the possibility of some form of *scientific cognition*, is shown by the fact that the primitive statements he envisages as regress-stoppers are not the simple truths of perception (cf. 72^{a}1–5 and 100^{a}3–11) but causally basic, real definitions—note ὅρους at 72^{b}26 (cf. 90^{b}24–7) and τὰ ἄμεσα at 72^{b}19 and 22 (cf. 72^{a}7–8). That the scientific cognition at issue in 1. 3 is directed at *necessary* truths is shown by the direct reference at 72^{b}30–1 (in **EH8**) to the official definition of unqualified knowledge in **EH1**. And, finally, that this scientific cognition involves *knowledge* of necessary truths is borne out not only by the **EH8–EH1** connection (assuming **EH1** does espouse the epistemic reading of the necessity condition—see appendix B), but also by Aristotle's failure to note that the sceptic's general rejection of *knowledge* which they derive from their regress against *demonstrative knowledge* could be resisted, not only for the reason given at 72^{b}18–25, but also on the grounds that, even in the absence of demonstration, induction, as well as other forms of argument relying on bottom-up J-priority, enables us to *know* the truth of universal statements that in fact represent demonstrable conclusions (cf. 72^{b}28–30); Aristotle's silence on this point is intelligible if he is concerned here with knowledge of the *necessity* of such statements, since this sort of knowledge is something which these non-demonstrative forms of argument cannot (at least as a rule) provide. (Granted, a regress argument could easily be redeployed against the idea that induction and other forms of inference relying on bottom-up J-priority are capable of justifying any sort of knowledge claim; but, as I shall have to show elsewhere, Aristotle has already effectively defused this bottom-up version of the justificatory regress at 71^{a}11–17.)

aim solely at knowledge; for, although there is some reason to think that the principle utilizes only the concept of J-priority, the idea that explanatory considerations also have a role to play in Aristotle's formulation of the argument is not without good support of its own. Thus, in order to determine the precise sense of ἐπίστασθαι ἁπλῶς in **EH6**, we shall have to go further and examine the remaining premises that would be needed to generate regress arguments both against the single state of knowledge and against the epistemic pair of knowledge and scientific understanding.

If the regress argument of 1. 3 is explicitly attacking only the possibility of knowledge in a non-explanatory sense, then its conclusion will be derived from **D** (which will be understood as bearing the idea of J-priority) together with the following two premises about the relationship between knowledge and demonstration:

K→K$_d$ If you have knowledge of a statement, then your knowledge of that statement must come by way of demonstration.

K$_d$→K$_p$ If your knowledge of a statement comes by a way of demonstration, then you must know the premises of that demonstration.

If, on the other hand, the argument at work in the text is also meant to cover scientific understanding, then it depends on the two principles above (with a qualification to be introduced below regarding **K$_d$→K$_p$**),[25] along with **D** (understood as also carrying the idea of

---

[25] A regress against scientific understanding could be generated more parsimoniously by dropping both **K→K$_d$** and **K$_d$→K$_p$** and then conjoining **U→U$_d$** with the following replacement for **U$_d$→K$_p$**:

U$_d$→U$_p$ If your scientific understanding of a statement comes by way of demonstration, then you must have *scientific understanding* of the premises of that demonstration.

But it is hard to square this version of the regress with Aristotle's response at 72^{b}18–25, since his solution would then consist in rejecting **U→U$_d$** and declaring that we can have *scientific understanding* of indemonstrable first principles; yet numerous obstacles stand in the way of this view of his response to the regress, including the fact that Aristotle commits himself to **U→U$_d$** by identifying unqualified knowledge with demonstrative knowledge in 1. 2. (Aristotle is, however, presumably committed to **U$_d$→U$_p$** for premises that are themselves demonstrable from statements prior in the order of explanation; and it is worth noting that this restricted version of **U$_d$→U$_p$**, together with **U→U$_d$** and **D**, is sufficient to foreclose the possibility of scientific understanding on the hypothesis of the first limb of the regress, which treats the sets of linearly ordered demonstrative premises as having infinite members.)

E-priority), as well as the following two premisses about the relationship between understanding, knowledge, and demonstration:

$U \rightarrow U_d$ If you have scientific understanding of a statement, then your scientific understanding of that statement must come by way of demonstration.

$U_d \rightarrow K_p$ If your scientific understanding of a statement comes by way of demonstration, then you must *know* the premisses of that demonstration.

Let us now try to decide which set of premisses best answers to Aristotle's condensed presentation of the regress in 1. 3.

First of all, we should note that the statement in $K \rightarrow K_d$ plainly corresponds to the key principle at 72^b12-13 ($\phi\alpha\sigma\grave{\iota}\nu \langle\tau\grave{o} \delta\iota' \, \dot{\alpha}\pi o\delta\epsilon\acute{\iota}\xi\epsilon\omega\varsigma$ $\dot{\epsilon}\pi\acute{\iota}\sigma\tau\alpha\sigma\theta\alpha\iota\rangle \, \epsilon\hat{\iota}\nu\alpha\iota \, \tau\grave{o} \, \dot{\epsilon}\pi\acute{\iota}\sigma\tau\alpha\sigma\theta\alpha\iota \, \mu\acute{o}\nu o\nu$), which is the premiss Aristotle will go on to reject in his solution to the regress at 72^b18-25, where he counters the sceptics with the claim that demonstration is unnecessary for *knowledge* of first principles (cf. n. 25). (Although Aristotle will reject $K \rightarrow K_d$ in an unrestricted form, 72^a25-6 commits him to the principle for some form of knowledge, and not merely for scientific understanding, of *demonstrable* statements.) The absence of explanatory considerations from the sceptical requirement that all 'knowledge' be demonstrative is borne out by, among several other considerations, the fact that this requirement is shared between the sceptics and the advocates of circular demonstration (72^b15-16); for it is highly implausible that the latter group would have required that a circular demonstration explain and produce scientific understanding of its several conclusions, rather than merely justify and yield knowledge of them, since otherwise these thinkers would have left themselves badly exposed to the easy objection of 72^b25-32, which does stem from the Aristotelian demand that demonstrations explain (see Appendix A on **EH8**).

In comparison with $K \rightarrow K_d$, its yoke-fellow in $K_d \rightarrow K_p$ has a less secure position in Aristotle's presentation of the second limb of the regress. Although (given the points about $K \rightarrow K_d$ in the preceding paragraph) this principle undoubtedly lies behind 72^b8-10 in the first limb of the argument, and although it would ultimately be needed in the second limb to block the possibility of *knowing* demonstrable conclusions (as well as the possibility of having scientific understanding of demonstrable conclusions whose premisses are themselves demonstrable), $K_d \rightarrow K_p$ is completely unnecessary to derive the statement in the protasis of **EH6** that knowledge of first principles is impossible, which is a point that follows directly from **D** and $\mathbf{K} \rightarrow \mathbf{K_d}$ by themselves (cf. 72^b11-13); and, for this reason, $\mathbf{K_d} \rightarrow \mathbf{K_p}$ would also be unnecessary to derive an explicit conclusion in **EH6** against the possibility of having *scientific understanding* of the immediate consequences of explanatory first principles. But if the entire conditional in $\mathbf{K_d} \rightarrow \mathbf{K_p}$ does makes an explicit appearance in Aristotle's presentation of the second limb of the regress, it would appear in **EH6** in the form of what is effectively its contrapositive ('If you don't *know* the first principles, then you cannot *know* anything by way of demonstration'). And at least the consequent of $\mathbf{K_d} \rightarrow \mathbf{K_p}$ does seem to occur in negated form as the protasis of **EH6** (εἰ δὲ μὴ ἔστι τὰ πρῶτα εἰδέναι); for the verb εἰδέναι, making its only appearance in the argument, is evidently used advisedly there for conveying the more generic notion of *knowledge* to characterize the sort of non-explanatory cognition we need in connection with first principles. (Aristotle's reluctance to characterize our cognition of first principles as ἐπιστήμη is likewise borne out by the generic ἄγνωστος at 72^b12, as well as by the equally generic γνωρίζειν at $^b24-5$, for whose non-ingressive sense—which, incidentally, dashes hopes of finding a faculty of 'intuition' in 1. 3—see ἡ γνωρίζουσα ἕξις at 99^b18; note also the use of ἀρχὴ ἐπιστήμης in contrast to ἐπιστήμη at 72^b23-4; cf. 100^b12-14.) As for the antecedent of $\mathbf{K_d} \rightarrow \mathbf{K_p}$, it would appear in negated form in the apodosis of **EH6** if either or both of the expressions ἐπίστασθαι ἁπλῶς or ἐπίστασθαι κυρίως served there to indicate a form of knowledge that is being viewed as independent of the explanation condition. But, whether or not $\mathbf{K_d} \rightarrow \mathbf{K_p}$ actually surfaces in his explicit presentation of the second limb of the regress, this is certainly a principle to which Aristotle is committed (at least for some form of knowledge); for it is tantamount to the requirement of (top-down) J-priority that he places on demonstrative premises at the end of 1. 2, and it therefore effectively represents one instance of the general principle on priority in inferential knowledge acquisition with which he opens the *Posterior Analytics* (71^a1-2).

If we now turn to the additional premises needed to generate a regress that also explicitly targets the possibility of scientific understanding, we can first simply remind ourselves that the statement in $\mathbf{U} \rightarrow \mathbf{U_d}$ represents an obvious consequence of the formal identification Aristotle effects in the first part of 1. 2 between unqualified knowledge, with its explanation condition, and demonstrative knowledge. He could therefore easily insert this principle into his formulation of the regress through a regulation use of ἐπίστασθαι ἁπλῶς in the apodosis of **EH6**.

As for the principle in $U_d \to K_p$, it has much the same status with respect to the text as does its counterpart $K_d \to K_p$, which it closely resembles. For reasons noted above in connection with $K_d \to K_p$, then, (1) if the entire conditional in $U_d \to K_p$ does play a part in Aristotle's version of the regress, it would appear in **EH6** in the form of what is effectively its contrapositive ('If you don't *know* the first principles, then you cannot have *scientific understanding* of any statement by way of demonstration'); (2) the consequent of $U_d \to K_p$, identical to that of $K_d \to K_p$, evidently appears in negated form in the protasis of **EH6**; and (3) the antecedent of $U_d \to K_p$ would occur negated in the apodosis of **EH6** if either or both of the expressions ἐπίστασθαι ἁπλῶς and ἐπίστασθαι κυρίως serve there to indicate the specific state of scientific understanding. The principle in $U_d \to K_p$ is itself, as we saw (n. 16), a simple consequence of the explanation condition placed on unqualified knowledge in **EH1**, and thus represents in effect yet another instance of the general principle on priority in inferential knowledge acquisition which opens the *Posterior Analytics*. Like its companion in $U \to U_d$, then, $U_d \to K_p$ is a basic epistemological principle plainly articulated in 1. 2, and Aristotle could therefore inject both of these principles into the conclusion of the regress argument in **EH6** through the simple expedient of employing ἐπίστασθαι ἁπλῶς there in a manner faithfully adhering to the official definition of the expression in **EH1**.

Thus, from this examination of the premises that might go into Aristotle's version of the regress in 1. 3, we see that we still cannot exclude the possibility that the argument has scientific understanding as an explicit target. The argument could be read as attacking knowledge exclusively only if we are prepared to say that $K_d \to K_p$ but not $U_d \to K_p$ is at work in generating the apodosis of **EH6**, and hence only if we are willing to reject the idea that the expression ἐπίστασθαι ἁπλῶς there carries the sense officially assigned to it at the start of 1. 2.[26] But, although my discussion to this stage has

---

[26] It might be thought that we could assign ἐπίστασθαι ἁπλῶς its official meaning while still denying that $U_d \to K_p$ plays a role in Aristotle's reasoning were we to say that the argument he presents depends solely on his conception of top-down J-priority; for $K_d \to K_p$ would then suffice to preclude satisfaction of the epistemic

remained largely neutral on this lexical question, we should now admit to ourselves that, other things being equal (and we have seen already that they are at least equal here in 1. 3), we must assign this occurrence of the expression the sense we have found it bears in the surrounding chapters 1. 2 (**EH1** and **EH2**—see below for **EH7**) and 1. 4 (**EH3** and **EH4**), as well as the sense carried by its official synonym εἰδέναι ἁπλῶς, which appears shortly after in 1. 3 itself (**EH8**). Given the weight of these nearby parallels, then, along with the strong expectation that Aristotle would want to register in the text the consequences that the regress would have for the explanatory form of cognition which he introduced at the start of 1. 2, we must finally conclude that ἐπίστασθαι ἁπλῶς in **EH6** does indicate the state of scientific understanding, and that what is lying behind the use of the expression in this occurrence is the explanation condition on unqualified knowledge from **EH1**.

But we can gain further support for this reading of **EH6** by raising the question whether ἐπίστασθαι κυρίως likewise serves to indicate the state of scientific understanding. And our difficulty in deciding whether $K_d \rightarrow K_p$ or $U_d \rightarrow K_p$ represents the premiss that Aristotle relies upon in generating the apodosis of **EH6**, as well as our earlier inability to decide between the justificatory and explanatory readings of the principle in **D**, now tells in favour of allowing the second of the two epistemic expressions that appear in the conclusion of the regress to indicate knowledge in a non-explanatory sense; for, on this interpretation, we can say that Aristotle's failure to specify the sort of priority at work in **D** was deliberate: he wants to keep this principle about demonstration sufficiently general to cover both E-priority and J-priority so that in the apodosis of **EH6** he can draw two separate conclusions from the regress argument—the one denying the possibility of scientific understanding, the other deny-

---

version of the necessity condition, and this alone, regardless of the explanation condition, would undermine the possibility of scientific understanding. Now, the first thing to note about this objection is that it concedes what is the most important point for the overall purpose of this study, namely, that ἐπίστασθαι ἁπλῶς here in 1. 3 carries the sense officially assigned to it at the start of 1. 2; for on this reading, while the necessity condition would actually determine Aristotle's use of the expression in this case, what he says about unqualified knowledge would be perfectly in keeping with the explanation condition as well. As we shall see below, however, there is actually no need to plump for one or the other of the explanation and necessity conditions, since Aristotle is best understood to be relying on both in drawing the conclusion of **EH6**; and, on this most preferred reading, it will be the explanation condition that determines his use of ἐπίστασθαι ἁπλῶς here.

ing the possibility of knowledge in a non-explanatory form. And it should be noted that a double inference of this sort is made all the easier by the fact that the key premisses needed for sceptical conclusions against each of these epistemic states (i.e. $U_d \rightarrow K_p$ and $K_d \rightarrow K_p$) share the selfsame consequent, namely, the very statement which gets negated in the protasis of **EH6** by the sceptical denial that we can know first principles.

For consider how the regress argument works on this double-barrelled reading. If the sets of linearly ordered demonstrative statements are finite, then, as the sceptics argue, since there are no premisses prior to the 'primary truths', we are precluded from demonstrating (by **D**) and hence knowing (by $K \rightarrow K_d$) the ultimate premisses of demonstration ($72^b 11$–13). But, as Aristotle proceeds to report in **EH6**, if we cannot know ($\epsilon i \delta \epsilon \nu a \iota$) the ultimate premisses of demonstrations, then two things follow for our cognition of their conclusions: given the explanatory considerations at work in $U \rightarrow U_d$ and $U_d \rightarrow K_p$, we would be deprived of *scientific understanding* of those conclusions (i.e. we could not know them $\dot{a}\pi\lambda\hat{\omega}s$: in the precise Aristotelian sense of $\dot{\epsilon}\pi i\sigma\tau a\sigma\theta a\iota$), and, given the justificatory requirements in $K \rightarrow K_d$ and $K_d \rightarrow K_p$, nor ($o\dot{v}\delta\dot{\epsilon}$) could we even have *knowledge* of them (i.e. we could not know them $\kappa\upsilon\rho i\omega s$: in any proper sense of $\dot{\epsilon}\pi i\sigma\tau a\sigma\theta a\iota$).

Thus no impediments hinder and decided advantages favour the conclusion that Aristotle's version of the regress argument explicitly targets two different epistemic states (or at least two aspects of the same epistemic state).[27] But since the preceding account of **EH6** offers an unorthodox view of Aristotle's handling of the epistemological regress in 1. 3, and since it does so by offending against interpretations, firmly entrenched within the commentary tradition, which assimilate $\dot{\epsilon}\pi i\sigma\tau a\sigma\theta a\iota$ $\dot{a}\pi\lambda\hat{\omega}s$ to $\dot{\epsilon}\pi i\sigma\tau a\sigma\theta a\iota$ $\kappa\upsilon\rho i\omega s$ both here and elsewhere, I should pause to note some of the further

---

[27] As would be the case if, as there is good reason to believe (see n. 24 and appendix B), Aristotle restricts the focus of his version regress in 1. 3 to scientific cognition of necessary truths and also holds that, at least paradigmatically, knowing the necessity of demonstrative conclusions and knowing the explanation why they are true are one and the same state under different descriptions. In that case, then, he might also have expressed the sceptical conclusion in the apodosis of **EH6** through the language of *Post. An.* $75^a 14$–15: $\dot{\epsilon}\pi i\sigma\tau\dot{\eta}\sigma\epsilon\tau a\iota$ $o\ddot{v}\tau\epsilon$ $\delta\iota\dot{o}\tau\iota$ $o\ddot{v}\tau\epsilon$ $\ddot{o}\tau\iota$ $\dot{a}\nu\dot{a}\gamma\kappa\eta$ $\dot{\epsilon}\kappa\epsilon\hat{\iota}\nu o$ $\epsilon\hat{\iota}\nu a\iota$. In other words, Aristotle would be showing that the regress argument, if sound, would preclude satisfaction of each of the two conditions he placed on unqualified knowledge in the official definition of **EH1**: the explanation condition and the epistemic reading of the necessity condition.

philosophical and philological advantages the proposed account has over such 'single-state' interpretations, which can offer their simpler formulations of the argument in 1. 3 only at the cost of failing to do full justice to the actual data of Aristotle's text.

First of all, by having the two modifiers determine distinct cognitive states, the above reading yields a passage that is philosophically richer and more fully engaged with Aristotle's central tenets about demonstration and scientific cognition; and since this reading depends only on basic epistemological principles to which Aristotle expressly commits himself in 1. 2, it relies on no idea that would not be fully intelligible in the light of what we have learned in the treatise to this point. Moreover, if it is correct to assume that the original version of the regress argument operated with a less stringent conception of demonstration, i.e. one requiring only J-priority for demonstrative premises, then it would have been left to Aristotle to bring out the consequences of the regress for his own special form of explanatory demonstration; in that case, since the original regress concerned *knowledge* while Aristotle is also concerned with its specific consequences for the state of *scientific understanding* that he has been analysing in 1. 2, it would behove him to mention both forms of cognition in presenting the conclusion of the regress in **EH6**. Indeed, since in 1. 2 Aristotle himself required that demonstrative premises be prior to their conclusions both in terms of explanation and in terms of (top-down) justification, this alone provides good reason for him to remark how the sceptics' denial of the possibility of knowing first principles would undermine his conception of unqualified knowledge in both its aspects: as a form of understanding and as a form of knowledge as well (cf. $75^a14–15$).[28]

In addition to these more philosophical points, the following lin-

[28] The reading proposed here has the additional philosophical merit of closing the major gap that was exposed in Burnyeat's account of Aristotelian ἐπιστήμη by T. Irwin, *Aristotle's First Principles* (Oxford, 1988), 530 n. 24. In 'Understanding Knowledge' Burnyeat maintains that the epistemic state of concern to Aristotle in the *Posterior Analytics* is best taken as a form of understanding rather than as a form of knowledge; Irwin resists this contention on the grounds that, although regress and circularity are problems that have traditionally been raised in connection with the justification of *knowledge* claims, Burnyeat says little about how his thesis can accommodate Aristotle's treatment of these problems in 1. 3. On the account proposed above, however, it becomes wholly plain how Aristotle can regard the regress argument as posing a threat not only to justification and knowledge (with special focus here on top-down justification and knowledge of necessary truths) but also to explanation and understanding. (The commentary on **EH8** in appendix A will do the same for Aristotle's treatment of the circle.)

guistic considerations likewise favour the idea that Aristotle intends
ἐπίστασθαι ἁπλῶς and ἐπίστασθαι κυρίως to indicate different forms of
cognition. First, while it is true that Aristotle can use the two modifiers ἁπλῶς and κυρίως interchangeably when the 'unqualified sense'
of a term yields the same reference as its 'proper sense'—whether
the latter is judged by a standard of propriety taken from ordinary
speech or from philosophical discourse (see e.g. *Cat.* 14^{b}24–5, *GC*
317^{a}32–4, *NE* 1147^{b}7 and 31 with 1148^{a}1, and 1157^{a}29–32 with
1157^{b}4–5; see also n. 29)—the negative particle οὐδέ ('nor' or 'nor
even'), which introduces κυρίως in **EH6**, does not normally call for
an epexegetical construction of its sequel. Second, the proposal that
the two expressions determine distinct states in this case allows us
to deliver the grudging prose of the *Posterior Analytics* from un-
motivated redundancy; for Aristotle could hardly be attempting to
explicate at this stage in the treatise the already well-defined term
ἐπίστασθαι ἁπλῶς by the undefined and freshly appearing idea of
knowing κυρίως. Besides, it is hard to see how Aristotle could have
thought that κυρίως might serve as a helpful gloss on ἁπλῶς at all:
this is the only occurrence of ἐπίστασθαι κυρίως in the treatise, and
nowhere in the corpus does the expression receive the sort of stan-
dardization given to ἐπίστασθαι ἁπλῶς by the official definition in
1. 2; indeed, it would even be a mistake to pursue a single reference for ἐπίστασθαι κυρίως in all of its occurrences in the corpus,
since in that case we would find Aristotle contradicting himself.[29]

---

[29] For instance, at *De anima* 417^{a}28–9 we are told that it is the person who is actually exercising linguistic knowledge with an individual subject before the mind (τόδε
τὸ A) who is ἐπιστάμενος κυρίως (cf. *NE* 1098^{a}3–7), whereas at *NE* 7. 3, 1147^{b}13–
17, it is the non-actualized knowledge of universal statements that is declared to
be ἡ κυρίως ἐπιστήμη. But there is no contradiction between the two passages; for
κυρίως serves in these cases simply to signal that the expression it modifies is to be
taken in accordance with its proper or primary usage in *philosophical* discourse (see
e.g. *Metaph.* 1015^{a}13–15, *Pol.* 1280^{a}9–11, and *NE* 1157^{a}25–32), and from different
philosophical perspectives the same expression can be regarded as having different
proper or primary usages. So, from the perspective of the *De anima* psychologist,
the primary use of an epistemic verb (especially one indicating an applied form of
cognition, like literacy) will refer to the actualization of a general cognitive capacity
on individual subjects, while its use in connection with the capacity itself will be
parasitic, since from this perspective capacities are defined in terms of their corresponding activities (see e.g. 415^{a}16–20). On the other hand, from the vantage-point
of an epistemologist trained in the Academy (especially when discussing Socrates, as
Aristotle at *NE* 7. 3), the proper use of ἐπιστήμη will refer exclusively to knowledge
of universals (cf. *Metaph.* 987^{a}29–^{b}7 and 1078^{b}12–32), since 'scientific cognition' is
then the epistemic state of primary philosophical interest, while knowledge of particulars will be ἐπιστήμη only in a loose and vulgar sense. (There is yet another use

Finally, the term κυρίως commonly indicates that a term is to be taken in accordance with its proper usage in *ordinary* language—as opposed to metaphorical and other non-standard usages, including even the technical usages of philosophical discourse (see e.g. *Top.* 123ᵃ33–7, *Poet.* 1457ᵇ1 ff., and *Metaph.* 1045ᵇ34–1046ᵃ1)—and, for several reasons, this is just the role ἐπίστασθαι κυρίως is best suited to play in the context of **EH6**: (1) this is no doubt the kind of cognition which the sceptics originally sought to undermine through their version of the regress argument, i.e. 'knowledge' as commonly understood, without the additional, technical requirement that it be *explanatory* knowledge; (2) the most relevant contrast with ἐπίστασθαι ἐξ ὑποθέσεως is provided not by scientific understanding but by 'knowledge' in its everyday acceptation, since claiming to *know* the consequent of a conditional statement simply in virtue of knowing the conditional itself would involve a rather infelicitous use of ἐπίστασθαι, one which departed most saliently from popular rather than from precise Aristotelian usage; and, finally, (3) the expression against which ἐπίστασθαι ἐξ ὑποθέσεως ('knowledge based on an assumption') is immediately juxtaposed in **EH6** is not in fact ἐπίστασθαι ἁπλῶς ('knowledge in the unqualified sense') but ἐπίστασθαι κυρίως ('knowledge, properly speaking'), which interposes itself between the two, thereby occupying a position in the text that perfectly reflects the intermediate epistemic status of knowledge in relation to *explanatory knowledge*, on the one side, and a state that cannot properly be regarded as *knowledge* at all, on the other. Simply put, then, in our passage ἐπίστασθαι κυρίως represents ἐπίστασθαι as used in ordinary speech, indicating a form of knowledge which demands justification but which need not be explanatory,[30] while ἐπίστασθαι ἁπλῶς stands for ἐπίστασθαι as used

of ἐπιστήμη κυρίως at *Metaph.* 1003ᵇ16–17, which tells us that 'knowledge' κυρίως actually refers to knowledge of first principles—the very form of knowledge that in the *Posterior Analytics* Aristotle is concerned to distinguish from ἐπιστήμη ἁπλῶς by giving it the special title νοῦς. Still, there is an obvious epistemological sense in which scientific cognition of first principles is primary while that of derivative truths is secondary; for, without the former, one cannot in the truest sense of 'knowledge' have the latter.)

[30] This is not to say that ἐπίστασθαι κυρίως here ranges over everything that would be accepted as knowledge in common life; for, as we have seen (n. 24), in his formulation of the regress Aristotle restricts his focus to top-down J-priority and thus, implicitly but fairly clearly, to knowledge of necessary truths. Rather, the point is that the expression in this case carries the basic and general idea behind ordinary usage that, in order for an intellectual state to count properly as *knowledge*, as opposed

in 'precise speech', indicating the consummate form of explanatory knowledge which is scientific understanding.

So, having securely established that the occurrence of ἐπίστασθαι ἁπλῶς in **EH6**, like those in **EH2–5**, carries the precise sense assigned to it in the official definition of **EH1**, we can now return and complete our survey of Aristotle's use of the expression.

The last of the seven occurrences of ἐπίστασθαι ἁπλῶς outside of 1.1 appears in the following passage from the end of 1.2 (unjustly given short shrift by commentators), where Aristotle invokes a fourth and final endoxon about true knowledge by taking on board the Platonic notion (see esp. *Tim.* 51 E 4; cf. 29 B 4–C 1) that the bearer of ἐπιστήμη must be immune to any argument which would, were it presented to him, rationally commit him to renouncing the truth of the statement he knows:

EH7 The person who is going to achieve demonstrative knowledge [τὴν ἐπιστήμην τὴν δι' ἀποδείξεως] . . . must also fail to accept as more convincing and better known any statement which is inconsistent with the first principles and which could yield a deduction [συλλογισμός] of an opposing false belief, since it is necessary for the person who knows in the unqualified sense [τὸν ἐπιστάμενον ἁπλῶς] to be incapable of being persuaded ⟨by dialectical argument[31]⟩ to change his belief [ἀμετάπειστον]. (1.2, 72ᵃ37–ᵇ4)

Although it is possible that Aristotle intends this further requirement of rational 'unpersuadability' to be an independent condition on unqualified knowledge, the following considerations (in addition to the language of **EH1** itself—see n. 15) make it more likely that he considers unpersuadability to be bound up with the account of unqualified knowledge given at the start of 1.2. First of all, in its numerous occurrences as an example in *Topics* 5 (130ᵇ15–18, 133ᵇ28–31, 133ᵇ36–134ᵃ3, 134ᵃ34–ᵇ1, 134ᵇ16–18; cf. 6, 146ᵇ1–2), rational unpersuadability is regarded as a non-defining *idion* of ἐπιστήμη, where the term ἐπιστήμη is evidently used in a generic sense of *scientific cognition* that covers (at least) both νοῦς

to opinion or mere belief, it must be accompanied by adequate justification—an idea which holds just as much for scientific knowledge of necessary truths as it does for quotidian forms of cognition.

[31] That Aristotle expects us to supply the phrase ὑπὸ λόγου can be gathered from the passages in *Topics* 5 (to be cited in the text; cf. [*Def.*] 414 B 10–C 4) where the unpersuadability condition on ἐπιστήμη finds expression, as well as from the appearance of συλλογισμός within **EH7** itself.

and scientific understanding. (That the unpersuadability condition here in 1. 2 is likewise meant to hold for both of these epistemic states is implied by **EH7** itself; for Aristotle there requires that one be unpersuadable with respect to first principles in order *to* be unpersuadable with respect to demonstrative conclusions.) Moreover, elsewhere Aristotle himself evidently endorses the idea that, for someone to have scientific cognition of any statement, whether first principle or derivative truth, she must lack stronger commitment to any belief which is inconsistent with that statement; for she would otherwise be susceptible to *ad hominem* refutation, and, like Plato, he regards the ability consistently to defend a thesis and rationally to withstand attempts at dialectical or elenctic refutation as a necessary condition on at least those forms of cognition that are for him most interesting philosophically.[32] Thus, since Aristotle makes unpersuadability a condition on scientific cognition in general, and since scientific understanding entails scientific cognition (at least owing to the epistemic component of the explanation condition, if not also to the epistemic version of the necessity condition), the unpersuadability condition on scientific understanding would in fact emerge from the definition in **EH1**. But even if unpersuadability is meant to be an independent requirement on unqualified knowledge and neither the necessity nor the explanation condition determines Aristotle's use of ἐπίστασθαι ἁπλῶς in **EH7**, it is nevertheless plain that this occurrence of the expression at the end of 1. 2 is not only fully compatible with the (then partial) definition of unqualified knowledge advanced at the start of the chapter, it is also fully intended to be compatible with that definition.

So, having exhausted the occurrences of ἐπίστασθαι ἁπλῶς outside of 1. 1, we are now in a position to draw some solid conclusions concerning Aristotle's use of the expression. In each of the reviewed passages containing ἐπίστασθαι ἁπλῶς (with the possible exception of **EH7**), when Aristotle is not actually defining the expression (as in **EH1**) or referring back to that definition and explicitly mention-

---

[32] For Plato, consider the epistemological significance generally accorded to the elenchi of the early dialogues, noting in particular the *ad hominem* refutation of Nicias' Socratic definition of courage at *La.* 199 c–200 a; see also e.g. *Rep.* 534 b 8–c 6. For Aristotle, consider the function of 'peirastic' arguments (see e.g. *SE* 165^b^4–7, 169^b^23–5, 171^b^4–6, 30–2, and 183^a^37–^b^8), which is how he designates those dialectical arguments that, in the vein of Socratic elenchi, are designed to test for the presence of expert knowledge (whether in the form of ἐπιστήμη or τέχνη); see also e.g. *SE* 165^a^24–8.

ing the necessity condition on unqualified knowledge (as he does
in **EH2** and **EH3**), either the necessity condition or the explanation
condition determines what he does say in connection with the cognitive state designated by ἐπίστασθαι ἁπλῶς. And even in those cases
where one or the other of the two conditions (or both, perhaps, in
the case of **EH7**) is not directly engaged by Aristotle's actual reasoning, the points he does make about the state he calls ἐπιστήμη
ἁπλῶς are clearly in keeping, and clearly intended to be in keeping,
with both of the requirements placed on unqualified knowledge in
the official definition of **EH1**. Given these findings, along with the
fact that throughout these passages unqualified knowledge is either
directly or indirectly associated with demonstration (in the unqualified sense) and demonstrative knowledge, both of which themselves
require satisfaction of the explanation and necessity conditions (see
nn. 9 and 17), it will be difficult to escape the further conclusion,
already suggested in Section 2.1, that in all of these occurrences
the technical coinage ἐπίστασθαι ἁπλῶς bears a single, determinate
sense and refers to one and the same epistemic state—the state of
true ἐπιστήμη which is explicitly and formally defined in **EH1** and
which Aristotle goes on in 1. 2 to identify with the epistemically
perfect state of demonstrative knowledge or scientific understanding.

2.3 ἐπίστασθαι ἁπλῶς *in* Post. An. *1. 1*

Seen against the backdrop of the official definition at the start of
1. 2 together with Aristotle's uniform usage of ἐπίστασθαι ἁπλῶς
elsewhere in book 1 of the *Posterior Analytics*, the occurrence of the
expression in 1. 1, at least as it must be understood on the received
view, immediately stands out in all of its blushing singularity.

Recall from Section 1 above that on the received view Aristotle
is using ἐπίστασθαι ἁπλῶς in **B3** to indicate the cognitive state of
having explicit knowledge of a singular statement whose subject
is the particular triangle inscribed in the semicircle ('T') which
gets introduced as his example in **A2**. That T is intended to be an
individual entity is shown beyond question by the framing statements in **A1** and **A3**, which expressly treat the example in **A2** as
illustrating an epistemological point that applies generally to all individuals that fall in actual fact under known universal truths. Aristotle describes T as 'this triangle here in the semicircle' (τόδε τὸ ἐν

τῷ ἡμικυκλίῳ τρίγωνον), then, not because he has some specifically
mathematical point to make about the example (cf. 79ᵃ7–10),³³ nor
certainly (as the addition of τόδε further shows; cf. 77ᵃ1–3) because
his general point is meant to apply exclusively to species (such as
the right-angled triangle), but simply to indicate that the particular
triangle he has in mind is featuring in a geometrical diagram, and
hence represents a concrete particular—so also e.g. Pacius (273. 5)
and Zabarella 637 E–F. In the parallel passage at *Prior Analytics*
2. 21, 67ᵃ13–14, Aristotle achieves this same effect of introducing
a physical instantiation of the angle-sum theorem for triangles (his
favourite illustration of a universal truth) to stand for any individual instantiating any sort of universal truth by characterizing that
triangle as a 'perceptible triangle' (note also the generalization at
67ᵃ26). Besides, had Aristotle there or here wanted to make clear
that he had in mind a certain *type* of triangle falling under the
angle-sum theorem, his natural reflex would have been to reach
for τὸ ἰσοσκελές (see e.g. 73ᵇ38 ff., 74ᵃ32 ff., 85ᵃ27–8, ᵇ6 ff., 38 ff.,
and 91ᵃ3–5). Thus, for these reasons, the exemplary triangle T in
A2 is going to have to be an individual and material entity with a
non-renewable lease on existence (say, a triangle drawn on papyrus
or on a wax tablet), and hence an entity that lacks the ontological
constitution and metaphysical stamina needed to support the universal, omnitemporal, and necessary truths of Aristotelian science.
And since, at least on the received view, T is also the subject that we
need to supply for the proposition which **B3** tells us could form the
content of a state designated by ἐπίστασθαι ἁπλῶς, Aristotle would
have to be using this technical expression in 1. 1 to indicate an epistemic state whose object is a singular, contingent, and impermanent
fact.³⁴

But such a use of ἐπίστασθαι ἁπλῶς in 1. 1 would be astounding,

---

³³ For some recondite mathematical interpretations of Aristotle's example see e.g.
Detel ad 71ᵃ17 and T. Heath, *Mathematics in Aristotle* (Oxford, 1949), 37–8; these
scholars do not trouble themselves much, however, about how Aristotle could have
expected his audience to catch their unusual and involved interpretations from his
casual locution in **A2**, especially when the sentences embracing and characterizing
his example point in the direction of a completely different, more general, and much
simpler epistemological point.

³⁴ M. Ferejohn, 'Meno's Paradox and *de re* Knowledge in Aristotle's Theory of
Demonstration', *History of Philosophy Quarterly*, 5 (1988), 99–117, uniquely offers an interpretation of **B** in which the object of ἐπίστασθαι ἁπλῶς is not a singular
statement exemplifying a universal truth but the universal truth itself. Among its
other drawbacks, however, this departure from the received view will not stand
comparison with the received text.

for several reasons. First of all, knowledge of a singular, impermanent fact, like the fact that T has 2R, obviously fails to measure up to the necessity condition explicitly placed on unqualified knowledge in the formal definition of **EH1** (not to mention Aristotle's general requirement that the objects of scientific cognition be universal truths—see e.g. 87^{b}28–39, 88^{b}30–3, and *NE* 1140^{b}31–2). And Aristotle himself could hardly be more explicit on the point; for not only does he constantly reaffirm the necessity requirement on scientific understanding, often in connection with the very expression ἐπίστασθαι ἁπλῶς (see e.g., in addition to **EH2–4**, 74^{b}6, 36–9, 75^{a}12–13, and 19–20), but also, in **EH5**, just after restricting the conclusions of demonstrations to omnitemporal truths, he expressly bars impermanent facts from serving as the objects of 'unqualified knowledge', since such facts obtain 'only at a certain time' (note the sequel at 75^{b}26–36, as well). Thus, in the light of these considerations, were we to accept the received view, this is what we would find ourselves looking at: in 1. 1 Aristotle is wheeling out his technical innovation ἐπίστασθαι ἁπλῶς, the linguistic vehicle which, as we saw in 2.1, he carefully manufactured in book 1 of the *Posterior Analytics* for the precise purpose of conveying the most fundamental concept of knowledge in his epistemological system, and he is using this weighty and uncommon expression to refer there, not to the state of scientific understanding which it is designed and defined to pick out, but instead to what is for him the non-scientific grasp of a singular and ephemeral truth—a cognitive state that signally fails to satisfy the official and all-important definition that he explicitly lays down for this key expression less than fifteen lines later at the start of 1. 2, in the passage around which the rest of the treatise revolves. This would be an odd spectacle, surely.

But, what's more, since, as we saw in 2.2, the occurrences of ἐπίστασθαι ἁπλῶς in **EH2–7**, the only other appearances of the expression in the corpus, all conform to the formal definition in **EH1** and serve to pick out the ideal state of scientific understanding, the use of ἐπίστασθαι ἁπλῶς in 1. 1 would also be at once without parallel and startlingly incongruous with his otherwise fastidious use of this crucial technical term in the first eight chapters of the *Posterior Analytics*. For this reason too, then, the delinquent use of ἐπίστασθαι ἁπλῶς in 1. 1 would convict Aristotle of a philosophically appalling disregard for precise diction.

And what makes such a deviant occurrence of ἐπίστασθαι ἁπλῶς in

1. 1 tax faith all the more is that there was simply no good reason for Aristotle to be employing the expression in this anomalous, contradictory, and misleading way. If he had wanted to mark the contrast between potential and explicit knowledge of a singular statement in order to solve the Paradox of Knowing Universals, as on the received view, then he held in readiness other, more common technical locutions for doing so, and for doing so in a more transparent and less confounding manner. He could have easily and more effectively brought forward for this purpose the distinction between εἰδέναι δυνάμει and εἰδέναι ἐνεργείᾳ, which he in fact employs later on in book 1, at 1. 24, 86ᵃ22–9, and which commentators generally appeal to for the exegesis of ἐπίστασθαι ἁπλῶς in 1. 1. Or, if he somehow felt the need to mark potential knowledge with the qualifier καθόλου, he could have availed himself of the basically equivalent and equally plain distinction between ἡ καθόλου ἐπιστήμη and ἡ καθ᾽ ἕκαστον ἐπιστήμη—the very distinction he deploys in the parallel passage at *Pr. An.* 2. 21, 67ᵃ16–21, when solving that selfsame paradox.

In sum, then, were the received view correct, Aristotle's use of the coinage ἐπίστασθαι ἁπλῶς in 1. 1 would flout, and flout needlessly, its official and neighboring definition by bearing a reference that is both unprecedented for the expression and staggeringly anomalous *vis-à-vis* his otherwise unvarying employment of this vital *terminus technicus*. And what the reader needs to bear in mind at this point is that all of this senseless slovenliness would be transpiring in the introduction to one of the most important treatises in the corpus— a treatise which, moreover, is specifically devoted to analysing the properties of the official referent of ἐπίστασθαι ἁπλῶς, and an introduction which, to judge from other instances of the genre, with their similarly sententious curtain-raisers, we have every reason to believe Aristotle would have exercised considerable care in planning and composing. Given these consequences, it should not seem unfair to conclude that what the received view of 1. 1 perforce offers us in its construal of ἐπίστασθαι ἁπλῶς is an unaccountable and incredible lexical aberration on Aristotle's part.

What resources do advocates of the received view have at their disposal for meeting this grave accusation? It is hard to say, since, what is nearly as astonishing as the lexical aberration itself, commentators on the *Posterior Analytics* have manifested little if any unease about what we have seen to be the deeply unsettling discord between the use of ἐπίστασθαι ἁπλῶς in 1. 1 and both its formal definition at the start of 1. 2 and Aristotle's otherwise scrupulous use of the expression. Only the commentaries of Detel and Barnes venture remarks which could, if acceptable, weaken to some extent the force of this otherwise jolting linguistic anomaly; for Detel apparently wants to account for Aristotle's use of the expression in 1. 1 by arguing that the 'unqualified knowledge' spoken of there does at least *partially* satisfy the definition of unqualified knowledge furnished at the start of 1. 2, while Barnes offers a general interpretation of the locution ἐπίστασθαι ἁπλῶς which would allow its 'referent' to be completely context-dependent. Let us look first at the proposal of Detel.

Although, as we have just seen, the epistemic state marked by ἐπίστασθαι ἁπλῶς in 1. 1 clearly comes up short against the necessity condition, evidently nothing bars that state from meeting the second, independent requirement that Aristotle formally imposes on unqualified knowledge in its official definition at the start of 1. 2, namely, the explanation condition (see n. 14). And, without explicitly announcing this to be his intention, Detel (ad 71ᵃ17) apparently tries to exploit this loophole in order to mitigate the conflict between the two uses of ἐπίστασθαι ἁπλῶς in 1. 1 and 1. 2 when he offers the idiosyncratic suggestion that Aristotle elects to use ἐπίστασθαι ἁπλῶς in 1. 1 because he wants to indicate that the epistemic state referred to there is not merely explicit or actualized knowledge but also a form of 'explanatory knowledge' (*begründetes Wissen*); for, according to Detel, Aristotle's intention there is to make clear that our illustrative syllogism yields knowledge not merely of the fact that T has 2R but also of the fact that it has this property *because it is a triangle.*

Owing to the serious discrepancy with the necessity condition, however, even if Detel's suggestion concerning ἐπίστασθαι ἁπλῶς in 1. 1 were correct, we would still have to charge Aristotle with a needlessly and surprisingly sloppy employment of this all-determining technical term; for, although Detel's thesis would allow us to assign Aristotle some reason for his use of ἐπίστασθαι ἁπλῶς in 1. 1, that reason would, in view of the arguments adduced above, be an exceptionally poor one. Yet, owing to a host of further difficulties from which it suffers, Detel's proposal cannot in fact be used to give the occurrence of ἐπίστασθαι ἁπλῶς in 1. 1 even the semblance of intelligibility.

First, by burdening ἁπλῶς with the ideas of both *explicitness* and *explanatoriness* Detel has that simple term shouldering a semantic load that is a good deal too heavy for it. Second, it is difficult to see how Aristotle could have intended his audience to pick up the notion of *explanatoriness* while leaving behind the idea of *necessity* through his use in 1. 1 of the uncommon expression ἐπίστασθαι ἁπλῶς; for the component terms in the expression do not readily lend themselves to such a construal, especially in the context of 71ᵃ17–30, and, if we turn for help to the official definition that comes shortly afterwards, we get both concepts wrapped together as part of a single semantic package. Third, if Aristotle had wanted to convey the idea of explanatoriness without that of necessity, he would have done much better to use the language of 'knowing why' (εἰδέναι διότι), which recurs throughout the *Posterior Analytics* (see e.g. 74ᵇ30, 75ᵃ16–17, 32, 79ᵃ2–3, 11–12, 14–16, and esp. 85ᵇ34). Fourth, the idea of explanatoriness is extraneous to the solution of the Paradox of Knowing Universals, which Aristotle is supposed to be addressing in **B**; for this puzzle arises whenever we know a universal statement without knowing one of its instantiations, ir-respective of the explanatory status of that universal. Yet, given Detel's reading of ἐπίστασθαι ἁπλῶς as indicating an epistemic state that fuses both explicit and explanatory knowledge, the distinction that would constitute Aristotle's solution to the paradox would actually apply only in cases in which we know an *explanatory* uni-versal. Thus, contrary to his own explicit instructions on how to solve a paradox (see e.g. *Top.* 160ᵇ23–35), Aristotle would have left the puzzle standing for such universal statements as *every celestial non-twinkler is near the earth*, since a universal major of this kind fails to explain the truth of its singular conclusions (that is, a newly discovered planet will not be near the earth *because it is a celes-tial non-twinkler*—see the well-known and important discussion of scientific explanation at *Post. An.* 1. 13, 78ᵃ22 ff.). Fifth, what is a closely related point, explanatory considerations play no role at all in Aristotle's criticism of the alternative solution to the paradox in the subsequent passage at 71ᵃ34–ᵇ5, where, in fact, such consid-erations could have been deployed to devastating effect, since the outlandish, knower-relative universal statements recommended in the alternative solution can hardly be made to carry out an explana-tory function. (For more on the alternative solution and Aristotle's actual objection to it, see n. 4.) Finally, there is no direct suggestion of the idea of explanatoriness in (*a*) the occurrences of 'actualized knowledge' in *Pr. An.* 2. 21 (ἐπίστασθαι τῷ ἐνεργεῖν at 67ᵇ5 and ἡ κατὰ τὸ ἐνεργεῖν ἐπιστήμη at 67ᵇ9), which, despite the differences in nomenclature, Detel cites as parallels for his construal of ἐπίστασθαι ἁπλῶς in 1. 1,[35] nor in (*b*) the occurrences of ἡ καθ' ἕκαστον ἐπιστήμη, which, together with ἡ καθόλου ἐπιστήμη, constitutes the distinction Aristotle actually uses to solve the Paradox of Knowing Universals in 2. 21 (67ᵃ16–21). While it is true that 'actualized knowledge' and 'particular knowledge' in 2. 21 *refer* to states of explicit knowledge that could also be accompanied by an explanation (e.g. 'this animal here is sterile *because it is a mule*'), nevertheless, it is not this concomitant feature of those states that Aristotle is calling attention to there; for it is the *explicitness* of actualized and particular knowledge that presents the most important and most salient contrast with potential and universal knowledge. (The absence of the idea of explanatoriness from the concept of actualized knowledge gains further, striking corroboration from the only other explicit appearance of the idea of knowing ἐνεργείᾳ in the *Posterior Analytics*; for in 1. 24 the principal argument Aristotle advances in favour of 'universal' demonstrations is based on the distinction between actualized and potential knowledge (86ᵃ22–9; cf. 86ᵃ10–13), and he expressly distances this argument from the earlier arguments at 85ᵇ23–7 and 85ᵇ27–86ᵃ3, where explanatory considerations were in play.) Thus, if the idea of explanatoriness were part of the *mean-*

[35] Detel seems to think that 'actualized knowledge' in 2. 21 must convey more than merely the idea of *explicit* knowledge of a syllogistic conclusion on the grounds that 67ᵇ3–5 expressly contrasts actualized knowledge with knowing τῇ οἰκείᾳ ἐπιστήμῃ ('by specific knowledge'), which he apparently takes to be synonymous with 'particular knowledge' and which he certainly takes to cover explicit knowledge of both sorts of singular statements that occur in a simple syllogism, i.e. minor premisses and conclusions. But Aristotle's contrast is best preserved there—as I have shown in greater detail in my 'Aristotle's Solution to Meno's Paradox: *Posterior Analytics* I.1' (Ph.D. diss., University of Texas, 1994), ch. 6—if we understand 'specific knowledge' to be indicating only explicit knowledge of the *species-identifying* statement in the minor premiss of a simple syllogism (e.g. 'this animal here is a mule'), and not also explicit knowledge of the *property-attributing* statement in the syllogistic conclusion (e.g. 'this animal here is sterile'), which is what 'particular knowledge' and 'actualized knowledge' both refer to in 2. 21—with 'particular knowledge' leaving open the question of how the explicit knowledge of that non-identifying statement was acquired, i.e. whether by a simple syllogistic inference or otherwise (e.g. by perception), but with 'actualized knowledge' carrying the additional information that the explicit knowledge of the singular conclusion has actually been gained syllogistically on the basis of prior knowledge of its subsuming universal truth (whether explanatory or not) and hence from an earlier state of having had *potential* knowledge of that singular statement.

ing of 'actualized knowledge', as Detel suggests, then Aristotle did a cunningly thorough job of concealing this fact from others; for he never explicitly mentions a connection between explanatoriness and actualized knowledge, and no inference that he draws in connection with that form of cognition betrays the presence of the idea in his thought.

For all of the preceding reasons, then, while the epistemic state referred to by ἐπίστασθαι ἁπλῶς in 1. 1 may in fact satisfy a tolerant version of the explanation condition on scientific understanding, Aristotle is not telling us there that it does.

Instead of attempting to conciliate the state of 'unqualified knowledge' in 1. 1 with the requirements placed on 'unqualified knowledge' in its official definition at the start of 1. 2, Barnes takes a different tack: he puts forward an account of the locution ἐπίστασθαι ἁπλῶς that would allow it to be applied to epistemic states that need not have much in common at all.³⁶ On this view, it would be misguided to look for a single referent behind every occurrence of ἐπίστασθαι ἁπλῶς in Aristotle, since the locution is not in fact a denoting expression at all. Rather, in accordance with the general function of ἁπλῶς, which is to negate the force of a particular qualification explicitly or implicitly attached to a particular term in a particular context, the modifier in the expression ἐπίστασθαι ἁπλῶς serves simply to nullify some qualification or other attached to another occurrence of ἐπίστασθαι either explicitly appearing or meant to be understood in the same context, thereby allowing the verb to carry the signification it would ordinarily have in that context without the cancelled qualification. And since the epistemic state indicated by an occurrence of ἐπίστασθαι that is modified by ἁπλῶς thus depends on the particular form of qualified knowledge with which that state is contrasted, the reference of ἐπίστασθαι when modified by ἁπλῶς can vary according to context. Naturally, given the orientation of Aristotle's reflections in the *Posterior Analytics*, 'knowing in an unqualified sense' will typically be used there in connection with the state of scientific understanding, in contrast with some defective and qualified form of ἐπιστήμη which falls short of the cognitive ideal; but this is by no means the only role the expression can play. Thus, given the standard, 'de-qualifying' function of ἁπλῶς, along with a highly generic use of ἐπίστασθαι (answering

---

³⁶ My understanding of Barnes's position is derived from the remarks in his commentary ad 71ᵃ24 as well as from an extremely generous personal communication.

not to the species *scientific understanding*, nor even to its proximate genus *scientific cognition*, but—what, it must be interjected, would be extremely unusual for the *Posterior Analytics*—to the epistemic summum genus *know*), ἐπίστασθαι ἁπλῶς can function in 1. 1, not to denote the state of scientific understanding, but merely to wipe out the special qualification on the adjacent ἐπίστασθαι καθόλου ('know in a universal way'), leaving behind an instance of ἐπίστασθαι as ordinarily understood ('know, period'), and hence, in this case, an instance of explicit knowledge of a singular, contingent truth.

Now, what the preceding argument shows is that, even though we can cite no parallel case in which he does so, Aristotle could have applied ἐπίστασθαι ἁπλῶς to an instance of ordinary, non-scientific knowledge of a singular statement *in some context or other*. Yet the question we must face is this: could Aristotle have used this locution to indicate particular knowledge *here* in the opening chapter of the *Posterior Analytics*? In addition to the arguments assembled just above (i.e. the proximity of ἐπίστασθαι ἁπλῶς in 1. 1 to the official definition of this uncommon expression at the start of 1. 2, its startling incongruity with the otherwise undeviating use of this key *terminus technicus*, the ready availability of unproblematic technical alternatives for marking explicit knowledge of singular statements, and the fact that all of these oddities would be occurring in the very introduction to a treatise dedicated to a close study of the official referent of ἐπίστασθαι ἁπλῶς), as well as the arguments advanced in Section 2.1 in favour of an 'absolute' construal of the expression in the *Posterior Analytics* (see esp. n. 10; cf. n. 44), the following considerations likewise point firmly to a negative answer to our question.

First of all, only two chapters later, at 1. 3, 72^{b}30–1 (see the discussion of **EH8** in Appendix A), Aristotle shows himself especially solicitous to circumscribe a determinate extension over which ἐπίστασθαι ἁπλῶς can range—and understandably so, given the fundamental and all-deciding role which, as we saw in Section 2.1, this epistemic expression is designed to play in the treatise.

Second, if for some reason, inscrutable to us, Aristotle felt compelled to forgo the admirable technical alternatives at his command and decided to indicate the state of particular knowledge by attaching ἁπλῶς to an epistemic term, then he at least could have distanced his point in section **B** from the soon-to-appear formal definition of ἐπίστασθαι ἁπλῶς by coupling this modifier with a verb of cognition other than the epistemologically resonant ἐπίστασθαι, such as the duller verb γινώσκειν. (Although γνωρίζειν serves repeatedly in section **A** to indicate the *acquisition* of knowledge, it too would have been preferable here, whether in its ingressive or its non-ingressive sense—for the latter of which see e.g. 72ᵃ39 and ᵇ24.³⁷) Besides, if Aristotle had wanted an epistemic verb for conveying the supremely generic idea of knowledge *tout court*, as on the proposal under review, he could have made no better selection than the completely generic γινώσκειν.³⁸ Indeed, because this verb and its cognate noun γνῶσις never undergo the sort of philosophical regimentation to which ἐπίστασθαι and ἐπιστήμη are subjected by Aristotle (and by Plato before him), and because they therefore fail to carry the overtones of an exclusively high-grade, scientific form of cognition that are typically present in ἐπιστήμη and kin, Aristotle often employs the generic terms γινώσκειν and γνῶσις to indicate by default what is for him the epistemologically uninteresting and non-scientific species of cognition that is represented by explicit knowledge of a singular truth whose subject is a corruptible

³⁷ Aristotle also would have done better to repeat the performance of **B2** and attach the modifier ἁπλῶς to εἰδέναι again in **B3**, instead of switching, much more problematically, to ἐπίστασθαι there; for, although εἰδέναι ἁπλῶς elsewhere serves as a synonym for ἐπίστασθαι ἁπλῶς as defined in **EH1** (see appendix A), the verb εἰδέναι too typically displays more generic propensities than ἐπίστασθαι (see e.g. 71ᵇ30–1, 94ᵃ20, and esp. 97ᵇ17), making it a more suitable term for indicating particular knowledge. And, besides, just the linguistic differences between εἰδέναι ἁπλῶς and ἐπίστασθαι ἁπλῶς would have allowed Aristotle to avoid the more jarring clash that we actually find in our text between the (unnecessary) talk of 'unqualified knowledge' in **B3** from 1. 1 and the official definition of ἐπίστασθαι ἁπλῶς at the start of 1. 2. Note also, finally, that ἐπίστασθαι disappears again in the passage following **B** at 71ᵃ30–ᵇ5, where Aristotle exclusively uses εἰδέναι in his presentation and criticism of the alternative solution to the paradox that he himself is supposed to be addressing in what precedes; given the received view, then, Aristotle would clearly have been under no compulsion to switch back and forth between εἰδέναι and ἐπίστασθαι in **B**, as he actually does. (Why, after avoiding the term at 71ᵃ30–ᵇ5, Aristotle then returns to ἐπίστασθαι at the end of 1. 1 (71ᵇ6), just before offering his definition of ἐπίστασθαι ἁπλῶς in 1. 2, is an important question to ask, but one whose answer must be given elsewhere.)

³⁸ The generic character of γινώσκειν and γνῶσις is shown by the fact that these terms are deliberately used to refer to a number of cognitive states for which ἐπίστασθαι and ἐπιστήμη would generally be unfitting labels: not only (as will be shown in the text) to knowledge of contingent singular truths (failing the necessity condition) and to knowledge of first principles (failing the explanation condition), but also to knowledge of the meanings of terms (see n. 40) and even to knowledge of one's possession of scientific understanding (76ᵃ26–7). The generic character of these terms is also revealed by Aristotle's use of them to contrast cognition in general with action (see e.g. *NE* 1095ᵃ5–6, 1179ᵃ35–ᵇ2, *EE* 1214ᵃ10–12, and *Protrep.* B 52 Düring).

individual (see e.g., in addition to the passages from the *Posterior Analytics* cited below, *Metaph.* 981ᵃ15–16, ᵇ9–11, *GA* 731ᵃ31–3, and *Protrep.* B 76 Düring)—a type of cognition which, when it gets covered at all by any special category in the official epistemic taxonomy of the *Posterior Analytics*, finds itself disparaged with the Platonic slur of δόξα (see 1. 33, 88ᵇ30–89ᵃ3; cf. e.g. 100ᵇ7, *NE* 1140ᵇ27, and *Metaph.* 1039ᵇ30–1040ᵃ2).

And furthermore, both in 1. 1 and at the start of 1. 2 Aristotle does in fact show himself fully responsive to the semantic differences between the specific ἐπίστασθαι and the generic γινώσκειν. Nothing reveals this more clearly than the much-remarked fact that, in **EH1** itself, when expressing the epistemic component of the explanation condition in the definiens of his formal definition of the species ἐπίστασθαι ἁπλῶς ('scientific understanding'), Aristotle deliberately avoids circularity by employing the generic and nondescript γινώσκειν ('know')—cf. *Phys.* 184ᵃ10–12, *Metaph.* 982ᵃ25–6, 994ᵇ29–30; for the related use of γινώσκειν and kin in connection with knowledge of explanatory first principles see e.g., in addition to the passages cited below, *Post. An.* 92ᵇ38, 93ᵇ18, *De anima* 402ᵇ17, and esp. *GA* 742ᵇ32–3. But likewise, in the opening sentence of the *Posterior Analytics*, when Aristotle is making his sweeping pronouncement on the abstract epistemic prerequisites for any act of inferential knowledge acquisition, γνῶσις is his obvious epistemic term of choice, since the prior 'knowledge' which that general principle requires is meant to cover the full spectrum of cognitive states—everything from perceptual knowledge of singular statements to scientific insight into first principles. Similarly too, in the stretch of 1. 1 falling between its first line and section **B** (including, it should be observed, section **A**, which, like **B** on the received view, is directly focused upon our knowledge of singular statements in a syllogistic context), Aristotle resolutely eschews the terms ἐπίστασθαι and ἐπιστήμη when referring to kinds of cognition that include states taking as their objects singular statements, first principles, or other items which are unsuitable to be the objects of ἐπίστασθαι in the precise sense in which he is obviously already looking forward to using the term—see (προ)γινώσκειν at 71ᵃ6 and 8 (cf. ᵇ31–2 and 72ᵃ28), as well as γνῶσις in **A1**³⁹ (cf. the several

---

³⁹ If we resist Ross's emendation of the plural relative pronoun at 71ᵃ19 (see n. 1), as I shall suggest elsewhere we should, then the ensuing occurrence of γνῶσις would likewise be used in connection with knowledge of singular statements.

occurrences of γνωρίζειν in **A**).[40] (Consider also another passage in which it behoves Aristotle to be circumspect in selecting items from his epistemic vocabulary, namely, the final chapter of the *Posterior Analytics* (99ᵇ18 ff.), where he takes up the terminological aspect of the question about our knowledge of first principles raised just after the definition of ἐπίστασθαι ἁπλῶς in 1. 2, asking whether or not the scientific grasp of first principles should be called a form of ἐπιστήμη, precisely speaking: 99ᵇ18, 21, 22, 27, 29, and 38–9 all employ γνῶσις, γινώσκειν, and γνωρίζειν to indicate knowledge of singular statements or knowledge of first principles—cognitive states for which ἐπίστασθαι and ἐπιστήμη would clearly have been inappropriate tags there.)

As a matter of fact, it is not until he comes to **B** itself, the precise point in 1. 1 where he will be attaching the important modifier ἁπλῶς to a verb of cognition, that Aristotle for the first time in the *Posterior Analytics* even employs the term ἐπίστασθαι in more than a passing way (cf. ἐπιστήμη at 71ᵃ3). Indeed, what needs special underscoring, the language which gives us our first serious introduction to ἐπίστασθαι in the treatise reveals that Aristotle's decision to use this particular expression in this context is a completely self-conscious one—note φατέον ἐπίστασθαι in **B1**, where the legislative talk of 'we should say', occurring as it does within the highly sensitive linguistic atmosphere at the start of the *Posterior Analytics*, hardly makes for a convincing prelude to an unusually slack and wholly generic use of that portentous verb. And, what is also worthy of special notice, the intentional hyperbaton in (at least) the second clause of **B2**, which has the effect of placing stress on ἁπλῶς by holding it back from its natural position next to the verb and deferring its placement until the end of the sentence, shows that Aristotle is fully deliberate in his use of this second element in the compound expression ἐπίστασθαι ἁπλῶς, as well. Finally, note well, too, that the sentential adverb ἴσως ('presumably' here), which precedes φατέον ἐπίστασθαι in **B1**, is likewise indicative of mindfulness, disclosing in this case that the prescriptive lexical decision lying behind the phrase 'we should say ἐπίστασθαι' was actually sanctioned by the antecedent reflection 'there seems to be no reason

---

[40] Aristotle's concern in 1. 1 with the proper selection of items from his extensive epistemic vocabulary is further manifested by his deliberate use of the verb συνιέναι in order to indicate the specific form of cognition (γνῶσις, 71ᵃ1–2) that is represented by *linguistic comprehension*—see 71ᵃ7–8 and 15; cf. ᵇ31–3.

why not'! But since on the received view there would be no reason at all for him to be (and, as we have seen, plenty of reasons for him *not* to be) abandoning the generic γινώσκειν which he is careful to use in surrounding texts and which would have allowed him to put some distance between his already ill-advised talk of 'unqualified knowledge' in **B** and the completely different and all-important definition of ἐπίστασθαι ἁπλῶς coming up at the start of 1. 2, Aristotle's purposeful switch to the pregnant ἐπίστασθαι at the exact moment when he will be unnecessarily and incongruously yet emphatically modifying epistemic verbs with the crucial expression ἁπλῶς would seem to bespeak a sudden and momentary fit of what—since it cannot now be regarded as inattention—would have to be wilful and incomprehensible defiance.

For these additional reasons, then, this second line of defence for the received view can do little more than the first to prevent our earlier conclusion from going through: the occurrence of ἐπίστασθαι ἁπλῶς in 1. 1 remains an inexplicable and prodigious linguistic abnormality.

Having suffered these reverses, die-hard partisans of the received view will perhaps find their best remaining defence in the claim that, even when we count among them the two conforming instances of εἰδέναι ἁπλῶς from 1. 3 and 1. 4 (**EH8** and **EH9**, to be discussed in Appendix A), the occurrences of ἐπίστασθαι ἁπλῶς in Aristotle are too few in number for its use in 1. 1 to constitute a truly glaring lexical anomaly, proximity to the official definition of the expression notwithstanding. Yet, after our earlier review of the birth and brief career of this uncommon technical locution, whose sole reason for existence in the first eight chapters of the *Posterior Analytics* was, as we learnt above (see esp. n. 12), to announce and then faithfully communicate a precise and fundamental conception of knowledge that represents the vital link uniting the lay and philosophical endoxa about ἐπιστήμη to Aristotle's own conception of the cognitively ideal state of ἀποδεικτικὴ ἐπιστήμη, this defensive position will have to be taken up in the vicinity of the last ditch.

Virginia Polytechnic Institute and State University

APPENDIX A
εἰδέναι ἁπλῶς

In Section 2 we learnt that, as understood on the received view, the occurrence of ἐπίστασθαι ἁπλῶς in *Post. An.* 1. 1 constitutes a most unnerving lexical anomaly. But this deviant use of ἐπίστασθαι ἁπλῶς in **B3** is preceded in the second clause of **B2** by an occurrence of εἰδέναι ἁπλῶς that would likewise serve to indicate a state of explicit knowledge whose supplied object would have to be the contingent, singular truth that T has 2R.[41] I show here that this construal of εἰδέναι ἁπλῶς in 1. 1 is subject to the same problems, albeit in somewhat less blatant form, that were discussed above in connection with the occurrence of ἐπίστασθαι ἁπλῶς in 1. 1; for, as we shall see, Aristotle elsewhere employs εἰδέναι ἁπλῶς as a synonym for ἐπίστασθαι ἁπλῶς, and hence as an alternative technical locution for referring absolutely to the ideal state of scientific understanding.

Outside of 1. 1, we encounter two occurrences of εἰδέναι ἁπλῶς, both of which turn up, unsurprisingly, in the very same habitat in which all of the occurrences of ἐπίστασθαι ἁπλῶς have their residence: the early chapters in book 1 of the *Posterior Analytics*, where Aristotle is treating the central properties of demonstrative knowledge or scientific understanding.[42] Consideration of Aristotle's use of εἰδέναι ἁπλῶς in its two occurrences outside of 1. 1 will reveal that the expression shares with ἐπίστασθαι ἁπλῶς the

[41] The first clause of **B2** contains another occurrence of εἰδέναι ἁπλῶς, one which, on the received view, would have to be indicating the state of having ordinary, explicit knowledge of the singular *existential* statement that T exists. I pass over this occurrence here since, in addition to the lexical problems it shares with its successor, this first occurrence of εἰδέναι ἁπλῶς in **B2** raises special philosophical difficulties that must be taken up elsewhere—in connection with the other doctrinal peculiarities in 1. 1.

[42] At 1. 22, 83ᵇ32–84ᵃ6, where Aristotle returns to his solution to the sceptical regress argument of 1. 3, we find the two expressions εἰδέναι δι' ἀποδείξεως ἁπλῶς and ἐπίστασθαι δι' ἀποδείξεως ἁπλῶς, in each case set in opposition to an ensuing ἐξ ὑποθέσεως; but it is not immediately clear that these expressions are to be counted as further instances of εἰδέναι ἁπλῶς and ἐπίστασθαι ἁπλῶς, respectively, since it is not clear that we are meant to take ἁπλῶς together with the verbs ἐπίστασθαι and εἰδέναι rather than with the noun ἀπόδειξις (for ἐξ ὑποθέσεως as a qualification on ἀπόδειξις cf. e.g. 92ᵃ6–7 and ᵃ35). In favour of taking ἁπλῶς with ἀπόδειξις is the fact that our two locutions would otherwise involve pleonasm: since there is no unqualified knowledge that is not demonstrative knowledge, ἐπίστασθαι ἁπλῶς by itself would have sufficed to indicate scientific understanding, making δι' ἀποδείξεως otiose (the points made here about ἐπίστασθαι ἁπλῶς hold for εἰδέναι ἁπλῶς as well; cf. 84ᵃ4). Granted, there is also no demonstrative knowledge that is not unqualified knowledge; but this is true only when the term ἀπόδειξις is understood in accordance with its official definition in 1. 2 rather than in some looser sense, and, as we saw in sect. 2.1, Aristotle will often attach ἁπλῶς to ἀπόδειξις for the purpose of assigning that term its precise, technical value. The expression ἐπίστασθαι ἁπλῶς, in contrast, being effectively an

technical function of expressing the concept of *true knowledge* as defined by the explanation and necessity conditions in **EH1**.

In the following passage from 1. 3, while presenting his first argument against circular demonstration, Aristotle uses—or rather, he evidently mentions (see n. 10 above)—the expression εἰδέναι ἁπλῶς in order to direct attention back to the official definition of ἐπίστασθαι ἁπλῶς at the start of 1. 2:

EH8 If ⟨an argument proceeding⟩ in this way [i.e. in the way induction does, from what is prior to us to what is prior by nature] ⟨can count as a 'demonstration'⟩, then the expression 'knowing in the unqualified sense' [τὸ εἰδέναι ἁπλῶς] would not have been properly defined [ὡρισμένον], but would carry a double significance [διττόν]. (1. 3, 72ᵇ30–1)

Aristotle here considers a potential problem for his definition of unqualified knowledge in **EH1**: given his commitment to the principle that demonstrations produce unqualified knowledge (71ᵇ17–19), if he grants official recognition to a lax usage of ἀπόδειξις and allows that arguments establishing a conclusion prior by nature on the basis of premisses prior and better known to us can also constitute 'demonstrations', then he would be obliged to concede that these arguments too generate unqualified knowledge. But, as he observes in **EH8**, the expression 'knowing in the unqualified sense' would in that case refer to two quite different types of epistemic state, only one of which is covered by the definiens in **EH1**, and hence his formal definition would have erred on the side of narrowness. Though not as clearly stated as one might wish, the reason Aristotle thinks 'unqualified knowledge' would come to have this twofold reference is none the less plain: unlike the epistemic states generated by the explanatory demonstrations defined in 1. 2, the states issuing from the 'demonstrations' on audition in this stretch of 1. 3 would fail to meet the explanation requirement of **EH1**; for these would-be demonstrations proceed from facts prior to us, and such facts do not explain but are explained by facts prior by nature (71ᵇ31; cf. 98ᵇ16–21).[43] In short, then, if a non-explanatory argument were

Aristotelian coinage, would not need the supplementary δι' ἀποδείξεως to ensure proper construal.

In any event, even if we were to place the two expressions in 1. 22 on the roll of instances of ἐπίστασθαι ἁπλῶς and εἰδέναι ἁπλῶς, they would nevertheless comport perfectly well with both the official definition of **EH1** and Aristotle's invariable use of those expressions outside of 1. 1; for in each case—as is likewise true for the occurrences in **EH6** and **EH8**, which both come from 1. 3, a chapter Aristotle is plainly harking back to here in 1. 22—it would be the explanation condition that primarily determines Aristotle's use of these expressions (note πρότερα at 83ᵇ33, as well as ἐπάνω at 84ᵃ2; cf. 82ᵃ23–4), while what he says about the states they pick out is clearly in keeping with the necessity condition as well.

⁴³ Aristotle's complaint against these upside-down 'demonstrations' is plainly

accorded the status of being an ἀπόδειξις, the expressions εἰδέναι ἁπλῶς and ἐπίστασθαι ἁπλῶς would refer not only to the preferred state of scientific understanding, but also to a humbler, non-explanatory form of knowledge.

Aristotle introduces this problem, however, only to solve it: in the next sentence (72^b31-2) he preserves univocity for 'knowing in the unqualified sense' by rejecting the protasis of **EH8**, maintaining instead that only an argument proceeding from premisses prior in the order of nature can qualify as a *true* demonstration (ἀπόδειξις ἁπλῶς; cf. 72^b25); for, obviously, only an argument travelling in this direction can supply explanations and thus explanatory knowledge. Thus what we find driving the use of εἰδέναι ἁπλῶς in **EH8** (as was also the case with the occurrence of ἐπίστασθαι ἁπλῶς in **EH6**, from earlier in 1. 3) is the explanation requirement on unqualified

not that they are incapable of justifying a knowledge claim, since induction, the paradigm of an argument exemplifying this sort of 'bottom-up' J-priority, is readily admitted to issue in (non-demonstrative) knowledge of demonstrable universal truths (72^b29-30). Nor does his objection depend on his special notion of 'top-down' J-priority, which is connected with knowledge of the necessity possessed by demonstrative conclusions (see the discussion of **EH6** in sect. 2.2). For one thing, Aristotle does not explicitly take up discussion of the necessity condition on unqualified knowledge until the start of 1. 4 (73^a21 ff.). For another, although he speaks of the need for the premisses of a true demonstration to be both πρότερα and γνωριμώτερα (72^b26-7)—terms which, to avoid redundancy, are best taken here to express the distinct ideas of E-priority and top-down J-priority, respectively (for the solo use of γνωριμώτερον in this sense see e.g. 72^b1 and 100^b9-10)—the decisive move against circular demonstration is couched exclusively in the causal language of πρότερα and ὕστερα (72^b27-8; for the solo use of πρότερον in this sense see also e.g. 76^a19-20 and 87^a31-3). What's more, the assumption of linearity on which Aristotle's criticism depends is more intuitively obvious when it concerns explanation rather than justification (cf. 98^b16-19); thus the idea of linear E-priority, unlike that of linear J-priority, could be introduced into the argument without elaboration, which, in fact, Aristotle fails to provide here in his first criticism, but which he does offer in his second criticism, when he is concerned with the issue of justification—note also the switch from ἀποδεικνύναι ('demonstrate', in the technical sense) at 72^b25 in the first criticism to the more generic δεικνύναι ('prove') at 72^b35 and 73^a6 in the second, as well as 73^a13 and 17 in the third (cf. e.g. 71^a8-9). On the other hand, if Aristotle were here relying on an undefended assumption of linear J-priority, not only would his first, bare objection be largely redundant in the light of his second, developed criticism, it would also beg the question against advocates of the circle; for these thinkers pointedly reject the assumption of linearity. (It cannot be objected that, on the reading proposed here, Aristotle's first argument against circular demonstration would then be guilty of *ignoratio elenchi*; for, while it is true that champions of the circle evidently would not themselves have claimed that circular demonstrations serve to explain the truth of demonstrative conclusions, rather than merely justify belief in their truth, Aristotle need not be assuming they did: in his first objection (72^b25-32) he simply reveals that circular demonstrations cannot do the explanatory work that he himself requires of a demonstration, while his subsequent objections (72^b32-73^a20), especially the second (72^b32-73^a6), show that circular demonstrations cannot do what the proponents of the circle themselves want demonstrations to do, either.)

knowledge from **EH1**. And the fact that Aristotle can direct us back to the formal definition of unqualified knowledge in 1. 2 by mention of the expression εἰδέναι ἁπλῶς reveals, not only the compatibility of **EH8** with the necessity condition in **EH1**, but also the official synonymity of the two locutions εἰδέναι ἁπλῶς and ἐπίστασθαι ἁπλῶς.

Our second passage containing εἰδέναι ἁπλῶς comes from the end of 1. 5 (74ᵃ32–ᵇ4), which offers a brief discussion of the criterion for deciding when someone knows 'universally', in the strong sense given that term in 1. 4, a consequence of which, as Aristotle sees it, is that a general statement predicating a non-essential property of its subject is universally true if and if only its subject and predicate terms are coextensive (73ᵇ32–74ᵃ3; cf. 74ᵃ35–ᵇ4 and 99ᵃ33–5); thus, to know 'universally' in the case of non-defining predications is a matter of knowing a 'commensurate universal' (and, no doubt, knowing it as such—cf. δοκεῖ at 74ᵃ6—though in what follows I ignore this refinement for simplicity's sake):

EH9 So when do we not know universally [οἶδε καθόλου] and when do we know in the unqualified sense [οἶδεν ἁπλῶς]? (74ᵃ32–3)

Now, it is just possible that εἰδέναι ἁπλῶς serves here to indicate, not unqualified knowledge in the technical sense of **EH1**, but simply ordinary, non-universal knowledge—in which case ἁπλῶς would function in the way Barnes claims it does in 1. 1 (see Section 2.3 above), namely, to strip a neighbouring and qualified epistemic term of its modifier, leaving behind a case of 'knowledge' as it would be understood in that context without that particular qualification. (In fact, ἁπλῶς would here be eliminating the same qualifier as in 1. 1, i.e. καθόλου, though here bearing a different sense.) In that case, the second question in **EH9** would be merely a gloss on the first, and Aristotle would be asking: when do we fail to occupy the more sophisticated state of knowing universally? that is, when do we *merely* know?

But such a reading is belied by Aristotle's ensuing response; for his answer contains only a single epistemic term, εἰδέναι without modification, and he employs the term to indicate not plain knowing but (at least) the state of knowing universally:

It's clear [from what has been said in the preceding, at 73ᵇ32 ff.], then, that (*a*) if what it is to be a triangle and what it is to be an isosceles triangle were the same in each and every case, ⟨then you would know universally⟩; but (*b*) if they are different and not the same, and ⟨having 2R⟩ belongs to ⟨the isosceles triangle⟩ in so far as it is a triangle, then you do not know ⟨universally⟩ [οἶδεν]. (73ᵇ33–5)

Presupposing that the properties of triangularity and having 2R are coextensive, Aristotle here imagines a hypothetical situation in which someone knows the general statement that every *isosceles triangle* has 2R without

knowing that every *triangle* does. In that case, (*a*) if the properties of triangularity and 'isoscelarity' were identical, then the properties of isoscelarity
and having 2R would be coextensive, and so the person would know universally; but (*b*) if the properties of triangularity and isoscelarity are not
identical (i.e. if not all triangles are isosceles), then isoscelarity and having
2R would not be coextensive, and so the person would not know universally.

Now, if Aristotle's reason for attaching the modifying expressions καθόλου and ἁπλῶς to εἰδέναι in the questions of **EH9** were to distinguish the
cognitive states of *knowing universally* and *merely knowing*, then it would
be remarkable that he would completely dispense with those modifiers in
his answer; for he would have left it unclear which of the two contrasted
states he was talking about there. Or rather, even worse, since on the suggested reading εἰδέναι ἁπλῶς is synonymous with εἰδέναι unmodified, the
unadorned εἰδέναι in which Aristotle couches his answer would mislead
us into thinking that he was referring to plain, non-universal knowledge,
whereas in fact he clearly intends to refer at least to the state of knowing universally (cf. 85ᵇ38–86ᵃ3). For these further reasons, then, it is far
preferable to think that—for the purposes of the question at hand, at any
rate—Aristotle is not intending to give differential treatment to the distinct
states marked by εἰδέναι καθόλου and εἰδέναι ἁπλῶς, but is instead treating
them as sufficiently similar to one another and different from non-universal
knowledge so that his answer in terms of unmodified εἰδέναι can apply to
both knowing universally and 'knowing in the unqualified sense'. In that
case, his answer should be read as follows: if the protasis of (*a*) were true,
then one would know, i.e. both universally and in the unqualified sense,
while if the protasis of (*b*) is true, then one would not know, i.e. neither
universally nor in the unqualified sense. And the unmodified εἰδέναι in Aristotle's answer can cover both of the states indicated in the questions of **EH9**
only if εἰδέναι ἁπλῶς serves there to refer, not to ordinary, non-universal
knowledge, but to the ideal state of scientific understanding.

Of course, in a question about our knowledge of the non-essential but
necessary and coextensive properties of a subject, as in Aristotle's example, knowing universally is insufficient for scientific understanding (see
e.g. 74ᵃ27–30, where the two states are distinguished); for one could know
a commensurate universal without *knowing the explanation why* it is true,
as would occur if one had not yet discovered the essence or causally primitive properties of the subject of that universal truth. Nevertheless, if
Aristotle is ignoring this possibility here and assuming that explanation
follows immediately upon the apprehension of the universal truth, or even
accompanies it (as in cases of discovering 'the that' and 'the why' at the
same time—see e.g. 93ᵃ16–18 and 35–6), then he could treat his ascription
of universal knowledge in the apodosis of (*a*) as licensing an ascription of
scientific understanding as well; and since, on the other hand, a person who

knows a non-commensurate universal without knowing the commensurate universal which that statement exemplifies is in no position properly to explain either statement (see e.g. 85ᵇ7–8), the denial of universal knowledge in the apodosis of (*b*) suffices for denying scientific understanding as well.

Thus, Aristotle's answer to the questions in **EH9** strongly favours an 'absolute' use of εἰδέναι ἁπλῶς there to refer to the state of unqualified knowledge as defined in **EH1**, with the explanation condition being foremost in his mind—since this would constitute the most salient difference between scientific understanding and knowing universally (see Appendix B), and hence would explain why he bothers to mention both states here—and with the necessity condition being perfectly compatible with what he says about the state of 'knowing in the unqualified sense'. Besides, it should really come as no surprise that Aristotle would want to return to the state of scientific understanding at the end of the continuous study in 1. 4–5, since this investigation was initiated for the express purpose of gaining insight into the nature of the premises required by the demonstrations that will issue in unqualified knowledge (see **EH3** and **EH4**, which likewise come from the uninterrupted investigation in 1. 4–5). We can conclude, then, that (as we should have expected after consideration of **EH1–8**, anyway) the use of εἰδέναι ἁπλῶς in **EH9** is wholly in keeping with the official definition of unqualified knowledge in **EH1** as well as with Aristotle's unvarying use of ἐπίστασθαι ἁπλῶς and εἰδέναι ἁπλῶς outside of the problematic opening chapter to the *Posterior Analytics*.⁴⁴

Thus, the preceding review of the two occurrences of εἰδέναι ἁπλῶς beyond the frontiers of 1. 1 shows clearly that the appearance of this expression in that initial chapter, which on the received view must indicate a cognitive state that obviously fails to meet the necessity condition on unqualified knowledge, generates the same set of problems as does the occurrence of ἐπίστασθαι ἁπλῶς immediately following it; for εἰδέναι ἁπλῶς in 1. 1 would (1) violate the nearby and formal definition of its technical synonym ἐπίστασθαι ἁπλῶς at the start of 1. 2; (2) be both without parallel and out of keeping with Aristotle's otherwise meticulous use of the synonyms εἰδέναι ἁπλῶς and ἐπίστασθαι ἁπλῶς in the early chapters of the *Posterior Analytics*; and (3) accomplish (1) and (2) for no good reason at all, since Aristotle was well equipped with other, more effective technical devices for indicating the state of having explicit knowledge of a singular truth. What the received view offers us in its reading of εἰδέναι ἁπλῶς in

---

⁴⁴ In fact, **EH9** speaks eloquently in favour of the absolute usage of εἰδέναι ἁπλῶς and ἐπίστασθαι ἁπλῶς in Aristotle; for unless these expressions had been groomed by the official definition of ἐπίστασθαι ἁπλῶς at the start of 1. 2 to be denoting phrases in their own right, Aristotle could hardly have juxtaposed εἰδέναι ἁπλῶς to a qualified occurrence of εἰδέναι, as he does here, and expected his audience to take ἁπλῶς *not* to be playing the context-relative, 'de-qualifying' role it normally plays in other connections.

1. 1, then, is yet another lexical anomaly. Since εἰδέναι ἁπλῶς makes fewer appearances in Aristotle than ἐπίστασθαι ἁπλῶς, and since the term εἰδέναι itself generally carries less of an epistemological charge than ἐπίστασθαι, this anomaly may not be quite as shocking as was the use of ἐπίστασθαι ἁπλῶς in 1. 1; but, given the official synonymity of the two expressions (as well as the emphatic placement of ἁπλῶς in the second clause of **B2**), the occurrence of εἰδέναι ἁπλῶς in 1. 1 none the less adds just one more lexical irregularity to the short passage at 71ᵃ17–30 which is already teeming with linguistic and doctrinal oddities.

APPENDIX B
Aristotle's Two Accounts of Justification

I discuss here Aristotle's two accounts of justificatory priority: 'bottom-up' J-priority, which is inversely correlated with explanatory priority, and 'top-down' J-priority, which is directly correlated with explanatory priority. The apparent incompatibility between these two mirror-image accounts of justification and J-priority is a notorious crux in the interpretation of Aristotle's epistemology, and reactions to it have divided scholars into two basic camps: the first, emphasizing the *probative* aspect of Aristotelian ἀπόδειξις and privileging the model of the mathematical sciences—moves tradition-ally associated with the ideas of axiomatic foundationalism, 'self-evident' first principles, and a rationalist faculty of 'intuition' for apprehending these indemonstrable 'certainties'—tends to downplay the importance of bottom-up justification, treating it as producing not *knowledge* but at best merely *probable true belief* (see e.g. Ross ad 71ᵇ19–23); the second camp, stressing the *explanatory* dimension of Aristotelian ἀπόδειξις and taking its cue from the natural sciences (with their empirical justification of statements about less evident causes on the basis of statements about the more evident phenomena, which generally requires that one *know* the de-monstrable 'that' before the indemonstrable 'why'—see e.g. 89ᵇ29–31 and 93ᵃ16 ff.), tries to explain away Aristotle's talk of top-down J-priority as an awkward restatement of the explanation condition on *scientific understand-ing* (see e.g. Detel ad 72ᵃ28).

Preferable to either of these dismissive and one-sided views, however, would be a reading which allows, as Aristotle obviously intends to al-low, that bottom-up and top-down justification can each warrant bona fide knowledge claims in connection with statements that fall within the same science and that, in a sense, represent the very same states of affairs (see Burnyeat, 'Understanding Knowledge'—though what follows constitutes a rejection of his hazy and apparently psychologistic solution to our problem in terms of what he calls 'intellectual habituation'). Such an account can best be achieved here, I suggest, by thinking of Aristotle's two forms of justification as relating to the same statements under different *modal* descriptions, with bottom-up justification from sense perception warranting claims to know that a demonstrable statement *is true* and top-down justification from first principles warranting claims to know that that same statement *is necessarily true*. In that case, we could allow the definition of J-priority in the text of Section 2 to stand for bottom-up J-priority, and then offer the following account of top-down J-priority:

> *p* has top-down J-priority over *q* iff knowledge that *p* is necessary is required for knowledge that *q* is necessary, but not vice versa.

A full defence of this interpretation of Aristotle's two accounts of justification and J-priority cannot be undertaken here; but brief mention may be made of some of the additional attractions this more elegant suggestion has over the above-mentioned alternatives, whose respective strengths it takes over by allowing us to do full justice to Aristotelian demonstrations in their dual capacity as both *proofs* and *explanations*, in the natural as well as the mathematical sciences.

First of all, the suggested view of top-down justification obviously comports well with the epistemic reading of the necessity condition on unqualified knowledge (see n. 15 above), and there is good support for that reading; for even if the amphibolous expression of the necessary condition in **EH1** does not explicitly endorse the epistemic reading, Aristotle evidently does reveal a commitment to it at 75^{a}14–15 (see also Barnes ad 71^{b}9).[45] Moreover, since for Aristotle the essence of a subject both explains why the subject has the necessary non-essential properties it does (e.g. 99^{b}21–3) and also constitutes the source of their necessity (see the remarks above on **EH4**; cf. *Metaph.* 1015^{b}7–15), it would be natural for him to adopt, alongside the view that knowledge of essences is required for *knowledge of the explanation why* those non-essential properties hold (e.g. 90^{a}31–4), the suggested account of top-down J-priority according to which knowledge of the necessity of essential properties is required for *knowledge of the necessity* of non-essential properties (see 75^{a}12–17—which, however, need only demand a necessary and not also an explanatory middle for knowledge of the necessity of demonstrative conclusions). And, in that case, we could readily appreciate how demonstrations can be necessary (note δεῖ at 72^{a}25) as well as sufficient for satisfying both the explanation condition and the epistemic version of the necessity condition on unqualified

---

[45] Note also Aristotle's hesitations at 72^{a}28 and 36–7, which are best understood, not in the light of 71^{a}17–24 (*pace* Ross ad 72^{a}28), but in connection with the question, left open by Aristotle here, whether a necessary syllogistic conclusion can be derived from premisses one of which is not itself necessary—cf. 75^{a}1–17.

knowledge (particularly if Aristotle holds that what assures us of the necessity of non-essential properties is our recognition of the explanatory
linkage connecting them to the essential properties we already know to be
necessary). By the same token, the logical equivalence between E-priority
and top-down J-priority would also become intelligible, since a statement
would be prior in the order of explanation if and only if it was also prior
in the order of knowledge of necessities, with both sorts of priority representing proximity to the explanatory and necessary essence of the subject
of that statement. Furthermore, on the suggested account, the curious and
seemingly problematic talk by which Aristotle expresses the idea of top-
down J-priority at the end of 1. 2—i.e. that first principles must be 'known
more' (εἰδέναι μᾶλλον) than demonstrative conclusions—can be understood
straightforwardly and charitably (though not, in the final analysis, without
running into some philosophical difficulty) as a statement of the requirement that we have greater justification for claiming to know the *necessity* of
first principles than that of demonstrative conclusions; for our derivative
knowledge of the necessity of non-essential properties would be dependent on our direct knowledge of necessity of first principles (cf. 72^{a}29–32).
(This same point is easily extended to what are basically the equivalent requirements of *being more convinced* (πιστεύειν μᾶλλον) about first principles
than about their conclusions, and of *knowing* the first principles *beforehand* (προγινώσκειν), at least when the latter demand pertains to top-down
J-priority—see n. 22 above.) Finally, this account does not commit the
empiricist Aristotle to the unappealing rationalist idea of an intuitive faculty for apprehending essences and their necessity—*νοῦς ex machina*, as it
were—an idea which, despite continued parroting, is wildly implausible
for the natural sciences and in fact finds very little textual support in the
Posterior Analytics (2. 19, the text in the *Posterior Analytics* on which this
view has generally rested, quite plainly regards νοῦς as a state or ἕξις and
not as a faculty or δύναμις at all—see 99^{b}18, 25, 100^{a}10, and ^{b}6; cf. 99^{b}32–
5, which concerns the 'faculty' of perception; see also Barnes ad 100^{b}5).
Rather, the suggested reading allows that claims to know that a particular
statement represents the essence of its subject may be justified discursively
through bottom-up J-priority (see e.g. *Post. An.* 2. 8, 2. 19, 100^{b}3–5; *Top.*
101^{a}36–^{b}4; *Pr. An.* 46^{a}10–27; and *De anima* 402^{b}16–25); knowledge of the
necessity of this essence-defining statement is then gained, not from some
occult intuitive faculty, but simply as an immediate consequence of the
overarching metaphysical principle that real definitions, representing as
they do not only the eternal but also the causally basic structure of reality,
are necessarily true—see e.g. *Metaph.* 1015^{b}6–15. (See further n. 24.)

   Against the suggested reading of top-down J-priority, it will be argued
that Aristotle's epistemological theory does not always require knowledge
of explanatory essences for knowledge of the necessity of non-essential

properties; for instance, at 1. 4, 73^{b}32 ff. (see the discussion of **EH9** in Appendix A), Aristotle offers an extensional test for καθόλου, and hence necessary, predications, and this test could evidently be performed even without knowledge of the explanatorily primitive properties of a given kind (but cf. 75^{a}28–35). Let us concede the gist of this objection without more ado. What we should then do is not to forgo the attractions of the suggested account by abandoning it altogether, but merely to qualify this conception of top-down J-priority by saying that it holds only 'paradigmatically'— as we must likewise qualify Aristotle's explicit account of bottom-up J-priority at 72^{a}1–5, e.g. for our knowledge of the law of non-contradiction, which is among the most universal statements but which at the same time is also best known to us (see *Metaph.* 1005^{b}11–18; cf. *Post. An.* 71^{a}11–17, 72^{a}14–17, and 76^{b}23–4). Aristotle's view of these two forms of J-priority involves some degree of abstraction from actual epistemological practice; it constitutes a highly general and idealized but none the less illuminating picture of how knowledge acquisition proceeds on the way to and from first principles (cf. e.g. *NE* 1095^{a}32–^{b}1), with the linear stages along these two epistemological routes being objectively marked off by the metaphysical standard of E-priority, which, in actual knowledge acquisition, at least as Aristotle views it, would correlate with some regularity both inversely with bottom-up J-priority and directly with top-down J-priority as understood on the interpretation proposed here.

ARISTOTLE AND THRASYMACHUS

DOMINIC SCOTT

No bound to riches has been fixed for man.
SOLON, fr. 13. 71

THERE has been considerable interest recently in the kind of audience Aristotle is addressing in the *Nicomachean Ethics* and in the
nature of the arguments that he uses. On the basis of some passages,
it has been argued that he is not aiming to convert anyone who does
not already aspire to the moral life; instead he demands that his audience must have been brought up with beliefs in the value of justice
and the other virtues, beliefs to which he can appeal throughout the
course of his argument.[1] If one accepts this view, it is then tempting
to see a strong contrast between his aims and those of Plato, especially in the *Gorgias* and *Republic* book 1. In these works we find
interlocutors who deny the value of justice and claim that *eudaimonia* ('happiness') is to be found in pursuing its exact opposite—
untrammelled *pleonexia*. Proceeding dialectically and professing to
use only premises that they can accept, Socrates attempts to refute
their challenge and steer them towards the life of justice.[2]

There are certainly some texts which, prima facie, suggest that

© Dominic Scott 2000
Earlier versions of this paper were given at Cornell University and the 1999 Pacific
division meeting of the APA. I have benefited greatly from all those who commented,
and especially from Harold Hodes, Terry Irwin, Stephen Menn, Christopher Rowe,
and Jennifer Whiting.

[1] See M. F. Burnyeat, 'Aristotle on Learning to be Good' ['Learning to be Good'],
in A. O. Rorty (ed.), *Essays on Aristotle's Ethics* [*Ethics*] (Berkeley, 1980), 69–92 at 81;
J. Lear, *Aristotle: The Desire to Understand* [*Aristotle*] (Cambridge, 1988), 192–7;
and I. Vasiliou, 'The Role of Good Upbringing in Aristotle's Ethics' ['Upbringing'], *Philosophy and Phenomenological Research*, 56 (1996), 771–97. Not everyone
accepts this interpretation. Irwin has argued that Aristotle, no less than Plato, can
be read as addressing his arguments to a moral sceptic. I discuss some of his views
in the appendix.
[2] Lear, *Aristotle*, 193, talks of 'a radical departure from Plato'.

Aristotle refuses to address the likes of Callicles and Thrasymachus and that he presupposes a commitment to the recognized virtues.[3] At the same time, there is a particularly famous passage in the *Nicomachean Ethics* which, at the very least, raises a question-mark over this interpretation. In *NE* 1. 7 Aristotle constructs an argument out of the claim that *eudaimonia* consists in the fulfilment of the human 'function' (*ergon*). It is from this argument that he extracts a crucial premiss for the rest of the work, viz. that *eudaimonia* consists in virtuous activity. Few commentators doubt that this argument is fundamental to the structure of the entire work. Yet, as many of them have pointed out, it is remarkably similar to the final argument of *Republic* book 1, where Socrates is engaged in the last phase of his attempt to refute Thrasymachus' challenge to justice.[4] If there is supposed to be a radical discontinuity between Platonic and Aristotelian ethics, what use would Aristotle have had for an argument borrowed from a text which almost epitomizes the anti-sceptical project?

The central focus of this paper will be upon this apparent tension between the supposed aims of the *Nicomachean Ethics* and the obvious provenance of one of its central arguments. In attempting to resolve it, we shall come to see that Aristotle's relation to the anti-sceptical project found in certain Platonic works is more complex than is usually imagined: neither a matter of straightforward continuity, nor a complete break. I shall start in Section 1 with a comparison between the two function arguments and then, in Section 2, turn to those texts that give rise to the impression that he has a very different project from Plato.

A note about terminology: I shall use the expression 'moral intuitions' to refer to beliefs in the choiceworthiness of the virtues of character that Aristotle discusses in the course of the *Nicomachean Ethics*. I shall call the opposition to such beliefs 'moral scepticism' or simply 'scepticism'. A good deal of my discussion will focus on whether or not an argument uses moral intuitions as premisses and so operates within a certain moral viewpoint. I shall use the terms

---

[3] 1. 4, 1095[b]4–8; and 10. 9, 1179[b]7–31.

[4] See e.g. A. Grant, *The Ethics of Aristotle*, 4th edn., rev. (London, 1885), i. 449; J. A. Stewart, *Notes on the* Nicomachean Ethics *of Aristotle* [*Ethics*] (Oxford, 1892), i. 97–8; J. Burnet, *The Ethics of Aristotle* (London, 1900), 34; R. A. Gauthier and J. Y. Jolif, *L'Éthique à Nicomaque*, 2nd edn. (Louvain and Paris, 1970), ii/1. 54–5; and T. D. Roche, 'On the Alleged Metaphysical Foundation of Aristotle's *Ethics*' ['Metaphysical Foundation'], *Ancient Philosophy*, 8 (1988), 49–62 at 59.

'internal' and 'external' to distinguish arguments that rely upon moral intuitions and those that do not.

1. Virtue and the human function

(a) The function argument in Republic book 1

Plato's function argument addresses the question who lives better and is happier, the just or the unjust person (352 D 2–4). My aim in this section is not to provide an exhaustive analysis of the argument, but to draw attention to two features of it that will be particularly salient when we turn to *NE* 1. 7.

The first concerns the position against which Socrates is arguing. Thrasymachus sets out his view extensively at 343 B 1 ff., claiming that the greatest happiness is to be found in 'perfect' injustice (343 E 7–344 C 8), *pleonexia* on the grandest scale. The person who epitomizes this life is the tyrant—someone for whom there are no limits on what he can take or from whom. As he affirms a little later on (349 C 6–9), the unjust person overreaches everyone in everything, always grabbing the most for himself.

It is important to note that the ideal of *pleonexia* as 'having more' without limit, once laid out at 344 A–C, becomes seminal to the whole work, even when Thrasymachus himself ceases to be an interlocutor.[5] Glaucon, in renewing his challenge, cites the example of Gyges, whose ring enables him to step outside all social bounds in the pursuit of his desires. The same motif appears in book 9 with the critique of a character who embodies the most extreme form of injustice, the tyrant. We are told repeatedly that, in his pursuit of 'lawless' desires, there are no limits, no sources from which he will not take.[6] This passage also draws out a theme that was always implicit in Thrasymachus' original challenge, viz. that the need for unlimited power is driven by the presence of ever increasing desire in the soul of the tyrant. *Pleonexia* on the grandest scale follows naturally from the total collapse of psychological restraint.

The conception of *eudaimonia* against which Plato battles in the *Republic* also figures in the *Gorgias*'s comparison of the just and

---

[5] At a number of places Socrates indicates that he still has Thrasymachus' position in view: cf. 358 A 7–8; 367 A 5–C 5; 545 A 8–B 1.

[6] 571 D 1–4; 573 D 6–575 A 7; cf. also 591 D 6–9.

unjust lives.[7] The tyrant motif surfaces when Polus, in his encomium to injustice, refers to the example of Archelaus (470 D 5–471 D 2; cf. 469 C 7). But the connection between the conception of *eudaimonia* as unlimited *pleonexia* is clearest when Callicles enters the argument. Here is the way in which he describes his conception of the ideal life:

The fine and just according to nature is this, what I'm speaking freely of to you now—the man who is to live rightly should let his appetites grow as large as possible and not restrain them, and when these are as large as possible, he must have the power to serve them, because of his bravery and wisdom, and to fill them with whatever he has an appetite for at any time. (491 E 6–492 A 3)[8]

Shortly afterwards, and with Callicles' complete agreement, Socrates clarifies this ideal in the following terms:

Do you say that a man must not restrain his appetites, if he's to be as he should be, but should let them grow as great as possible, and find fulfilment for them from anywhere at all and that virtue is this? (492 D 5–E 1)

As in the *Republic*, there is a very close association between intemperance (*akolasia*) and *pleonexia*. Both notions imply the absence of restraint, whether internal and psychological (*akolasia*), or external and social (*pleonexia*).

It is also worth noting that Plato's target in the *Gorgias* and the *Republic* was not the ideal of a few maverick extremists, but had a very wide appeal, as is made clear when Glaucon and Adeimantus rearticulate it in *Republic* book 2.[9] Indeed, a closely related point had already been made by Socrates in the *Apology*:

I shall never cease to practise philosophy, to exhort you and in my usual way to point out to any one of you whom I happen to meet: '. . . are you not ashamed of your eagerness to possess as much wealth, reputation and honours as possible, while you do not care for nor give thought to wisdom and truth, or the best possible state of your soul?' (29 D 4–E 3)[10]

The fact that he feels the need to propagate this message to every-

---

[7] For the connection between justice and *eudaimonia* see *Gorg.* 491 E 5 ff. and 507 C 8 ff.

[8] Translations of the *Gorgias* are from T. Irwin, *Plato's Gorgias* (Oxford, 1979).

[9] Cf. e.g. 358 A 4 ff.

[10] Trans. G. M. A. Grube, in *Plato: Complete Works*, ed. J. Cooper (Indianapolis, 1997).

one, 'young or old, foreigner or fellow citizen' (30 A 3–4), points to
the broad attraction of the rival position.

The second feature of Plato's function argument that will be central to our comparison with the *Nicomachean Ethics* concerns its
structure. Socrates starts by establishing the existence of a 'function' (*ergon*) for each thing, defined as either what it alone can do or
what it does best (352 E 2–3). To illustrate the first case he appeals
to the function of eyes and ears and, for the second, uses examples
of artefacts (352 E 5–353 A 5). In the next stage he introduces the
notion of a virtue (ἀρετή): anything that is to perform its function
successfully must possess its own particular virtue. Again the point
is illustrated with reference to the sense organs (353 B 14–C 11).

These general points settled, Socrates goes on to consider the
case of human beings. The soul has a function, something it alone
can do—managing, ruling and deliberating. All these are said to be
peculiar (ἴδια) to it (353 D 7). He also adds, but does not further
explain, that life is the function of the soul. If the soul has a function, it must also have a virtue without which its function could not
be successfully fulfilled (353 D 11– E 5). So by this point we have
reached the conclusion that the soul's successful activity requires
virtue. At 353 E 7–8 Socrates identifies the soul's virtue with justice and so concludes that the soul's successful activity, and hence
happiness, require justice.

Obviously, without the premiss that justice is the virtue of the
soul, Socrates would be unable to secure the overall conclusion that
justice is necessary for happiness. But this premiss is not supported
within the function argument itself; it is accepted as having been
agreed in an earlier passage: 349 B 1–350 C 11. Thrasymachus had
originally argued that injustice was a virtue and a form of wisdom
(348 E 1–4). But having agreed that the unjust person tries to outdo
the unjust as well as the just, he was refuted by Socrates' list of
examples showing that no one who has virtue in their domain en-
gages in competition or *pleonexia* with their peers. Justice, rather
than injustice, is the virtue of the soul.

On its own, therefore, the function argument of 352 D 8–354 A 9
is insufficient to fend off the sceptical challenge: although it establishes that virtue in *some* sense is necessary for *eudaimonia*, parties
who differ radically about what counts as virtue could still agree
with its conclusion: at 348 C 1– E 4 Thrasymachus had called virtue
what most people call injustice; in the *Gorgias*, Callicles had made

a similar inversion, identifying virtue with luxury, intemperance, and freedom (492 C 4–5). Unless it is supported by 349 B 1–350 C 11, the function argument is neutral as to what kind of virtue, moralistic or Thrasymachean, is required for happiness. It is an important structural feature of Socrates' reply to Thrasymachus that he needs a separate argument (henceforth 'the *pleonexia* argument') as a way of establishing that the virtue required to fulfil the human function is indeed justice.

(b) The function argument in Nicomachean Ethics *1. 7*

Aristotle proposes to investigate *eudaimonia* by reference to the human function at *NE* 1. 7, 1097^{b}22 ff. First, he tries to show that humans do indeed have a function. After citing experts in the different crafts and asserting that in every case they have a function, he asks:

> Have the carpenter, then, and the tanner certain functions or activities, and has man none? (1100^{a}13–14)[11]

To strengthen his case, he points out that individual parts of a human—e.g. eyes, hands, or feet—each have a function, so that a human being as a whole must surely have one too. His next move is to ask what it is. He surveys the functions of plants and other animals and, eliminating what is held in common with other organisms (such as life or perception), identifies the human function as activity of the soul according to reason (1098^{a}7–8). This is not yet the conclusion of the argument because, to achieve the good, we must not just engage in our characteristic activity, but must do so in the best way, i.e. with virtue. *Eudaimonia* therefore consists in activity in accordance with virtue.

There is no doubting the similarities between this argument and the final section of *Republic* book 1. Most importantly, they both arrive at the conclusion that virtue is necessary for *eudaimonia*, and they do so by a very similar sequence of steps involving the notion of there being a function for human beings. Moreover, there are striking similarities at a more detailed level. Both make use of the notion of something being special or peculiar to humans,[12] and both exploit two kinds of analogy: bodily parts and crafts. At a more

---

[11] Translations of the *NE* are by W. D. Ross, rev. J. O. Urmson, in *The Complete Works of Aristotle*, ed. J. Barnes (Princeton, 1984), with slight modifications.
[12] 353 D 7 and 1097^{b}34.

detailed level still, even some of Socrates' examples (horses, eyes) turn up in Aristotle's version.

There are, of course, points where Aristotle's argument differs from Plato's, but most of these appear to be modifications aimed at improving the argument—making it better able to establish the conclusion that Plato originally had in mind. For instance, where Socrates and Thrasymachus had simply accepted that humans have a function, Aristotle makes some attempt to argue for it (1097^b25–33). Again, when it comes to specifying the nature of our function, Aristotle seems to be trying to be more systematic. Plato gave us a list of candidates, including managing, ruling, and deliberating. Aristotle, in using reason to identify our function, could be seen as trying to find out what underlies Plato's more miscellaneous list; and, while giving a more unified approach than Plato, he also promises something more precise with his distinction between prescriptive and obedient reason (1098^a4–5), so we need not accuse him of replacing Plato's miscellaneity with vagueness. Plato also added 'living' to his list of items constituting the human function, but never explained how this is to be compatible with the peculiarity requirement. Here again Aristotle attempts to be more precise. Living takes different forms, so the nutritive and perceptive kinds are excluded as being common to other living things (1097^b33–1098^a3). Later, however, he does define the human function as life *of a certain kind* (1098^a13), obviously referring to the life of a rational being.

Whether or not my comparison is too partisan in favour of Aristotle, none of these differences undermines the claim that Aristotle is continuing Plato's project of arguing that virtue is a necessary condition for *eudaimonia*.[13]

Let us now compare the two arguments on the point we made about the structure of Plato's argument: on its own, it merely showed that virtue in some sense is necessary for *eudaimonia*. He needed the support of his previous *pleonexia* argument to rule out Thrasymachus' conception of virtue. On this point, the comparison becomes more complicated. On the one hand, it does look as if there is nothing in Aristotle's premisses to lead to the conclusion

[13] There is a potentially important difference in the way that the two passages define a function. Plato gives two options—either what is peculiar to something or what it can do best. Aristotle mentions only the first. Nevertheless, this still does not affect the point at issue in this paper. For further differences see J. M. Cooper, *Reason and Human Good in Aristotle* [*Reason and Human Good*] (Cambridge, Mass., 1975), 145–6 n. 2.

that *eudaimonia* requires moralistic virtue. As some commentators have argued, all we know about the good life is that it requires the use of reason in accordance with virtue, which is, as yet, some unspecified kind of excellence.¹⁴ Like Plato, he cannot be taking the argument as establishing the conclusion that moralistic virtue is necessary for *eudaimonia*.

On the basis of this, one may be tempted to make a further claim—that Aristotle is in exactly the same position as Socrates before he recalled the *pleonexia* argument. The fact that Aristotle lays great emphasis on reason seems of little help here: this does exclude the purely bestial life of gratification, but is not enough to rule out the positions of Thrasymachus and Callicles. Both of them see wisdom as integral to *eudaimonia*; in so far as they propose a life of gratification, it is one endorsed by reason and self-awareness.¹⁵

However, although Aristotle's conception of virtue is just as indeterminate as Plato's before the *pleonexia* argument was invoked, it is not clear that he sees himself as in exactly the same position. He claims to have proved that *eudaimonia* consists in activity of the rational soul: this is clear from 1. 7 itself, and also from the following chapter, where he takes himself to have shown that the human good consists in the goods of the soul (i.e. virtuous activities) and not in externals (1098ᵇ19–20). Now this conclusion is incompatible with the most obvious reading of the Thrasymachean ideal, where bodily and external goods presumably constitute the final goal: the reason for pursuing externals without limit is most likely to be that they are good in themselves, and not subordinate to anything else. So even without a determinate conception of virtue, the argument causes difficulties for Thrasymachus and Callicles.¹⁶

Nevertheless, the outcome of the argument is still vague. Even though the good is identified with activity of the rational soul, we have not ruled out the possibility that it may involve, rather than consist in, the unlimited pursuit of externals. So Aristotle needs

¹⁴ See J. McDowell, 'The Role of *Eudaimonia* in Aristotle's Ethics', in Rorty, *Ethics*, 359–76 at 366, and Vasiliou, 'Upbringing', 782, 787.

¹⁵ Cf. *Gorg.* 489 E 6–9; 497 E 3–6; *Rep.* 348 D 1–E 4.

¹⁶ One could dispute my reading of *NE* 1. 7 and claim that *eudaimonia* merely *involves* the use of reason: such a position would be consistent even with the most natural understanding of the Thrasymachean ideal. For this weaker reading of 1. 7 see T. Irwin, 'The Structure of Aristotelian Happiness', *Ethics*, 101 (1991), 382–91 at 390. The stronger reading seems more plausible, however, since Aristotle is emphatic about identifying *eudaimonia* and virtuous activity: aside from 1098ᵇ19–20, see 1099ᵃ29–31, 1099ᵇ26, 1100ᵃ13–14, and 1102ᵃ5–6.

the *pleonexia* argument, or a surrogate, to reach a more determinate account of virtue and so clinch the results of the function argument.

There is no sign of the *pleonexia* argument in the rest of 1. 7, nor of any surrogate, and in the following chapter he turns to compare the results of his argument against widely held views about the nature of *eudaimonia*. So far, then, Aristotle seems to be borrowing only one part of the final section of *Republic* book 1.

At this point, one might be tempted to say that Aristotle does not try to fill the gap in the function argument as Socrates had done, using a further argument with premises that Thrasymachus could accept; instead, he now takes an unashamedly intuitionist route, drawing on conventional beliefs about virtue to fill in the sketch of 1. 7.[17] If this is correct, he does not after all borrow Plato's anti-sceptical argument in its entirety but only a fragment which, on its own, cuts less ice with the sceptic; his own supplement to that argument presupposes a conventional view about the content of the virtues.

It would, however, be premature to give up hope of finding a non-intuitionist replacement for the missing *pleonexia* argument. Although Aristotle does make extensive use of moral intuitions throughout the *Nicomachean Ethics*, the interpretation I have just sketched exaggerates the role that they play, and allows them to dominate the work too soon. Having concluded in 1. 7 that virtue in some sense is required for *eudaimonia*, he continues this line of argument in two later passages, 1. 13 and 2. 5–6, with the explicit aim of giving a more determinate account of virtue, and so of improving upon the conclusion of 1. 7. Both these chapters contain arguments that do not presuppose moral intuitions. In other words, the second half of 1. 7 starts a line of argument that is postponed (by a survey of the appearances in 1. 8 and a discussion of fortune in 1. 9–11), but then resumed in 1. 13; the argument is then further interrupted for a discussion of education in 2. 1–4 but resumed, yet again, in 2. 5–6. In the next two subsections I propose to see if we can find the *pleonexia* argument or a surrogate in either 1. 13 or 2. 5–6.

(c) Nicomachean Ethics *1. 13*

That this chapter picks up the strand of argument from 1. 7 is clear from the way it begins:

---

[17] For an approach along these lines see Vasiliou, 'Upbringing', esp. 781.

Since *eudaimonia* is an activity of the soul in accordance with perfect virtue, we must consider the nature of virtue. (1102ᵃ5–6)

Aristotle then fulfils his promise to invesitgate virtue by laying the foundations of his moral psychology, first by discussing the different elements of the soul. He initially divides it into the irrational and the rational (1102ᵃ27–8) and then subdivides the former into one part, the vegetative, which is not responsive to reason (1102ᵇ29–30), and another, unnamed part which is (1102ᵇ13 ff.); this is the part by which we feel desire and emotion. A crucial idea throughout the *Nicomachean Ethics* is that these can in some way be moulded by reason. As for the rational part, he hints at the end of the chapter that this can be subdivided into what will later turn out to be practical and theoretical components (1103ᵃ5–6). But most of this chapter has been concerned with the practical kind of reason—the part of the soul that gives commands to the appetitive to obey—and with the relation between the two. In the course of this discussion, he modifies his earlier way of contrasting them as rational and non-rational, by allowing that the appetitive and emotional element can be called rational in a sense in so far as it is responsive to reason (1103ᵃ1–3).

So how far has 1. 13 narrowed down the conclusion of the function argument? One thing it has done is to explain a rather cryptic reference to two 'parts' of the rational principle in 1. 7, 1098ᵃ4–5:

. . . one part has such a principle in the sense of being obedient to one, the other in the sense of possessing one and exercising thought . . .

But although we have a clearer picture of the different aspects of reason, what have we now learnt about virtue, which was meant to be the focus of the chapter? At the end of 1. 13, and the beginning of 2. 1, Aristotle explains that virtue should be divided along the lines of the distinctions within the soul now established. Thus there are intellectual virtues (practical and theoretical—the subject-matter of *NE* 6) and, corresponding to the appetitive/emotional part, virtues of character, which involve feeling the right degree of emotion or desire.

This does mean that by the beginning of *NE* 2, we have a more determinate conception of the good life than we were left with at the end of 1. 7. We have now been told that it will involve using practical reason to inform and mould our emotions and actions. Yet, informative as this is about virtue, it fails to bring us any closer to a moralistic conception of virtue. For all the talk of bringing appetites into line with reason, the likes of Callicles or Thrasymachus might claim that reason demands that they be maximized without limit.

(*d*) *The doctrine of the mean:* Nicomachean Ethics 2. 6

If 1. 13 does not fulfil our expectations, we should not yet abandon hope, because Aristotle resumes his investigation of the conclusion of the original function argument in 2. 5–6. In these chapters he offers a definition of virtue, starting in 2. 5 with the *genus*: virtue is a 'disposition' (ἕξις). At the beginning of 2. 6 he again admits that this is not enough (presumably it is still too indeterminate) and attempts to supply the *differentia*. This is indeed the chapter where Aristotle gives a more specific account of virtue, and in the first part (up to 1106^b35) he does so by arguing that it is a mean.

It is essential for understanding this passage and its role in the structure of the work to realize that it is a direct continuation of the function argument. This is clear from the way it begins, restating what the argument of 1. 7 had told us about virtue:

We may remark, then, that every virtue both brings into good condition the thing of which it is the virtue and makes the function of that thing be done well; e.g. the virtue of the eye makes both the eye and its function good; for it is by the virtue of the eye that we see well. Similarly the virtue of a horse makes a horse both good in itself and good at running and at carrying its rider and at awaiting the attack of the enemy. Therefore, if this is true in every case, the virtue of man also will be the state which makes a man good and makes him do his own function well. (1106^a15–24)

This directly recalls the gist of 1. 7, 1098^a7–15—viz. that a thing can only perform its function well through its virtue. The examples of the function of a horse and that of an eye repeat those of 1. 7, 1097^b30 and 1098^a2. In effect, his question now is: given the connection established in 1. 7 between virtue and function, what more can we learn about the nature of virtue? Aristotle now provides an inductive argument from crafts to virtue. In anything continuous and divisible there is a more or less and a mean. He then distinguishes between the mean relative to us and relative to the object; to illustrate this distinction he gives the example of a trainer prescribing differing amounts of food for his athletes. This brings him to conclude at 1106^b5–7: 'every expert avoids excess and deficiency but aims for the mean'. Every art achieves its function well by

aiming at the mean—indeed the very accuracy of such arts consists
in their hitting the mean so precisely that anything added or taken
away would destroy the achievement. Now he draws his conclusion:

If virtue is more exact and better than any art, as nature also is, then it
must have the quality of aiming at the mean. (1106^b14-16)

Arts achieve a good of a certain sort and are also remarkable for
their accuracy (1106^b9-14). Thus virtue, which, like any craft, is
concerned with what is continuous and divisible, but is even better and even more accurate,[18] must also be something that aims at
the mean.[19]

  To bring out the continuity between 1. 7 and 2. 6, remember
how a crucial move in the earlier one involved an *a fortiori* argument from the crafts:

Have the carpenter, then, and the tanner certain functions or activities, and
has man none? (1097^b28-30)

In 1. 7 he argues that human beings have a function, by appealing
to the fact that a craftsman has one. In 2. 6 he further argues that
humans achieve their function by hitting a mean with the appeal
to the fact that a craftsman achieves his function by hitting a mean
(*meson*).[20]

  In this passage Aristotle provides an argument, henceforth the
'*meson* argument', that continues the line of thought of 1. 7. Since
he proceeds inductively, without relying on intuitions, he has not
lurched from the indeterminate conception of virtue of 1. 7 straight

---

[18] A good explanation of this point is given by Stewart, *Ethics*, i. 196.

[19] The doctrine of the mean makes a brief appearance in 2. 5, when Aristotle
illustrates the way in which dispositions can be praised or blamed (1105^b25-8).
However, he uses the doctrine only by way of illustration; he need not be taken to
be presupposing its truth at this point. In 2. 6 it is clear that he makes an attempt
to argue for the doctrine *ab initio*.

[20] At 1106^a24-6, just after saying 'the virtue of man also will be the state which
makes a man good and makes him do his own function well', he adds: 'how this will
be we have stated already, but it will be made plain also by the following consideration of the nature of virtue'. Commentators have long asked which passage Aristotle
is referring to here. Some look back to 2. 2, 1104^a11 ff., where, in the course of discussing moral education, he says that virtues are produced and preserved by actions
lying in the mean. But this is about how the virtue is developed, while 1106^a24-6
is about how virtue—*once it has been developed*—will fulfil the function. The mystery, however, disappears once we read 2. 6 as a direct continuation of the function
argument: the back-reference of 1106^a24-5 is to 1. 7, specifically 1098^a7-12, where
Aristotle asserts the connection between a thing's having its virtue and achieving its
function, precisely the link just mentioned in 1106^a23-4.

into a moralized one. Rather, there is an intermediate phase in which he extends the function argument to show that the virtue required by *eudaimonia* must fit into a certain pattern, a triad in which the virtue is opposed by two extremes. In doing this, he has moved a step closer towards showing that the intuitive conception of the virtues is indeed that required for *eudaimonia*.

At this point, one might object that the doctrine of the mean is too indeterminate to be of any use in bridging the gap between the original function argument and the account of moralistic virtue espoused in the central books. To say that virtue is a mean between extremes leaves open too many rival conceptions of virtue in the field. In fact, at the beginning of the next chapter Aristotle himself concedes that his definition of virtue is still rather indeterminate ($1107^{a}28$).

Yet, indeterminate though it may be in some respects, the doctrine of the mean is nevertheless incompatible with the sort of position against which Plato had fought. We saw above that the target he had in mind involved the maximization of desire and, with it, the removal of social constraints, allowing one to take without limit from anyone. Such a conception of *eudaimonia* is clearly excluded by the doctrine of the mean. This point is not undermined by the fact that someone who followed the Calliclean or Thrasymachean prescription might in practice be forced to limit their ambitions (because, for instance, they were not very good at covering their tracks or had not acquired enough power in their city). Such restraint would merely be a concession to circumstances; in itself, the ideal has no place for limits, and this is the point at which it is incompatible with Aristotle's theory, on which the existence of limits is a mark of success.[21]

The interpretation I mentioned above was that Aristotle starts by borrowing a fragment of the anti-sceptical argument, and then

---

[21] A. W. H. Adkins, 'The Connection between Aristotle's *Ethics* and *Politics*', in D. Keyt and F. D. Miller (eds.), *A Companion to Aristotle's Politics* (Oxford and Cambridge, Mass., 1991), 75–93 at 79–80, claims that the doctrine of the mean is still too indeterminate to exclude the immoralist ideal. Presumably he means that Callicles or Thrasymachus could appropriate the doctrine, but invert the usual moralistic scheme of virtues and vices: what Aristotle calls 'intemperance' they could call the mean, and 'temperance' the deficiency. Yet, although both Plato and Aristotle allow that the immoralist will engage in some kind of relabelling (*Gorg.* 491 E 2–492 C 8, *Rep.* 348 E 1–4 and 560 D 2–561 A 1; *NE* 2. 8, $1108^{b}19$–26), such inversions do not operate with a *triad* of character states—a mean and two extremes. Because the immoralist treats the pursuit of excess as the ideal, there can be only one virtue and *one* vice, the deficiency, even if it is capable of being instantiated to different degrees.

abandons it, relying on intuitions instead. But I am proposing that, when read together, *NE* 1. 7 and 2. 6 constitute a strand of argument that follows the final assault on Thrasymachus much more closely than has been recognized. Not only does he borrow the function argument from Plato but, in 2. 6, he has a surrogate for the *pleonexia* argument that serves to narrow down his notion of virtue and help exclude the same conception of *eudaimonia* against which Plato had battled.[22] What is also striking is that Aristotle develops his surrogate to the *pleonexia* argument out of the function argument itself. Where Plato had thought that line of argument exhausted, Aristotle finds more mileage in it.[23]

2. Preaching to the converted?

If I am right about the continuity between *Republic* book 1 and *Nicomachean Ethics* 1–2, we need to confront those texts that have been taken to suggest a radical departure on Aristotle's part from the Platonic enterprise: what is the evidence for saying that he refuses to address the sceptic and that he uses moral intuitions as premises? Where the second question is concerned, we need in particular to focus upon whether he actually says that all his arguments will depend on intuitions: if so, there would be an immediate problem in accounting for the fact that the *ergon–meson* argument is so obviously external.

In this section I wish to show that he does indeed refuse to address the sceptic, but still recognizes the need for external, anti-sceptical arguments for the purposes of reinforcement, to prevent the possibility that his audience might drift away from the values of their upbringing.

---

[22] Although the *pleonexia* and *meson* arguments are distinct, there is some similarity between them (e.g. both use a craft analogy). See J. Adam, *The* Republic *of Plato*, 2nd edn. (Cambridge, 1963), i, 50, and J. P. Maguire, 'Thrasymachus . . . or Plato?', *Phronesis*, 16 (1971), 142–63 at 153, who compares the *pleonexia* argument to Aristotle's treatment of justice in *NE* 5. For brief anticipations of the doctrine of the mean in later sections of the *Republic* see 591 E 1–3 and 618 E 4–619 B 1.

[23] One further difference between the arguments of *Rep.* 1 and *NE* 1–2 is that, while Aristotle tries to show that *eudaimonia* requires all the virtues, Plato seems to be arguing for the narrower conclusion that it requires the virtue of justice. This does not undermine my claim that Aristotle has an externalist argument which excludes the Thrasymachean ideal. (If anything, it makes Aristotle's enterprise look all the more ambitious.)

(a) The nature of the audience

In 1. 3, 1095^{a}4–11, Aristotle describes the young as unsuitable for ethics lectures. They tend to follow their passions, and yet the aim of ethics is not knowledge but action:

> For to such persons, as to the incontinent, knowledge brings no profit; but to those who desire and act in accordance with a rational principal, knowledge about such matters will be of great benefit. (1095^{a}8–11)

On its own, this text excludes those who follow passion rather than reason, but is otherwise somewhat vague. At 10. 9, 1179^{b}7–31, however, in a passage that focuses directly on the efficacy of ethical argument, Aristotle is more specific about who will and who will not benefit from his lectures. As in 1. 3, he excludes those who are ruled by passion, but the whole passage is more complex. Again he contrasts two sets of people, the passionate and the well brought-up. The former, now identified with 'the many' (1179^{b}10), are too distracted by bodily pleasure to be susceptible to reason. But this passage makes a further point: as well as being ruled by bodily pleasure, the many 'have not even a conception of what is noble and truly pleasant since they have never tasted it' (^{b}15–16).

By contrast, anyone who is to benefit from his lectures must be brought up to be 'a true lover of the noble' (1179^{b}8–9); 'the soul of the student must first have been cultivated by means of habits for noble joy and noble hatred, like earth which is to nourish the seed' (^{b}24–6). He concludes that the character of the student 'must somehow be there with a kinship to virtue, loving what is noble and hating what is base' (29–31). In other words, the student must already aspire to certain types of behaviour which are genuinely noble. So 10. 9 demands more by way of upbringing than 1. 3: it repeats the negative point—that the audience be free from excessive passion—but adds that they must already have certain moral dispositions. Furthermore, in making this requirement, Aristotle can hardly avoid requiring his audience to hold certain beliefs, e.g. that a specific type of action is noble and choiceworthy.

This passage confirms that Aristotle cannot be addressing the sceptic: Callicles and Thrasymachus had no habits for noble joy and hatred, and lacked the requisite judgements. In fact, it is not just the out-and-out opponents of intuitive morality who are excluded, but anyone who starts from an agnostic position and has yet to form a view about the value of the moral virtues.

(b) *Arguing from the 'that'*

Next we need to ask whether Aristotle claims that all his arguments depend on intuitions. Chapter 10. 9, as we have just seen, implies that the audience are required to hold certain moral beliefs, and it is natural to infer that such beliefs will be used as the premises of his arguments. Is this in fact the case?

When castigating the many, Aristotle complains that they are too biased in favour of their own pleasures to be responsive to reason:

What argument would remould such people? It is hard, if not impossible, to remove by argument the traits that have long been incorporated in the character. (1179^{b}16–18)

Their upbringing, and what they take pleasure in, constitutes an obstacle to their accepting the conclusions of any opposing argument. By contrast, those who are well brought up are willing to be persuaded. Their love of the noble, and the pleasure they take in it, will make them receptive to argument.

The emphasis here is on the motivation and dispositions of the audience: moral beliefs are required because their possession is entailed by having these dispositions. So far, however, there is nothing to say that such beliefs have a logical function, supplying premises for the arguments, and it remains possible that some of the arguments will have non-moral premises.

But 10. 9 contains a further reason why a good upbringing is required if one is to benefit from argument. Again, we need to start with his criticism of the many. In addition to the fact that their own desires for pleasure constitute an obstacle to accepting the argument, they also lack any conception of what is noble (1179^{b}15–16). A little later on he comments:

. . . he who lives as passion directs will not hear the argument that dissuades him, nor *understand* it if he does; and how can we persuade one in such a state to change his ways? (1179^{b}26–8; emphasis added)

Here he accuses them of a certain kind of blindness. To them, the idea that a virtuous act is noble and choiceworthy in itself will seem incomprehensible; perhaps the virtues might be instrumentally useful, but they will be burdensome. Without a conception of what it is like to treat moral virtue as choiceworthy in itself, without having 'tasted' of its pleasures, they are barred from properly understanding the argument. Conversely, the well brought-up will be able to make sense of the arguments precisely because they already have the necessary beliefs and intuitions in place.

If this is right, then 10. 9 does contain a commitment to using moralistic premisses in the arguments of the *Nicomachean Ethics*. Another text that makes the same point is a methodological passage from 1. 4:

> For, while we must start with what is familiar, things are so in two ways—some to us, some without qualification. Presumably, then, we must begin with things familiar to us. Hence anyone who is to listen intelligently to lectures about what is noble and just and, generally, about the subjects of political science must have been brought up in good habits. For the 'that' is a starting-point, and if this is sufficiently plain to him, he will not need the reason as well, and the man who has been well brought has or can easily get starting-points. (1095^{b}2–8)

He has just referred to a distinction between moving towards principles and moving from them. This is the difference between discovering the first principles, propositions that are epistemologically basic, and proceeding from these to understand (by way of proof and explanation) propositions which seemed intuitively plausible ('more familiar to us'). It is clear that, when Aristotle talks of principles being 'familiar without qualification', he means what is epistemologically basic. He then says that we must start from what is more familiar to us and, as he goes on to talk of these as principles, he must be using 'principle' in two senses, corresponding to 'the more familiar in nature' and 'the more familiar to us'. The latter kind of principle is said to be a grasp of the 'that'. Because he immediately goes on to imply that this is acquired by habituation, a number of commentators rightly infer that the type of principle at issue is a judgement of the sort that involves a commitment to the moral virtues, e.g. 'this type of action is noble'.[24] Accordingly, this passage, like 10. 9, can be used to show that moral intuitions will indeed play a role in Aristotle's arguments.

But does either of these passages commit Aristotle to saying that *all* his arguments, or all sections of them, will be based upon moral

---

[24] For this reading of the 'that' see Stewart, *Ethics*, i. 54–6, and Burnyeat, 'Learning to be Good', 71–2 with n. 3.

intuitions? Neither text commits Aristotle to this extreme position; and, in another passage that talks about grasping the 'that' as a starting-point, he takes up the weaker position that only some of his arguments are internal:

> Nor must we demand the cause in all matters alike; it is enough in some cases that the 'that' be well established, as in the case of the first principles; the 'that' is a primary thing and a first principle. Now of first principles, some come by induction, some by perception, some by a certain habituation, and others too in other ways. (1. 7, 1098ᵃ34–ᵇ4)

Here he gives a list of the different ways in which principles (ἀρχαί)[25] are grasped, one of which is habituation. This passage therefore incorporates the point of 1. 4 that ethical enquiry uses moral intuitions. It shows, however, that not all starting-points are won by habituation and adds induction and perception to the list of possibilities. There is no reason to assume that these are not methods relevant to the starting-points of ethical, as opposed to scientific, enquiry: the function argument makes use of induction, a point made explicitly in the *Eudemian Ethics* version (1219ᵃ1–2). We should not therefore take 1. 4 to be saying that all the starting-points of ethical argument come from habituation.

(c) Clarification and reinforcement

Aristotle's remarks about the nature of his starting-points can be reconciled with the fact that the *ergon–meson* argument is an external argument. At the same time, our analysis of 10. 9 shows that he cannot be addressing or converting the sceptic. What, then, is his purpose in revisiting the argument of *Republic* book 1?

One possibility is that he is redeploying the argument not for the purposes of conversion, but of clarification. He takes an audience who have had the appropriate upbringing but have not yet reflected systematically on the nature of the human good. The *ergon–meson* argument is intended to make their previously hazy conception of *eudaimonia* more precise. One of the more specific aims he may have is to clarify the relative weighting of various goods.[26] The audience

---

[25] I take it that, as in 1. 4, 1095ᵇ6, he uses ἀρχαί to mean 'what is more familiar to us'. This is clear from the fact that perception is included among these ἀρχαί (cf. *Post. An.* 1. 2, 72ᵃ1–3).

[26] See S. Broadie, *Ethics with Aristotle* [*Ethics*] (Oxford, 1991), 23: Aristotle aims to 'show the goods which we initially value in such a light that we shall end by valuing them only as they ought to be valued'.

arrives with beliefs in the choiceworthiness of a number of different things—not just moral virtue, but also pleasure, honour, friendship, wealth, and health. Here, the function argument in particular leaves us clearer about the primacy of psychic over external goods.

If Aristotle were redeploying the argument of *Republic* book 1 solely for the purpose of clarification, he would presumably have no interest in the fact that it is external, i.e. independent of any particular moral viewpoint. Any potential it may have for converting the sceptic is purely incidental. What might interest him instead is that it introduces a metaphysical dimension into the work and furthers the process of clarification by making connections between the human good and human nature.

There seems no doubt that clarification is at least one of Aristotle's purposes in reusing the argument of *Rep* book 1. There are plenty of signals in the early chapters of *NE* 1 and elsewhere that he conceives of his task as one of giving increasing determination to his audience's conception of the good.[27] It could be that this is all he has in mind. Another possibility, however, is that he has a further aim—one that, on a scale of similarity, lies somewhere between conversion and clarification.

Consider an audience of people who have been brought up to hold certain moral beliefs. As they start to reflect on the human good, there is the possibility that they might do so badly. For example, they might be tempted to infer that, if *eudaimonia* is the supreme good, more choiceworthy than anything else,[28] and if such things as bodily pleasure and money do genuinely count as goods, *eudaimonia* ought to involve having as much of them as possible: after all, the more good in one's life, the better. The danger of such slippage will apply even if they start by admiring justice and recoiling from its opposite. Bad reflection on the final good will influence them and may undermine the effect of their upbringing. This danger can be offset by an argument which is independent of their upbringing and which shows the incompatibility of *eudaimonia* with the unlimited pursuit of external goods.

The same point applies if we imagine that some members of the audience not only aspire to justice and temperance, but already believe them to be necessary for *eudaimonia*. Again, there is no reason why this belief could not be destabilized by bad reflection, and so again an anti-sceptical argument can serve to counteract this danger.

---

[27] e.g. 1097^{b}22–4, 1098^{a}20–2.   [28] Cf. 1097^{a}28 and ^{b}14–22.

Another aim in *NE* 1–2 might therefore be construed as reinforcement: Aristotle does depart from the Platonic project of addressing the sceptic, but still uses anti-sceptical arguments to prevent
the possibility of slippage. In thinking of the distinction between
conversion and reinforcement, it is crucial to distinguish between
addressing a sceptic and refuting scepticism. Where conversion is
concerned, one attempts to change a person; to do so, of course,
one targets their position, using anti-sceptical arguments. But it
is possible to target the sceptical position without addressing the
people who actually hold it.

The difference between reinforcement and clarification, on the
other hand, is that the former is essentially defensive and involves
focusing on a specific belief or set of beliefs that the audience is
in danger of espousing. If Aristotle's aim were merely clarification,
not only would he be uninterested in converting the likes of Callicles and Thrasymachus, he would not even be attempting to single
out their position for the purposes of refutation.

So can we show whether he is concerned to reinforce as well as
clarify his audience's intuitions? First of all, there is an immediate objection to be answered: why should Aristotle think that the
well brought-up need any reinforcement? Someone trained in good
habits will surely be impervious to the results of bad reasoning:
in 10. 9 it is said to be impossible—or at least very difficult—for
reason to counteract the effects of habituation ($1179^{b}16$–18).

This passage, however, needs to be treated with caution. Consider
the following text from *Pol.* 7. 13:

For people do many things contrary to their habits and their nature, because of reason, if they are persuaded that it is better to do otherwise.
($1332^{b}6$–8)[29]

Here he clearly affirms the power of reason to override habit. It is
possible that in doing so he simply contradicts 10. 9, but there is a
way of reconciling the two passages. The specific point in *NE* 10. 9
concerns the inability of reason to overrule *bad* habits. We generate
a contradiction between the two texts if we assume that the *Politics*
passage is talking of the effects of reason on *all* kinds of habit. Yet
it may only be concerned with the effects of reason on good habits,
and claiming that bad reasoning can undermine a good upbringing.

---

[29] Translations of *Pol.* 7 are by R. Kraut, *Aristotle:* Politics, *Books VII & VIII*
(Oxford, 1997).

Although this removes the contradiction, it immediately raises the question of why there should be an asymmetry between the effects of reason on good and bad habits. The answer is that those who are well brought-up, aside from being orientated towards the noble, are also susceptible to rational persuasion (1095^a10–11), while those who have become accustomed to 'gratify' their appetites (1168^b19 ff.) insulate themselves from reason. There is, however, a price to be paid for a good upbringing: being amenable to rational persuasion carries the risk that when the argument is bad, good habits may be undermined.[30]

(d) The evidence of Politics *7. 1*

To show that Aristotle does use the *ergon–meson* argument to reinforce his audience's intuitions against the Thrasymachean challenge, it would help to have some more direct evidence that he thought the challenge actually merited a response in the first place. Some might doubt this: although Plato thought that the ideal had a worryingly powerful attraction, Aristotle might simply have seen it as a maverick position unworthy of serious consideration.

Again, we need to turn to *Politics* 7, this time the first chapter, where he briefly summarizes his views on *eudaimonia*, and does so with reference to the three classes of goods: psychic, bodily, and external.[31] Everyone, he says, is agreed that we need some share of the psychic goods—the virtues of courage, temperance, justice, and wisdom.

> But . . . they disagree about quantity and superiority. For in the case of virtue they believe that to have a certain amount is sufficient; but in the case of wealth, property, power, reputation, and all such things they seek increase without limit. (1323^a35–8)

He then argues that the goods of the soul ought to be increased indefinitely, whereas the other types of good merely have instrumental value: beyond a certain point, further pursuit of them is either useless or harmful (1323^b7–12). What is striking about this passage is that it shows Aristotle targeting the view that external

[30] For this way of interpreting *NE* 10. 9 and *Pol.* 7. 13 I am indebted to R. Kraut, 'Aristotle on Method and Moral Education', in J. Gentzler (ed.), *Method in Ancient Philosophy* (Oxford, 1998), 271–306 at 284–7. The same general point appears in Broadie, *Ethics*, 24: 'Aristotle says that good arguments do not make us good people, but it does not follow that bad ones might not help to make us bad.'

[31] Cf. *NE* 1. 8, 1098^b12–14.

or bodily goods should be increased without limit: the maximizing ideal is a line of thought that needs to be confronted, not dismissed out of hand.

Despite the evidence of this passage, our objector may be unimpressed. The view that Aristotle confronts here at least allows that justice (like the other virtues) is to some degree choiceworthy and has a place in the best life (1323ᵃ27–34). This seems quite different from the Thrasymachean ideal.

The two positions, however, are much closer than one might at first think. In *Pol.* 7. 1 Aristotle is considering the relative weighting of psychic goods and those of the other two kinds and, in describing the rival view, draws a double contrast with his own. First, he requires the goods of the soul (the virtues) to be maximised indefinitely, and the other goods to be placed within a limit; for the rival, this position is simply reversed. Second, Aristotle thinks that non-psychic goods are to be sought for the sake of the soul; again, the rival reverses this and makes the virtues merely instrumental for acquiring the other goods (1323ᵇ18–21). This in turn explains why each party places a limit on what it takes to be subordinate goods: in the rival's case, the virtues have a limit because they should only be pursued as far as they are useful, while externals, being unconditionally good, should have no limit.

So Aristotle's rival in *Pol.* 7. 1, like Callicles and Thrasymachus, takes the *ideal* to be the life of maximizing external and bodily goods. Admitting an element of what Callicles would call 'conventional' justice for instrumental reasons is merely a concession to circumstances. In thinking of the intimate connection between these two positions, it is useful to compare Glaucon's challenge to Socrates at the beginning of *Republic* book 2. At 358 B 1 ff. he presents himself as articulating a single position—the Thrasymachean ideal, resuscitated from book 1. It is natural enough that he goes on to use the example of Gyges (359 B–360 D) freed from all social constraints, this is someone who embodies the Thrasymachean ideal in his unlimited pursuit of *pleonexia*. As part of the same position, however, Glaucon also cites the widespread opinion that justice merely has instrumental value. That his exposition moves seamlessly from this view back to the Thrasymachean ideal brings out the fundamental similarity between the two views: the instrumentalist approach to justice is really the

Thrasymachean ideal forced to accommodate itself to the realistic setting of everyday life. Similarly, the fact that Aristotle's rival in *Pol.* 7. 1 takes justice to be merely instrumental for acquiring the other goods, which are themselves worth pursuing without limit, points to the underlying similarity to the Thrasymachean ideal.[32]

Pol. 7. 1 is not the only point in the work where Aristotle shows an interest in targeting the pleonexic rival. In two other places he mentions one of its specific applications, the view that there should be no limit to the acquisition of wealth.[33] What is particularly striking is that in one of these (1256^b31–4) he cites no less a figure than Solon as having believed this view. With such a reputable sponsor, this is a view which would have been all the more difficult for Aristotle to ignore.[34]

So Aristotle does have an interest in targeting the position that so concerned Plato in the *Gorgias* and the *Republic*, and the *ergon–meson* argument is tailor-made to perform that task: it allows that such things as money, pleasure, and honour are undoubtedly goods of a kind; yet in the best life we do not attempt to get as much of them as possible. On the contrary, a requirement of maximizing what *is* unconditionally good (i.e. virtue) is that we actually place restrictions on our pursuit of the external goods.[35]

---

[32] W. L. Newman, *The Politics of Aristotle* (Oxford, 1902), iii. 311–12, draws out the close parallel between Aristotle's target in *Pol.* 7. 1, 1323^a37–8, and the popular view criticized by Socrates in *Ap.* 29 D 9–E 1 ('are you not ashamed that you give your attention to acquiring as much money as possible, and similarly with reputation and honour?'). We noted above the very close affinity between Socrates' targets in *Ap.*, *Gorg.*, and *Rep.* 1–2. If Newman is right to think that Aristotle is consciously imitating *Ap.* 29 D–E in *Pol.* 7. 1, it is all the more plausible that he would consider the Thrasymachean position a worthy target.

[33] Cf. 1256^b30–7 and 1257^b30–1258^a14, both concerned with the art of household management. In the first passage he supports his case with analogies from other crafts (1256^b34–6), as he does in *NE* 2. 6. It is also interesting that the second passage links the desire for unlimited pursuit of wealth to the belief that *eudaimonia* consists in the satisfaction of unlimited bodily desire (1257^b40–1258^a6).

[34] The fragment in question is quoted at the beginning of this paper. Solon is a figure whom Aristotle takes very seriously. In *NE* 1. 10, where he expresses his disagreement on the subject of fortune and *eudaimonia*, he feels the need to argue his case at some length.

[35] To be more precise, in *Pol.* 7. 1 Aristotle makes two points about external goods: they are subordinate to internal goods (which actually constitute *eudaimonia*) and they have a limit. The first of these points is established by the *ergon* argument (cf. 1. 8, 1098^b12–20), the second by the *meson* argument.

3. Conclusion

In this paper I have argued that external argument does play a significant role in the *Nicomachean Ethics*. This is not to deny, of course, the importance of internal argument. The two exist side by side. So, for example, in 1. 8 Aristotle shows how the conclusion of the function argument is consistent with widely held views, and in the process appeals to a moralistic conception of virtue (1099ᵃ18–20). Again, 2. 1–4 constitute a mini-treatise on the acquisition of virtue and, throughout it, the examples show that he is thinking of virtue in a moralistic sense.³⁶ He also uses intuitions to give a further specification of virtue after 2. 6. Recall that, at the beginning of 2. 7 he describes his account as still rather general. In the more detailed account of the virtues between 3. 6 and 5. 11 intuitions play a conspicuous role: he continually appeals to what he expects his audience to praise and blame, articulating and crystallizing ways of thinking with which he expects them to be familiar.³⁷ Nevertheless, internal arguments do not completely dominate the work: in two of the best known passages, 1. 7 and 2. 6, Aristotle, like Plato, has an interest in external argument *qua* external. He therefore shows more continuity with Plato than is often supposed.

In comparing Platonic and Aristotelian uses of ethical argument, I have not discussed how the *Nicomachean Ethics* relates to later books of the *Republic*. To do so would require an extended treatment in its own right, as the problems involved are highly complex. Nevertheless, I would like to close by making two broad points about the relation between the *Nicomachean Ethics* and *Republic* book 2 onwards on these issues.

How does what happens after *Republic* book 1 compare with the intuitionist approach that Aristotle follows in *Nicomachean Ethics* 3–5? Here there is, prima facie, a significant difference. Although Thrasymachus ceases to participate in the argument after book 1, his challenge remains the focus of attention: Glaucon and Adeimantus profess themselves to be dissatisfied with

---

³⁶ For justice as an ἀρετή see 1103ᵇ1, 15–16; 1105ᵃ17–20, ᵇ2–12.

³⁷ I noted above that, for Vasiliou, 'Upbringing', 781, intuitions seem to take over from external argument as soon as 1. 7 is over; on my view, they take over eventually, but not before the field of candidates for *eudaimonia* has been significantly narrowed by the *meson* argument.

Socrates' argument and restate the case against justice more articulately than Thrasymachus had done. In what follows Plato does attempt to provide a determinate account of justice and to show that, so conceived, it leads to *eudaimonia*. Presumably he attempts to do this without making moralistic assumptions, otherwise he would not be meeting the challenge posed at the beginning of book 2.

To the extent that Plato reaches a more determinate conception of justice in books 2–9 than in book 1, and does so without appealing to moralistic intuitions, there is a discontinuity with Aristotle's intuitionistic approach after *NE* 2. This issue is complicated because just how determinate a conception Plato does reach in the later books of the *Republic*, and just how far argument does rest on premises that Callicles and Thrasymachus could accept, is open to question. We could only get a precise idea of the continuity or otherwise of these two works as a whole once we have answered these questions.

Nevertheless, even if there is a clear discontinuity on this point, on another there is more continuity, viz. the character of the audience. When Glaucon and Adeimantus take over Thrasymachus' challenge, they do so in a very different spirit. They play devil's advocate, not endorsing the argument that injustice leads to *eudaimonia*, but presenting it as something proposed by others. They want it to be refuted and Socrates' view to prevail (367 B 1).

In response, Socrates testifies to their ambivalence:

. . . there must indeed be a touch of the god-like in your disposition if you are not convinced that injustice is preferable to justice though you can plead its case in such a fashion. And I believe that you are really not convinced. I infer this from your general character, since from your words alone I would have distrusted you. (368 A 5– B 3)[38]

This confirms that Glaucon and Adeimantus are asking the same question as Thrasymachus, even though they have a very different character.[39] They may have been well brought up and have the right intuitions, but they are in danger of being undermined by bad reflection. The ensuing argument is intended to set that right. So it turns out that, so long as we start from the second book of the

---

[38] Trans. P. Shorey, *Plato:* The Republic (Cambridge, Mass., 1937).
[39] On this see D. Scott, 'Platonic Pessimism and Moral Education', *Oxford Studies in Ancient Philosophy*, 17 (1999), 15–36 at 26.

Republic, we can find some continuity between Plato and Aristotle on the question of the psychology of the audience.

So the relation between Platonic and Aristotelian approaches to ethical argument turns out to be more complex either than business as usual or a complete break. In terms of how both works begin (*Republic* book 1 and *NE* 1–2), the logical structure of the arguments is close, but the people addressed are different: Plato in *Republic* book 1 aims at conversion, Aristotle at reinforcement. But if one thinks of the two works in their entirety, things are almost inverted: from *Republic* book 2 on, the type of audience directly addressed is much closer to Aristotle's, and both works can be said to involve reinforcement. But *Republic* books 2–9 is more ambitious than the *Nicomachean Ethics* about how much can be achieved without intuitions and relies much more extensively upon external argument than the *Nicomachean Ethics*

Clare College, Cambridge

APPENDIX
A Metaphysical Basis for Aristotle's Ethics?

One of the most significant contributions to the recent debate over the aims and scope of the *Nicomachean Ethics* has been made by T. Irwin. In a series of articles culminating in his book *Aristotle's First Principles*, he has argued that Aristotle, no less than Plato, can be read as addressing his arguments to a moral sceptic.[40] What is also distinctive of Irwin's work is the claim that Aristotle bases his ethics on the theories of the *Physics*, *Metaphysics*, and *De anima*. The place where Aristotle most conspicuously relies on such support is, allegedly, the function argument of *NE* 1. 7. Here Irwin thinks that Aristotle borrows a metaphysically loaded account of human nature from his other works in order to establish the link between *eudaimonia* and virtue. Thus, the *Nicomachean Ethics* is to be seen as continuing an extended argumentative strategy that begins in the *Physics*.

To do justice to Irwin's interpretation would require a long review

[40] See T. Irwin, 'The Metaphysical and Psychological Basis of Aristotle's Ethics', in Rorty, *Ethics*, 35–53; 'First Principles in Aristotle's Ethics', in P. A. French (ed.), *Studies in Ethical Theory* (Midwest Studies in Philosophy, 3; Morris, 1978), 252–72 at 260–2; and *Aristotle's First Principles* (Oxford, 1988), esp. 347–9 with n. 8. This approach also appears in J. Whiting, 'Aristotle's Function Argument: A Defense', *Ancient Philosophy*, 8 (1988), 33–48 at 45.

article in its own right. Here I shall comment only briefly on my reasons for being reluctant to accept his overall view. As far as the nature of the audience is concerned, if his claim is that the *Nicomachean Ethics* is actually intended to convert those who do not already consider the moral virtues choiceworthy, he faces a considerable obstacle in the form of 10. 9. Nevertheless, if he were to claim merely that Aristotle attacks a sceptical *position*, he would be on much firmer ground, although there is still a question about the prominence of this type of argument in the *Nicomachean Ethics*. For Irwin it seems to dominate the whole work; I have portrayed it as one strand, a particularly important one, that helps launch the argument, but I am not claiming that it pervades the work.

As far as the nature of Aristotle's argument is concerned, Irwin faces a number of hurdles.[41] First, given the striking similarities between *Republic* book 1 and *NE* 1. 7, it is not clear that the latter needs to be seen as the continuation of the *Physics*, *Metaphysics*, and *De anima*. None of the differences between the two passages calls for any explanation involving these works. Furthermore, at certain points in *NE* 1 Aristotle warns against asking for too much precision or explanation in ethics.[42] One of these passages comes immediately after the function argument (1098^{a}20–^{b}8) and is therefore specifically telling us not to rest *that* argument on excessively precise starting-points or in-depth explanations. One should therefore be very cautious before looking for support from *Metaph. Γ* 1–5, as Irwin does. The science of metaphysics aims for explanation at the deepest level, and the principle under investigation in those chapters, the principle of non-contradiction, is the most basic of them all.[43] One might say that to follow Irwin's path through the metaphysical works and thence into the *Nicomachean Ethics* is almost exactly what Aristotle is telling us not to do. Again, in *NE* 1. 13 (1102^{a}23–8) Aristotle admits that the student of political science needs some grasp of psychology, but adds that he should not delve into the subject too far. He then makes a reference not to the *De Anima*, but to certain exoteric works (26–7). Unlike Irwin, therefore, I do not see the *Nicomachean Ethics*, and the function argument in particular, as the ethical continuation of Aristotle's metaphysical works. That argument existed long before Aristotle the metaphysician came on the scene.

In creating a distance between the *Nicomachean Ethics* and the metaphysical treatises, however, I do not wish to go to the other extreme

---

[41] These have been discussed in more detail by Roche, 'Metaphysical Foundation'. See also Vasiliou, 'Upbringing', 782–3.

[42] 1094^{b}11–1095^{a}2, 1095^{a}30–^{b}8, 1096^{b}27–31, and 1098^{a}20–^{b}8.

[43] *Metaph. Γ* 3, 1005^{b}32–4: φύσει γὰρ ἀρχὴ καὶ τῶν ἀξιωμάτων αὕτη πάντων.

and remove all traces of Aristotle's metaphysical interests from his ethical views. Three points are worth noting here.

First, I am not denying that there is, in some sense, a metaphysical basis for Aristotle's ethics. The very claim that human beings have a 'function' is metaphysical, committing Aristotle to some form of teleology. Again, it is very close to one that Socrates (and indeed Thrasymachus) accepts in *Republic* book 1. In fact, by talking about a justice rooted in nature, Callicles may also be committed to a metaphyiscally grounded ethics (482 E 5 ff.). But there is a distinction between basing a theory on a metaphysical claim and deriving it from technical metaphysical theories developed in a series of works in the Aristotelian corpus.

Nor am I saying that the conclusions of the function argument, and of the *Nicomachean Ethics* in general, are incompatible with Aristotle's metaphysics. Indeed, Aristotle could doubtless have written a treatise in which he brought out the interconnections between these different areas of his work. But such a project would have had a reflective rather than a practical function.

Finally, I do not wish to deny that Aristotle uses conclusions from his metaphysics at later points in the *Nicomachean Ethics* to elaborate his theory. This is indeed what happens in book 6 (at least he uses the epistemology of the *Analytics*, which rests on metaphysical claims about essences) and perhaps in 10. 7–8, where both the *Metaphysics* (especially *Λ*) and the *De anima* could plausibly be said to be in the background.[44] But this is different from saying that he uses his metaphysics to launch the *Nicomachean Ethics*.

[44] For the claim that the theory of the *De anima* is invoked in *NE* 10. 7–8 see Cooper, *Reason and Human Good*, 175–7.

ARISTOTLE ON THE FANTASTIC ABILITIES OF ANIMALS IN *DE ANIMA* 3.3

CATHERINE OSBORNE

1. Fixing the problem: can animals have a successful life without νοῦς?

MY topic in this paper concerns the connection between the objects of perception and the objects of thought. Do we think about, or know, the same objects as we perceive? It is easy to suppose that Aristotle, given his hostility to Plato's separation of Forms, must have a clear and unambiguous anti-metaphysical answer to this question: there had better be no parallel set of objects occupying a thought-world. And, we might expect, Aristotle's unambiguously anti-metaphysical answer should surely have some appeal for those modern philosophers who find anti-metaphysical Aristotelianism congenial.

However, things turn out to be less simple once we recognize that the question about the connection between objects of knowledge and objects of perception is also a question about the relationship between animal behaviour and human behaviour. If we accept a distinction between rational animals and irrational ones, and if we suppose that the difference is not confined to private thoughts but manifests itself in differences in their behaviour, and in the correct explanation of their behaviour, then we are committed to saying that irrational animals govern their behaviour on a somewhat different basis from the rational ones. In what, then, does the difference consist? If it is that the lack of an intellectual capacity (say, thought) precludes access to that capacity's range of objects

© Catherine Osborne 2000

I am grateful to the audiences at the Southern Association for Ancient Philosophy 1997 meeting, and at a Swansea work-in-progress seminar, who responded to earlier versions of this paper, and to David Sedley for written comments.

(say, concepts), then the division between rational and irrational animals introduces surreptitiously a Platonic distinction between objects of thought and objects available to non-rational perception. It is quite common to find philosophers of language urging us to believe that it can be no proper explanation of the dog's behaviour to say that it expects its master to come home, since the dog has no concept of 'master' or 'home' or 'coming'. These are linguistic tools, they might say; they belong to language-users and apply to nothing that could figure in the dog's own life; so that if we do use them to describe the dog's behaviour, that can only be because we, linguistic, concept-using creatures, are speaking of things that we find significant in the dog's life.

So should we bow to this pressure and say that although *we* might pace anxiously waiting for the return of a loved one, the dog's apparently similar restless anticipation does not really reflect the same kind of experience at all? Aristotle does draw a distinction between rational and irrational animals, and he does claim that a distinctive capacity of the soul, νοῦς, is present in the one group and lacking in the other. Does this, then, commit him to separating objects of thought from objects accessible to creatures whose faculties end at the five senses? Must he then provide a different explanation of apparently similar behaviour, because things that we might have in mind when choosing how to act would be totally missing from the perceptible world with which the beast was interacting? I shall argue that this does not follow on Aristotle's view: that animals without intellect are not thereby missing out on the objects of thought; nor do they live in an inadequate or ill-directed way; nor do the factors that explain their actions differ in any way from the factors that explain the corresponding behaviour in a human agent. In other words, I am suggesting that Aristotle can coherently preserve a distinction between intellect and the other faculties, without thereby breaking the evident continuity of human and animal behaviour, or separating the objects of thought from the objects of perception.

Let us start by asking what is being denied when Aristotle denies that non-human animals have the intellectual capacities of the soul. Certain famous parts of the Aristotelian corpus treat something called νοῦς as a thing detached, abstract, and divine, something that can exist in separation and belong to beings that lack any kind of particular interaction with changing things.[1] The detachment of

[1] Cf. *Metaph.* Λ 9, and *De anima* 3. 5.

the νοῦς matches the fact that it is unrestrictedly open to abstract thought and pure enquiry. The fact that humans, as well as the divine, possess such a faculty explains why the successful human life includes not only practical action but also some kind of pure reflection; correspondingly, the successful life for the divine is a life of pure thought. Since nothing in the life of the divine involves action or decision-making, it seems clear that the characteristic activity of this abstract νοῦς that is 'the most divine thing' cannot be essentially bound up with practical or purposive action.

On the other hand when, in *De anima* 3. 4, Aristotle turns from a discussion of animal perception to consider the faculty that is νο-ητικόν, the cognitive functions for which he has still to allow room in the intellectual part of the soul include a whole range of judgements and opinions, knowledge, science, calculation, and guesswork that are by no means abstract or theoretical, but apparently include our entire understanding of the world. It might seem that many of these cognitive functions would be vital to our ability to act and make decisions in daily life.[2] Do we not need to form opinions about our environment and what is in it, making (if possible) true judgements and predictions and building up an understanding of the behaviour of things? Could anyone operate successfully without such beliefs? If animals lack the ability to form beliefs, can they have any hope of getting what they want in life?

Much writing since Aristotle has presupposed some such in-adequacy in the intellectual capacities of other animals, and their consequent lack of intelligent behaviour. The story goes something like this: if animals lack intellect, they cannot have concepts; if they lack concepts, they cannot have anything in mind: no intentions, no purposes, no plans—they cannot even formulate a desire for *x* rather than *y*; if they lack plans or desires, they cannot choose to act on the basis of those plans, or consider alternative courses of action towards a given end; if animals do not choose to act for a precon-ceived purpose, their actions are random and unintended; hence animal behaviour is arbitrary and ineffective—they have no desires that could be fulfilled or frustrated, and consequently no notion

---

[2] Aristotle himself seems to suggest this at the start of *De anima* 3. 10, but then proceeds to confine the actual effecting of movement to inclination alone. Purposive inclination can equally be provided by φαντασία without thought, and even deliber-ation turns out to be the ability to derive one presentation from a plurality provided by φαντασία, 434ᵃ9–10.

of success or failure; their behaviour is indistinguishable from the unintentionally purposive behaviour of a machine.

As I have suggested, I shall argue not only that such reasoning bears no relation to Aristotle's own, but also that Aristotle's account can provide a more coherent and promising analysis for both human and animal behaviour: one that avoids the trap of supposing that concepts, of a linguistic or theoretical sort, are presupposed in purposive action.[3] I shall suggest that we should understand Aristotle to say that all, or virtually all, animals act for a reason, and that humans act for a reason in exactly the same way, without appeal to any abstract concepts. What moves all animals, human and non-human alike, Aristotle argues in the *De anima*, is inclination ($\emph{ὄρεξις}$), and inclination is always purposive.[4] There are, of course, intellectual capacities peculiar to humans and some of these can have a bearing on purposive action, but evidently only if they can alter the attractiveness of the appearance of a given object of desire, since the object of desire is what arouses the inclination and initiates voluntary motion. For instance, intellectual tasks include the ability to reflect on the reasons or purposes, calculating which is better and thereby rendering one or another reason more attractive to the will, which, along with desire, is simply a form of inclination.[5] Thus by evaluating *reasons*, and not merely actions, human agents can deliberate, and decide for or against a particular course of action, not on the grounds that it is unattractive, but because the reasons for it are unsound, which consequently renders it unattractive.[6] Such a capacity for reflection, or beliefs about value, will not make the behaviour itself any more purposive than that of other animals, who similarly choose the action that is rendered most attractive in the cirumstances, and choose it purposely and for a reason.

We might say that the reflective possibilities provided by intellect, such as the evaluation of reasons and choices rather than results alone, change the character of the behaviour and open up additional

---

[3] A similar interest in Aristotle's account of animal behaviour, and the presence or absence of concepts in accounting for it, motivates Richard Sorabji's discussions in 'Intentionality and Physiological Processes', in M. C. Nussbaum and A. O. Rorty (eds.), *Essays on Aristotle's* De anima [*Essays*] (Oxford, 1992), 195–225, and in his *Animal Minds and Human Morals* (London, 1993), but his discussion focuses on the rich perceptual content ascribed to animals, while retaining the duality of perceptual vs. conceptual objects that I am concerned to question.

[4] *De anima* 3. 9, e.g. 432^{b}13; 3. 10, 433^{a}15.   [5] *De anima* 3. 10, 433^{a}23.
[6] 433^{a}23; cf.3. 11, 434^{a}9.

kinds of explanation. Nevertheless, such evaluative responses seem irrelevant to the animal's capacity to enjoy success or failure in its purposive actions, though they do open the way for a different kind of assessment of the source of success or failure, and for the possibility of a failure at a different level of ethical responsibility—a level at which the appropriate responses would include remorse, regret, and culpability, rather than frustration or disappointment.

Thus it would be a mistake, I think, to confuse acting on purpose (intentional animal behaviour) with reflecting on, or analysing, the reason for acting so (reflective evaluation), or with deliberating about the correct evaluation of competing options (practical deliberation). It seems to me that the ability to engage in reflective analysis of one's choices and actions has nothing to do with whether one is or was acting as one intended or for a purpose or, indeed, whether one made such a choice between conflicting desires, preferring to act on one rather than another.[7] In fact the reflective analysis is detached from action in a way that would indeed make it plausible to treat it as an activity of thought, a theoretical evaluation, belonging in Aristotle's account of the faculties of intellect (though in practice very little is said of such practical applications of the intellect in the chapters on intellect). On the other hand, to say that such theoretical evaluation is specially human implies no commendation of it over the ordinary purposive activity of all animate beings, but is merely to observe that it will figure in any judgement of how successful a *human* life is. Similarly, denying that it enters the lives of other animals is not to deny that they act purposively, for reasons of which they are aware, and that they can be successful or frustrated. It does mean that it is nonsense for us to assess their lives by our own reflective criteria, by which we evaluate the reasons for action and the corresponding moral responses to it.

Before turning to Aristotle's analysis of the purposive behaviour of animals, we must first ask whether Aristotle ever implies that animals act arbitrarily without intentions. In a difficult passage of

---

[7] When Aristotle says that debating whether to do this or that is a function of λογισμός and not an option for animals without the λογιστικόν (434ᵃ8), he need not mean that other animals cannot choose to do this rather than that when faced with alternatives. They will presumably (as we generally do) choose to do the one that seems immediately more attractive. Beings with intellect and a sense of time can, if they think of it, calculate the future outcome and thereby effect a different evaluation and hence different preference (433ᵇ5–7). Aristotle seems here to think principally of choices between immediate and long-term goals, rather than between two immediately attractive options, such as face Buridan's ass.

De motu animalium Aristotle compares the behaviour of animals to the movements of some kind of mechanical toy.[8] His terminology is uncannily anticipatory of Descartes's famous claim that animals are automata.[9] Animals move, says Aristotle,

in just the same way that mechanical devices [αὐτόματα] move as soon as a small movement occurs . . . (701[b]2–3)

However, the striking verbal resemblance between Descartes and Aristotle is actually deceptive. Admittedly, the details of Aristotle's mechanical illustrations are hard to reconstruct—he refers, apparently, to two machines that carry out operations by themselves, but neither is identifiable precisely. However, his point is clear: that the physical structure of an organic body affects the way it will respond to stimulus. For example, one of his illustrations is of a little cart (701[b]3). If the cart is constructed so as to have the left wheel larger than the right wheel, it will turn clockwise in a circle when pushed, whereas if it is constructed with wheels equal in diameter it will go straight. In the same way, not everything in an animal's behaviour is voluntary, in the strong sense, or chosen from various alternatives. An animal may respond in a characteristic way—say a bee buzzes— not because it chose to buzz rather than sing, but because buzzing is the automatic effect of having one's body so constructed. Aristotle's other example (701[b]2–3 and 8–10), which is some kind of machine in which a small movement of rods and pulleys produces a much more pronounced movement at the other end of the mechanism, illustrates how quite extensive movements can be reflex responses to tiny stimuli from the environment. A third illustration introduced half a page later (701[b]25–8), of a boat, in which minimal movement of the rudder at the stern effects a considerable swing at the bows, illustrates the same point. Aristotle's idea is that these reflexes are not purely determined by the environment: on the contrary, they would not occur as they do if the animal were not so constructed as to respond in that way, so that the explanatory force lies as much or

---

[8] *De motu anim.* ch. 7, 701[b]2–13. For details on the problems of this text see M. Nussbaum, *Aristotle's* De motu animalium [*DMA*] (Princeton, 1978), commentary ad loc.

[9] Cf. Descartes, *Discourse on Method*, pt. 5 (381 ff.). Descartes's account of the common sense, imagination, memory and sensation in this passage suggests that he is directly borrowing from Aristotle, though Descartes (either deliberately against Aristotle or as a result of a tendentious reading of Aristotle) drastically eliminates the conscious cognition that Aristotle had attributed to these forms of awareness.

more in an analysis of the organs in which the response occurs as in whatever external environmental stimulus initiates the movement. Nevertheless, although the responses are end-directed (just as the little cart seems to be made with uneven wheels so that it will turn in a circle), the animal itself is not choosing to act for that end at the moment when it acts on a reflex, any more than the cart chooses to move in a circle when pushed.

So far Aristotle's point seems compatible with Descartes's claim that the apparently goal-directed behaviour of animals is merely a reflex response in an automaton, a device constructed to respond automatically to environmental stimuli. But Aristotle immediately goes on to highlight a difference between the behaviour of his machines and that of the animals, which is that animals adapt their behaviour in response to the environment. In practice the little cart must have either equal wheels, in which case it goes straight, or unequal wheels, in which case it goes in a circle. If it could change the size of its wheels it could determine for itself whether it goes straight or in a circle. Animals, by contrast with machines, can change the shape and size of limbs and organs so as to adapt the resulting movements, and they do that intentionally—'intentionally', that is, in a technical sense, in that the changes are brought about by what we would call mental events[10] in the animal's consciousness. Evidently the animal has, after all, elected to act in its own way in a sense in which the little cart has not.

Thus Aristotle is saying that even if reflex responses account for much of the animal's behaviour, this does not make it a mere automaton, because it adapts to produce these goal-directed responses, and is prompted to do so by the intentional objects of states of awareness. These intentional states are also responses to the environment, but where animals differ from machines is in making appropriate movements to alter their subsequent behaviour, in response not to the physical stimulus but to the intentional content of the mental state.

But what is the intentional content of a mental state? This question clearly invites us to reflect on Aristotle's notion of φαντασία. Indeed, I hope that in approaching φαντασία from this direction, we may clear up some remaining difficulties in the interpretation of Aristotle. Let us begin this way: one task that faces Aristotle, in contrast to Plato, is the need to account for the common intentional

---

[10] φαντασίαι, αἰσθήσεις, and ἔννοιαι, 701ᵇ17–18.

content of different mental states; whereas for Plato, in his most
Platonic mode, the objects of knowledge differed from the objects
of opinion or perception, so that there were parallel worlds of epistemic items, one set available to knowledge and the other to sensation,[11] for Aristotle, by contrast, the same item can and must figure
as the intentional object of more than one mental state. My suggestion is that φαντασία is the explanation that Aristotle offers for
this interchange of objects between the different cognitive faculties.
φαντασία or 'imagination'[12] is not, on this account, a distinct faculty,
alongside sensation and thought, but rather, as I hope to show, the
capacity to furnish the various faculties with intentional objects of
determinate kinds, thereby accounting for the common objects that
figure in perception, thought, and knowledge. To support my claim
I shall indicate how it provides Aristotle with what he needs, and
point to the relative coherence and perspicuity of the discussion of
φαντασία in the *De anima* when read in this way.

Of course there is a sense in which the intentional objects of
different faculties are not the same. Throughout his discussion of
perception, Aristotle makes it clear that distinct faculties of perception (sight, hearing, smell, and so on) have distinct ranges of objects
(colour, sound, scents, etc.) together with some shared ones (shape
and number, for instance). One sense cannot properly perceive the
exclusive objects of another sense.[13] Since it is the special objects
that are directly perceivable, whereas the item to which they belong
(Diares' son) does not directly present itself to the senses as such,
it might seem controversial to claim that for Aristotle the faculties

---

[11] Plato also has to account for the connection between the objects of thought and
the particulars that bear their names. This is the perennial question of 'participation',
but it remains a connection between two items, not just one.

[12] The translation 'imagination' is problematic. See the discussion in Malcolm
Schofield, 'Aristotle on the Imagination' ['A on I'], in J. Barnes, M. Schofield,
and R. Sorabji (eds.), *Articles on Aristotle*, iv (London, 1979), 103–32 at 103–7
(=Nussbaum and Rorty, *Essays*, 249–77 at 249–53). Schofield finds the term not
wholly objectionable, since he sees Aristotle collecting a set of phenomena that
include imagination, among others. The term 'imagination' has been used more
recently by Michael Wedin, *Mind and Imagination in Aristotle [M&I]* (New Haven,
1988), whose understanding of the range of phenomena to be included matches my
own. I am not comfortable, however, with the pseudo-visual implications of 'image',
since it implies that the mind is structured to think solely in terms of visual images,
whereas φαντασία must in fact serve to construe the materials of taste, smell, hearing,
and even touch, even though Aristotle tends to give primacy to visual examples.
Perhaps the idea of creating an impression (not physically but mentally) is better
than the notion of forming an image. I should therefore prefer to translate φαντασία
as 'impressionability'.   [13] *De anima* 2. 6, 418[a]11.

of thought and perception do not pertain to different sets of objects. My point is this, that while the effect in a particular sense is, say, colour, the same object thus perceived as coloured may also be perceived as, say, sweet. Perception as a whole grasps not two objects but one, namely a sweet white object, though the particular modalities of perception are sensitive to colour or taste exclusively. Similarly the faculty of thought has a single object in mind when it also thinks or knows of the sweet white object, and that object will be the very same sweet white object that perception grasped. It is not just that the *source* of both the sensation and the thought are ultimately the same, a single external object in the world, but that both are about that object, and not about some double of it, nor about some separate form to which it bears some resemblance. I take it to be uncontroversial, therefore, though perhaps it needs to be stated, that for Aristotle, perception and thought differ neither in their objects, nor in the ultimate source of their objects. Rather, I imagine that they differ partly in how they make contact with the object (and here I shall suggest that φαντασία needs to perform a role) and partly in how they manipulate those objects (including, perhaps, whether they construct them as universals—but that is an issue to be treated in more detail on another occasion).

To sum up, then, it seems that I can see and taste an iced bun, I can think of the iced bun, I can remember the iced bun after eating it, and I can dream about it: in each case one and the same iced bun figures as the object of my attention. The four events differ not in the object that each is about, but only, perhaps, in the story that one might tell about what was happening in my mind, and as with any mental event there would be two irreducible stories to tell, one physiological and one epistemological.

My first claim, then, is that φαντασία must belong in Aristotle's explanation of intentional objects. I hope to show that it can allow perceptions and thoughts to be *about* objects in the world, and that, in the process, it can also explain how relevant objects in the animal's environment might be picked out for attention and construed in ways effective for the animal's own concerns—so that the bird finds, or indeed dreams of, berries or nest-building materials, not just red blobs or brown streaks. In this respect my interpretation will be not dissimilar to other recent contributions to this discussion. Indeed, I shall argue that φαντασία is not itself a faculty but is subservient to the faculties, and in that respect my thesis takes up Michael Wedin's persuasive analysis in *Mind and Imagination in Aristotle*, while Victor Caston has also linked φαντασία with intentionality in his 'Aristotle and the Problem of Intentionality'.[14]

My second claim is that if φαντασία is identified, as I am suggesting, as the source of common intentional content across different mental states, then we can expect to find it playing four distinct roles in the various cognitive processes to which it contributes— two roles concerned with taking in structures objectively presented in the environment, and two concerned with presenting such structures for attention. I shall call these two kinds of role 'receptive' and 'presentational' respectively, and for technical terminology for the structures involved I shall speak of 'forms', meaning thereby the pattern that is identified as salient when an object is perceived as a thing of a certain kind or as manifesting a certain kind of property or feature.

On the presentational side, we shall identify (*a*) the ability to construe some currently available perceptual field in the light of familiar forms previously encountered, so that it presents itself to the attention as a set of discrete objects of interest (thus allowing for what we call 'seeing as');[15] and (*b*) the ability to recall or present the same forms for contemplation (allowing for something 'coming to mind', which might include recognition). On the less familiar receptive side, we need (*a*) the ability to register or figure out new forms—that is, to pick out new objects in the environment (noticing a new or unfamiliar kind of thing)[16]—and (*b*) the ability

---

[14] ['Intentionality'], *Philosophy and Phenomenological Research*, 58 (1998), 249–98; Caston clarifies several issues in more detail than I do here, including those relating to particularity of objects. Cf also V. Caston, 'Why Aristotle Needs Imagination', *Phronesis*, 41 (1996), 20–55.

[15] I have classified this capacity as a 'presentational role' despite the fact that, viewed another way, it is clearly a way of receiving input from the environment. I am suggesting that the notion of 'seeing as' has to be explained not simply by the presence of an objective form hitting us from outside, as it were, but by the ability to pick out, recognize, or identify that item as a particular kind of thing. This capacity would belong to φαντασία in so far as one recognizes it in terms of familiar forms presented from previous experience by φαντασία. Thus, although the perception is receptive, the role of φαντασία in construing it is active and consists in presenting a certain form with which to construe what is given.

[16] This will be distinct from 'seeing as' if, as I am assuming here, we cannot see something as an *x* unless we have taken prior notice of an *x*. We must then presuppose that noticing an *x* for the first time is possible, though different, and does not employ but rather constructs a new form in the repertoire; otherwise we commit Aristotle to innate ideas. Wedin calls this 'acquisition of [re]presentational

to stash away and retain those forms in some kind of storage facility (making a mental note of something and remembering it). However, we need not expect Aristotle to present these four tasks systematically, for while each would constitute a classic example of φαντασία at work, not all figure in the explanation of every one of the activities or responses for which φαντασία is typically invoked,[17] and this will be one reason why attempts to reconstruct a so-called 'doctrine of φαντασία' from Aristotle's intermittent allusions tend to look inconsistent or muddled. In connection with different activities, as we might expect, Aristotle points sometimes to a receptive role, sometimes to a presentational one, sometimes one that directs attention to objects outside, sometimes one that provides them from within.[18] In my view, he never attempts a systematic analysis.

Thus, I suggest, φαντασία will turn out to make sense if we identify it with the ability to pick out significant forms in the environment, and to use them when contemplating the objects to which they belong, whether present or absent.[19] In approaching Aristotle's text we need to distinguish which aspect of the process is invoked in each context.[20] To confine the analysis to a reasonable

structures' (*M&I* 39–45), but I would prefer to avoid the idea that the structures are representational, which implies that what we think of or notice are representations or images of the things: rather, I would maintain that we have in mind the things themselves. In my view the structures we acquire are not representational, viewed in place of the real world, but rather tools of analysis with which we construe a world directly available to perception, and which enable us to think or dream again about that world in its absence.

[17] We might also ask whether every animal that employs one of the features of φαντασία must necessarily employ them all. The ability to construe objects in the perceptual field (to hear a bell, to see a flower) might seem to be something of which animals are capable independently of whether they memorize any of those observations or ever subsequently recall them in their absence.

[18] Schofield, 'A on I' 130–1 (=276), suggests that someone might try to patch up the unity of Aristotle's theory by identifying different sorts of exercise of the imagination in the different passages. In a sense that task, together with an explanation of why the various sorts of exercise form a systematic analysis of a single feature, is what I have attempted here.

[19] I shall suggest that the initial source of these forms is the world (we see the shapes as flowers because flowers out there have prompted a 'flower' form to lodge itself as an interpretative model in the soul), not our soul (the soul being so constructed as to have 'flower' as an interpretative model with which to construe the perceptual field). The latter would imply that the *phantastic* ability could present such forms to thought or the imagination independently of perception. Aristotle seems to think that we depend upon perception for thought.

[20] Some progress on similar lines has been made by Dorothea Frede, 'The Cogni-

scale I shall focus here on the most problematic text, namely *De anima* 3. 3.

2. *De anima* 3. 3

First of all we should notice, as Schofield does in his classic article, what Aristotle is trying to do in this passage.[21] His topic hitherto has been the kinds of awareness attributable to perception alone, concluding in 3. 2 with the awareness of which sense an object is presented to, and the ability to compare objects of different sense modalities. The third chapter starts to move on, turning to the capacities that belong to intellect; but first Aristotle asks whether we are right to divide cognition into the two faculties of perception and thought. If we think of both sensation and thought as kinds of being aware of (αἰσθάνεσθαι) something, Aristotle suggests, then perhaps consciousness should be taken to be simply one single faculty?[22] Against this idea, chapter three defends the distinction between perception and thought, and crystallizes it: for although some cognitive abilities appear to muddy the division, in that they seem not clearly to belong to one without the other, this (Aristotle suggests) is because φαντασία is involved, and φαντασία is not perception.

Thus I would claim that chapter 3 is not attempting to provide an account of what φαντασία is, or of what it does. Unlike those recent scholars who have sought to identify φαντασία as a specialist

tive Role of Phantasia' ['Cognitive Role'], in Nussbaum and Rorty, *Essays*, 279–95, who observes that the term φαντασία can be used interchangeably for a capacity and for the exercise and products of that capacity. Sorting these out helps to clarify some apparent difficulties in reading *De anima* 3. 3. My point is further that the capacity is exercised in a number of different activities, and these are not distinguished clearly in the text (because the text is not concerned to list the functions of φαντασία systematically).

[21] Schofield's analysis of the context and occasion of the discussion seems to me absolutely right, 'A on I' 126–7 (=271–2), but I shall explore it myself at some length, since on my account the structure is a key to the absence, in this chapter, of any theory of φαντασία.

[22] 427ª21. This result follows at once on any view (e.g. Locke or Berkeley) whereby the object of attention is always an idea, whether derived from sense or from thought; Berkeley tries to salvage a distinction by suggesting that ideas re-presented by the mind are distinguishable from those perceived from without, but it remains true that the idea perceived is effectively the same, and is the internal mental entity. I take it that Aristotle's rejection of any such collapse of the two forms of cognition shows that it must be wrong to take him to be anticipating Lockian or Berkeleian ideas, or any kind of internal representation perceived from within.

faculty for giving access to some definite, or indefinite, set of quasi-sensory experiences,[23] and indeed in contrast even to Wedin—who finds here what he calls a 'canonical theory'—I do not think that we can, or should even try to, identify a *theory* or *definition* of φαντασία in *De anima* 3. 3. It is wrong, in my view, to suppose that Aristotle's text is as it is because it bears the mark of 'the untidy-genius syndrome',[24] aiming to provide a clear definition but signally failing through the negligence of a scholar too eminent to pay heed to the deferential readers who battle through the wandering trail of his stream of consciousness. On the contrary, we mistake the purpose altogether if we try to pick up a definition here; that is not what the passage is about. And, I should emphasize, that will be true equally of the passage at the end of chapter 3, in which Aristotle identifies a potential physiological underpinning whereby φαντασία could emerge with its recognizable pattern of results and prerequisites.[25]

   Thus, despite their appreciation of the dynamics of book 3, both Schofield and Wedin search the text in 3. 3 for a theoretical account of φαντασία. By contrast, on my reading the chapter seems to sideline φαντασία, as a phenomenon that figures neither in the account of perception nor in that of intellect; it is of interest only in so far as its role in both can lead to confusion of the two. Thus the chapter is concerned to make a clear division between perception and thought, and, in order to clear the path for that division, φαντασία must be disentangled from both sides of the route, lest it obstruct the scythe.

---

[23] Currently the most influential theories of this sort are: (*a*) the classic work of Schofield, 'A on I', who identifies a capacity for apprehending 'non-paradigmatic sensory experience' (i.e. a loose family of experiences that are similar to, but diverge from, the standard case of successful perception); cf. also D. Modrak 'Phantasia Reconsidered', *Archiv für Geschichte der Philosophie*, 66 (1986), 47–69; (*b*) the work of Nussbaum (*DMA*) and others in which the idea of 'seeing as' is given priority, together with Dorothea Frede 'Cognitive Role', and the earlier theories against which Schofield was arguing (whereby φαντασία is involved in all apprehension of sensory data, or is a Kantian-style interpretative system for processing sensory input); and (*c*) the work of Caston, especially 'Why Aristotle Needs Imagination' and 'Intentionality', in which φαντασία is designed to allow for intentional content of a non-conceptual kind specifically with a view to analysing mental states that are open to error.   [24] Frede, 'Cognitive Role', 280–1.
[25] It is here that Wedin finds 'the core of the canonical theory' (*M&I* 24), and Frede finds 'the definition of *phantasia* itself' ('Cognitive Role', 281). For my own account of this physiological passage (428[b]10 ff.), which I take to be an attempt to allow physiological space for the likely occurrence of one rather fundamental receptive process on which the presentational capacities of φαντασία must depend, see below, p. 279.

In consequence, the prime concern is with marking φαντασία off *vis-à-vis* perception, on the one hand, and a variety of kinds of thinking, on the other, in such a way as to enable Aristotle to draw the line between perception and thought accurately. His aim is to draw it differently from his predecessors, both the early thinkers who failed to make an adequate division between perception and thought at all,[26] and anyone who thinks that φαντασία involves both αἴσθησις and δόξα working together (thereby implying that any animal that uses φαντασία must have intellect).[27]

Is Aristotle trying to put φαντασία within perception (so that animals without intellect can have φαντασία included in perception), or within thought (so that animals with φαντασία thereby do some sort of thinking)? The answer will turn out, I think to be 'neither', because φαντασία is really something quite different, not itself a mode of awareness at all; but since the chapter never says what φαντασία is, it is also hard to find the answer to the question of where it belongs in relation to its cognate capacities, a difficulty aggravated by the repetitive structure of the chapter, which appears to be constructed from two versions not worded identically. A brief glance at the odd construction of the chapter may help to indicate what I mean.

Halfway through our chapter, the sentence at 427^{b}27 reads like the beginning of a new section on thinking (νοεῖν), as though the division between perception and thought were uncontroversial and φαντασία (to be discussed first) belonged to thought:

Concerning thinking, given that it is different from perceiving, and its two aspects seem to be (*a*) φαντασία and (*b*) ὑπόληψις, we must speak about the latter once we have first drawn the defining line round φαντασία. (427^{b}27–30)[28]

But this is odd, for two reasons. One is that φαντασία suddenly ap-

---

[26]   427^{a}21: Empedocles and Homer are mentioned.

[27]   Aristotle rejects this suggestion that φαντασία is some combination of two things at 428^{a}24. He is usually taken to be objecting to suggestions made by Plato, *Soph.* 264 A–B and *Tim.* 52 A 7 (I find both references unconvincing, but the issue does not affect the present argument).

[28]   I would not deny that, if one were inclined to see an attempt to define φαντασία in this chapter, one might appeal to the phrase περὶ φαντασίας διορίσαντας to support the claim that Aristotle intended the chapter to provide a definition. However, even if that were so, I would suggest that that statement, and with it the stated aim, belonged to an earlier version of the chapter, which had assumed a simplified identification of φαντασία as one kind of thinking (cf. 427^{b}28), a confusion just such as is challenged by the finished chapter that we now have. In any case, the phrase can equally be

pears to be listed as one aspect of thinking, whereas the immediately preceding passage had implied that it was only a *precondition* for thought; the other is that the distinctions that then follow (428ᵃ5– 428ᵇ9), which aim to show that φαντασία is not identical with one of the other kinds of cognition, nor with a combination of perception and thought, retrace bits of the same ground as the earlier part of the chapter. One possible explanation for this incoherence is that Aristotle's discussion of φαντασία had once started at 427ᵇ27, and that the preceding passage (up to 427ᵇ26) was added later as a supplement, perhaps when Aristotle realized that the basic distinction between thought and perception could not thus be taken for granted, and should itself be established first. That would explain why he might have inserted the passage which discusses the ancients' confusion of the two, 427ᵃ17–ᵇ14.

If this is right, we might fruitfully suggest that the claim at 427ᵇ28, that φαντασία belongs in a discussion of thought rather than perception, had once served merely as a tentative and preliminary generalization, prior to a more precise location of it as distinct from both, since, ultimately, both parts of the chapter seem agreed in isolating φαντασία as identical with neither perception nor any of the other kinds of cognition.

Going back to the start of the chapter, then, we may, if I am right, be dealing with Aristotle's revised and more sophisticated preamble, designed to facilitate progress towards a discussion of what is distinctive about intellect. Aristotle begins this preamble by asking why some early thinkers assimilated perception and thought. If the issue is how perception and thought can have the same objects, that is not explicit, except in the mention of the fact that both kinds of cognition pick out real things, 427ᵃ21;²⁹ rather, Aristotle begins with classification issues. Traditionally, he tells us at what we now read as the start of chapter 3 (427ᵃ17), the defining characteristics of soul are put into two sorts: (*a*) motion and (*b*) consciousness or awareness—i.e. all kinds of awareness, including thought. But now a problem arises because the general term for awareness has to be

read as simply indicating a concern to 'mark φαντασία off' from adjacent capacities, without thereby explaining or analysing it in its own right.

²⁹ In so far as the issue of ensuring that perception and thought have the same objects is ever made explicit, this is not until 432ᵃ3–14, where the opposition to Platonic separation, and the role of φαντάσματα in ensuring that it is not required, is eventually spelt out.

αἰσθάνεσθαι, which is also the specific term for perceptual awareness:[30]

and it seems that both thinking and knowing are a kind of awareness [αἰσθάνεσθαι] of something (for in both these the soul discriminates and identifies a real thing) (427ᵃ19–21)

Hence, Aristotle observes, early thinkers tried to explain *all* sorts of awareness—i.e. both thought and sense perception—on the perceptual model 'like is perceived by like'.

Aristotle responds to this problem, first with a short digression on whether this model can allow for being deceived.[31] A 'like by like' model of awareness will turn out to be problematic for both perception and thought, because the cause inevitably resembles the subjective experience, and hence there can be no erroneous impressions. Aristotle will, in due course, appeal to φαντασία in accounting for error, but it is not clear that the mention of error *here* is particularly designed to call forth a discussion of φαντασία. Rather, the puzzle is over the failure of the 'like by like' model as a tool for explaining cognition of any sort. The difficulty applies alike to perceptual error and vain thoughts, whenever our impressions fail to match what is actually producing them, but it seems to be a side issue in the development of the chapter since it has no bearing on the division between the two kinds of cognition.

Aristotle returns at 427ᵇ6 to the difference between perception and thought. Regardless of whether the 'like by like' model was itself flawed, Aristotle now tries to show that assimilating the two faculties must be wrong in any case. He points to two factors that show this: (1) the different distribution of the faculties and (2) whether they tell the truth or not. At the same time the analysis becomes more complicated, since knowing and thinking, which had up to

---

[30] Aristotle explains this general sense of αἰσθάνεσθαι (= consciousness or cognition in general) in the parenthesis at 427ᵃ20: when the soul discriminates or identifies a real object it is *aware* of it, and that happens in both thinking and perceiving. It seems likely that the ambiguity between a general sense and a perceptual sense of αἰσθάνεσθαι is explored in the first part of Plato's *Theaetetus* in the discussion of the claim that to know is to be aware of something, αἰσθάνεσθαι, which likewise leads into a discussion of things that 'appear to be of a certain sort to someone' (φαίνεσθαι), which is essentially one of the effects of φαντασία in the present account in Aristotle.

[31] *De anima* 427ᵃ29–ᵇ6. Caston ('Why Aristotle Needs Imagination') has suggested that this comment on the need to explain error is central to the chapter and underpins what is to be said about φαντασία (as explanatory of non-veridical experience). I take a different line in what follows, whereby error is only one factor that happens to be useful in the attempt to define the extensions of the various concepts at issue.

this point been lumped together (τὸ νοεῖν καὶ φρονεῖν, 427ᵃ19), are now broken down into various types as Aristotle attempts to mark off each capacity individually from perception, by its distribution or its fallibility, or both.

The first distinction, between perception and φρονεῖν, is supposed to be obvious on the basis of the distribution: while all animals have perception, the other faculty called φρονεῖν belongs to only 'a few' (427ᵇ7–8). The point seems straightforward until we wonder which animals those few kinds are, and what is the faculty that they possess: on one alternative the few animals who possess it will be humans only, and the capacity is practical wisdom that involves deliberation, what we know as φρόνησις elsewhere; on another alternative the few animal kinds include some non-human species, and the capacity is a kind of savvy, or understanding of the world, that allows such creatures to behave in quite complex and intelligent ways and to plan for the future. The latter alternative seems to be favoured by the fact that there appears to be a contrast, emphasized twice by the repeated οὐδέ, at 427ᵇ8 and 11, between this φρονεῖν and the next item on the list of kinds of cognition to be contrasted with perception: this time the candidate is νοεῖν, but it is immediately unpacked as a generic term under which a variety of kinds of cognition fall, including knowledge, true and false opinion, and, significantly, φρόνησις. *This* φρόνησις must surely be what we know as practical wisdom, the sort that involves rationality; but it seems that the previous reference to φρονεῖν must be to something else, something that is not a brand of νοεῖν and is not a rational capacity confined to humans. Indeed, the term νοεῖν (thinking) has hitherto appeared paired with φρονεῖν as two types of cognition that together form the thought side of the perception/thought divide (427ᵃ18, 19, 26, 28). The present passage appears to treat the two in succession in a manner consistent with supposing that they were two coordinate, mutually exclusive, and jointly exhaustive kinds of cognition.[32]

'Thinking', νοεῖν, in all its guises is now (427ᵇ8–11) said to be distinct from perceiving (*a*) with respect to fallibility, because perception of proper sensibles is invariably true (whereas thinking

---

[32] Later in the chapter (427ᵇ27, which I have suggested above may be earlier in composition) and in chapter 4 νοεῖν appears to be a generic term for all the faculties on the thought side of the thought/perception divide.

includes right and wrong varieties),[33] and (b) with repect to distribution, because perception is common to all animals, while thinking belongs only to animals that also have λόγος (perhaps meaning 'language').[34]

Thus by the time we reach the first mention of φαντασία in the course of our heavily reworked chapter, the opening topic has clearly been established: it focuses on how the dividing line is to be drawn between the two principal cognitive faculties, perception and thought. Aristotle appears satisfied that he has drawn a clear distinction between the two that will ensure that no experience classified under one could be a function of the other faculty in disguise. It is at this point that φαντασία enters the arena to complicate the simple twofold division between perception and thought.

(a) Introducing φαντασία

φαντασία is first mentioned at 427[b]14. As we have just seen, Aristotle has been affirming a distinction between thinking and perceiving on the grounds that thought, unlike perception, is peculiar to animals that have λόγος. Mentioning φαντασία is evidently supposed to clarify that point; Aristotle says:

For φαντασία is distinct from both perception and thought, and φαντασία does not occur without perception, and without φαντασία there is no supposing [ὑπόληψις]. (427[b]14–16)

What exactly is the word γάρ doing at the start of this sentence (427[b]14)? It might indicate an explanation for the immediately preceding claim, that no animal without λόγος thinks, or for the more general claim (427[b]8–10) that thought is distinct from perception. Assuming that it is the first,[35] φαντασία figures in what must be

---

[33] Of the varieties of thinking (νοεῖν) φρόνησις, ἐπιστήμη, and δόξα ἀληθής are thinking rightly, and some unnamed opposites are doing it wrongly, 427[b]9–11. Further on, Aristotle observes that it is possible to have false thoughts (διανοεῖσθαι ψευδῶς, 427[b]13). The argument from fallibility looks weak if we observe that perception also comes in true and false forms: it is only perception of the proper sensibles that is infallible. Given that there are branches of thought (knowledge, etc.) that are necessarily correct, the point would need to be expanded in some way that revealed a fundamental difference in the truth ascribed to perception.

[34] 427[b]14. There are a number of complexities in Aristotle's sentence 427[b]8–14 that I have just summarized, but it appears that Aristotle denies that animals without λόγος engage in the activity identified as διανοεῖσθαι or perhaps in anything included under νοεῖν—i.e. φρόνησις, ἐπιστήμη, δόξα ἀληθής, and so on (427[b]10).

[35] On the other alternative, φαντασία figures in a further justification for distin-

an attempt to explain away apparent counter-examples of intelligent behaviour on the part of animals without λόγος. To spell out the unstated suggestion, Aristotle would grant that some animals without λόγος, though they do not actually *think*, may still behave in some ways *as though they were thinking*, and suggest that φαντασία, not thinking, is what enables them to act intelligently. His actual statement, that φαντασία is not identical with either thought or perception, would be designed to allow that such behaviour need not presuppose thought since it could be dependent upon φαντασία instead.

In any case, Aristotle implies that people confuse thinking and perceiving as a result of ignoring the distinctive role of φαντασία which forms a basis for a certain sort of thought, here called ὑπόληψις. But what is this ὑπόληψις, which I have translated 'supposing', for which φαντασία is apparently a precondition? Here we encounter a difficulty, for the next passage (427ᵇ16–26) concludes by claiming that there are a number of different subspecies of ὑπόληψις, which include ἐπιστήμη, δόξα, φρόνησις and their opposites. This is exactly the same list as the subspecies of 'thinking' (νοεῖν) given earlier at 427ᵇ9–10; it therefore seems to follow that our present ὑπόληψις or 'supposing' is a generic term synonymous with the earlier generic category of 'thinking', νοεῖν; and since the latter apparently involves assent to the view in question,[36] so presumably does the former.

We may use this observation to cut through an impasse in the next sentence of our present passage, 427ᵇ16–17, where the text in the majority of manuscripts seems to say

But that thinking [νοεῖν] and supposing [ὑπόληψις] are not the same thing, is plain. (427ᵇ16–17)

Not only does this claim contradict what we have just deduced about the synonymity of 'thinking' and 'supposing', but the immediately following statement refers to 'this experience'[37] apparently

---

guishing thought and perception as such. Aristotle would be anticipating a particular tendency to confuse them due to the confusing nature of φαντασία, such a confusion being eradicated if we can keep φαντασία distinct from both.

[36] This, I think, is implied by the claim that thinking can be right or wrong (427ᵇ9), and is picked up, I believe, by the suggestion that judging necessarily results in claims that are truth-valued (427ᵇ20–1).

[37] τοῦτο τὸ πάθος, 427ᵇ17; the following points assert that 'this experience' is under our control to operate at will, by contrast with δοξάζειν (which we might take to be

with reference to φαντασία, despite the fact that φαντασία was not mentioned in 16–17. Plainly sense demands that in 16–17 Aristotle did not state a contrast between ὑπόληψις and νόησις (which we now know to be synonymous), but rather between *one or other—i.e. both—of those two capacities* on the one hand and φαντασία, which becomes 'this experience', on the other.[38] Aristotle contrasts thinking and φαντασία, on the grounds that the former is a judgement that is involuntary, and true or false, and involves assent and appropriate responses.[39] By contrast, φαντασία is something in which we engage at will, does not involve being right or wrong (because it is not an assertion), and does not invite the corresponding reactions.[40]

(b) Presentational φαντασία (1): φαντασία vs. opinion, 428ᵃ18–24

In the light of my claims about the double construction of the chapter, I now want to suggest that we should couple the passage just examined, in which φαντασία is contrasted with thought, including knowledge and opinion, with a passage a page later that explores the same contrast. At 428ᵃ16–18 Aristotle swiftly distinguishes φαντασία from ἐπιστήμη and νοῦς, on the grounds that it can be false whereas these are always true; at 428ᵃ18–24 he deals with factors that distinguish φαντασία from opinion (δόξα), and at 428ᵃ24–ᵇ9 he infers that it is not to be identified with any combina-

an alternative expression for ὑπόληψις), which we cannot withhold at will, since one inevitably has an opinion, whether right or wrong. The context implies that the voluntary experience, which is associated with envisaging imaginary models in memory exercises, must be φαντασία.

[38] Most of the manuscripts and ancient commentators have ὅτι δ' οὐκ ἔστιν ἡ αὐτὴ νόησις καὶ ὑπόληψις, φανερόν. Ross's excision of νόησις is sufficient to secure the sense we need, which can also be achieved by substituting φαντασία for νόησις in line with emendations inserted in two of the manuscripts.

[39] We might illustrate the claim by considering my response to a wasp: this takes the form of an involuntary judgement; that is, (*a*) if I take it for a wasp, I take it for a wasp and I cannot choose not to; (*b*) it either is or is not what I take it to be, so I inevitably make either a true or a false judgement; and (*c*) to 'take it for a wasp' is to assert that it is one and to react accordingly—if I did not react, I would not have judged that it was one.

[40] Perhaps I can picture the wasp as a fighter aircraft instead; then we do not expect responses appropriate to the presence of such an aircraft, any more than we would when watching a film of fighter aircraft. Two further kinds of recognition in this case would also invite a reference to φαντασία: first, recognizing aeroplanes in a film as aeroplanes (this seems to be an ability to construe what it is that is presented); second, the judgement that says 'this is actually a wasp' or 'this is only a movie': although this is a judgement it *depends upon* an ability to construe the environment as recognizable objects. In addition, it is an assertion about what is actually there.

tion of opinion and perception. To distinguish it from opinion he observes that opinion entails belief (πίστις) but animals do not have πίστις, though they can, and many do, have φαντασία.[41] Furthermore, he continues at 428ᵇ2–9—in exploring considerations that clinch the claim that φαντασία is not a combination of opinion and perception—the fact that the sun can appear one foot wide, while at the same time we can believe and assert that it is in fact enormous, shows that what we believe is different from how things look. Here it seems that φαντασία is somehow responsible for our ability to *see it as* a foot across, but evidently this cannot incorporate a judgement from opinion since belief or ὑπόληψις is itself simultaneously asserting a contrary judgement, to the effect that the sun is huge. The argument works only on the assumption that seeing the sun as a foot across is typically and evidently a task effected by φαντασία, so that any suggestion that that is a kind of opinion, or must include an input from opinion, can be ruled out by the presence of belief in a contrary claim. We might suggest that seeing the sun as a foot across illustrates a typical contribution of φαντασία because it must be φαντασία that presents preconceived measures of size and shape with which to construe the likely dimensions of the apparent object—but without thereby requiring that we ever assert that it is an object of that size or shape. At the same time one can have a true supposition (ὑπόληψιν ἀληθῆ, 428ᵇ3), implicitly asserting that it is not as it appears, but must be larger than the Earth.[42]

Opinion (δόξα) is, as we have now twice been told, a species of supposing. In the cases we have considered this is typically in the form of taking something to be an *x* or a *y* (some kind of primary or secondary substance) or to have properties *F* or *G*. Thus we may schematize the various cognitive activities discussed so far as follows: the activities collected as ὑπόληψις or νοεῖν typically involve implicit assertion in the form of *taking something to be* an *x* or a *y* or to have property *F* or *G*, either truly (ἐπιστήμη, φρόνησις, δόξα ἀληθής) or falsely (opposites of those forms of cognition); the activities included under perception typically involve *seeing, hearing, or otherwise perceiving something as* an *x* or a *y* or as having the property *F* or *G*, without implying an assertion to that effect; the activity

---

[41] 428ᵃ19–22.

[42] The example of the sun, which reappears in *De insomniis* 458ᵇ28, is well discussed by Wedin, *M&I* 76–81, who addresses earlier discussions in Schofield, 'A on I', and Nussbaum, *DMA* 248–9.

for which φαντασία has been mentioned as responsible here (but not necessarily typically) includes *presenting some form x* or *y* (e.g. a species or secondary substance), or the form of some property *F* or *G*, as a tool with which to construe the relevant perceptual field.

It is unsurprising that, in the two passages that attempt to distinguish φαντασία from some branch of supposing such as opinion, Aristotle focuses on examples that involve a *presentational* role for φαντασία. The temptation to think that φαντασία might belong in supposing, and that it involves getting things right or wrong, arises when we find that our ability to identify something as what it really is, or, equally, to identify it wrongly, can come from φαντασία. How does this differ from knowing or believing that it is an *x*, or taking it for *x*? The similarity comes in the fact that φαντασία is what provides the tools that enable us to construe an *x* in our environment: because of φαντασία things look a certain way to us. Aristotle chooses an example such as the appearance of the sun, where we might find ourselves initially tempted by the idea that an opinion is involved; the difference, which is what has to be brought out for Aristotle's point to come home, here and earlier in 427^{b}20–1, focuses on the assertoric nature of thoughts, and therefore on their truth-telling, by contrast with the non-assertoric, non-truth-valued nature of the construals based on φαντασία. So far, then, the only role of φαντασία that we have explored has been its role in presenting the tools with which to construe things that are currently present to perception.[43]

(c) Presentational φαντασία (2): φαντασία vs. perception, 428^{a}6–16

Two hints in chapter 3 imply that truth values belong only to certain kinds of judgements, namely the kind that involve assertion.[44] In the second of these passages, 428^{a}4–5, perception is included among the judgemental faculties, so that perception is conceived as judging how things are, and can correspondingly be false or true depending

[43] I have explored primarily the example of seeing the sun as a foot wide, rather than the example at 427^{b}18–20 of conjuring up some image for mnemonic purposes. The latter also invokes φαντασία in a presentational role, without entailing assertion, and hence not entailing the corresponding truth value that an assertion would have. It differs in that there is no corresponding perception; also the mnemonic example stresses the idea of calling up presentations by choice, a contrast with opinion that I have omitted from the summary merely for simplicity.

[44] 427^{b}20–1 δοξάζειν δ' οὐκ ἐφ' ἡμῖν· ἀνάγκη γὰρ ἢ ψεύδεσθαι ἢ ἀληθεύειν; 428^{a}4 καθ' ἃς κρίνομεν καὶ ἀληθεύομεν ἢ ψευδόμεθα. A similar implication emerges from the distinction between saying and asserting in 3. 7.

on whether things are as it perceives them to be. In so far as φαντασία has, at 427ᵇ21, been distinguished from intellectual judgements that imply assertion, there is a sense in which it is not a candidate for such truth values. Something similar seems to be implied by the notion that we see the sun as a foot wide, yet we do not change our mind nor contradict ourselves when we claim otherwise. No truth claim is ever made in the observation that it looks thus and so.

Yet there is another way in which it can still make sense to ask whether our non-committal impressions are true. Aristotle will say that φαντασία can be false as well as true (428ᵃ18), and he means thereby to distinguish between impressions that do, and those that don't, correspond to the way things really are. The distinction between true ones and false ones does not undermine his claim that φαντασία is not in the business of assertion, and, in that sense, not truth-apt. The distinction between the two questions about truth roughly corresponds to the difference between ψεύδεσθαι ἢ ἀληθεύειν (lying or telling the truth, 427ᵇ21, 428ᵃ4) on the one hand, which is the issue for assertions, and ἀληθής ἢ ψευδής (true or false, 428ᵃ15, 18) on the other, which is the issue for impressions.

Perception, like the presentations of φαντασία, appears to be a candidate for truth and falsity of the latter sort.[45] To discover why we might be tempted to confuse φαντασία with perception, and why in fact they should be distinguished, Aristotle picks up the fact that φαντασία (again in a presentational role, though not the same one that figured above) can present forms that are not concurrently presented in the surroundings, unlike perception, which is always of something that is actually there.[46] On this account, such φαντασίαι count as 'false', where 'truth' is a matter of matching up with items in the surroundings.

This change of focus helps to explain what might otherwise seem an enigmatic observation at 428ᵃ11–12, to the effect that perceptions are always true whereas the majority of φαντασίαι are false. Aristotle is saying neither that perceptions assert the truth, nor that φαντασίαι

---

[45] At 428ᵃ4 perception is listed as one of the judgemental faculties which are truth-telling in the former sense, as though perceiving were a form of asserting. However, the subsequent comparison between perception and φαντασία focuses on the relative prevalence of presentations that are not true of anything present in the environment, and hence turns to the latter kind of truth value.

[46] Thus we are told that something can appear to us (e.g. in sleep) when the sense is not only not perceiving but not functional at all (428ᵃ6–8). The mention of the visions experienced by the blind (ᵃ15) seems to be an afterthought that forms an additional contribution to this same argument.

assert lies. Rather, perception is importantly *'true of'* the objects that it perceives,[47] in the sense that it invariably has a corresponding object that is perceived (there is no perception without an external object that is perceived), whereas the kind of presentations for which φαντασία is here held responsible are paradigmatically the ones that do not correspond to any present reality; the majority of such presentations are not true of anything since there either is no corresponding object present at the time, or it is not as we envisage it. Doubtless there *might* by chance be a murderer downstairs when my fevered imagination constructs the prospect of one from the creakings in the night; and this accounts for the claim that it is only *the majority* of such φαντασίαι, and not all of them, that are false in this sense. Thus I think it is unnecessary to suppose that Aristotle is saying that most of the presentations for which φαντασία could ever figure as an explanation are bogus; rather, in a restricted class of such presentations, i.e. the ones that occur when our senses are idle, almost all of them lack any accurate correspondence with the immediate environment at the time.

To contrast φαντασία with perception, then, Aristotle naturally again focuses on a particular presentational role that is characteristically associated with φαντασία, one in which φαντασία might easily be taken to present forms that are indistinguishable from the objects of perception. And of course, if I am right, the objects or forms that it thus presents are indeed indistinguishable from the objects of perception. But φαντασία must still be distinguished from perception, for it is not itself the perception of those forms, nor does it present them to be perceived. No: perception is of things outside, and is true of those things; it cannot be a case of perception if what is observed is not there.

Thus, to indicate the contrast between perception and φαντασία accurately, Aristotle focuses attention on the second of the two kinds of presentation for which φαντασία is responsible, the one in which it is responsible for calling to mind forms not concurrently given in the environment. We may thus schematize the cognitive activities that are distinguished in this second contrast as follows: the activities attributed here to *perception* typically involve seeing, hearing,

---

[47] 'True of' is Wedin's formulation: he introduces this helpful distinction between the two kinds of truth value at *M&I* 76. We can also express the point by taking Aristotle to have recognized that 'perceive' is always a success verb, whereas the conversational implicature of 'looks' or 'appears' is frequently an invitation to scepticism (428ᵃ12–15). On this see further below.

or otherwise perceiving some sensible object that *is genuinely there* (so that the perception counts as true); the activities attributed here to φαντασία, not necessarily typically, include presenting some form of *x* or *y* or of property *F* or *G* when there is no such object there, so as to construe items that are there as what they are not, or to envisage items that are not there at all. The lack of correspondence with what is there qualifies such presentations for the designation 'false'.

Thus a different activity associated with φαντασία has been picked out for attention in drawing the contrasts with perception, as opposed to the earlier contrast with thought; but this is not, I suggest, the result of any confusion on Aristotle's part: it simply reflects the need to identify the relevant feature that will precisely mark the required distinction. In neither case are we being offered a full account of the functions for which φαντασία is responsible; rather we are looking at selected functions relevant to the distinction at issue.

The distinction with perception raises two other points. One is the distribution of the two capacities:

Furthermore, perception is always present, but φαντασία is not, whereas if they were actually the same, it would be possible for φαντασία to occur to all the animals; but this seems not to be the case (e.g. to the ant or bee or maggot). (428^{a}8–11)

The point of this passage is clear though the details are not. Here, as elsewhere, Aristotle claims that all animals have some form of perception; that seems the most plausible way to understand 'perception is always present'. But should it not be the case that φαντασία is universal too, so as to provide *all* animals with the capacity to construe their environment and act appropriately?[48] If that is not so, why might one cite bees or ants as examples in which it is not present? Or are these intended to be examples in which it is present, by contrast with maggots? In other works Aristotle affirms that the ant and bee, as a result of their pure and thin bloodless fluid, have particularly fine perception and intelligence, better even than the beasts that have blood,[49] so it might seem particularly surprising to find them denied φαντασία. But then what about maggots?

One solution may be to remind ourselves once again that Aristotle

---

[48] This expectation seems to be reflected in Aristotle's questions about the explanation of movement on the part of 'incomplete' animals at 433^{b}31–434^{a}5.

[49] *PA* 650^{b}19–27.

is, at this point, concentrating on one particular role of φαντασία, when it presents forms that are not simultaneously available in the immediate environment. Answering 'but it seems not' (428ᵃ10) to the suggestion that all beasts would have to be endowed with the capacity for such φαντασία might be contextually understood to deny such creatures only the fantasies of absent objects, not the abilities identified earlier in distinguishing φαντασία from thought. Some might still have *that* capacity, but if perception were simply identical with φαντασία any animal with perception would thereby have the full range of experiences for which φαντασία is invoked, including ideas of absent objects. Aristotle would be saying that φαντασία must be distinct from perception to allow that this need not be so.

Alternatively, we may favour a reading whereby Aristotle denies presentations of absent objects only to the most basic of creatures, in this case the maggot. There are textual variants and several ways of reading the phrase that mentions ants, bees, and maggots, of which arguably the most plausible is 'it seems that φαντασία is not present in all animals, for example, contrast ants or bees with the maggot'.[50]

In any case, in order to show that φαντασία is not just the same thing as perception, it is enough to show that *some* animals with perception lack *some* of the effects attributable to φαντασία.[51]

(d) Presentational φαντασία (1) (again): φαντασία vs. perception again

The final mark distinguishing φαντασία from perception returns us, apparently, to the role that we first picked out for φαντασία in distinguishing it from thinking above—that is, the presentation of appropriate forms with which to construe the present environment in perception. Aristotle observes that we characteristically speak of things 'appearing to us' in contexts where the perception is hard to construe. When it is obvious, we don't say 'it appears to be a man',

[50] The manuscripts say δοκεῖ δ' οὔ, οἷον μύρμηκι ἢ μελίττῃ ἢ σκώληκι ('but it seems not, as for the ant or bee or maggot'); some of the ancient commentators paraphrase the passage as if it ascribed φαντασία to the bee but denied it to the maggot, and that sense is allowed, though not required, by Ross's preferred emendation (from Förster) δοκεῖ δ' οὔ, οἷον μύρμηκι ἢ μελίττῃ, καὶ σκώληκι.

[51] Of course, one might want to say that this argument is not quite adequate, since the absence of some effect might be due not to the absence of the capacity but to an animal failing to exercise the capacity or it being suppressed due to other conditions of the animal's habitat or lifestyle.

whereas we do when we are unsure whether we have seen what is really there.[52] This suggests that φαντασία is required to help with the work of figuring out what it is that we are seeing, in the latter cases, where we cannot see clearly, but not in the former. Even the way in which φαντασία contributes to the ability to construe the objects of perception, then, is not identical with the act of perceiving but a separate task.

This might imply that the clearer case of perception does not involve φαντασία. Perhaps when we plainly and clearly see a man, this is simply incidental perception: there is no need to say that we see it 'as a man' as though one might see it as anything else. If so, φαντασία only comes in when we have to pick out items of interest from a fuzzy perceptual field, when construing it is a task beyond mere perception.

This may be what Aristotle has in mind,[53] in which case perhaps the unproblematic perceptions can serve as the source from which φαντασία derives the forms that it will subsequently employ. This suggests an initial passive role for φαντασία, namely tracing the forms of objects given in perception. Then, once we have clearly seen a man, say, that form will figure in the repertoire with which we attempt to construe future experiences. It will now be possible to see something else *as a man*, which in turn will allow those of us with intellect to form an opinion or *take it to be a man*.[54]

(e) Receptive φαντασία (1): the physiology of derivative authenticity

So far, because of the distinctions that needed to be drawn between φαντασία and thought, on the one hand, and φαντασία and perception, on the other, Aristotle has focused on what I have called presentational roles of φαντασία, whereby it presents forms for attention, supplying those forms required to construe objects of sense as meaningful structures and producing similar presentations in dreams and fantasies. By contrast, the last part of the

---

[52] 428ª12–15.

[53] I do not think that this is the only possible account to be given of this example. An alternative is that Aristotle does suppose that φαντασία is required to explain even how we see the clear example as a man, but that he notes that the characteristic use of 'appears' in the unclear case suggests that this one and not the clear case is the paradigm in which the work of φαντασία is most evident, and in which it is plainly not merely integral to the perception but has to be distinguished from the unclear perception.

[54] More needs to be said on this procedure: cf. *Post. An.* 2. 19.

chapter (428^{b}10 ff.) is, I think, best interpreted as alluding to a quite different role, one that has not figured in the earlier parts of the chapter—a receptive role whereby, in virtue of φαντασία, we can register the structures or forms that will be used in subsequent activities requiring presentations supplied by φαντασία, including all those mentioned in the chapter so far.[55] My suggestion is that, in the light of issues about truth that have figured in the discussion of those other activities, Aristotle sums up with an appeal to the likely physiological explanation of our ability to store such forms, in order to clarify at the same time some further ways in which one might ask whether the forms count as true. From 428^{b}10 onwards Aristotle first speaks of the possibility of a change being set up as a result of perceiving, and of the resemblance between the change so caused and the perception itself. Eventually he suggests that the necessary and sufficient conditions of such a change, were it to occur, would correspond exactly to the necessary and sufficient conditions of φαντασία, and thereby infers that φαντασία is to be identified with such a change (429^{a}1–2). This physiological section mentions only passive experiences resulting directly from perception. Taken as an account of the presentational roles of φαντασία mentioned in the earlier part of the chapter, it is wholly mysterious, for there seems little reason to suppose that presentations such as we get in dreams or memory are the mechanical effects of simultaneous perceptions, and no way of seeing how events caused by the perceptions could constitute the kind of presentations that are supposed to help in construing or interpreting obscure objects of perception. If, on the other hand, we read this section as an account of a quite different phenomenon, namely the passive reception of forms that are later to recur as intentional objects in the kind of experiences discussed earlier, we shall make much better progress.

Thus, if we take it this way, we now encounter φαντασία as the process of registering forms that impinge in the course of perception, i.e. one aspect of what I called receptive φαντασία. It is said to be a change that occurs; it only occurs with perception; it occurs to things that are currently perceiving[56] and it is about the same things as the perception is of. In other words, while we are perceiving, at

---

[55] The account offered by Aristotle in 428^{b}10–429^{a}8 is of physiological processes, and he does not spell out exactly what psychological events they belong to. I take the emphasis on concurrent perception and passivity to imply the receptive role.

[56] αἰσθανομένοις, 428^{b}12.

the same time receptive φαντασία is registering the same thing as the perception is about. This is not impossible, Aristotle suggests, because there is no reason why the change or motion involved in actual perception itself should not also initiate another similar change which will then have similar intentional content to the perception. Such a secondary effect would have all the defining conditions of receptive φαντασία: it could not occur without perception, nor in things not currently perceiving; a creature that had it would be able to carry out a wide range of activities and undergo experiences on the basis of it; and it could be true or false ($428^{b}14$–17).

The last of these features might seem problematic, for how could something that is merely receptive of the same changes as take place in perception be false, any more than perception can? Aristotle immediately proceeds to explain, but it helps to bear in mind that the notion of 'truth' here is evidently not the truth-telling of assertions, but rather the kind of truth invoked in the comparison between φαντασία and perception,[57] namely whether the experience in question matches up with a corresponding object in the environment at the time. Perception itself, Aristotle points out, differs in its truth (in this sense) depending on its objects: perception of a proper sensible is always true of its proper object (sight is of colour and in so far as a colour is seen, there is such a colour that is seen); perception of incidental sensibles may sometimes be false (if I see what I take to be my dog, there may indeed be a dog there, or it might have been a sheep, though I can't be wrong about it being white); while perception of common sensibles is the area where Aristotle thinks that we most often get a false impression (if I observe what I take to be the dog going away, it or something like it may indeed be going away, but conceivably it is really coming nearer). But now, it seems, receptive φαντασία gets its materials from all these sorts of observations, and hence it has exactly the same opportunities for acquiring input that doesn't exactly match up with the things it derives from:

The change occasioned by the actuality of perception will differ as it comes from the three forms of perception. The first is true *while perception is present*, but the others would be false *both while perception is present and in its absence*, and particularly whenever the object perceived is far away. ($428^{b}25$–30)

[57] $428^{a}11$–12.

First we should remember that all presentations, even of proper
sensibles, must automatically count as 'false' in this sense when they
occur in the absence of the relevant perceptible object, given that
things would then not match up with them.[58] However, those are
not the experiences that we are currently asked to consider. Instead
we are now primarily concerned with the change initiated *during
perception*, while the object perceived must be present to be perceived. In this case, we are told, the truth or falsity of the secondary
effect will 'differ' (428^{b}26)—i.e. differ in truth value—because a
perception that is invariably true will have a corresponding effect
in the receptive φαντασία that is similarly invariably true (true of a
corresponding special object) while it is concurrent with the true
perception, whereas the other kinds of perception may sometimes
be false impressions themselves. Such false impressions will insti-
gate correspondingly false forms in the repertoire of φαντασία, even
while we are still perceiving the wrongly identified object. This
would explain how we might acquire a fantastic repertoire of quite
non-existent forms, derived none the less from perception.

(f) Receptive φαντασία (2): sticky forms

Of the four roles that we initially distinguished for φαντασία we have
now found three arising in the course of *De anima* 3. 3—two active
roles (the presentation of forms whereby we construe our current
perception as recognizable objects; the presentation of the same
forms in the absence of corresponding perceptible objects) and one
receptive role (the registering of forms presented to perception, at
the time of perception). One role has so far been ignored, and that
is the retention of the forms over time, while they are neither being
perceived nor presented for attention. Aristotle merely alludes to
this in summing up the chapter:

And because these stick and are similar to perceptions, animals carry out
many activities on the basis of them—some because they do not have intellect, as with the beasts, some because the intellect is sometimes shrouded
as a result of emotion, illness, or sleep, as with human beings. (429^{a}4–9)

[58] That is, if I see a green frog, the appearance of greenness that strikes me is
true, for there is a green frog. If, however, in the absence of anything green at all,
I get a presentation from φαντασία of a green frog, the greenness impression will be
false even though frogs, were they there, would be green, and even though green is
a colour and proper to sight; for there is nothing green there in fact.

Nothing is said here about how or why the forms stick. Aristotle is not giving a complete summary of the functions of φαντασία (many of which are explored in other treatises) but identifying the features that indicate its different place in animal life as compared to the several cognitive functions to which it contributes.

(g) φαντασία *disposed*

It seems that we can now summarize the range of cognitive roles attributed to thought, perception, and φαντασία like this: ὑπόληψις or νοεῖν involved implicit assertion, whether truly or falsely, that something is an *x* or has the property *F*; the activities included under perception involved, first, non-assertively perceiving something as an *x* or a *y* or as having the property *F* or *G*, and, second, perceiving some sensible object that is genuinely there; the sense in which what is perceived is 'genuinely there' has also now turned out to be variable depending on whether it is a proper sensible or one of the incidental or common sensibles; the activities attributed to φαντασία, not necessarily exhaustively, included two presentational roles, namely (*a*) presenting some form as a tool for construing the perceptual field, and (*b*) presenting some form when there is no such object there, and two hints at receptive capacities, namely (*a*) registering the proper, incidental, and common sensibles as they occur to perception, and (*b*) retaining those forms for future use.

It will be noticed, however, that a distinction between presentational roles, on the one hand, and receptive roles, on the other, is helpful for φαντασία, but does not apply to the cognate faculties from which it is, in each case, being distinguished. Modes of cognition like supposing, interpreting, thinking, knowing, or perceiving are not faculties that present objects to the mind for attention; they are the mind's attention to such objects. Neither perception nor knowledge creates or supplies its own objects: rather the objects must be, so to speak, objective, otherwise it would not be perception or knowledge, even if there is a sense in which the mind can actively select its objects for attention. In so far as the soul itself plays any role in actually forming the objects of its attention, that will surely be the task of φαντασία. However, by speaking of presentation, I am not suggesting that φαντασία presents an alternative inner set of objects to perception or thought, as though one watched an internal slide show of fantastic images, a virtual world. The effect is rather that in presenting a form, φαντασία is directing our attention not to an internally created image, but to the world that is so construed. We remain observers of the forms directly encountered in perception, not observers of our inner cognitive experiences, partly, of course, because our inner cognitive experiences are nothing else but the actuality of their objects of attention. To explain our ability to construe a vague perceptual field as recognizable objects of attention, or to recall the same objects in memory, for reflection and judgement by the intellect, Aristotle seems to suggest that we shall seek the explanation in φαντασία.

3. Conclusion

I have tried to suggest that φαντασία is not an extra pseudo-faculty that kind-of-thinks, and thereby somehow makes up for a lack of concepts in animals, but rather that it is not a faculty of judgement or interpretation at all, but the source of the intentional objects to which we attend. Why is it important, then? Because by avoiding a dualism of the intentional objects of the two faculties of sense and thought, and by ensuring that the objects of both are actually the objects we encounter in experience of the real world, Aristotle is cutting away any possibility of the move that we started this paper with, the claim that because animals do not have access to the world of thoughts they cannot have anything in mind when they act. That problem only arises if we suppose that there is some special kind of mental object that we humans would be thinking of, which cannot be the same object as an animal lacking intellect might see and choose. My plate of roast chicken appears to me to be food; so is that notion of 'food' a special object of thought and not something that I see? Not according to Aristotle, for food is an object that I can perceive as well as dream of. And hence the next-door cat can see the food, just as well as I can, and can also envisage the likelihood that he will find such food if he creeps in through the open door from which the familiar smell is emerging, and consequently do so on purpose. For it is quite certain that he does not come in unintentionally.

Aristotle offers us an explanation of how our ability to perceive relevant objects in our environment and our ability to think of such objects in their absence are not unconnected, and how the thoughts are of the same items as we experience in perception. His insistence (in the chapter that we have been considering) that thought is nevertheless distinct from perception shows not that it is of a different range of objects, nor that it is necessary for purposive action, but only that the mode of attention to the objects is distinct. The last sentence that I quoted at 429ᵃ7–9 implies that we follow our fantasies only when our brains are switched off, so to speak; but in fact this is evidently incorrect, as *De anima* 3. 10, with its account of the motivating force of ὄρεξις, based on φαντασία, eventually reveals. What this means is that were we to look more closely we would discover that our actions are really chosen on the basis of a likely outcome that we envisage, which presents itself to us as an attractive or unattractive experience. In this, I suggest, Aristotle would claim that we are not only acting on purpose, and sometimes intelligently, but also behaving in no way differently from the beasts.

University of Liverpool

DID EPICURUS DISCOVER
THE FREE WILL PROBLEM?

SUSANNE BOBZIEN

1. Introduction

I N 1967 Epicurus was credited with the discovery of the problem of free will and determinism.[1] Among the contestants were Aristotle and the early Stoics. Epicurus emerged victorious, because—so the argument went—Aristotle did not yet have the problem, and the Stoics inherited it from Epicurus. In the same year David Furley published his essay 'Aristotle and Epicurus on Voluntary Action', in which he argued that Epicurus' problem was not the free will problem.[2] In the thirty-odd years since then, a lot has been published about Epicurus on freedom and determinism.[3] But it has

© Susanne Bobzien 2000
Versions of this paper have been presented at Cambridge, Berne, Yale, and Cornell Universities. I am grateful to members of my audiences for stimulating discussion; and I thank David Sedley, Tad Brennan, Gail Fine, Terry Irwin, and especially Charles Brittain for helpful written comments on earlier drafts of this paper.

[1] By Pamela Huby in 'The First Discovery of the Freewill Problem' ['Freewill Problem'], *Philosophy*, 42 (1967), 353–62.

[2] D. Furley, 'Aristotle and Epicurus on Voluntary Action' ['Voluntary Action'], in his *Two Studies in the Greek Atomists* (Princeton, 1967).

[3] e.g. J. Annas, *Hellenistic Philosophy of Mind* [*Mind*] (Berkeley, 1992), ch. 8; E. Asmis, *The Epicurean Theory of Free Will and its Origins in Aristotle* (Ph.D. diss., Yale University, 1970); ead., 'Free Action and the Swerve: Review of Walter G. Englert, *Epicurus on the Swerve and Voluntary Action*' ['Free Action'], *OSAP* 8 (1990), 275–91; I. Avotins, 'The Question of *Mens* in Lucretius 2. 289', *Classical Quarterly*, NS 29 (1979), 95–100; id., 'Notes on Lucretius 2. 251–293', *Harvard Studies in Classical Philology*, 84 (1980), 75–9; P. Conway, 'Epicurus' Theory of Freedom of Action' ['Epicurus' Theory'], *Prudentia*, 13 (1981), 81–9; W. G. Englert, *Epicurus on the Swerve and Voluntary Action* [*Epicurus*] (Atlanta, Ga., 1987); D. Fowler, 'Lucretius on the *Clinamen* and "Free Will" (II 251–93)', in Συζήτησις: *Studi sull'epicureismo greco e romano offerti a Marcello Gigante* [Συζήτησις] (Naples, 1983), 329–52; N. Gulley, 'Lucretius on Free Will' ['Free Will'], *Symbolae Osloenses*, 65 (1990), 37–52; P. Huby, 'The Epicureans, Animals, and Freewill', *Apeiron*, 3 (1969), 17–19; K. Kleve, 'Id Facit Exiguum Clinamen', *Symbolae Osloenses*, 55 (1980), 27–31; S. Laursen, 'Epicurus *On Nature* Book XXV', *Cronache ercolanesi*,

only rarely been questioned again whether Epicurus, in one way or another, found himself face to face with some version of the free will problem.[4] In this paper I intend to take up the case for those who have questioned the point, combining a fresh perspective on the debate with a selection of new arguments and a detailed textual analysis of the relevant passages. Let me begin with a brief sketch of the problem of freedom and determinism which Epicurus is widely taken to have been concerned with.

The *determinism* Epicurus defends himself against is usually understood as *causal* determinism: every event is fully determined in all its details by preceding causes. These causes are commonly pictured as forming an uninterrupted chain or network, reaching back infinitely into the past, and as governed by an all-embracing set of laws of nature, or as manifestations of such a set of laws of nature.

On the side of *freedom*, Epicurus is generally understood to have been concerned with freedom of decision (the freedom to decide *whether or not* to do some action) or freedom of choice (the freedom to choose *between* doing and not doing some action)[5] or freedom of the will (where the freedom to will to do something entails the freedom to will not to do it, and vice versa; I call this *two-sided* freedom of the will). Epicurus is taken to have introduced an *indeterminist* conception of free decision or free choice or two-sided free will:

---

18 (1988), 7–18; id., 'Against Democritus—Towards the End', in M.Capasso *et al.*, *Miscellanea Papyrologica* (Florence, 1990), 3–22 at 21–2; id., 'The Summary of Epicurus' On Nature Book 25', *Papiri letterari greci e latini* (1992), 143–54; id., 'The Early Parts of Epicurus, *On Nature*, 25th Book' ['Early Parts'], *Cronache ercolanesi* (1995), 5–109; id., 'The Later Parts of Epicurus, *On Nature*, 25th Book' ['Later Parts'], *Cronache ercolanesi* (1998), 5–82; A. A. Long, *Hellenistic Philosophy* (New York, 1974), 56–61; A. A. Long and D. N. Sedley, *The Hellenistic Philosophers* [Long–Sedley; LS] (Cambridge, 1987), i. 102–12; ii. 104–113; P. Mitsis, *Epicurus' Ethical Theory* (Ithaca, 1988), ch. 4; J. S. Purinton, 'Epicurus on "Free Volition" and the Atomic Swerve' ['Free Volition'], *Phronesis*, 44 (1999), 253–99; T. Saunders, 'Free Will and the Atomic Swerve in Lucretius', *Symbolae Osloenses*, 59 (1984), 37–59; D. N. Sedley, 'Epicurus' Refutation of Determinism' ['Determinism'], in Συζήτησις, 11–51; id., 'Epicurean Anti-Reductionism', ['Anti-Reductionism'], in J. Barnes and M. Mignucci (eds.), *Matter and Metaphysics* (Naples, 1988), 295–327; R. W. Sharples, *Cicero* On Fate *and Boethius* The Consolation of Philosophy *IV. 5–7, V* (Warminster, 1991), 172–7, 195; id., 'Epicurus, Carneades and the Atomic Swerve' ['Epicurus'], *BICS* (1991–3), 174–90.

[4] Besides Furley there is Conway, 'Epicurus' Theory'. Authors have, however, become more careful on this point: see e.g. Mitsis, *Epicurus' Ethical Theory*, and Laursen's publications (see n. 3).

[5] Or alternatively to choose between doing one action or another.

agents are free in this sense only if they are causally undetermined (or not fully causally determined) in their decision whether or not to act or their choice between alternative courses of action; undetermined, that is, by external and internal causal factors alike. There is assumed to be a gap in the causal chain immediately before, or simultaneously with, the decision or choice, a gap which allows the coming into being of a spontaneous motion. In this way every human decision or choice is directly linked with causal indeterminism. The assumption of such indeterminist free decision, free choice, or two-sided free will does not presuppose that one specifies an independent mental faculty, like e.g. a will, and indeed it is not usually assumed that Epicurus' theory involved such a faculty.

The 'free will problem' that Epicurus is assumed to have faced is then roughly as follows: If determinism is true, every decision or choice of an agent between alternative courses of actions is fully determined by preceding causes, and forms part of an uninterrupted causal chain. On the other hand, if an agent has (two-sided) freedom of the will, it seems that the agent's decision or choice must not be fully determined by preceding causes. Hence, it appears, determinism and freedom of the will (freedom of decision, freedom of choice) are incompatible.[6]

I do not believe that Epicurus ever considered a problem along the lines of the one just described. In particular, I am sceptical about the assumption that he shared in a conception of free decision or free choice akin to the one I have sketched. (I also have my doubts that he ever conceived of a determinism characterized by a comprehensive set of laws of nature; but this is a point I only mention in passing.) To avoid misunderstandings, I should stress that I do believe that Epicurus was an indeterminist of sorts—only that he did not advocate indeterminist free decision or indeterminist free choice.

Why do I surmise that Epicurus did not deal with a concept of free decision or choice? I have first an external reason, as it were: it is my view that neither Aristotle nor the early Stoics nor any contemporaries of Epicurus were concerned with such a concept.

---

[6] This is the kind of free will problem C. Giussani (*Lucreti Cari De Rerum Natura Libri Sex*, i (Turin, 1896), 125–69) and C. Bailey (*The Greek Atomists and Epicurus* [*Greek Atomists*] (New York, 1928), 318–23, 433–7) connected with Epicurus, and which the majority of more recent scholars take him to have dealt with: so e.g. Asmis, 'Free Action'; Gulley, 'Free Will'; Huby, 'Freewill Problem'; Purinton, 'Free Volition'; Sedley, 'Determinism'; Sharples, 'Epicurus'.

However, in this paper I want to focus exclusively on Epicurean philosophy.[7] I argue—negatively—that nothing in Epicurus' extant writings and in our other sources for Epicurus' philosophy provides any unambiguous evidence that Epicurus ever discussed a free will problem as just described;[8] and—positively—I suggest that Epicurus was caught in a related, but different, set of problems, for which we do have some direct evidence. One can best understand *why* Epicurus was concerned with a different problem if one realizes that he worked with different models of agency and moral responsibility from those attributed to him by many modern scholars who see him as a proponent of indeterminist freedom of decision or choice.

The concept of indeterminist freedom that has been attributed to Epicurus presupposes that agents are free only if they are undetermined (or not fully determined) *in their decision or choice* by external and internal factors alike. The stipulation of the absence of these determining factors is typically linked with a model of agency that is based on the following distinction: on the one hand, there are the possible causal influence factors, some external to me (the agent), like the environment, some internal to me, such as my character dispositions. On the other hand, there is myself, the one who decides, causally detached not only from external impacts, but also from my past experiences, from my present character and dispositions, from my desires and inclinations, perhaps even from my memories and factual beliefs. I, the one who decides, am thus identified with some sort of a decision-making faculty which is detached from the rest of 'me', where this rest includes my character and my present mental dispositions. This decision-making faculty has control over all the other factors and can in principle decide against any one of them. Thus the entity that makes decisions is not identified with

---

[7] For the Stoics see my *Determinism and Freedom in Stoic Philosophy* [*Determinism*], (Oxford, 1998), ch. 6. For Aristotle, the Peripatetics, the Middle Platonists, and the general development of the problem of free decision and causal determinism see my 'The Inadvertent Conception and Late Birth of the Free-Will Problem' ['Inadvertent Conception'], *Phronesis*, 43 (1998), 133–75.

[8] Whether Epicurus discussed free will depends on what one means by 'free will'. For example, if one intends 'free will' to render Lucretius' 'libera voluntas' (see below, sect. 4), and to mean whatever element of Epicurus' doctrine Lucretius meant to capture by this phrase, then Epicurus evidently was concerned with free will. My concern is only to show that he did not discuss a problem of free will that involves a conception of freedom of decision or choice as adumbrated in the main text.

the whole person (body, soul, and mind), nor even the whole mind, but is causally independent of large parts of that person or of that mind. I call this the independent-decision-faculty model of agency. It is often, and sometimes explicitly, taken to underlie Epicurus' philosophy.[9]

This model and the concept of free decision or choice on which it is based are commonly linked with the following conception of moral responsibility: I can be held morally responsible for an action of mine only if I could have decided or chosen to act otherwise, or if I was free to decide or choose otherwise. This conception of responsibility is typically backed up with the fact that people are generally convinced that they could decide and act otherwise than they do, and with suggestions that moral emotions like regret or guilt indicate that we are free to decide and act otherwise.

Epicurus, I suggest, operated with a different conception of moral responsibility and with a different model of agency; a model which does not causally sever a person's present character and mental dispositions from that person *qua decision-maker*. Rather, Epicurus identified the agent with the person's mind (or large parts thereof), including the person's system of beliefs, memories, character dispositions, desires, and emotions. In this model, what volition a person forms, and what action they perform, fully depends on the overall disposition of the person's mind at the time of forming the volition. It is considered essential for the causal attribution of an action to me as a person that it is the person as I *am* when I form the volition who is (at least in the main)[10] causally responsible for what action is performed. I call this the whole-person model of agency.[11]

In this model, moral responsibility for an action is typically *not* based on the causal undeterminedness of the agent's *decision*, but, on the contrary, on the fact that the action is dependent on the person's present overall disposition of their mind. What makes an agent morally responsible, and an action voluntary, is what for

---

[9] Explicitly e.g. in Asmis, 'Free Action', 283; Sharples, 'Epicurus', 178, 187–8; it is implicit in e.g. Bailey, *Greek Atomism*, 435, and in Sedley 'Determinism', at 49 and before.

[10] Epicurus allowed for a multiplicity of causes for human behaviour; see below, p. 317 with n. 64.

[11] Two Lucretius passages could perhaps be adduced as providing some support for the assumption that Epicurus worked with the whole-person model of agency: '. . . that is still nothing to us, who are constituted by the conjunction of body and spirit' (Lucr. 3. 845–6, trans. Long–Sedley) and 'the mind and the spirit are firmly interlinked and constitute a single nature' (Lucr. 3. 136–7, trans. Long–Sedley).

convenience I shall call the *autonomy* of the agent. By 'autonomy'
I intend to indicate nothing but the fact that the agent, *and not
something else*, causes the action (or is at least its main cause), and
that the agent is not compelled or forced to act. This second concept
of moral responsibility is thus not grounded on a concept of freedom
to decide or choose otherwise, but on a notion of agent autonomy.[12]

Characteristically, in the whole-person model of agency agents
can influence their ways of acting and behaving only *indirectly*, by
changing the basis of their actions, i.e. their mental dispositions
(since their volitions and actions are a function of these dispositions). There is in this model no space for indeterminist freedom of
decision. For the fact that agents act in accordance with their overall
mental disposition is considered a *necessary condition* for attributing the action to them, whereas indeterminist freedom of decision
takes the *detachment* of the decision-making faculty from (most of)
the rest of the person's mind as a necessary condition. The concept
of an internally undetermined decision *made by the agent* would be
difficult to incorporate in this conceptual framework; and so would
be the free will problem in the form sketched above.

In the whole-person model of agency the main problem that
arises from a deterministic assumption is how, if everything, including my actions, were necessitated by something other than me,
I, the agent, could still rightfully be considered as being myself
causally and hence morally responsible for my actions. I call this
the problem of necessitation and agent autonomy.

In the following I aim to show that all the surviving texts which
have been adduced as evidence that Epicurus dealt with a free will
problem as set out above are in fact compatible with the assumption
that Epicurus did not work with an independent-decision-faculty
model of agency or a concept of moral responsibility based on
freedom to decide otherwise; and that there is a reasonable amount
of evidence that Epicurus worked with a whole-person model of
agency and a concept of moral responsibility based on the idea of
agent autonomy as just described; and accordingly, that his problem
was not the one commonly assumed, but a problem of necessitation
and agent autonomy.

Why, then, is it such a popular view among philosophers that
Epicurus dealt with a free will problem as described above, or at

[12] Evidence that Epicurus had this concept of moral responsibility is provided in
sect. 3 below.

least with some of its main aspects? Apart from less relevant factors
such as that it would be nice if Epicurus had anticipated the modern
discussion of causal determinism and free decision-making, and
even nicer if he had anticipated, with his swerve, the 'solution'
some modern libertarians squeezed out of the theory of quantum
mechanics—apart from such factors, there is one important reason:
many of the key expressions used in those Epicurean passages that
are commonly held to be about indeterminist choice appear to be
ambiguous in such a way that—although they never state the problem of free decision and causal determinism directly—they *can* be
read as alluding to it. These are, in particular, phrases and terms
like 'free volition', 'freedom', 'being without master', 'beginning of
motion', 'moving oneself', and 'that which depends on us' (τὸ παρ'
ἡμᾶς). When, in the following pages, I analyse those passages that
have been adduced as evidence that Epicurus dealt with indeterminist freedom of decision or choice, I shall, on the way, also spell
out the ambiguities and vagueness in the key expressions involved.

2. τὸ παρ' ἡμᾶς

There is, in the extant Epicurean texts, no Greek term for freedom of decision, freedom to do otherwise or free will.[13] The Greek
expression in Epicurean sources which is most often regarded as
an indication that some such freedom is at issue is παρ' ἡμᾶς. This
expression occurs in Epicurus' *Letter to Menoeceus* 133–4, and we
find it twice in one sentence in Epicurus' *On Nature* 25. (It also appears in some later Epicurean texts. The related expression ἐφ' ἡμῖν
does not occur in surviving passages by Epicurus.) Both passages
from Epicurus have been understood as dealing with freedom of
choice. However, I believe that this interpretation is based on an
inadequate understanding of the expression παρ' ἡμᾶς. For the expression could be taken either as what I call 'causative one-sided'
or as what I call 'potestative two-sided', and only the former does
the passages justice, whereas only the latter could provide support
for the view that Epicurus was concerned with free choice. Let me
explain the difference between these two ways of understanding the
phrase παρ' ἡμᾶς.

---

[13] ἐλευθερία, in *Gnom. Vat.* 77 (τῆς αὐταρκείας καρπὸς μέγιστος ἐλευθερία) does not
denote freedom of decision, or—two-sided—freedom of the will.

The interpretation of παρ' ἡμᾶς as two-sided potestative commonly assumes a verb of being (rather than of happening or becoming) to go with the phrase: something *is* παρ' ἡμᾶς. When I call παρ' ἡμᾶς 'two-sided', I mean that if some action, e.g. walking, is said to be παρὰ σέ, this can be read as short for 'it is παρὰ σέ *whether or not* you walk'. On this understanding of the expression, the class of things that are παρ' ἡμᾶς includes precisely 50 per cent unrealized possibilities. Thus, when at a certain time it is παρὰ σέ whether you walk, then it is παρὰ σέ whether you don't walk, too; but you will be able only either to walk or not to walk at that time—not both. Hence either one or the other will remain unrealized. By 'potestative' I mean that if some action or occurrence is understood as παρ' ἡμᾶς, we are taken to have some sort of *power* to bring it about or not bring it about. A good translation of παρ' ἡμᾶς in its two-sided, potestative reading is 'up to us'.

This two-sided potestative understanding of παρ' ἡμᾶς entails neither determinism nor indeterminism.[14] But it is often understood as indeterminist, in the following way: it is assumed that walking is up to me at a certain time if at that time *whether or not* I will walk is causally undetermined (not fully determined) and depends on my free decision. Epicurus is commonly interpreted as using the expression παρ' ἡμᾶς both as two-sided potestative and as indeterminist.[15] When the expression is understood in this manner, the 'we' or 'us' (ἡμᾶς) in it is given the status of an active decision-maker. We can *decide* freely *whether or not* we walk (or choose freely between walking and not walking).

This is quite different in the case of what I call the one-sided causative παρ' ἡμᾶς. This interpretation of παρ' ἡμᾶς usually assumes a verb of happening or becoming (rather than of being) to go with the phrase: something *happens* or *comes to be* παρ' ἡμᾶς. By 'causative' I mean to indicate the fact that the prepositional phrase 'παρὰ y' in 'x happens παρὰ y' refers to something which is a (main) cause or reason of x. Thus here translations such as 'because of us'

---

[14] For a determinist reading compare what I say about the related expression ἐφ' ἡμῖν in 'Inadvertent Conception', 143–4, or in *Determinism*, 281–2.

[15] For a two-sided potestative reading see Long–Sedley, vol. i, 20 C 1 (trans.) 'that which we develop is up to us' (γίνεσθαι παρ' ἡμᾶς), interpreted as 'it is up to us whether or not we develop a particular characteristic *c*' or 'whether or not we develop *c* or not *c*'; further Annas, *Mind*, 129 n. 18; Englert, *Epicurus*, 129, who assumes that τὸ ἐφ' ἡμῖν and τὸ παρ' ἡμᾶς are equivalent; similarly Purinton, 'Free Volition', 261–2.

or 'due to us' are preferable. When I call the phrase 'one-sided', I mean that if an action happens (comes to be) παρ' ἡμᾶς then its opposite does not happen (come to be) παρ' ἡμᾶς. If at a certain time my walking happens because of me, then it is not the case that my not walking happens because of me, too; for in that case my not walking does not happen at all. Here the natural understanding of the phrase is that it expresses who has the *causal responsibility* for the action in question. 'The walking happens παρὰ σέ (because of you)' can be paraphrased as 'you are the *cause* of your walking'. When understood as one-sided causative, 'whether-or-not' paraphrases of παρ' ἡμᾶς are impossible. The general idea is that, when sifting through the things *that actually happen* one distinguishes: well, this came to be by necessity, and that happened because of you, and so forth.

The one-sided causative παρ' ἡμᾶς, too, can be made use of in an indeterminist as well as a determinist theory. However, whereas the two-sided παρ' ἡμᾶς can be used to express an element of undeterminedness, by implying that we, *qua* decision-makers, can freely decide between alternative options, the one-sided παρ' ἡμᾶς cannot be so used. Its function is rather to indicate who bears the causal responsibility for an event. It does not imply the possibility of free choice. (The one-sided causative παρ' ἡμᾶς is, however, compatible with the assumptions that *we* can be the cause of our actions only if, say, we are not forced in our action, or if we have a general two-sided capacity for acting and not acting, or if it is in some sense possible for us—or up to us, ἐφ' ἡμῖν—both to act and not to act. I return to this point at the end of Section 3.)

Now, it is my view that in Epicurus, and quite generally in Hellenistic philosophy in the context of determinism and moral responsibility, the phrase παρ' ἡμᾶς was generally understood as one-sided and causative. There are several good reasons for assuming this.

First, in all the Epicurean (and related) texts in which παρ' ἡμᾶς is connected with a verb, this verb is always γίγνεσθαι, never εἶναι, and thus fits the causative understanding better. It is true that γίγνεσθαι can mean 'to be'. However, 'to come to be' or 'to happen' usually fits the context better (see below), and the consistency in the use of γίγνεσθαι rather than εἶναι also suggests this latter meaning. (It is also, I believe, a more common use of παρά with personal accusative.)

Second, παρ' ἡμᾶς occurs repeatedly as one of a triad of expressions for kinds of causal factors. Take first the above-mentioned passage from the *Letter to Menoeceus*:

Whom do you believe to be better than the one . . . who would denounce ⟨fate⟩, which some introduce as mistress of all things, ⟨saying that some things happen by necessity,⟩ others by chance, and others again because of us, since necessity is not accountable to anyone, and chance is an unstable thing to watch, whereas that because of us is without master, and culpability and its opposite are naturally attached to it; for it would be better to follow the myths of the gods than to be enslaved by the fate of the natural philosophers. For the one indicates some hope for pardon from the gods if we honour them, but the other comes with inexorable necessity.[16] (Epic. *Men.* 133–4)

In this passage παρ' ἡμᾶς is contrasted with the expressions 'by necessity' (κατ' ἀνάγκην) and 'by chance' (ἀπὸ τύχης). These latter two expressions are both used to refer to causes (i.e. to that *because of which* some things happen), and as one-sided: if something happens by necessity, then its opposite does not happen; and again, if something happens by chance, then its opposite does not happen. Since παρ' ἡμᾶς is co-ordinated and treated as on a par with these two expressions, it is natural to infer that it has the same function of establishing the cause of an actual event. And this implies that it, too, is used as causative and one-sided.[17]

This finds support in the fact that in Stobaeus' report of Epicurus' tripartition παρ' ἡμᾶς has been substituted by the Peripatetic expression κατὰ προαίρεσιν and the three expressions are taken to denote so many kinds of being caused:

. . . αἰτιῶν ποικίλων προαιρέσεως, τύχης καὶ ἀνάγκης. Ἐπίκουρος κατ' ἀνάγκην, κατὰ προαίρεσιν, κατὰ τύχην. (Stob. *Ecl.* 1. 4–5 =Diels *Doxogr.* 326. 1–4)

[16] ἐπεὶ τίνα νομίζεις εἶναι κρείττονα τοῦ . . . τὴν . . . ὑπό τινων δεσπότιν εἰσαγομένην πάντων ⟨κατ⟩αγγέλλοντος ⟨εἱμαρμένην καὶ μᾶλλον ἃ μὲν κατ' ἀνάγκην γίνεσθαι λέγοντος,⟩ ἃ δὲ ἀπὸ τύχης, ἃ δὲ παρ' ἡμᾶς, διὰ τὸ τὴν μὲν ἀνάγκην ἀνυπεύθυνον εἶναι, τὴν δὲ τύχην ἄστατον ὁρᾶν, τὸ δὲ παρ' ἡμᾶς ἀδέσποτον ᾧ καὶ τὸ μεμπτὸν καὶ τὸ ἐναντίον παρακολουθεῖν πέφυκεν· ἐπεὶ κρεῖττον ἦν τῷ περὶ θεῶν μύθῳ κατακολουθεῖν ἢ τῇ τῶν φυσικῶν εἱμαρμένῃ δουλεύειν· ὁ μὲν γὰρ ἐλπίδα παραιτήσεως ὑπογράφει θεῶν διὰ τιμῆς, ἡ δὲ ἀπαραίτητον ἔχει τὴν ἀνάγκην.

⟨κατ⟩αγγέλλοντος: cf. Hdn. 5. 2. 2 δοῦλοι ὅσοι δεσπότας κατήγγελον· ἂν γελῶντος Long–Sedley; διαγελῶντος Usener. ⟨εἱμαρμένην . . . λέγοντος,⟩: Usener (cf. also *Gnom. Vat.* 40, where γίνεσθαι κατ' ἀνάγκην occurs three times); ⟨εἱμαρμένην ἀλλ' ἃ μὲν κατ' ἀνάγκην ὄντα συνορῶντος⟩ Long–Sedley.

[17] The tripartition is also found in S.E. *M.* 5. 46: τῶν γινομένων τὰ μὲν κατ' ἀνάγκην γίνεται τὰ δὲ κατὰ τύχην, τὰ δὲ παρ' ἡμᾶς . . . The passage *M.* 5. 46–8 may well be an argument put forward by later Epicureans.

Moreover, in *On Nature* 25 we find Epicurus talking about τὴν καθ' ἡμ[ᾶς] . . . αἰ[τίαν].[18] Similarly, the later Epicurean Diogenianus speaks about τὴν παρ' ἡμᾶς αἰτίαν,[19] and he uses the phrase παρ' ἡμᾶς as one-sided causative throughout.[20]

A strong reason for the assumption that Epicurus used παρ' ἡμᾶς as one-sided causative is finally provided by the way it occurs in Epicurus' *On Nature* 25:

Consequently, that which we develop (characteristics of this or that kind) comes to be at some point absolutely because of [παρά] us; and the things which of necessity flow in through our passages from that which surrounds us, at one point come to be because of [παρά] us and because of [παρά] the beliefs of ours which are from us ourselves.[21] (Epic. *Nat.* 25; Arr. 34. 26; Laursen, 'Later Parts', 33)

In its last part this sentence contains the following parallel construction:

. . . the things which of necessity flow in . . . from our surroundings come to be because of [παρά] us and because of [παρά] the beliefs of ours which are from us ourselves.

I take it that παρά (with accusative) has the same meaning in both phrases, since they are syntactically co-ordinated. But in the phrase 'παρὰ our beliefs' we cannot construe παρά as two-sided potestative. We cannot understand our beliefs as a decision-maker in the way we can see ourselves; we cannot paraphrase 'our beliefs make a decision as to *whether or not* we develop characteristic *c*'. Our beliefs cannot actively decide anything. They are specific beliefs which we actually have, and if something depends on them, that can here only mean that they determine *that* we develop one way *and not* the other—not *whether* we develop one way *or* the other. But if παρά is one-sided causative in the case

---

[18] Laursen, 'Early Parts', 99. 1056 corn. 1 pz. 3 z. 1 col.2 = Arr. 34. 7. This is Laursen's reading of the papyrus.

[19] *Praep. Evang.* 6. 8. 34. Cf. also [Plut.] *Epit.* 27. 3 (Diels, *Doxogr.* 322. 5–8) for Plato: τὴν παρ' ἡμᾶς αἰτίαν.

[20] *Praep. Evang.* 6. 8. 2, 6, 23, 30 (with γίνεσθαι), 6. 8. 32 (with συμβαίνειν). A passage in pseudo-Plutarch (*Epit.* 27. 4; Diels, *Doxogr.* 322. 9–14) suggests that the Stoics used παρ' ἡμᾶς as one-sided causative. The formulation in Philod. *Sign.* 36 is neutral with respect to a one-sided or two-sided reading.

[21] ὥστε παρ' ἡμας ποτε ἁπλῶς τὸ ἀπογεγεννημένον ἤδη γείνεσθαι, τοῖα ἢ τοῖα, καὶ τὰ ἐκ τοῦ περιέχοντος κατ' ἀνάγκην διὰ τοὺς πόρους εἰσρέοντα παρ' ἡμᾶς π[ο]τε γε[ίνε]σθαι καὶ παρὰ τὰς ἡμετέρας ἐξ ἡμῶν αὐτῶν δόξ[ας . . . (Epic. *Nat.* 25; Laursen, 'Later Parts', 33)

of our beliefs, it should also be one-sided causative in the case of παρ' ἡμᾶς.[22]

The interpretation of παρ' ἡμᾶς as one-sided causative obtains additional confirmation from the context in which the sentence in *On Nature* 25 belongs. It is the last sentence before a gap in the papyrus. The question discussed by Epicurus that leads up to the sentence (Arr. 34. 24–5; Laursen, 'Later Parts', 29–31) is whether we are morally responsible for our bad actions, if there is a correlating badness in our original constitution (i.e. the one we are born with). Epicurus' answer is that if we act through our initial disposition, we cannot be held responsible; but if, when pursuing the bad actions, we ourselves as we developed (presumably once we reached adulthood) are the cause, then we can be morally criticized, even if what we do is in line with our initial constitution. I assume that in the above-quoted sentence that contains the expression παρ' ἡμᾶς Epicurus is still in some way concerned with this same question. Thus the surrounding context of our sentence does not deal with alternative choices, or with a decision-making power of any sort (nor do any other passages from *On Nature* 25, as far as I can see). Rather, the context is human mental and especially moral development, and the general question is what or who is causally responsible for our dispositions and actions.

The occurrence of the phrase παρ' ἡμᾶς in Epicurean writings is, then, no evidence for the claim that Epicurus discussed the free will question as set out in Section 1, since the phrase is used by him not as two-sided and potestative, but as one-sided and causative.

3. The digression in *On Nature* 25

Next I consider the so-called digression in Epicurus' *On Nature* 25 (34. 27–30 Arr.; LS 20 C 2–15; Laursen, 'Later Parts', 35–42; I follow Laursen's edition of the text). In it Epicurus digresses from the book's main topic of human psychological development in order to refute the necessitarian views of an opponent. This passage has sometimes been taken to be concerned with the topic of the compatibility of determinism with free choice. It contains a series

---

[22] Contrast Long and Sedley, who translate παρ' ἡμᾶς as 'up to us' and παρὰ τ[ὰς] ἡμε[τέρα]ς [ἐ]ξ ἡμῶν αὐτ[ῶν] δόξ[ας . . . as 'dependent on beliefs of our own making' (Long–Sedley, vol. i, 20 C 1).

of arguments against a philosophical view that is incompatible with Epicurus' own. The structure and philosophical strength of these arguments have been analysed in detail by David Sedley.[23] Here I primarily intend to follow up the question of what philosophical problems Epicurus is concerned with in the passage, and what information it provides on his concepts of action and of moral responsibility.

The main thesis of Epicurus' opponent was that everything is caused by necessity, or that everything is necessitated (LS 20 C 5 and 13; Laursen, 'Later Parts', 36, 41). Thus his is a position of universal necessitation. The repeated use of phrases such as ἡ κατὰ τὸ αὐτόματον ἀνάγκη (LS 20 C 2, 3; Laursen, 'Later Parts', 35, cf. 41) makes it clear that the mechanical necessitation of the atomists is at issue, and not teleological predetermination. Necessity is not some mysterious divine power; it is broken down into various *causal* factors. In the case of human behaviour, the two factors that are explicitly mentioned are our initial congenital constitution (ἡ ἐξ ἀρχῆς σύστασις), as necessitating us internally, and the mechanical external necessity of that which happens to surround us and which we perceive (LS 20 C 2–3; Laursen, 'Later Parts', 33, 35). Epicurus' opponent believes that our actions are a function of necessitating hereditary and environmental factors.

By contrast, Epicurus concedes that *some* occurrences are necessary,[24] but maintains that we are the cause of our actions and that they are not necessary. He takes it for granted that the same action cannot be caused both by necessity and by ourselves. The reason for this seems to be that he construes necessity in terms of compulsion or force (e.g. LS 20 C 10), and considers it a necessary condition for *us* to be the cause of our actions that we are not compelled. Epicurus believes that his opponent faces the problem that in his theory he cannot guarantee the *causal* responsibility of the agents for their actions. In all the arguments of the digression the underlying question is *who* or *what* is the cause of, or causally responsible for, human action. Epicurus considers two candidates: necessity on the one hand, us ourselves on the other (LS 20 C 2, 5; Laursen, 'Later Parts', 35, 37).

Where Epicurus uses the terms αἰτία, αἴτιος, and αἰτιᾶσθαι, they have sometimes been taken as denoting moral responsibility. How-

---

[23] Sedley, 'Determinism'.

[24] See also Epic. *Men.* 133–4 (quoted above); *Nat* 25, Arr. 34. 24 (discussed below).

ever, the surviving parts of Epicurus' *On Nature* 25 (Laursen,
'Early Parts', 'Later Parts') suggest that Epicurus used the expressions αἰτία, αἴτιος, and αἰτιᾶσθαι indistinguishably in order to
express the *causal* responsibility of something, or its being a cause.
For example, they are all also used of things such as atoms, the environment, our nature, etc. This suggests strongly that their meaning
is not that of having *moral* responsibility.[25] Epicurus talks of moral
responsibility in terms of praise and blame and similar *evaluative*
expressions (see below).

The opponent's problem, as Epicurus presents it, is, then, not
that he is unable to accommodate in his theory that our actions
and decisions must be *causally undetermined*, or that we can *choose
freely* between alternative courses of actions. Rather, Epicurus and
his opponent seem to share the assumption that my actions are
caused and in that sense determined. The opponent's problem is
that on his theory it is difficult to see how I myself can be causally
responsible for my behaviour, since he claims that *something else*,
i.e. necessity in the form of hereditary and environmental factors,
is fully causally responsible for it.

I quote the text in chunks, with some comments interspersed, in
order to make it apparent that it does not deal with free choice or
free decision, but with the question of whether we, the agents, or
necessity cause our actions. (Suspension points indicate lacunae in
the text; all italics are mine; the Greek text is Laursen's, but I have
kept Long–Sedley's numbering for convenience.)

(2) ⟨And we can invoke against the argument that our behaviour must be
caused by our initial constitution or by environmental factors⟩[26] by which
we never cease to be affected, ⟨the fact that⟩ we rebuke, oppose, and reform
each other *as if we have the cause also in ourselves*, and not only in our initial
constitution and in the mechanical necessity of that which surrounds and
penetrates us.[27] (3) For if someone were to attribute to the very processes
of rebuking and being rebuked the mechanical necessity and always . . .

---

[25] e.g. τὴν ἀνάγκην . . . πάντα αἰτιᾶσθαι (Laursen, 'Later Parts', 41; Long–Sedley
20 C 13); καὶ τὴν αὐτὴν ἀμφότερα κέκτηται μὲν αἰτίαν . . . ἡ ἀρχὴ εἶχε τὴν αἰτίαν, εὔχομεν
δὲ καὶ ἡμεῖς (Laursen, 'Later Parts, 43); διὰ τὴν ἐξ ἡμῶν γεινομένην αἰτίαν . . . διὰ τὴν
φυσικὴν αἰτίαν (Laursen, 'Later Parts', 46–7).

[26] Long–Sedley add '⟨And we can invoke, against the argument that our eventual
choice between these alternatives must be physically caused either by our initial make-
up or by those environmental influences⟩' (my italics). But nothing in the text
suggests that choice is at issue.

[27] Namely by means of perception; cf. Epic. *Nat.* 25 (Laursen, 'Later Parts', 33;
LS 20 C 1), quoted above.

understand ... (4) ... when he blames or praises. But if he were to act in this way, he would be leaving intact the very same behaviour ⟨i.e. praising and blaming⟩ which we think of as concerning ourselves, in accordance with our preconception of the cause;[28] and he would have changed the name ⟨only⟩. (5) ... so great an error. For this sort of account is self-refuting, and can never prove that everything is of the kind which we call 'by necessity'; but he debates this very question on the assumption that his opponent talks nonsense on account of himself. (6) And even if he goes on to infinity saying that, again, he does *this* action of his by necessity, always appealing to arguments, he is not reasoning it empirically *so long as he goes on imputing to himself the cause for having reasoned correctly and to his opponent that for having reasoned incorrectly*. (7) But unless he were to stop attributing his actions to himself, and to pin it on necessity instead, he would not even ...[29] (Epic. *Nat.* 25; Arr. 34. 27–8; Laursen, 'Later Parts', 35–7)[30]

In this section the opponent faces the charge that he pragmatically refutes himself when he argues his position of universal necessitation. Epicurus provides him with the alternatives of either attributing causal responsibility to himself and his interlocutor and not to necessity—because the opponent in fact attributes evaluative criticism to his and his interlocutor's verbal acts—or giving up his argument. Epicurus' main argumentative step is this: when someone evaluates a person's acts morally or veridically, they implicitly attribute causal responsibility to that person for that act. Freedom

[28] I follow Laursen's reading (cf. next footnote, sentence (4)). However, I do not quite understand what it means. I hope it still means the same as what David Sedley (in 'Determinism') suggested, viz. that our observation of blaming and praising produces our preconception of us as causes of our actions.

[29] (2) ἐστήκει, ὧν οὐ ... ἀπολείπει τὰ πάθη τοῦ γίνεσθαι, ... νουθετεῖν τε ἀλλήλους καὶ μάχεσθαι καὶ μεταρυθμίζειν ὡς ἔχοντας καὶ ἐν ἑαυτοῖς τὴν αἰτίαν καὶ οὐχὶ ἐν τῇ ἐξ ἀρχῆς μόνον συστάσει καὶ ἐν τῇ τοῦ περιέχοντος καὶ ἐπεισιόντος κατὰ τὸ αὐτόματον ἀνάγκῃ (3) εἰ γάρ τις καὶ τῷ νουθετεῖν καὶ τῷ νουθετεῖσθαι τὴν κατὰ τὸ αὐτόματον ἀνάγκην προστιθείη καὶ ἀεὶ τοῦ ποθ' ἑαυτῷ ὑπάρχοντος, ... συνιέναι ... (4) μεμφόμενος ἢ ἐπαινῶν· ἀλλ' εἰ μὲν τοῦτο πράττοι, τὸ μὲν ἔργον ἂν εἴη καταλεῖπον ὃ ἐφ' ἡμῶν αὐτῶν κατὰ τὴν τῆς αἰτίας πρόληψιν ἐννοοῦμεν, τὸ δ' ὄνομα μετατεθειμένος ... (5) τοσαύτης πλάνης. περικάτω γὰρ ὁ τοιοῦτος λόγος τρέπεται, καὶ οὐδέποτε δύναται βεβαιῶσαι ὡς ἔστιν τοιαῦτα πάντα οἷα τὰ κατ' ἀνάγκην καλοῦμεν ἀλλὰ μάχεταί τινι περὶ αὐτοῦ τούτου ὡς δι' ἑαυτὸν ἀβελτερευομένῳ. (6) κἂν εἰς ἄπειρον φῇ πάλιν κατ' ἀνάγκην τοῦτο πράττειν ἀπὸ λόγων ἀεί, οὐκ ἐπιλογίζεται ἐν τῷ εἰς ἑαυτὸν τὴν αἰτίαν ἀνάπτειν τοῦ κατὰ τρόπον λελογίσθαι εἰς δὲ τὸν ἀμφισβητοῦντα τοῦ μὴ κατὰ τρόπον. (7) εἰ δὲ μὴ ἃ ποιεῖ ἀπολήγοι εἰς ἑαυτόν ἀλλ' εἰς τὴν ἀνάγκην τιθείη, οὐδ' ἂν ...

[30] In my rendering of the digression I have made use freely of Long–Sedley's excellent translation, but have modified it in line with Laursen's new readings of the text, and in some other places in order to bring out my understanding of the text more clearly.

of decision or free choice is not involved in the argument; nor is freedom to do otherwise anywhere explicitly mentioned.

This passage also provides important insight into *Epicurus' concept of moral responsibility*. Epicurus takes the fact that we blame each other, and try to reform each other, as an *indication* that the cause of our actions lies in ourselves, or that the actions happen through ourselves (LS 20 C 2, cf. C 8). The concept of blame presupposes that the beings that are blamed were themselves causally responsible for their behaviour. It *makes no sense* to blame individuals for certain events, if those events came about through necessity (LS 20 C 3). There are several other passages that confirm that Epicurus based his concept of moral responsibility for an action on that of our causal responsibility for it: (1) Epic. *Nat.* 25, Arr. 34. 25 (Laursen, 'Later Parts', 29) implies that if an action of a certain kind is caused by the initial constitution of a person, in response to the environment, then the person is not to be blamed. However, if an action *of the same kind* is caused by the person herself, and thus not (exclusively) by the initial constitution, then the person is to be blamed for it. (2) In Epic. *Men.* 133 the things that happen because of us are said 'to have praise and blame naturally attached to them'. With the above interpretation of that which happens because of us (παρ' ἡμᾶς), this suggests that when I am *causally* responsible for something happening, then I can be held *morally* responsible for it. (3) Similarly, Epic. *Nat.* 25, Arr. 34. 21 (Laursen, 'Later Parts', 19–20; LS 20 B 1–4) suggests that if a person (or their 'developments') is causally responsible for something, then they can be held morally responsible for it.

Back to Epicurus' 'digression':

(8) . . . using the word 'necessity' of that which we call '. . . by ourselves', he is merely changing a name; but he must prove that we have a preconception of a kind which has faulty delineations *when we call that which ⟨comes⟩ through ourselves causally responsible* . . .[31] (Epic. *Nat.* 25, Arr. 34. 28; Laursen, 'Later Parts', 37)

Epicurus' point in (8) is that we have a preconception that we are causally responsible for our actions by means of that which comes through ourselves, i.e. presumably our own beliefs (δόξαι, LS 20

---

[31] (8) . . .]φ ἡμῶν αὐτῶν καλούμενον τῶι τῆς ἀνάγκης ὀνόματι προσαγορεύειν ὄνομα μόνομ μετατίθεται. δεῖ δ' ἐπιδίξ[α]ι ὅτι τοιοῦτό τι ᾧ μοχθηρ[οί εἰσι τύ]ποι προειληφότες τὸ δι' ἡμῶν αὐτῶν αἴτιον καλοῦμεν, οὐτιδ[. . .

C 1) and impulses (ὁρμήματα, ὁρμαί) or desires (προθυμίαι, LS 20 C 9–11); and that his opponent is unable to show that we are mistaken about having this preconception. This argumentation is *not* a version of the modern one that we have the intuition, or know by introspection, that we *could have acted or decided otherwise.* The preconception is not that we have an ability to act or to decide otherwise, but that we (by means of our beliefs, impulses, and desires), and not something else, are causally responsible for what we do.

(9) . . . but to call necessity ⟨empty⟩ as a result of your claim. If someone won't show this, and has no auxiliary element or impulse in us which he might dissuade from those actions which we perform *calling the cause of them 'through ourselves'*, but is giving the name of necessity to all the things that we desire to do in accordance with our position, *calling the cause of them 'through ourselves'*, he will be merely changing a name. (10) He will not be modifying any of our actions in the way in which in some cases the one who sees what sort of things are necessitated usually dissuades those who desire to do something in the face of compulsion. (11) And the mind will be inquisitive to learn what sort of action it should then consider that one to be which is performed in some way *out of ourselves through our desire to act.* For he has nothing else to do but to say . . . [32] (Epic. *Nat.* 25, Arr. 34. 29; Laursen, 'Later Parts', 39)

The point of the argument (9)–(11) is in short this: if saying 'our actions happen by necessity' is to be more than just another way of saying 'our actions happen through ourselves', then our recognition of their necessity would have to change our behaviour, as our behaviour is generally changed when it is pointed out to us that something must necessarily occur. For then we will not desire and endeavour to do anything to prevent the necessitated thing from occurring, because there is no point in doing so. Similarly, if our actions were necessitated, there would be no point in doing anything about them; in particular, there would be no point in making an effort to bring them about. Thus Epicurus seems to envisage necessity as some kind of compulsion, and to presuppose that if

---

[32] (9) ἀλλὰ κενὸν καὶ τὸ δι᾽ ἀνάγκην καλεῖν πρὸς ὧν φάτε. ἂν δὲ μή τις τοῦτο ἀποδείξει, μηδ᾽ ἔχει ἡμῶν τι συνεργὸν μηδ᾽ ὅρμημα ἀποτρέπειν ὧν καλοῦντες δι᾽ ἡμῶν αὐτῶν τὴν αἰτίαν συντελοῦμεν, ἀλλὰ πάντα ὅσα νῦν δι᾽ ἡμῶν αὐτῶν ὀνομάζοντες τὴν αἰτίαν πως προθυμούμεθα πράττειν κατὰ χώραν ἀνάγκην προσαγορεύων, ὄνομα μόνον ἀμείψει; (10) ἔργον δ᾽ οὐδὲν ἡμῶν μετακοσμήσει, ὥσπερ ἐπ᾽ ἐνίων ὁ συνορῶν τὰ ποῖα κατ᾽ ἀνάγκην ἐστὶν ἀποτρέπειν εἴωθε τοὺς προθυμουμένους παρὰ βίαν τι πράττειν. (11) ζητήσει δ᾽ ἡ διάνοια εὑρεῖν τὸ ποῖον οὖν τι δεῖ νομίζειν τὸ ἐξ ἡμῶν αὐτῶν πως πραττόμενον τῇ προθυμίαι τοῦ πράττειν. οὐ γὰρ ἔχει ἀλλ᾽ οὐθὲν πράττειν ἢ φάναι . . .

our actions are necessitated, they will happen even if we do not
desire to bring them about; by contrast, if we are the causes of our
actions, our desiring to act will be causally connected with the action itself.[33] Freedom of decision, free choice between alternatives,
or freedom to do otherwise are not part of the argument.

If any surviving passage from Epicurus deals with what Lucretius renders as *voluntas* (volitional act), I suppose it is this one.
In any case, we can extract from this passage what Epicurus regards as essential characteristics of human action. (1) Human action is not necessary—that is, it does not happen by force (βία).
(2) The agent has an impulse (ὅρμημα) towards the action and desires (προθυμεῖσθαι, προθυμία) to perform it. Impulse (ὅρμημα) or
desire (προθυμία) are the two candidates for Lucretius' *voluntas*. I
assume that physically they are motions in the agent's mind that
are directed at the action. They are our contribution (συνεργόν) to
the action. They are not portrayed as choices *between* alternatives,
or decisions *whether or not* to do something; they are volitions, impulses, desires *to do* something. (3) Epicurus repeatedly says that
we call the cause of an action 'through ourselves' (δι' ἡμῶν αὐτῶν).
I assume that the causes through ourselves are precisely our impulse and desire. (And they are, I take it, called 'through ourselves'
because they are the result of our own beliefs and desires, which
when externally triggered, produce the impulse and desire;[34] and
they make us the cause of our actions.[35]

We can then also see what Epicurus meant when in the *Letter
to Menoeceus* he calls that which happens because of us (παρ' ἡμᾶς)
'without master' (ἀδέσποτον: see the passage quoted above). He
refers to the fact that the things which happen because of us are
not forced. More precisely, that *we* are not forced when we bring
them about. There is nothing that compels (us to do) them. In
particular, our actions are not subordinated to fate (or necessity),
which a few lines before was characterized as master (or rather

---

[33] This argument is reminiscent of the so-called Idle Argument (ἀργὸς λόγος, for
which see ch. 5 of my *Determinism*); cf. the presentation and criticism of the Stoic
refutation of the Idle Argument by the Epicurean Diogenianus for the emphasis on
προθυμία and σπουδή (Eus. *Praep. Evang.* 6. 8. 25, 29, 30) and on us as causes (ibid.
6. 8. 34, 38).

[34] Epic. *Nat.* 25, Arr. 34. 26; Laursen, 'Later Parts', 33, LS 20 C 1, and perhaps
Arr. 34. 31; Laursen, 'Later Parts, 44–5, suggest that in order to be causes ourselves,
we must have beliefs, and that these beliefs must be our own beliefs.

[35] Cf. Epic. *Nat.* 25, Arr. 34. 22; Laursen, 'Later Parts, 32–3; LS 20 B 1, τὴν . . .
αἰτίαν . . . ἑαυτῶν, and LS 20 B 5, τὴν ἐξ ἑαυτοῦ αἰτίαν, etc.

mistress, δεσπότις).[36] The contrast in this passage is thus the same as the one in the digression in Epicurus' *On Nature*.

(12) . . . supremely unthinkable. But unless someone perversely maintains this, or makes it clear what fact he is rebutting or introducing, it is merely a word that is being changed, as I keep repeating. (13) The first men to give a satisfactory account of causes, men not only much greater than their predecessors but also, many times over, than their successors, contradicted themselves unawares—although in many matters they had alleviated great ills—in this respect that they held necessity and . . . causally responsible for everything. (14) Indeed, the actual account promoting this view came to grief when it left the great man blind to the fact that in his actions he was clashing with his doctrine; and that if it were not that a certain blindness to the doctrine took hold of him while acting he would be constantly perplexing himself; and that wherever the doctrine prevailed he would be falling into desperate calamities, while wherever it did not he would be filled with conflict because of the contradiction between his actions and his doctrine.[37] (Epic. *Nat.* 25, Arr. 34. 30; Laursen, 'Later Parts', 40–2)

This last section of the digression presents again a pragmatic argument: Philosophers who hold that every event is caused by necessity 'contradict' themselves when they act. The point seems to be that one embarks on an action only if, while one acts, one thinks of oneself as not necessitated and as causally responsible for one's actions. Freedom of decision or choice is not at issue.

We can conclude that in the digression Epicurus' concern is to refute the view that our actions are necessitated, in the sense of being caused by something other than us. He does not discuss the question whether we are undetermined in our decisions. As a matter of fact, all his arguments *in this digression* could be consistently proposed by a compatibilist determinist. This does not rule out that Epicurus was an indeterminist—and I believe he was. All I suggest is that in the arguments of the digression what is at issue

---

[36] Cf. also δουλεύειν a few lines later.

[37] (12) . . . μάλιστα ἀδιανοήτων. Ἄν δέ τις τοῦτο μὴ παραβιάζηται, μηδ᾽ αὖ ὃ ἐξελέγχει γε ἢ ὃ εἰσφέρει πρᾶγμα ἐκτιθεῖ, φωνὴ μόνον ἀμείβεται, καθάπερ πάλαι θρυλῶ. (13) οἱ δ᾽ αἰτιολογήσαντες ἐξ ἀρχῆς ἱκανῶς, καὶ οὐ μόνον τῶν πρὸ αὐτῶν πολὺ διενέγκαντες ἀλλὰ καὶ τῶν ὕστερον πολλαπλασίως ἔλαθον ἑαυτοῖς—καίπερ ἐν πολλοῖς μεγάλα κουφίσαντες—ἐν το⟨ῦτο ἐναντιολογοῦντες τὸ⟩ τὴν ἀνάγκην καὶ ταυτομεγ[ ]ν πάντα αἰτιᾶσθαι. (14) ὁ δὴ λόγος αὐτὸς ὁ τοῦτο διδάσκων κατεάγνυτο καὶ ἐλάνθανεν τὸν ἄνδρα τοῖς ἔργοις πρὸς τὴν δόξαν συνκρούοντα· καὶ εἰ μὴ λήθη τις ἐπὶ τῶν ἔργων τῆς δόξης ἐνεγείνετο, συνεχῶς ἂν ἑαυτὸν ταράττοντα· ᾗ δ᾽ ἐκράτει τὸ τῆς δόξης κἂν τοῖς ἐσχάτοις περιπείπτοντα· ᾗ δὲ μὴ ἐκράτει στάσεως ἐμπιπλάμενον διὰ τὴν ὑπεναντιότητα τῶν ἔργων καὶ τῆς δόξης.

⟨ῦτο ἐναντιολογοῦντες τὸ⟩ add. Laursen, 'Later Parts', 42.

is not indeterminism or free decision or choice, but agent autonomy.

A remark on freedom to do otherwise (as different from freedom
of decision and freedom of choice). I have described the contrast
between necessity and that which happens because of us as that between compulsion and absence of compulsion. This is a common
Greek way of understanding necessity. For Epicurus, a person's
behaviour happens by necessity, if the person is compelled to behave that way. If a person's behaviour (action) results from their
having an impulse to act that is based on their present beliefs and
desires in response to some external stimulus, then the person is not
compelled in their behaviour (action). Freedom to do otherwise is
not explicitly involved. It has been objected, however, that if one's
action is not necessary, then this entails, or even means, that it was
possible for one not to act, and consequently that one was free (in
some sense) to do otherwise than one did; hence that Epicurus must
have held that we are free (in some sense) to do otherwise than we
do. I am unsure about how to respond to this objection. First of
all, I am inclined to think that Epicurus believed that it is usually
up to us (ἐφ’ ἡμῖν) whether or not we act, either in the sense that
if we had different beliefs or desires we would act differently, or in
the sense that we have some general two-sided capacity for certain
things, such as walking and not walking. And if someone wants to
call either of these 'freedom to do otherwise', so be it—as long as
they are aware that such kinds of freedom are in principle compatible with determinism. Second, however, I am uncertain whether
Epicurus ever *de facto* drew the connection between such freedom
and non-necessity;[38] although, again, it is likely that he thought it a
precondition for an action to happen because of us (παρ’ ἡμᾶς) that
it was up to us. Third, regardless of whether he expressly drew this
connection, my point is that we have *no evidence* for the assumption
that he ever regarded the compatibility of such kinds of freedom
with atomistic mechanical necessity or causal determinism as *problematic*. We do not know whether he did. In the surviving passages
he appears to discuss different—if related—problems.

---

[38] At Epic. *Nat.* 25, Arr. 34. 27; Laursen, 'Later Parts, 28 'but out of itself or out
of the cause out of itself being able to [*develop*] also something else' is contrasted
with necessity of *development*. For the context of the passage see below, sect. 6.

4. Lucretius, *De rerum natura* 2. 251–293 and 4. 877–891

The passage 2. 251–93 of Lucretius' *De rerum natura* has traditionally been adduced as the main evidence for the claim that Epicurus
was concerned with a free will problem as set out in Section 1. It
is, however, generally agreed that Lucretius' immediate concern
in the passage is a different one: he provides a—second—argument
for the existence of the swerve. This argument very roughly follows
modus tollens:

(A) If the swerve does not exist, neither does volition. (2. 251–60)
(B) But volition exists. (2. 261–83)
(C) Therefore the swerve exists. (2. 284–93)

Thus—on the assumption that Lucretius is sufficiently faithful as a
witness of Epicurean doctrine—we can infer that Epicurus regarded
the swerve as a necessary condition for the existence of volition.
However, Lucretius does not tell us anywhere in the passage *in
what way* the swerve is required for volition. As a consequence,
scholars have with much inventiveness and subtlety produced a
host of interpretations, each designed to answer this question.

Those who argue that the Lucretius passage shows that Epicurus
discussed free choice or free decision generally agree on the following point: the swerve is meant to help solve the free will problem;
its function is to provide the element of indeterminedness that Epicurus thought is needed for individual decisions or choices to be
free. Most commonly the assumption is that one or more swerves
are involved in the *formation* of *every* volition.[39] Since I do not
believe that Epicurus was faced with a free will problem as set out
in Section 1, I also do not believe that it is the role of the swerve
to preserve free choice or decision. Nor do I believe that it has to
feature in every act of volition.

Before I say anything more about the swerve, I want to present what I hope to be a consistent alternative interpretation of
the Lucretius passage. (It will be easier to follow the suggested
interpretation if the reader assumes at least hypothetically that Lucretius has at the back of his mind the disposition-dependency

---

[39] Asmis, 'Free Action'; So for Bailey, *Greek Atomists*; Gulley, 'Free Will'; Huby,
'Freewill Problem'; Purinton, 'Free Volition'; Sedley, 'Determinism'; Sharples,
'Epicurus'.

model of agency, and the problem of autonomous agency, and not
the independent-decision-faculty model and a free will problem as
set out in Section 1.) At the same time, I shall point out a number
of those ambiguities in the text which I have mentioned above and
which may have furthered the view that Lucretius was concerned
with freedom of decision or choice.

One possible ambiguity should be mentioned at the beginning,
since it stretches through the whole passage: this is the fact that
voluntas can be used equally for an act of volition and for a capacity
or power of volition. It seems to me that *voluntas* is always used
for volitional acts, and that when Lucretius refers to a power of
volition, he uses different phrases. But this is not very important.
What matters—and will be argued in this section—is that volitions are not acts of choosing-between or deciding-whether, but
our willing (or impulse or desiring) to perform an action; and that
accordingly our power of volition is not a power of choice-between,
or a decision-making faculty, but our ability to form in response to
external stimuli volitions in accordance with our own beliefs and
desires.

Let me begin, then, with section (A). In this section Lucretius
does more than just state, in a somewhat passionate way, that the
swerve is a prerequisite for volition. He also provides us with information about the determinism he attacks, and with an implicit
account of volition (*voluntas*):

(1) Moreover, if all motion is always linked, and new motion arises out of
old in a fixed order, and atoms do not by swerving make some beginning
of motion to break the decrees of fate, so that cause should not follow
cause from infinity, (2) from where does this free volition exist for animals
throughout the world? (3) From where, I ask, comes this volition wrested
away from the fates, through which we proceed wherever each of us is
guided by their pleasure and likewise swerve off our motions at no fixed
time or fixed region of space, but wherever the mind itself carries us?[40]
(Lucr. 2. 251–60)

(1) describes the predetermination of all events which the swerve
is said to prevent. The theory is one of causal determinism. There

---

[40] '(1) denique si semper motus conectitur omnis | et vetere exoritur ⟨motu⟩ novus
ordine certo | nec declinando faciunt primordia motus | principium quoddam quod
fati foedera rumpat, | ex infinito ne causam causa sequatur, | (2) libera per terras
unde haec animantibus exstat, | (3) unde est haec, inquam, fatis avulsa voluntas |
per quam progredimur quo ducit quemque voluptas, | declinamus item motus nec
tempore certo | nec regione loci certa, sed ubi ipsa tulit mens?'

is a sequence of causes which reaches back infinitely into the past; there is a fixed order of all motion; this order is in accordance with the 'decrees of fate'.[41] We can infer that this fixed order and those 'decrees of fate' also go back infinitely into the past, and that all motions are understood as being in this way eternally predetermined. (3) contains the implicit account of volition as that 'through which we proceed wherever each of us is guided by their pleasure and likewise swerve off our motions at no fixed time or fixed region of space, but wherever the mind itself carries us'.

I take this account in two parts. First, 'this volition . . . through which we proceed wherever each of us is guided by their pleasure' (2. 257–8). This phrase suggests that volition is the vehicle by means of which we pursue or realize the satisfaction of our desires. If I find smoking cigarettes pleasant, then an act of volition directed at my smoking will be a necessary step to get me to smoke. Volition is here described as the consequence of our pleasure directing us somewhere: if—in a situation of possible smoking—I find smoking pleasant, then, it seems, by means of a volition a motion towards getting a cigarette *will* be started.

For the second part of the sentence (2. 259–60) it is important to take it in its entirety and not to cut it off before the 'but'. We are presented with a contrast: we swerve off our motions through volition *not* at a fixed time or space, *but* wherever the mind itself carries us. Two things are unclear here.

First, what does mind (*mens*) mean in this sentence? Proponents of the view that Lucretius discusses free choice or decision have repeatedly suggested that when Lucretius says 'mind' here and later in the passage, what he actually means is volition, and that he is only speaking loosely.[42] I prefer to think that when Lucretius says 'mind' in our passage, what he means is actually mind. That is, he means the central part of the soul, which is located in the heart and which elsewhere he calls *animus* or *mens*.[43]

Second, the phrase 'neither at a fixed time, nor in a fixed space' can mean two things. It can mean '(spatio-temporally) at random'.

---

[41] 'Decrees of fate' in quotes, since (as in *Men.* 133–4) the reference should be to the 'fate of the natural philosophers', i.e. to mechanistic necessity, not to a theory of teleological determinism.

[42] e.g. Sedley, 'Determinism', 47 n. 65; Long–Sedley, ii. 111–12; Gulley, 'Free Will', 42.

[43] e.g. 2. 270 'animi . . . voluntate', and 3.1 39, 'consilium quod nos animum mentemque vocamus'. The Greek would be διάνοια, or something similar.

The opposite is 'not at random', implying 'with some order'. Or else, it can mean 'not at a *pre*determined time or space'. Here the opposite is 'at a predetermined time or space'. These two options differ: logically, the second does not require that the motion is random. I believe that Lucretius intended this second reading, i.e. that time and space of the motions are not fixed in advance, from eternity (cf. 2. 255 *ex infinito*).[44] For the *contrast* in our sentence is between 'swerving off a motion at a fixed time or space' and 'swerving off a motion wherever the mind carries us'. But if, as I take it, 'mind' means 'mind', and we 'swerve off' our motions[45] *where our mind carries us*, this cannot properly be described as a random motion. For our mind carries us wherever it carries us *in accordance with* our pleasure—as is implied by the first part of the sentence; and this is not at random: for without pleasure the mind would not carry us there.[46]

Lucretius' contrast is this: either our mind is the cause of our motion (by means of a volition), or something *else* (fate, necessity, our initial constitution, etc.) predetermines time and location at which our motion occurs (and thus is its true cause). This is a variation of a point we encountered earlier, in the digression of Epicurus' *On Nature* 25. To sum up, the implicit account of volition in (A) can be read as saying that it is an essential characteristic of a volition that it is initiated directly by the mind, in accordance with our desire, and that it is not predetermined by something else.

Section (A) also contains the one phrase which offers perhaps the main reason for the persistent assumption that Lucretius is discussing free will in the passage under consideration: *libera voluntas*. The meaning of the phrase is, however, not 'freedom of choice' or 'freedom of decision', nor does it denote or imply a faculty of the

---

[44] There is the parallel, with the prefixed order (*ordine certo*) from line 2. 252, and with the whole predeterministic scenario (*ex infinito, fatis*, etc.) from the first part of the sentence (2. 251–7). All this evokes the familiar idea of *pre*determination from infinity. Cf. Cic. *Fat.* 21 for *certo* with the sense of 'predetermined' and thus implying necessity. Similarly *certus* in Cic. *ND.* 1. 69.

[45] I agree with Sharples, 'Epicurus', 182, that Lucretius here has *our* movements in mind, not the swerving atomic movements in us.

[46] If in 2. 258 one reads *voluntas* instead of the commonly accepted emendation *voluptas*, a similar argument can be produced, by taking *voluntas* to signify individual instances of volition ('this volition . . . through which we proceed wherever each of us is guided *by it*'). For instance, if I have a volition to smoke (based on some belief of mine that it is pleasant, hence good for me), then this volition will guide me towards smoking a cigarette.

will capable of making un-predetermined choices between alternative courses of actions. Rather, an act of volition is free (*libera*), since it is *not forced* by fate, necessity, our initial constitution, etc. It is an unforced volitional act. Importantly, *libera voluntas* is pleonastic here: if the volition were not free or unforced, it would not be a volition.

Section (B) (2. 261–83) has the function of establishing the existence of volition. For this step in the argument reference to the swerve is not required, and we should not normally expect it. What Lucretius produces in this passage is an empirical argument that backs up the existence of volition by contrasting the phenomena of volitional movement of living beings with those of externally induced movement. Movement that is initiated by something external to the moving body is described as non-volitional (*invitus*: 2. 275, 2. 278) and as forced (*coactu* 2. 273, *cogat* 2. 278). Volitional motion, on the other hand, is unforced.[47] It is characterized as involving (at least) two kinds of motion in our passage (B), and as involving three kinds of motion in the passage on volition in book 4 which is often employed to illuminate our text (4. 877–91). First, there is the volition or desire of the mind (*mens avet* 2. 265; *studium mentis* 2. 268; *voluntas animi* 2. 270). It is itself a motion of the mind, and is initiated by the mind (4. 886, 2. 269–70). The mind, thus moved, then sets in motion the soul, which extends through the entire body (4. 887–8; hinted at at 2. 271). The soul, thus moved, in turn moves the body, and in this way sets in motion the whole living being (2. 266–8, 4. 890–1).[48] This enables Lucretius to say that the body follows the mind's desire (*studium mentis*, 2. 268). The phenomenological difference between volitional (and thus unforced) motion and forced motion of living beings is that in the former case there is an observable time delay between the formation of the will to act and the eventual movement of the entire body. And this—Lucretius maintains—can only be explained by the assumption of the existence of volition, which needs some time to internally mobilize the body via the soul. So far this step of the argument.[49]

---

[47] This is similar to the point that that which happens because of us (τὸ παρ' ἡμᾶς) is without master (ἀδέσποτον). I assume that that which happens because of us and our volitional movement are coextensional.

[48] Cf. also 3. 159–60 'facile ut quivis hinc noscere possit | esse animam cum animo coniunctam, quae cum animi vi | percussast, exim corpus propellit et icit.'

[49] Passage (B) has been used to argue that Lucretius was concerned with freedom

I have indicated above that, as regards the logical function of section (B) in the argument, we should be surprised if we found in it any discussion of the swerve. This fact has not prevented scholars from searching for traces of the swerve in virtually every line of it. Together with the parallel passage in book 4 (4. 877–91), this passage has repeatedly been exploited to back up the views that Epicurus considered the swerve as a necessary condition for free decision or choice, and that the swerve features in every instance of volition. The main reason for this, I suspect, is another characteristic ambiguity, namely that which we find in phrases like 'the beginning of motion' and 'setting oneself in motion'. For when something is said to bring about a beginning of motion, or to move itself, this can be understood in two rather different ways. First, it can refer to some *absolute beginning* of motion: something produces a motion, or causes itself to move, but is itself not fully causally determined to do so by any prior motion. There is a gap in the 'causal chain'. The motion is spontaneous.[50] Second, talk about moving oneself and producing a beginning of motion can refer to a *relative beginning* of motion: here a thing is said to move itself, or to produce a beginning of motion, if, given certain external or internal impacts, the thing will start to move because it is the sort of thing it is. For instance, two people are each offered a cigarette: one takes it and smokes it, the other does not. One is the sort of person

of action rather than freedom of the will (Conway, 'Epicurus' Theory'). Freedom of action is the freedom I have when there is nothing that prevents me from acting as I desire or choose to act. Freedom of action is lacking when I desire or have chosen to do something, but the realization of the action is prevented by physical hindrances, and my desire is thus frustrated. In this case things happen *against* my desire or will. Now it is true that (B) includes an adequate description of what we call free action. (Cf. also Lucr. 4. 877–8 'how it comes that we can step forward when we want to', where free action seems to be the topic.) However, I think that in (B) Lucretius is not primarily interested in free action. At least, his contrast is not between free action and prevention of free action, i.e. frustrated desire or choice. Rather it is between motion that has an internal beginning by means of the agent's desire and volition, and motion that has an external beginning, without the agent's desire or volition being involved. In this latter case something happens *without* my volition (2. 275, 278), but not necessarily *against* my desire. The contrast is between volitional and non-volitional motion, not between free action and thwarted intention. Lucretius makes use of the *phenomenon* of free action in order to back up his thesis that volition exists. This is how (B) starts ('for no doubt it is volition that gives these things their beginning for each of us, and it is from volition that motions are spread through the limbs') and this is how (B) ends ('So do you now see that . . . there is something in our chest capable of . . .', namely the power of volition).

[50] So e.g. Bailey, *Greek Atomists*, 435; Purinton, 'Free Volition', 255, 276.

who considers smoking pleasurable, the other is not. Here—given the external stimulus—it depends entirely on the person whether movements of taking the cigarette will be initiated.

If we look at the three relevant passages in Lucretius, we can see that none of them compels us to interpret them as postulating an absolute beginning of motion. Hence, none of them implies *direct* involvement of the swerve.

First 2. 261–2: 'his rebus sua cuique voluntas principium dat'. In this phrase *his rebus* refers to *motus* (our movements, i.e. our volitional actions) from 2. 259. We can then translate: 'volition gives our movements the beginning for each of us'. This phrase need not mean anything more than 'the motion of volition makes us move' (or 'makes our body move'), as contrasted with the case in which something external makes us (or our body) move. Nothing is said about what brings about the volition. Hence there is in this case certainly no reason to assume an absolute beginning of motion.[51]

Second 2. 269: 'initum motus a corde creari . . .', which can be translated as 'a beginning of motion is brought about by the mind'.[52] This case differs from the previous one in that, as far as the wording is concerned, the beginning in question could be absolute or relative. It could be understood as 'the mind, *qua* decision-making faculty, may, without being caused in any way to do so, produce a motion of volition'. This would mark an absolute beginning. Or, it could be understood that in a certain situation the mind, *because it is the way it is*, may produce a motion of volition. For example, in a situation of a certain kind, a smoker may start smoking a cigarette (owing to his beliefs and desires), whereas a non-smoker may do nothing (owing to her beliefs and desires). This would be a relative beginning.

The third passage, 4. 886, is similar to the second: 'ergo animus cum sese ita commovet ut velit ire . . .', in English: 'thus, when the mind sets itself in motion so that it wants to go forwards . . .'. This, too, can be easily read as being about a relative beginning of motion, e.g. in the following way: because of the mind's individual constitution, images of walking strike the mind, and presumably

---

[51] If *voluntas* denoted a power of volition, this could be understood as 'the capacity of volition, by producing volitions, gives animal movements their beginning of motion'. This too would be contrasted with an external beginning of motion, and need not express an absolute beginning, since it is not ruled out that there are causes that make the power of volition produce volitions.

[52] Or alternatively 'in the heart'.

appear to it as pleasant,[53] when it 'previews' them (4. 884–5). (Another mind, in the same situation, may not be struck by such images of walking as pleasant.) As a result, the mind sets itself in motion in accordance with the images. More precisely, it sets in motion its faculty of volition. But once the mind is set in motion, *that means* that it *velit ire*, wants to go forward, which I understand as 'it now has the volition to go forward'.[54]

Thus all three passages in Lucretius harmonize well with the assumption that in them Epicurus had only a relative beginning of motion in mind. Accordingly, none of them provides compelling evidence for the view that swerves are involved directly in each act of volition, or for the view that they provide the element of undeterminedness required in an act of free choice or decision.

This leaves us with the last section (C) of the Lucretius passage on the swerve (2. 284–93). In it the conclusion that the swerve exists is drawn from the premisses set out in (A) and (B); but we have again more than that. An explanation is added of why the conditional premiss is true. And here we finally obtain two valuable bits of information about the relation between volition and swerve. The first is in the first sentence:

Therefore in the atoms too one has to admit another cause of motions besides impacts and weights from which this power is born in us, since we see that nothing can come to be from nothing.[55] (2. 284–7)

The term 'power' (*potestas*) in this sentence is another chameleon expression. *Potestas* can denote a disposition or capacity, i.e. something which is possessed continuously, both when it is actualized and when it is not. *Potestas* can also denote something like energy or force (or power as in 'power station'), i.e. the force released in an instance of volition. Such a power is something we do not have continuously. It exists only as long as the volition lasts. The phrase

---

[53] Remember 2. 257–8 'voluntas per quam progredimur quo ducit quemque voluptas'.

[54] It is perhaps not without interest that Epicurus seems to have considered this kind of relative beginning of motion in the context of the formation of volitional action in *On Nature* 25 (Arr. 35. 10; Laursen, 'Early Parts', 44 and 91 on P.Herc. 1420. 2. 2). There he seems to hold that an external influence may affect different people differently. Simon Laursen considers this to be a parallel to the Lucretius passage in book 4 (4. 877–91) which I have just discussed.

[55] 'quare in seminibus quoque idem fateare necessest, esse aliam praeter plagas et pondera causam motibus, unde haec est nobis innata potestas, de nilo quoniam fieri nil posse videmus.'

'from which this power *is born in us*[56] (*nobis innata*) in the sentence suggests that Lucretius is talking about a capacity.

What capacity does Lucretius then refer to? As he calls it *'this* power', it must be a power he has talked about shortly before. No power is explicitly mentioned in the whole passage, but there is an implicit reference: with *potestas* Lucretius can only really refer to lines 2. 279–83:

> There is something in our chest that *is capable of* [*possit*] fighting and resisting at whose bidding the mass of matter is also forced at times to be turned throughout the limbs and frame . . .[57] (2. 279–82)

This something in our chest is (that aspect of our mind which is) the power of having volitions, i.e. the power which can make the body move. Again, this should be a capacity rather than some kind of energy. Thus the swerve is a necessary condition for our having this power of volition. It is then possible to understand the phrase 'from which this power is born in us' in the following way: The power of volition is a *capacity* which we acquire at some stage of our life; and the swerves are somehow responsible for the coming to be (and perhaps for the sustaining) of this capacity in us. But let us look at the next sentences:

> For weight prevents that all things come about by impact, by, as it were, external force . . .[58] (2. 288–9)

The mind's weight (presumably including its atomic structure— see below) is sufficient to warrant that the mind's movements are not completely externally forced. However, as the next sentence in Lucretius makes clear, the mind's weight is not sufficient to prevent its movements from being forced by *internal* factors:

> . . . but that the mind should not itself possess an internal necessity in all its behaviour, and be overcome and as it were forced to suffer and be acted upon, that is brought about by a tiny swerve of atoms at no fixed region of space or fixed time.[59] (2. 289–93)

---

[56] Or 'from which we have this inborn power'; it makes little difference whether one takes *innata* as attributive adjective of *potestas* or as predicative adjective belonging to *est.*

[57] '. . . esse in pectore nostro | quiddam quod contra pugnare obstareque possit? | cuius ad arbitrium quoque copia materiai | cogitur interdum flecti per membra per artus . . .'

[58] 'Pondus enim prohibet ne plagis omnia fiant | externa quasi vi.'

[59] 'sed ne mens ipsa necessum | intestinum habeat cunctis in rebus agendis | et

Similarly to the 'digression' in Epicurus' *On Nature* 25, in these lines necessity is connected with force or coercion.[60] The crucial distinction in 2. 288–93 is that between external and internal compulsion. The swerve is said to prevent *internal* necessity of the mind,[61] and thus the mind's being 'overcome and as it were forced to suffer'. (Nothing further is said about what the internal necessity is, and how it is going to be prevented by the swerve.) One's interpretation of this internal necessity or coercion will differ depending on what one takes Epicurus' model of agency to be.

Proponents of the independent-decision-faculty model will be prone to the following reading: they will understand the internal necessity of the mind as necessitation, or coercion, of *one part* of the mind (the power of volition)[62] by *other parts* of the mind, in particular by the person's *present* character dispositions.[63] These would—if the mind's motions were internally necessitated—in the case of *each action force* the power of volition to initiate movement in accordance with them. Thus, effectively, there would be no power of volition. The swerve's role in the case of each action would naturally be somehow to sever the decision-making power from the agent's present dispositions.

---

devicta quasi cogatur ferre patique, | id facit exiguum clinamen principiorum | nec regione loci certa nec tempore certo.'

mens *Lambinus*: res *OQ*.

[60] In *On Nature* 25 (quoted in sect. 3) forced and necessitated actions were contrasted with actions performed with impulse (ὅρμημα) and eagerness or desire to act (προθυμία). This seems to be the closest parallel in a text by Epicurus to Lucretius' *voluntas*. (If *studium* is a translation of προθυμία, *voluntas* may be a translation of ὁρμή, ὅρμημα, or a similar term. The power of volition would then have been a δύναμις of ὁρμή or ὅρμημα, and a volition (*voluntas*) a particular impulse to act or intention a person has, e.g. the impulse or intention to smoke a cigarette.)

[61] I adopt the generally accepted emendation of *res* to *mens*. But I think (*pace* Avotins, 'The Question of *Mens*') that if the original *res* were to be kept, this would not make much of a difference for my interpretation. For I take it that *omnia fiant* in 2. 288 need not refer to *semina* from 2. 284, but that it can just as well refer generally to the things that happen on the everyday level. This might also help explain the use of *quasi*, by which Lucretius qualifies the external force. The point of lines 2. 288–9 would then be that not all things react in the same way when externally pushed, for the reason that different things have different weights, which make them react in different ways. *Sed ne res ipsa* . . . in line 2. 289 could then be translated as 'but that a thing itself should not . . .', where by 'thing' Lucretius refers in an indeterminate way to all the things on the everyday level that may not be internally necessitated, the most important of which would be human beings, or their minds. Other such things might be all those things that develop or change in a random way.

[62] Or perhaps rather that which would be the power of volition if it were not necessitated in its activity. [63] e.g. Asmis, 'Free Action', 283.

The whole-person model of agency suggests a different interpretation of the internal necessity. In it, it is *presupposed* that a person's volitions to act (in response to environmental stimuli) are always fully determined by the person's *present* overall mental disposition as it is while the person forms the volition. The decision-making is understood as a 'function' of the mind as the mind is when it decides, and external circumstances. Since in this model there is no independent decision-making faculty, *mens* (2. 289) refers to the mind *qua* conglomerate of atoms in which are manifested a set of dispositions. The mind's internal force is distinguished *temporally* from a person's present overall mental disposition: internal coercion is coercion of someone's *present* overall mental state by *temporally prior* mental states or dispositions, which in turn were necessitated by temporally prior mental states, etc. back to a time at which the individual is thought not yet to be responsible for their actions. The necessitation thus concerns the *development* of the mind, not its decision-making. The difference between internal necessity and its absence concerns the point whether the person was internally forced to become, or develop into, the person they are when they set out to act. In the case of force, the action cannot be attributed to the agent, since the agent is not truly causally responsible, but some other factors which predate adult agenthood and which necessitate the agents in their action by necessitating their mental dispositions.

This raises the question what, in this interpretation, the internal factors would be that necessitate the agents in their action, if there were no swerves; or, in other words, what the internal necessity is. The answer, I believe, can be gauged from a passage from Epicurus' *On Nature* 25 which I have already quoted above in Section 3. In this passage Epicurus critically assesses the case for holding that all our actions are determined by a combination of internal and external necessity:

⟨And we can invoke against the argument that our behaviour must be caused either by our initial make-up, or by those environmental influences⟩ by which we never cease to be affected, the fact that we rebuke, oppose, and reform each other as if the cause lay also[64] in ourselves, and not just

---

[64] That is, we are a co-cause, presumably the main causes, but not necessarily the only cause. There are other passages to this effect in *On Nature* 25, e.g. Arr. 34. 31; Laursen, 'Later Parts', 43 ὅθεν καὶ τὸ τοῦ τέλους αὐτοῦ ἐπιλόγισμα εἶχε μὲν καὶ ἡ ἀρχὴ τὴν αἰτίαν· εἴχομεν δὲ καὶ ἡμεῖς.

in our congenital make-up and in the accidental necessity of that which surrounds and penetrates us (Arr. 34. 27; Laursen, 'Later Parts', 35; LS 20 C 2; Greek text above, n. 25)

A person's behavioural response to the environment thus seems *internally* necessitated, inasmuch as the cause of the behavioural response to the environment lies in the person's initial constitution, instead of in the person herself.[65] This is consistent with the assumption of the whole-person model that a person's behavioural responses to the environment are determined by the person's overall disposition of the mind when the person sets out to act. It can be interpreted as suggesting that if the person herself is not the cause of the action, this means that the person's overall disposition at that time is internally necessitated by the person's initial constitution (and thus by something that is temporally prior to the person's formation of a volition—or any volition, for that matter).

Returning to Lucretius 2. 288–93, it would then be the initial constitution that internally necessitates the mind in all its behaviour, and it would be the swerve's function to prevent this necessitation. Internal necessity corresponds to the weight of the atoms (see above). The internal necessity of the mind should thus correspond to the weight—and composition—of the mind atoms. And this is exactly what we can imagine the initial constitution to be: it is a collection of atoms, the precise composition and structure of which vary from person to person. This atomic composition and structure make up a person's mental dispositions, and are as such relatively firm; and they determine which of the impinging images the mind takes in and acts upon, and which not.[66] The mere penetration of the mind by individual atoms or groups of atoms (e.g. εἴδωλα) coming from outside will not usually lead to a change of the mental structure. However, swerves may lead to a new structure of these atoms, perhaps to the integration of incoming atoms into this structure, and it will be the partial change of atomic structure (or the development of structure) which prevents internal necessitation of our behaviour by our initial constitution. The swerve leads to changes in the structure of the mind. Hence the mind is not necessitated or compelled in its movements by its original structure. And our

---

[65] Note also Epic. *Nat.* 25, Arr. 34. 33; Laursen, 'Later Parts, 48, the contrast between δι᾽ ἡμᾶς, διὰ τὴν φύσιν, καὶ τὸ περιέχον.

[66] Cf. Epic. *Nat.* 25, Laursen, 'Later Parts', 33; LS 20 C 1, quoted above in sect. 2.

decisions and actions with which we respond to our environment depend (at least to a major extent) on the new structural elements of the mind, and are hence not internally necessitated.

I conclude, then, that the Lucretius passage on swerve and volition can be consistently read as based on the whole-person model of agency, and as treating internal necessity as necessitation of the *development* of the mind, as opposed to necessitation of its individual decisions. Individual decisions are generally fully determined by the person's mind as it is when the decision is made. *If* a swerve comes in at this point, it will usually have no effect on what decision is made, in the same sense in which a swerve that occurs in the mind in the process of perception will usually have no effect on the reliability of perception. In both cases the mental structure can be conceived of as so firm that a single swerve does not easily make a difference to our decision or perception. If it ever did, the result would be chance events; this possibility could have been used by Epicureans in order to explain the occasional apparent malfunction of our volitional or perceptual apparatus.

Proponents of the view that Lucretius discussed a free will problem as set out in Section 1, however, may not yet be satisfied. They have repeatedly objected that mind- or character-formation interpretations cannot satisfactorily explain Lucretius' phrase 'we swerve off our motions' (2. 259), which they take as strong evidence that there is a swerve involved in every act of volition. I shall attempt to show that Lucretius' analogy between the three types of atomic motions and the three types of motions on the everyday level is not as close as this. Rather, for all three types of motion the primary point of the analogy is that the atomic motion is a necessary condition for the corresponding type on the everyday level. First, *collision*: if atoms did not collide, everyday objects could not collide. However, the collision of objects is qualitatively different from atomic collision; it can involve penetration of a complex of atoms by one or more atoms, and the destruction of a complex or aggregate of atoms. Second, *weight*: if atoms had no weight internally directing their downward movements (their default movements), then objects would have no weight (and atomic structure) internally directing their movements and changes (their default movements). What is analogous to the necessary downward movement of an atom is the necessary movement or change of an object in accordance with its internal physical properties, which are determined by certain stable combinations of atoms. Again, the analogous movements are clearly much more complex than the atomic ones; they are also qualitatively different, as they need not be 'downward' movements at all. Third, the *swerve*: if atoms didn't swerve, there would be no volitions (and no chance movements). There are a number of corresponding elements: If there were no atomic swerves, all atomic movement would be a function of weight and collision of atoms. If there were no volitions, all movements of the mind would be a function of the mind's atomic composition and its collision with external things (e.g. 'images'). With atomic swerves, the mind can develop in such a way that its movements are no longer a function of the mind's weight and collision with external things. Like the swerves, and because of them, the volitional movements of the mind are not eternally predetermined. As it is the nature of the atoms to swerve, so it is our (mind's) nature to have volitions; and as the atoms swerve from their downward path, so do we, with our volitions, swerve from our path of hereditary development.

5. Cicero, *On Fate* 23, and Diogenes of Oenoanda 32. 1. 14–3. 14

A sentence from Cicero, *On Fate* 23, has been plausibly suggested as a parallel to lines 2. 288–93 in Lucretius:[67]

Epicurus introduced this theory ⟨i.e. of the swerve⟩ because he was afraid that, if the atom was always carried along by its weight in a natural and necessary way, there would be nothing free for us, since our mind would be moved in such a way as the movement of the atoms would compel it.[68]

The parallels to Lucretius are obvious. In addition, there are two elements in this sentence which we do not find in the *De rerum natura*. Cicero implies that we have some sort of freedom, which is contrasted with our mind being compelled; and he mentions explicitly what it is that would force our mind if there were no swerve, viz. the movement of the atoms. This sentence has been adduced as a proof that Epicurus used the swerve to save freedom

---

[67] Long–Sedley, ii. 112.

[68] 'hanc Epicurus rationem induxit ob eam rem, quod veritus est ne, si semper atomus gravitate ferretur naturali ac necessaria, nihil liberum nobis esset, cum ita moveretur animus ut atomorum motu cogeretur.'

of choice or decision, and not for the 'freedom' of the development of dispositions. However, just like the verses in Lucretius, this sentence is *compatible* with the view that the swerve secures the non-necessity of the development of our mental dispositions on the basis of the whole-person model of agency. This model here leads to the following interpretation: Cicero's emphasis is on the contrast between internal compulsion by the atoms and freedom from such compulsion. The argument works from the atomic level to the everyday level.

If there were no swerve, all atomic movement would be necessary. Whether movements at the everyday level are necessary depends on whether all movements at the atomic level are necessary. In particular, if all the atomic movements that 'make up' an everyday-level movement were necessary, so would be the corresponding everyday-level movement. (In this way atomic movement, since necessary, would transmit its necessity to the everyday-level movement and thus in a sense 'compel' it.) In particular, 'our mind would be moved in such a way as the movement of the atoms would compel it'. That is, combinations of collision and weight would fully determine the way the structure of the mind changes or develops and accordingly how the mind reacts to external influences. At any time our mental dispositions would be a function of our initial constitution and external influences, and so would, accordingly, our behaviour.

On the other hand, as there are swerves, we have freedom from compulsion and it is not the case that 'our mind would be moved in such a way as the movement of the atoms would compel it'. The reason is that, as a result of the swerving movements, not all atomic motions are necessary, and hence that they no longer convey necessity to all change at the everyday level. In particular—as swerves occur in our mind—our mental dispositions are not the result of compulsion by the atoms, and nor, accordingly, will be the volitions and actions that flow from it. Rather, they are free, i.e. uncompelled. (The phrase 'cum ita moveretur animus' could refer either to what would otherwise be our volitions or to the change of our mental dispositions. In the latter case the translation 'be changed' would be preferable to 'be moved'. For my point it is immaterial which way one reads the text. For when the swerve prevents necessitation of our mental dispositions, neither the mind's development nor its volitional movements are compelled or necessary.) Hence the passage is consistent with my proposed interpretation of Lucretius.

Almost immediately after the quoted passage, still in *On Fate* 23, a couple of sentences lend further support to the interpretation that Epicurus connected the swerves with the development of a person's mental dispositions rather than directly with every act of volition: after a remark that Democritus' position is superior to Epicurus', because he can do without the swerve, Cicero continues:

> More astutely, Carneades taught that the Epicureans could have maintained their position without this fictitious swerve. For, seeing that they taught that there could be some volitional movement of the mind, it would have been better to defend that than to introduce the swerve . . .[69] (Cic. *Fat.* 23)

Here the introduction of the swerve is *contrasted* with the existence of volitions of the mind. But if the swerve really was needed in the formation or execution of every volition, we would expect not a contrast, but rather the claim that a volition can exist *without* involving a swerve. For the sentence implies that the Epicureans believed that the volitional movements of the mind were at least not directly dependent on their introduction of the swerve. On the other hand, if, as I suggest, the swerve is *not* concerned with the formation or execution of volition directly, the text as it stands poses no problems.

It has also been claimed that a passage in Diogenes of Oenoanda (32. 1. 14–3. 14) is evidence that Epicurus introduced the swerve in order to preserve free will and freedom to do otherwise than we do.[70] Again, I disagree. Here is the passage:

> (1) Once prophecy is eliminated, how can there be any other evidence for fate? (2) For if someone uses Democritus' account, saying that because of their collisions with each other atoms have no free movement, and that as a result it appears that all motions are necessitated, we will reply to him: (3) 'Don't you know, whoever you are, that there is also a free movement in atoms, which Democritus failed to discover but Epicurus brought to light, a swerving movement, as he demonstrates from evident facts?' (4) But the chief point is this: if fate is believed in, that is the end of all censure and

---

[69] 'acutius Carneades, qui docebat posse Epicureos suam causam sine hac commenticia declinatione defendere. nam cum docerent esse posse quendam animi motum voluntarium, id fuit defendi melius quam introducere declinationem . . .'

[70] Purinton, 'Free Volition', 265–6, 299.

admonition, and even the wicked ⟨will not be open to blame.⟩[71] (Diogenes
of Oenoanda 32. 1. 14–3. 14, trans. Long–Sedley)

In this passage Diogenes gives two *independent* reasons for why
not everything is compelled by necessity or fate: The first, in (3),
implies that Epicurus introduced the swerve in order to prevent
universal necessitation—nothing more, and I assume it to go back
to the same arguments of Epicurus' which Lucretius reports. The
second reason, in (4), is that universal necessitation is incompatible with praise and blame—nothing more, and I assume it to go
back to Epicurean arguments such as those in the digression of *On
Nature* 25.[72] Thus the passage corroborates neither the thesis that
Epicurus introduced the swerve in order to preserve freedom to
do otherwise, nor the thesis that swerves were involved directly in
every volitional act.[73]

6. Epicurus on internal necessity and character development

Before I add the inevitable speculation about how the swerve was
thought to prevent the internal necessity of the mind, I want to
present some further evidence in support of the suggestion that
both Epicurus and Lucretius are concerned with the internal necessitation of the *development* of the mind, and generally with the
question of the autonomy of the agent, and—as far as our evidence
goes—not with the free will problem as set out in Section 1.

We have a second passage in Epicurus' *On Nature* 25 (Arr. 34.
24; Laursen, 'Later Parts', 28) which is concerned with internal

[71] [πῶς ἀνῃρημέ]νης οὖν | μαντικῆς σημεῖ|ον εἱμαρμένης ἔστιν | ἄλλο; ἂν γὰ[ρ] τῷ
Δημο|κρίτου τι⟨ς⟩ χ[ρ]ήσηται|λόγῳ, μηδεμίαν μὲν ἐλευθέραν [φ]άσκων | ταῖς ἀτόμο[ι]ς
κείνη|σιν εἶναι δι[ὰ] τὴν πρὸς | ἀλλήλας σ[ύν]κρουσιν | αὐτῶν, ἐν⟨θ⟩[ε]ν δὲ φαί|νεσθαι
κατ[η]ναγκασ|μένως π[άντ]α κεινεῖσ|θαι, φή[σομε]ν πρὸς | αὐτόν· "[οὔκουν] οἶδας, ὅσ|τις
ποτὲ εἶ, καὶ ἐλευθέ|ραν τινὰ ἐν ταῖς ἀτό|μοις κείνησιν εἶναι, ἣ[ν] Δημόκριτος μὲν οὐ|χ
εὗρεν, Ἐπίκουρος δὲ | εἰς φῶ[ς] ἤγαγεν, παρεν|κλιτικὴν ὑπάρχουσαν, ὡς ἐκ τῶν φαι-
νομέ|νων δείκνυσιν;" τὸ δὲ | μέγιστον· πιστευθεί|σης γὰρ εἱμαρμένης | αἴρεται πᾶσα
νουθεσ[ί]α καὶ ἐπιτείμησις καὶ | οὐδὲ τοὺς πονηροὺς [
The adjective ἐλεύθερος seems to be used in the context of physical determinism
not before the 1st cent. AD. (see my 'Inadvertent Conception').

[72] Purinton does not translate the δέ ('but') in (4), and runs the two reasons
together: 'According to Diogenes . . . the main reason that Epicurus posited the
swerve was to preserve the phenomena of "admonition and rebuke".' I do not think
that the text bears this out.

[73] Plut. *Stoic. repugn.* 1050 B–C, too, gives no hint about whether the swerve was
meant to come in in character formation or directly in the formation of volitions.

necessitation of the mind, and occurs a little before the previous one (Arr. 34. 27):

And if the first constitution of the development exerts some kind of compulsion in the mind,[74] and such a thing is not developed out of necessity to the point of (developing) these specific things, but on the one hand, such a thing is developed from such conditions out of necessity to the point where there comes to be a soul or rather a soul with a disposition and movement of this particular size, on the other hand, such a thing is not developed out of necessity to the point of (developing) a soul of this or that kind, or at least such a thing is not developed with necessity once it proceeds in age, but out of itself or out of the cause out of itself being able to [develop] also something else. (trans. Laursen, 'Later Parts', 51–2, modified)[75]

This passage is not easy to make sense of, in particular since we lack the immediate context. None the less, it provides some hints as to which things Epicurus thought to be internally necessary and which not. That an individual develops a soul and that that soul has a disposition and motion of a particular size are necessary. But the specific qualities of that soul and its specific developments *when it* (*or the person whose soul it is*) *advances in age* are not internally necessitated. Rather, *when the soul* (*or the person whose soul it is*) *advances in age*, it will be able to develop from itself, or from the cause from itself. Here, again, internal necessitation and lack thereof are concerned not with individual actions or volitions, but with what a person's soul *comes to be like*. The emphasis is on the non-necessity of the development of the mind, and in particular on the fact that we ourselves (or the cause from ourselves) are *causally responsible for the changes in our soul*, and that these changes are not necessary.

The possibility of influencing the development of one's soul dispositions is all-important, if what a person's soul is like at a certain time determines how the person sets out to act at that time. For the only way of getting oneself to act differently from the ways one tends to act is by changing one's dispositions to act. This holds in

---

[74] David Sedley points out to me that it would fit the context much better if one rendered this phrase as 'and if by the power of thought the first constitution is forcibly separated from the development', although, as he adds, this has the drawback of taking ἐκβιάζεσθαι plus genitive in an uncommon way.

[75] κἂν κατὰ διάνοιαν δέ τι ἐκβιάζηται ἡ πρώτη σύστασις τοῦ ἀπογεγεννημένου, μὴ ἐξ ἀνάγκης μέχρι τωνδί τινων ?ἐξ ἀνάγκης ?τοιοῦδε ἀπογεννωμένου ἀλλὰ μέχρι μὲν τοῦ ψυχήν γενέσθαι ἢ καὶ τοσαυτηνὶ διάθεσιν καὶ κίνησιν ἔχουσαν ψυχὴν ἐξ ἀνάγκης ?τοιοῦδε ἀπογεννωμένου ἐκ τῶν τοιουτωνί, μέχρι δὲ τοῦ τοιανδὶ ψυχὴν ἢ τοιανδὶ οὐκ ἐξ ἀνάγκης τοιοῦδε ἀπογεννωμένου ἢ οὐκ ἐπειδὰν προβῇ γε τῇ ἡλικίᾳ τοιοῦδε ἀπογεννωμένου κατ' ἀνάγκην ἀλλ' ἐξ ἑαυτοῦ δυναμένου καὶ τῆς ἐξ ἑαυτοῦ αἰτίας καὶ ἄλλο . . .

particular for moral development.[76] We become the causes of the changes of our mental dispositions, if we receive the right moral education, and use our intellect to assimilate this education. A passage in Lucretius confirms that Epicurus had this conception of moral development; it deals with the development of the human mind and is based on the whole-person model of agency:

... Likewise the human race. Even though education may produce individuals equally well turned out, it still leaves those *original traces of each mind's nature*. And we must not suppose that faults can be completely eradicated, so that one person will not plunge too hastily into bitter anger, another not be assailed too readily by fear, or the third type not be over-indulgent in tolerating certain things. There are many other respects in which the various *natures and consequently the behaviours* of human beings must differ, but I cannot now set out their hidden causes, nor can I find enough names for all the shapes of primary particles from which this variety springs. But there is one thing which I see I can state in this matter: so slight are *the traces of our natures which reason cannot expel from us*, that nothing stands in the way of our leading a life worthy of the gods.[77] (3. 307–22, trans. Long–Sedley, modified; my italics)

The relevant points in the passage are these: the initial nature of a human mind includes certain moral dispositions, which are present in different people in various strengths.[78] Through education people's minds can develop in such a way that these differences are by and large evened out. The reason is that by the use of our intellect we can modify our mental dispositions to a large extent. This passage corroborates the assumption that the Epicureans worked with a whole-person model of agency on two counts. First, it makes it clear that Lucretius took a person's mind to include that person's character dispositions. Second, it implies that Lucretius thinks that one's nature determines one's behaviour, and third, that in order

---

[76] Both before and after the quoted passage of *On Nature* 25 morality is at issue: pp. 23, 26, 29 Laursen.

[77] 'Sic hominum genus est. quamvis doctrina politos | constituat pariter quosdam, tamen illa relinquit | *naturae cuiusque animi vestigia prima.* | nec radicitus evelli mala posse putandumst, | quin proclivius hic iras decurrat ad acris, | ille metu citius paulo temptetur, at ille | tertius accipiat quaedam clementius aequo. | inque aliis rebus multis differre necessest | naturas hominum varias moresque sequaces; | quorum ego nunc nequeo caecas exponere causas | nec reperire figurarum tot nomina quot sunt | principiis, unde haec oritur variantia rerum. | illud in his rebus video firmare potesse, | usque adeo *naturarum vestigia* linqui | parvula *quae nequeat ratio depellere nobis,* | ut nil impediat dignam dis degere vitam.'

[78] This point has a close parallel in the talk of seeds (σπέρματα) in Epic. *Nat.* 25 (Arr. 34. 26).

to change one's behaviour, one has to change one's nature, i.e. the nature of one's mind, by the use of one's intellect.

The explanation on the atomic level of what happens when we modify our character (and how we become the causes of our dispositions, and consequently actions) seems to be provided by another passage from *On Nature* 25:

In this way whenever something is developed which takes on some distinctness from the atoms in a discriminating way[79]—not in the way as from a different distance—he receives the causal responsibility which is from himself; and then he immediately imparts this to his first natures and somehow makes the whole of it into one.[80] (Epic. *Nat.* 25; Arr. 34. 22; Laursen, 'Later Parts, 22)

It seems to me that Bob Sharples is right when he says about this passage: 'the obvious, indeed inevitable way of interpreting this in the atomic context is to say that we, by thought and effort, can modify our character, and hence also the atomic structure of our minds . . . the downwards causation in the passage . . . may thus relate to the process by which we modify our characters, and not to the explanation of free choice . . .' (Sharples, 'Epicurus', 186).

This passage seems to be concerned with absolutely essential occurrences in people's mental developments: namely, how they themselves *become* causes first of their dispositions,[81] and consequently of their actions. I understand it in the following way. A person may encounter beliefs, including value beliefs, which differ from those they have adopted and developed in line with their initial constitution. These different beliefs are then transmitted to the initial 'disposition of the soul' (the 'first natures') and made part of it, and as a result the overall disposition is—slightly—changed.[82] (Thus new beliefs are adopted, and beliefs inconsistent with a new belief may be discarded.) At that point the disposition is no longer

[79] Perhaps: 'in a way that pertains to judgement'?

[80] οὕτως ἐπειδὰν ἀπογεννηθῇ τι λαμβάνον τινὰ ἑτερότητα τῶν ἀτόμων κατά τινα τρόπον διαληπτικόν, οὐ τὸν ὡς ἀφ' ἑτέρου διαστήματος, ἰσχάνει τὴν ἐξ ἑαυτοῦ αἰτίαν, εἶτα ἀναδίδωσιν εὐθὺς μέχρι τῶν πρώτων φύσεων καὶ μίαν πῶς ἅπασαν αὐτὴν ποιεῖ.

[81] Whether this is (1) a unique event in a person's life, or (2) a gradual process, in which a person changes or confirms their beliefs one by one upon reflection, or whether (3) such events happen all through one's adult life, is unclear.

[82] For Epicurus our dispositions to act, and our emotions, are grounded on, and perhaps partially identical with, our beliefs. Remember also that at *Nat.* 25, Arr. 34. 26, the text suggests that that which happens because of us (παρ' ἡμᾶς) happens because of *beliefs of ours which are from us ourselves* (παρὰ τὰς ἡμέτερας ἐξ ἡμῶν αὐτῶν δόξας): see above, sect. 2.

(fully) the result of internal and external necessity, but in part the result of conscious, rational, influencing. When, then, someone acts from such a disposition, *they* are the cause of the action, and no longer 'the atoms', i.e. those of their initial constitution. Again, the way things work seems to be: presumably externally induced changes in beliefs lead to changes in dispositions (which in turn lead to changes in behaviour).[83]

Thus, not only do the Lucretius and Cicero passages on the swerve allow a consistent interpretation of the swerve as having its main function in the formation of one's mental disposition—there are also several other texts that support this interpretation; in fact, Epicurus' ethics as a whole is geared to the development of one's character or mental dispositions, as opposed to a canon of right and wrong actions to choose from.[84]

7. The atomic swerve, mental development, and moral responsibility

It remains for me to provide a plausible story about the function of the swerve within the proposed interpretation. In this context I consider the following points. (A) First, I address the two main objections that have been voiced against interpretations that see the swerve as being involved in the formation of character, rather

---

[83] In *Nat.* 25 (Arr. 34. 31; Laursen, 'Later Parts, 44–5) Epicurus may refer to the same kind of development; but this passage is rather badly preserved.

[84] For completeness, I should mention that Cicero presents in a number of short passages in different works some information about Epicurus' treatment of the Principle of Excluded Middle for future propositions (Cic. *Fat.* 21, 28, 37; *Acad.* 2. 97, *ND* 1. 70). These passages show that Epicurus feared that arguments of the family of the 'Mower' prove that if the Principle of Excluded Middle held for future propositions, then all future events would be certain or predetermined, and hence *necessary*. In order to escape this consequence, Epicurus apparently took the step of denying universal application to the principle. (For details see my *Determinism*, 75–86). Neither the arguments nor Epicurus' reply mention action, volition, choice, or freedom of any sort; free decision or free choice are not under discussion, but the non-necessity of future events more generally. This is confirmed by the example for non-necessity Epicurus chose: 'either Hermachus will be alive tomorrow, or he will not'. What is at issue is not whether Hermachus will or won't do something tomorrow, nor whether he will or won't decide to do something tomorrow, but (assuming that he was not suicidal) whether or not something will happen to him tomorrow—human death being one of those occurrences that were paradigms of fated events which would happen in the form of 'accidents', such as drowning at sea, being struck by lightning, dying of disease, etc.

than in each volition. (B) Second, if, as I argue, Epicurus was not concerned with a free will problem as set out in Section 1, and in particular not when he introduced the swerve, I have to show that he had some other real problem, so that the introduction of the swerve does not seem gratuitous.[85] (C) Third, if such a problem can be identified, it remains to be demonstrated how the swerve could in principle be thought of as contributing to its solution—even if we do not know how Epicurus actually envisaged this to work.

(A) Here are *the two main objections* that have been levelled against the view that the swerve, as described in Lucretius, plays a role in the formation of character.[86] First, it has been repeatedly objected that if one's character can be randomly altered by the swerve, Epicurus would have problems explaining why people's characters remain relatively stable.[87] The point has been memorably illustrated thus: 'a man of good Epicurean character will live in fear of an unpredictable event which may change him into a Stoic or something worse'.[88]

It is, however, important to see that this criticism is merely a special case of a more general objection which, in slightly different forms, arises equally for interpretations that consider the swerve as necessary for forming or exerting a volition. The general problem is this: once the swerves have been furnished with a specific function, how can it be ruled out that additional swerves occur that undermine, obstruct, or undo the workings of the swerve as one has determined them? For swerves are by definition random motions and thus can in principle happen at any place at any time. For instance, the problem would manifest itself as follows in an interpretation that favours the swerve in the formation of volition in order to preserve freedom of choice: if a swerve is *correlated* with my forming a volition for performing some action, what if, at the same time, or immediately afterwards, a second swerve counteracts the first, and as a result I have a volition for its opposite, or at least have no longer a volition for that action? Alternatively, if I *utilize*

---

[85] As Asmis, 'Free Action', esp. at 288, has convincingly shown, Englert's interpretation suffers from this defect.

[86] I hope to have dispelled the frequently made objection that character-formation interpretations do not square with the Lucretius and Cicero passages in sects. 4 and 5 above.

[87] Long, *Hellenistic Philosophy*, 61; Englert, *Epicurus*, 3; similarly Sharples, 'Epicurus', 187 n. 56; Purinton, 'Free Volition', 275–6.

[88] Long, *Hellenistic Philosophy*, 61, quoted by Englert and Purinton.

one swerve for a volition towards some action, what if, whoops, another one undoes this by rechannelling the atom to produce a volition for its opposite, or to result in no volition either way?

Thus any interpretation of the function of the swerve needs to tackle this problem in the particular guise in which it each time occurs. Solutions depend—as far as I can see—mainly on inventiveness. In the case of character-formation interpretations the criticism can easily be countered as follows. Generally, single swerves go unnoticed, since they are so tiny that they do not interrupt the course of events on the everyday level. In particular, the atomic structure of someone's mental dispositions is relatively fixed and stable, so that one swerve has usually little chance of doing much damage. It is only in certain developmental situations—which will have to be described in the respective interpretations—that single swerves can contribute to the initiation of a new development in a different direction (see below).[89]

The second main objection is this: how can a *random* movement like the swerve that happens in the course of the development of one's character introduce and guarantee moral responsibility of the agents in their actions? This, again, is a specific version of a more general problem with which any interpretation of the swerve is confronted. A random motion or a number of random motions cannot by themselves warrant moral responsibility, regardless of whether they occur in the process of developing one's character, or of forming or of exerting a volition, and regardless of whether the concept of moral responsibility is based on freedom of decision or on autonomous agency. (We do not know whether Epicurus was aware of this problem in one form or other, but I would like to think that he was.) This objection can be invalidated by the observation that Epicurus—like most ancient philosophers—generally thought that moral responsibility is based on the fact that agents are beings of a certain kind, namely, rational beings who have the capacity to base their actions on their rationality, i.e. their own beliefs. Epicurus' swerve thus is a necessary but not a sufficient condition for our

---

[89] *Ceteris paribus*, proponents of the involvement of the swerve in the formation or execution of volition seem actually to have a harder nut to crack. For in such interpretations a swerve typically comes in at a point where whether or not a certain decision is made (or action performed) depends fully on whether a swerve occurs. Thus, if *one* swerve can determine whether or not an action is performed, *one* further swerve may suffice to counteract the first, and lead to the opposite result.

having volitions and autonomous agency. I sketch below how this could work in the case of character-formation interpretations.

(B) My second point was: what was *Epicurus' problem* that led him to introduce the swerve? I assume that this was not a 'timeless' philosophical problem such as the free will problem as set out in Section 1, but a problem specific to the ancient defence of atomistic philosophies such as Democritus' and Epicurus'. (The usefulness of the swerve is after all restricted to such theories.) Atomists have to explain the entire universe, and everything that happens in it, in terms of atoms and their movements, and the void. The problem is then this: on the one hand, atomists have the enormous task thus to account for the order and regularity in the universe;[90] on the other, they have to explain the existence of chance events, i.e. disorderly events, and how human beings can be causes or can have volitions. The function of the swerve is thus to provide an explanation of the possibility of chance events[91] and volitions *without* undermining the atomistic explanation of the order in the universe.

The nature of this problem becomes clearer when one follows the ancients in their depiction of Epicurean atomism in two stages: first atomism without the swerve; then atomism with the swerve. Whether the first stage was thought to be historically real, or fictitious and merely an explanatory device, is immaterial in this context.

Atomism without the swerve is designed to meet the challenge to give a non-teleological, mechanical explanation of the order in the universe. In atomism without the swerve every movement would be necessary, both at the atomic level and at the everyday level. There are two kinds of necessitating factors, internal and external ones. At the atomic level these are internally the weight of an atom, and externally other atoms that collide with this atom. At the everyday level, concerning the movements of everyday objects, they seem to be the weight and atomic composition and structure of the object as

---

[90] Cf. e.g. Plot. *Enn.* 3. 1. 3. Given a philosophical climate in which teleological views are the norm, this is one of the major challenges Epicurus has to meet. We can gather this also from the fact that Lucretius gives the point a lot of space. The readiness of many modern philosophers to believe in physicalism, mechanism, and reductionism is quite a different scene, in particular, since no empirical sciences such as modern chemistry and molecular physics were available to the ancients.

[91] This is what Philodemus, *Sign.* 36. 11–17, and Plutarch, *Soll. an.* 964 E say— and (*pace* Bailey, *Greek Atomists*, 327, and A. A. Long, 'Chance and Natural Law in Epicureanism', *Phronesis*, 22 (1977), 63–88) I cannot see why this should not be what Epicurus said.

internally necessitating factors, and atoms and things or clusters of atoms external to the object, that 'collide' with it (and might enter it), as externally necessitating factors. The order and regularity in the world are explained as the result of the co-operation of these two factors. Such explanation proves most difficult in the case of objects of complex structure like plants and animals, where phenomena such as reproduction and self-motion need to be accounted for. Plants and animals display stable properties, stable patterns of behaviour, and patterns of development that follow a fixed temporal order; for example, all animals have a soul, birds generally build nests, all boys sprout a beard when approaching manhood.[92] The *properties* are explained by the types of atoms involved and their structural combinations and patterns of movements. The *patterns of behaviour* are explained as reactions to external stimuli that are determined by the atomic structure and movement of the object. The *developmental patterns* (for the development of both properties and dispositions) require some in-built 'time-release' in the atomic base of things, which will be activated by suitable external stimuli. An atomistic theory can thus in principle explain the order and complex structure of the world.

In this swerveless atomic theory the following difficulty arises. Being entirely the result of internal and external necessitating factors, all motions—both at the atomic level and at the everyday level—are necessary. But it was generally accepted among Hellenistic philosophers that it is an essential characteristic of voluntary behaviour (and of chance events) to be non-necessary. Hence in the—swerveless—atomic system voluntary behaviour appears to be precluded.

(c) *The swerve is introduced to solve this problem* by satisfying *two* conditions: positively, it needs to make voluntary action possible by preventing internal necessitation of certain states and movements; and negatively, it must not undermine the explanation of the order and regularity in the world in terms solely of atoms and void. If one assumes that the swerve's function—as described in Lucretius and Cicero—is to remove internal necessity from the agent's mental *dispositions*, we can imagine this to work as follows.

First, a note on the *frequency of the swerves*—a point on which our sources are silent.[93] Since the swerve is a third basic motion, and

[92] Lucr. 5. 849–54.
[93] Except if one accepts Kleve's argument ('Id Facit Exiguum Clinamen', 28) that

none of the texts about the swerve mentions a particular scarcity of swerves, we may assume that swerves happen quite frequently. However, the frequency is limited by the fact that the everyday level world appears generally ordered (although arguably less so to ancient philosophers than to Newton, say). Thus we can state, as it were, an upper and a lower limit for the frequency of the swerves: on the one hand, the swerves must occur sufficiently often to guarantee the possibility of a frequency of chance events and non-necessitated character developments (especially character changes) that corresponds to the frequency of such kinds of occurrences as we can 'observe' them happening; on the other hand, relative to the size of the deviation of a swerve (the ἐλάχιστον) and the time it takes, the force of a single swerve and the number of swerves must be restricted in such a manner that they do not interfere with the order of things at the everyday level. For instance, the reliability of sense perception has to be preserved, and those kinds of developments that show great regularity must not be interfered with. (The theory of quantum leaps may give us an idea of how this could in principle be possible.)

Next, the *removal of necessity*. What the introduction of the swerve does to the modalities of the atomic movements is uncertain. We can assume the following points. (1) Swerving movements are not necessary. (I assume, however, that they are *caused* by the atom, whose nature it is to swerve randomly every now and then— within the bounds of frequency determined above, although *when* these swerves happen is not fixed in advance. Atoms may thus be conceived of as having a built-in random generator as part of their nature.) (2) Any movement that is neither itself a swerve nor in any way the close or remote effect of a swerve is necessary (but given the eternity of the universe, it is uncertain whether Epicurus assumed such movements). (3) Certain kinds of movements are impossible, e.g. swerves that exceed one minimum, and 'upward' movements if there is no collision involved. (4) This leaves the majority of atomic movements, those which are not swerves but have a swerve somewhere in their 'causal history'. I am inclined to think that at least all such movement as would not have occurred if one of the preceding swerves had not occurred would be non-necessary, assuming some sort of transitivity of non-necessity.

Lucretius' 'etiam atque etiam' (2. 243) means 'again and again' and refers to the frequency of the swerves.

What the modalities of movements at the everyday level are is equally underdetermined by our sources. I assume that they roughly correspond to those of the atomic movements. (1) All those events or changes of an object in which no swerve has been causally effective are necessary. These will include facts such as that people will die by a certain age (since the clusters of atoms that make up humans just 'give up' after a certain time, and no swervings can prevent this from happening); that, given certain circumstances, human beings desire pleasure and shun pain. (2) All those events or changes that concern an object in which one or more swerves have been causally effective somewhere in their 'causal history' are non-necessary. Thus, whenever in a person the mental dispositions have been changed as a result of a swerving, all subsequent behaviour of that person that is (internally) co-caused by the part of the overall disposition thus changed is non-necessary. (Here it does not matter whether it would also have happened without the change; what matters is what was causally effective in its coming about.[94])

We can then see why on this interpretation *the swerves that happen in the mind do not lead to chaos* and why Epicureans have little reason to fear that they may suddenly metamorphose into a Stoic or something worse. We have to imagine the mind as a relatively stable atomic structure, but with a large number of developmental 'potentials' (σπέρματα, Epic. *Nat.* 25, Arr. 34. 26), with built-in time release, which ensures that certain developments do not happen before a certain age (certain potentials are not actualized before a certain age), or before other developments have happened. We can then imagine that at a time when new developments are due to start, swervings can be effective much more easily, determining the direction the development takes (out of a number of possible directions or 'trajectories'), whereas once a new property or characteristic is fully developed, single swerves are not strong enough to make a difference; thus most swerves that occur in the mind do not affect the mind's structure, and thus a person's mental dispositions. If we postulate a sufficient number of swerves, and a sufficient number of developmentally sensitive periods for individual potentials (we could even assume that a swerve is a necessary condition for triggering a new development in such sensitive periods), most specific mental dispositions, and hence most human behaviour, will

---

[94] See Epic. *Nat.* 25, Arr. 34. 24–5; Laursen, 'Later Parts', 29–30.

become non-necessary, it being in part the result of a causally effective swerve.

We can also now explain *how such random modifications of the
initial state of our mind could make* **us** *any more causally or morally
responsible* for our movements than if they flowed directly from
our initial make-up. As hinted above, the answer is roughly that
the swerve is no more than one of many necessary conditions for
moral responsibility. All the other necessary conditions have to be
found in the nature of those beings who are to be held responsible.
(This point can also be inferred from the fact that swerves serve to
explain chance events, too,[95] since there must then be factors other
than the swerve that account for the difference between chance
events and those events for which *we* are causally and hence morally
responsible.)

Swerves can lead to the development of the power of volition and
to moral responsibility only in the right kind of things. My point is
not that because of the fineness of the mind-atoms swerves initiate
noticeable changes only in the mind, and that this explains why
humans are morally responsible, but for instance plants are not.
For even if the swerves can have effects in the mind more easily,
this does not rule out that, at the right point in the development
of a plant, or if occurring in a sufficiently large number, they could
also, for example, change the constitution of a plant. Imagine that
a 'cluster of swerves' in some part of a plant brings about a change
in the plant's constitution. Imagine that the plant now grows an
extra leaf at the wrong place. This would hardly make the plant
morally responsible for the changes. Nor would one hold the whole
plant itself *causally* responsible. Rather, for Epicurus such a change
would be *by chance* (ἀπὸ τύχης).[96]

For an action that happens *because of us* (παρ' ἡμᾶς), i.e. of which
we are the cause, a lot more than this is required: only those beings
can become morally responsible that come with a primary constitution of a certain complexity. Human beings do—and arguably
some tame animals. The initial make-up of human beings is cat-
egorically different from that of plants. We are—or so Epicurus
thinks—from birth led by pleasure. Plants are not. From birth, too,

---

[95] Philod. *Sign.* 36. 11–17, and Plut. *Soll. an.* 964 E. Purinton's reading of the two
passages as referring only to the chance existence of the cosmos ('Free Volition',
261–2) is unconvincing.

[96] See e.g. Lucr. 4. 1223–6 for random variation in heredity.

we have a large number of potentials for developments. Plants do not. It lies in our atomic structure that we will develop a mind, preconceptions, memory, the ability to speak a language, and many more things which plants do not develop. And presumably we have to develop quite a bit before the swerves can exert their catalytic function in the process that leads to the development of a capacity for fully fledged volitions by means of which we can become the cause of our actions.

I surmise that Epicurus held that we ourselves become causes and morally responsible at the point when we start changing our disposition by way of developing our own thoughts, value judgements, and so on; when we become capable of reconsidering the judgements and desires we have adopted or developed solely as a result of hereditary and environmental impacts. Such reconsideration influences what we regard as pleasant, and thus in what circumstances we have a volition for something, and thereby initiate an action. I further suspect that this is what Epicurus is concerned with in much of *On Nature* 25.[97]

There are several different ways in which one can conceive of the relation between, on the one hand, the swerves' prevention of internal necessitation of our mental dispositions, and on the other, the way we become (and remain) ourselves the causes of our actions, so that the actions happen because of us, and we are morally responsible for them. I give the two possibilities which I find most plausible; there are others. I do not maintain that either of the two *was* Epicurus'. I merely intend to show that such explanations, which are based on a character-formation interpretation, are possible and that they are no more fantastic than the ones suggested by those who think that the swerve was meant to solve the free will problem as set out in Section 1.

The first possibility is what one may call the *minimalist* approach: Epicurus' change of his conception of atomic movement to the effect that in addition to their natural downward movements atoms have swerving movements introduces an element of non-necessity into the world. This solves the problem of autonomous agency as follows: adult human beings can be called the cause of their actions because (*a*) they influence the development of their character by way of their rationality or reason; (*b*) what their character is at any time

---

[97] See in particular Epic. *Nat.* 25, Arr. 34. 22, quoted above in sect. 6, with my comments.

is not a function of hereditary internal and circumstantial external influences, since swerves occur in the mind in the process of its development and have at crucial developmental moments effects on the changes of the atomic structure of the mind; this development, the resulting mental dispositions, and the actions flowing from those dispositions are thus not necessary. (*c*) It therefore makes no sense to call necessity, or the atoms (at preceding times), or the initial constitution of the mind the cause of the action. The person can be called the cause of their actions, and can be held morally responsible, because of (*a*) and (*b*), which, however, are not necessarily connected.[98]

The second possibility is some kind of *correlation* approach: There is a direct correspondence between (some of the) swerving movements in a person's mind and their conscious effort to change their mental dispositions. For instance, I study Epicurean ethics and, aiming at tranquillity (ἀταραξία), I try to adopt and follow the theory, try to change my old ingrained beliefs and prejudices, etc. In this context, making a conscious effort to believe firmly that *P*, and to replace non-*P* by *P*, happens—at least occasionally—simultaneously with swerving motions of mind atoms; and when it does it leads to a change of my character dispositions (the main constituents of which are beliefs) by integrating *P* into my system of firmly held beliefs. Exactly how the randomness of the atomic level can be the foundation of change is not explained in our texts. Perhaps Epicurus could not answer this. Agents are the cause of their actions, because their mental dispositions, which determine their volitions and actions, are the result of the agents' own changing of (or confirmation of) their beliefs.[99]

8. Conclusion

My overall goal in this paper was this: to show that there is no compelling textual evidence for the assumption that Epicurus was concerned with freedom of decision or choice or with a problem

---

[98] This approach is close to Furley's position in his 'Voluntary Action'; it also utilizes some of Conway's suggestions in his 'Epicurus' Theory'.

[99] This is a modification, in the light of the character-formation interpretation and the whole-person model of agency, of interpretations such as those by Sharples, 'Epicurus'; Mitsis *Epicurus' Ethical Theory*, 164–6; Gulley, 'Free Will', 46–51; Asmis, 'Free Action'. 291.

of free will as set out in Section 1. There is no evidence that he discussed, or even had a conception of, freedom of decision or freedom of choice. There is no evidence that he had a concept of moral responsibility that is grounded on freedom of choice, or on freedom of decision. There is not even any direct evidence that he thought that freedom to do otherwise was jeopardized by atomistic determinism. There is further no compelling evidence that the swerve played a role in the formation of volitional acts or decision processes. I hence suggest that the whole idea that Epicurus was concerned with the free will problem as set out in Section 1 is anachronistic, and that—at least as long as no positive evidence comes to light—the view that Epicurus thought there was such a problem, and that he endeavoured to solve it, should be dropped.

I have attempted to draw an alternative picture, based on the evidence we have. This picture suggests that Epicurus—in line with philosophers before and after him (Aristotle and the Stoics)—had a different concept of human agency and of moral responsibility: human actions are fully determined by the mental disposition of the agents when they set out to act. Moral responsibility presupposes not free decision or free choice, but the absence of coercion and autonomous agency, i.e. that the person, and not something else, is causally responsible for the actions for which they are to be held morally responsible. Autonomous human agency requires the ability of the agents to influence causally, on the basis of their own beliefs, the development of their behavioural dispositions.

In the context of his mechanistic atomism, Epicurus faced the problem that he had to explain the non-necessity of human agency (and chance events), without undermining the atomistic explanation of the order in the universe. The swerve—which is of use only *within* atomism—was meant to solve this problem by making the mental dispositions of adult human beings non-necessary (perhaps by allowing a person's rational attempts at altering their dispositions to gain a foothold). This is possible without great interruptions and 'out-of-character' developments, if one assumes a certain frequency of the swerves, a generally stable atomic structure of the mind, which is susceptible to influence by single swerves only when new developments or realizations of potentials are about to start. How exactly this was meant to work in detail we do not know.

The Queen's College, Oxford

PLATONIC ETHICS

A Critical Notice of Julia Annas, *Platonic Ethics Old and New*[1]

A. A. LONG

IN Julia Annas's *magnum opus, The Morality of Happiness* (Oxford, 1993), the author apologized for excluding 'systematic discussion' of Plato (18–20). She defended her decision by indicating why Plato is 'problematic' for that book's subject—the examination of 'explicit ethical theory'. Few would quarrel with her enumeration of the salient difficulties. They include the dialogue form, Plato's anonymity, the treatment within single dialogues of issues that go beyond ethics, the 'immensely different positions occupied by Socrates in different dialogues', the 'perennial "Socratic problem"', the 'increasing questioning' of Platonic chronology, and 'the status of Plato's arguments'. Regarding this last problem, she wrote:

Are the arguments put forward by Socrates simply Plato's own arguments? Or is Plato more interested in exploring arguments and issues than in building up a system of ethics in the first place? This would certainly explain why he chooses the form of writing that he does. The more seriously we take this possibility, the more problematic it becomes to see particular arguments as simply part of a single system of ideas.

Notwithstanding these cautionary remarks, Annas allowed it to be 'perfectly legitimate to try to extract a "Platonic ethics" from the dialogues':

But we should be aware that this involves both strong methodological assumptions and a very large amount of system-building and priority-choosing on our part. And equally, once we have extracted the framework of ancient ethical theory from later writers, it is legitimate to go back and

[1] Julia Annas, *Platonic Ethics Old and New* (Ithaca and London, 1999), pp. viii+ 196. This book is the publication of Cornell University's Townsend Lectures, which Annas delivered in 1997.

apply it to Plato's works, if we are both cautious and clear about our methodological assumptions. We need, in fact, a work or rather several works on Platonic ethics to help us understand the following: the distinguishing features of 'Socratic' ethics and how they differ from 'Platonic' ethics; the theory of the 'middle' and 'later' dialogues, and the relation of this both to the ethical theories of the Old Academy and to the later position of Middle Platonists such as Plutarch. It is clearly of great interest to examine the extent to which modern readers of the dialogues agree, or disagree, with later writers in the ancient world who read Plato in the light of more developed and explicit expectations about ethical theory.

I have excerpted at such length from *The Morality of Happiness* because in *Platonic Ethics Old and New* Annas turns to the Middle Platonists (hereafter MPs) in order to apply the methodology foreshadowed in the above passage. That, however, understates the interest and ambition of her new book. In the few years separating the two publications, Annas has become a strong proponent of a unitarian Plato and an even stronger opponent of what she calls 'the orthodox, developmental reading' (7). As support for pursuing these ends in this later book, she also invokes the MPs as allies, and there is far more to its aims and content than even these big goals. With help from the MPs, but clearly prompted by her quite independent reflections, Annas makes a case for numerous substantive and highly controversial interpretations of Platonic ethics. These include, most notably, three claims: first, that we should read Plato as consistently adumbrating the Stoic thesis that virtue is sufficient for happiness (hereafter VSH); second, that we should not read the *Republic*'s moral psychology as a radical new departure from ideas found in the so-called 'Socratic' dialogues; and third, that the ethical theory of the *Republic* is largely independent of that dialogue's political and metaphysical themes.

These matters by no means exhaust the pages of this fairly short book. Annas finds that the MPs can help us to a more unified view of Plato's various discussions of pleasure. In addition, they direct us to Plato's repeated statements that being virtuous is 'becoming like God', a feature of Platonic ethics which 'is invisible for modern readers' (6). Annas devotes the third chapter of her book to an analysis of this formula and its implications. Although I shall not discuss this chapter here, I recommend it as a part of her book that I found particularly fresh and rewarding.

This brief survey of contents will ensure, I hope, that readers who may not share Annas's interest or confidence in the MPs as interpretative guides to Plato do not, for that reason, overlook her book. Because it invites more extensive study than I have the space to pursue here, I shall focus on four main topics: Annas's treatment of the MPs and their value for her enterprise; developmentalism vs. unitarianism; her conception of moral theory and the eudamonistic tradition; and her detachment of ethics from politics and metaphysics in the *Republic*.

1. The Middle Platonists

Annas's Middle Platonists are a selection of the figures discussed in John Dillon's classic book of that title: Alcinous (formerly identified with Albinus), Arius Didymus ('not himself a Platonist, but an author who shares some sources with Alcinous': 1 n. 1), Apuleius, Plutarch, Philo of Alexandria, and the Anonymous Commentator on the *Theaetetus*.[2] Of these, she draws most heavily on Alcinous. Although she mentions Antiochus occasionally, she implicitly excludes him from the 'tradition', so far as her book is concerned, seemingly because his way of combining Stoic with Aristotelian ethics is too remote from Plato to serve as a fruitful approach to our own interpretation of Platonic ethics (44 n. 44). She also, quite surprisingly, virtually omits Eudorus, whose ethics do include some of the doctrinal interpretations she emphasizes in this book.[3]

It is generally supposed that attempts to interpret Plato doctrinally began with Speusippus and Xenocrates. Annas, however, calls her selected figures (all from the early Christian era) 'the first philosophers in a Platonic tradition to see their task as that of interpreting Plato's own texts systematically' (1). Why does she opt for this late date?

The answers to this question are crucial for understanding her book's rationale. Her chosen Platonists were all explicit eudaimonists;[4] and further:

---

[2] The last two are actually very minor figures in Annas's book. For Alcinous, she makes extensive use of J. Dillon's *Alcinous: The Handbook of Platonism* (Oxford, 1993).

[3] On Eudorus, whom Annas cites at 109 n. 36, see J. Dillon, *The Middle Platonists* (London, 1977), 123–5.

[4] Since Annas takes eudaimonism as 'explicit theory' to be 'surfacing' in Plato (2), one may ask why she exempts Speusippus and Xenocrates from her 'tradition'. The

They also see [Plato] in terms sharpened by later debate. In particular what is important for them is the debate between the Stoics and Aristotelians on the place of virtue in happiness . . . Writing from a standpoint in which issues have been clarified by discussion, the later Platonists do not hesitate to enroll Plato on the side of the Stoics; they describe his ethical views in Stoic terms, since they take it that Plato regards as central the points that the Stoics do. (3)

Annas anticipates and rebuts the objection that such Stoicized accounts of Platonic ethics may be anachronistic. Her ancient Platonists, she says, have the advantage over us of sharing his own eudaimonistic framework, and hence they did not 'as we do, have to work into Plato's ethical thoughts from the outside' (3). Moreover, she argues, when we study Plato's texts in this Middle Platonic way, we find 'that ancient Platonists and Stoics are right to see Plato as akin to the Stoics on some basic issues'. This is not to say that Plato has fully achieved the Stoics' clarity and determinacy; none the less, by following the lead of the MPs our attention to Plato will be focused in the right place.

The question of whether Platonic ethics anticipates Stoicism as distinct from the Lyceum is entirely pertinent. What troubles me about Annas's Middle Platonist support for this view is that she begins her book with blanket statements about their adopting the former of these two lines. Not only was that not the view of Antiochus (whom she marginalizes), but also Plutarch (surely the most scholarly of all the MPs) and Calvenus Taurus opted, like Aristotle, for a plurality of goods. We have to wait for a footnote in order to learn very briefly about this deviation.[5] It turns out, then, that while

answer seems to be that it is only 'after Aristotle [that eudaimonism] becomes the explicit framework within which ethical theories are presented and debated' (ibid.). As for Aristotle, he does not pretend to try 'to produce a just picture of Plato's own ideas' (ibid.).

[5] 32 n. 6: 'Among the ancient Platonists, only Plutarch and Calvenus Taurus seem to reject the idea [that (1) virtue is sufficient for happiness and (2) only the fine is good] in their own right (and so, presumably, as an interpretation of Plato), but we are not well informed as to why. What is striking is the unanimity of other Platonists on the interpretation in Stoic terms.' I find it curious that Annas is so down on Antiochus, who does accept (1) above. She ends her footnote: 'See Dillon's commentary on Alcinous's chapter 27, and his [*Middle Platonists*] on the ethical positions of the various Platonists.' What she doesn't say is that Dillon (*Alcinous*, xxii) finds Alcinous 'rather unexpectedly in agreement with the more Stoicizing (and Pythagoreanizing) wing of Platonism'. And see Dillon, *The Middle Platonists*, 44: 'All through the period the two alternatives [Peripatetic and Stoic] secured adherents.'

Annas is quite correct to regard the MPs as explicit eudaimonists, they do not form a group who consistently took Plato to be a Stoic *avant la lettre* in ethics. That does pertain to Eudorus, Alcinous, Atticus, Philo (hardly an exegete of Plato), and Apuleius; it does not apply to Antiochus, Arius Didymus, Plutarch, or Taurus. In other words, ancient Platonists were about as divided on this issue as moderns may be. This leaves open the possibility that Alcinous *et al.* have the better insight into Platonic ethics. But it undercuts Annas's big claims about how much her MPs as a 'tradition' can help us on *that* particular question.

One of the attractions of this book is its lively style and freedom from abundance of scholarly clutter. The main text is thoroughly approachable by readers of diverse backgrounds, and Annas has included a helpful 'Cast of Characters' with brief portraits of her chosen MPs and other relevant philosophers. Yet, precisely because she has made the book accessible, she risks misleading many readers because she gives so little background on Middle Platonism and on the handbook tradition represented by texts like Alcinous' *Didaskalikos* and Apuleius' *De Platone et eius dogmate*. She tells us that the MPs 'are not a unified school [but] a set of rather different people producing interpretations of Plato's ideas, taken to be a unified set of doctrines' (1). Beyond that, virtually nothing. The way she writes of how Alcinous 'interpreted' Plato could lead those unfamiliar with his kind of text to suppose that he sat down with the dialogues in front of him and compiled a digest of doctrines, though she does acknowledge the material he shares 'verbatim' with Arius Didymus (10). What her book lacks is any account of the centuries-long tradition of what such books were designed for, how they were composed, who their audience was. etc.[6] There is no mention of Jaap Mansfeld's Herculean studies of this subject in Annas's bibliography.[7]

A possible explanation for these omissions is that Annas takes all this background to be irrelevant to her project. What she finds attractive about 'the ancient doctrinal traditions of interpreting Plato' is that they are 'stimulatingly different from our own' (11). Sometimes in this book Annas seems to favour a postmodern approach

[6] Cf. Dillon, *Alcinous*, xxix: 'What we find in the *Didaskalikos* is not so much the direct utilization of Plato's dialogues as the relaying of a formalized distillation of them into *dogmata* which had been completed long before A[lcinous]'s time.'

[7] See especially J. Mansfeld, *Prolegomena: Questions to be Settled before the Study of an Author, or a Text* (Leiden, New York, and Cologne, 1994).

to Plato—the more alternative readings, the better.[8] But I don't
think that is this book's dominant message, which is rather, as I
have already said, that the MPs adopt a view of Plato's unity in
general and of his ethics in particular that Annas herself finds persuasive. In that case, it seems to me a serious lapse that she says
so little about their cultural context and methods of composition.
Still, whether or not one agrees with her that it is the MPs who are
'best fitted to wake us from our developmental slumbers' (165), she
has undoubtedly done a fine service in publicizing some of their
views with such enthusiasm.

2. Development vs. unity

The goal of the book's second chapter, 'Many voices: dialogue and
development in Plato', is to show what the MPs can offer those
who are unhappy about imputing to Plato an 'overall, linear development' (12) but who also want to remain sensitive to the dialogue
form. Annas highlights the intriguing claim by Arius Didymus that
Plato was '*polyphōnos*, and not *polydoxos*, as some suppose'.[9] Rather
than commenting on 'as some suppose' (which indicates that unitarianism was far from *de rigueur* at the time of Arius), Annas focuses
on *polyphōnos*, arguing that what Arius has in mind is Plato's 'ped-
agogical versatility': the use of different styles and approaches to
represent 'a single position' to different audiences.

Was Arius, though, sufficiently sensitive to 'the aporetic Socratic
dialogues'? They, after all, have always been a stumbling-block for
modern unitarians. Annas makes the very good point that Socrates
can be both aporetic and doctrinaire within the same dialogue (notably the *Theaetetus*), and she draws on Plutarch to show 'how a doctrinal Platonist can have a role for Socrates' negative ad hominem

---

[8] Cf. the following from her concluding chapter: 'Of course, we do not have to
read Plato as the ancients did. But we do not have to read him as the Victorians did,
either' (165); and from p. 7: 'I suspect that Plato studies are likely to become less
settled, more uncertain, and more open to wide differences of approach.' I can only
make sense of this last sentence on the assumption that what 'Plato studies' need to
be unsettled from are the few well-known books from which she explicitly distances
herself in the present volume. Annas's style in this book can veer quite startlingly
between caution and assertion.

[9] Cited by Stobaeus at ii. 55. 5–7 Wachsmuth and at ii. 49. 25 (corrected from
Annas's 49. 20, p. 13 n. 8).

arguments' (23) without succumbing to developmentalism.[10] She rightly stresses the 'adaptability' of the Socratic figure both inside and outside Plato, and she notes that for Albinus 'there is no one definite starting point for reading Plato's philosophy, since it is like a circle' (27).

All this is usefully said and well worth the pondering of modern interpreters. Yet I left this chapter (and the book as a whole) with the sense that Annas's presentation of developmentalism vs. unitarianism casts the alternative positions much too rigidly.[11] Staying within the field of ethics, we surely have no difficulty in agreeing that the Plato who wrote the *Laws* was the same philosopher who wrote the *Apology* and *Crito*; there are degrees of unitarianism and degrees of developmentalism. Even if it were true that 'all hopes of establishing a scientific ordering' of the 'dialogues have failed to materialize' (26), we know such things as that the *Sophist* is presented as a sequel to the *Theaetetus*, and I think we know that the *Laws* postdates the composition of the *Republic*. Is there nothing to be learnt from the fact that in the so-called Socratic dialogues Plato pays no explicit attention to such earlier thinkers as Heraclitus or Parmenides, whereas they loom large in just those works that modern scholarship has generally agreed to be later? The fact that the MPs show no interest in such things does nothing to discredit modern questions concerning Plato's different preoccupations at different stages of his long life.

Annas deplores developmentalism because, she says, we have no external controls on any secure facts that bear on Plato's 'intellectual biography' (28). Yet, even if we set aside everything from the dubiously authentic *Letters* and other testimonies, Plato's dialogues (to state an obvious banality) were composed at a particular time and place, and we know quite a lot from Isocrates and other sources about these. Annas insists that her approach to Plato via the MPs is not anachronistic. I would heed that plea more sympathetically if she had also asked what we can learn about Plato's ethical theory by situating it in the world of fourth-century Greece.[12]

[10] On the adaptability and plasticity of Plato's Socrates see my article 'Plato's Apologies and Socrates in the *Theaetetus*', in J. Gentzler (ed.), *Method in Ancient Philosophy* (Oxford, 1998), 137–64.

[11] Contrast the more nuanced, though broadly similar, approach of Charles Kahn in *Plato and the Socratic Dialogue* (Cambridge, 1996).

[12] See T. Irwin's illuminating study 'Common Sense and Socratic Method', in Gentzler, *Method in Ancient Philosophy*, 29–66.

3. Ethical theory and the eudaimonistic tradition

Both Vlastos and Irwin have argued that Socrates in the so-called Socratic dialogues upholds the thesis that virtue is sufficient for happiness.[13] Both of them also maintain that this is not the position that is argued for in the *Republic* or the *Philebus*. There and also in the *Laws*, to cite Irwin: '[Plato] falls short of claiming that we can be happy no matter what non-moral goods we lack and no matter what non-moral evils we suffer. Since Plato does not affirm this stronger claim, he does not revert to the Socratic view that virtue is sufficient for happiness.'[14] Hence, for both scholars, a principal reason for their endorsement of developmentalism.

My own problem with the Vlastos/Irwin line is not so much its claim that Plato came to differ from 'Socrates' over this issue but that highlighting it as an issue threatens to obscure what is startlingly bold and original about Platonic ethics throughout the corpus. One of the main attractions of Annas's book is her insistence on the power and strangeness of making happiness dependent on virtue. In her second chapter, 'Transforming your life', she has excellent things to say about 'the idea that [Platonic] virtue has a transformative power; it transforms your view of happiness by transforming your values and priorities' (49); and she succeeds in showing that this idea is as potent in the *Laws* as it is in the *Apology*. Must we, then, for our basic assessment of Platonic ethics select a single formula as best representing his view on the relation of virtue to happiness? Or may we, instead, propose that while Plato sometimes specifies other goods besides virtue, and sometimes says that other so-called goods are harmful rather than beneficial when detached from wise usage, and sometimes again that nothing is intrinsically good except virtue, such different formulations should not be pressed as yielding either major changes of mind or vacillation over essentials? For whether we approach Plato's ethics from its contemporary or from its later Platonic perspectives, no attentive reader of the whole corpus can doubt that its author consistently favours the view (*a*) that you cannot be genuinely happy without

[13] G. Vlastos, *Socrates: Ironist and Moral Philosopher* (Cambridge, 1991), 207–9; T. Irwin, *Plato's Ethics* (Oxford, 1995), 73–5. Annas contrasts her own opposition to developmentalism with Irwin and Vlastos (32 n. 1).

[14] *Plato's Ethics*, 346. But Irwin admits that 'The *Laws* . . . sometimes appears to assert the sufficiency thesis' (ibid.).

virtue and (*b*) that virtue is the central (if not the only) requirement of happiness.

My own distinct preference is for the second alternative. Why does Annas favour the first, and in particular, the Stoic formulation, attributed to Plato by Alcinous, that 'only the fine (*kalon*) [or morally valuable, Annas's gloss] is good'? Consider the following remark:

Plato's view indeed seems to parallel the basic Stoic insistence that the value of virtue is different in kind from the value of other kinds of thing, and that once we properly understand this difference, we will see that virtue is sufficient for happiness . . . (48)

and also:

Plato and the Stoics both display, in contrast with Aristotle, a concern with the special role and value of virtue, its difference from conventional kinds of good. Plato's grasp of the implications of this radical thought is not as firm or precise as that of the Stoics, and he has not rigorously thought through the implications, for the role of external goods, of holding that virtue is the only truly good thing, and is sufficient for happiness. This is not surprising; Plato is pioneering a eudaimonistic theory, and the Stoics have the benefit of explicit discussion such as Aristotle's. But this should not obscure the real similarities. (45)

Annas is not the first person to register the extent to which texts such as *Euthydemus* may be read as anticipating Stoic ethics.[15] Yet, that does not, in my opinion, warrant us in supposing that lack of 'rigorous' thought has inhibited Plato from going all the way, so to speak, or from making all his statements about goods verbally consistent with those texts. Would Plato's ethics be better if he turned out to be a card-carrying Stoic?[16] Should he not earn even greater respect from us if he demonstrates some flexibility and uncertainty over precisely what to say about other so-

---

[15] Cf. my discussion of *Euthyd.* 278 E 3–281 E 5 in *Stoic Studies* (Cambridge, 1996), 23–32, repr. from *CQ*, NS 38 (1988); and G. Striker, *Essays on Hellenistic Epistemology and Ethics* (Cambridge, 1996), 316–24. Neither of these papers is cited by Annas.

[16] Annas observes (103) that Antipater, who was the second head of the Stoa after Chrysippus, 'claimed that Plato agreed with them in much of ethics, particularly on the crucial issue of the sufficiency of virtue for happiness'. She does not also say that Chrysippus himself had criticized Plato for recognizing as goods such things as health: see Irwin, *Plato's Ethics*, 199–200. Thus Stoics, just like the MPs, were unable to agree with one another about where Plato stood on Annas's 'crucial issue'.

called goods, while consistently acknowledging the sovereignty of virtue?[17]

Few, I think, will agree with Annas that Aristotle lacks 'a concern with the special role and value of virtue', and she does not explain what it is about Aristotle's 'explicit discussions' that helped the Stoics to arrive at their view that virtue is the only truly good thing. Throughout this book Annas seems to assume that Stoic ethics in general, and this Stoic thesis in particular, are the apogee of Greek moral theory. Which brings me to my principal philosophical disagreement with her.

Although Annas has done so much in her earlier work to state the attractions and distinctiveness of ancient eudaimonism, she has wanted to hold on to the view, as she puts it, that:

The ancient theories are not theories of some alien mode of thought, but theories of morality, in the same sense that Kant's and Mill's theories are.[18]

I do not know enough about Kant and Mill to offer a firm opinion on this bold claim, but I suspect that it does not allow sufficiently for the fact that ancient eudaimonism together with the virtue which is its sole or principal constituent (or instrument) was first and foremost a theory about the kind of life that will be best for individual persons from their own perspective. One of the principal propositions of Annas's position (repeated in the present book) is that while the modern concept of happiness is 'rigid', ancient *eudaimonia* is construed so flexibly by the philosophers that it accommodates 'morality', though at the risk of making us so revise our conceptions of happiness that we have difficulty in seeing ancient ethical theories as theories of *happiness*. Maybe. Yet Stoics as well as Epicureans take it that the primary object of concern, even for full-fledged philosophers, is always oneself. Epictetus, for instance, constantly insists that we have responsibility solely for ourselves, and that nothing outside the self, including other persons, has any bearing on our happiness. It is our function as rational or would-be rational selves to cultivate the desires and attitudes that will enable us to perform our social roles well, but the motivation for doing so is that this 'moral' life (if we call it that) is the only route to

[17] Note Annas's exemplary words on the distinctiveness of the account of pleasure in the *Protagoras*: 'Why should Plato not have tried out a different view on a difficult matter?' (160).
[18] *The Morality of Happiness*, 452.

happiness, construed as perfecting our rationality and living free from frustration and emotional disappointment.

My point is that happiness does not seem to do enough work in Annas's model of eudaimonism to capture the self-regarding aspects of ancient ethics. To be sure, all Greek philosophical ethics strives mightily to show that altruism is not merely compatible with self-love but actually required by it. Even so, Annas's model assimilates the ancients too closely to the moderns for my satisfaction. Hence, as I interpret her, the constant focus in this book on VSH. She takes this in its Stoic formulation to amount to a theory of virtually 'pure' morality, and she would like, for that reason, to retroject it onto Plato as his would-be systematic and most important contribution to ethics.

4. The Inner City: ethics without politics in the *Republic*

I come now to the most provocative chapter of Annas's book, entitled as above. Here she mounts an onslaught against three assumptions that she thinks have seriously marred modern interpretations of Plato: first, that the *Republic* is a contribution to political theory; second, that it is the most important and central of the dialogues; and third, that it is the natural culmination of a development from the Socratic dialogues. Instead, we are recommended to read the work 'as one dialogue among many in which Plato develops an argument about the sufficiency of virtue for happiness'. If we follow this advice, 'we shall have done a great deal to restore balance and proportion to our study of Plato's thought' (95). In most of this chapter Annas advances very strong views of her own, but before discussing those, I should indicate what she finds in the ancient interpretative tradition to support her thesis.

According to Alcinous (27. 5), VSH is to be found in many of Plato's works, 'but particularly in the whole of the *Republic*'. Further, Alcinous 'deals with politics separately, after ethics, the emotions, and friendship' (93). For Albinus, the *Republic* sketches the education needed for acquiring virtue (89 n. 45). Annas asks us to take strong note of the fact that 'in the ancient world, the political aspects of the *Republic* were treated separately from the main moral argument' (93), and she invokes Aristotle's treatment of Plato in his *Politics* as an indication of this separation. As to why we should let the MPs, who are so much later than Plato, influence our own interpretations:

> Where ethical theory is concerned, this is not a good objection . . . For it is remarkable that once eudaimonistic theory gets established, it carries on quite indifferently to changes in historical and political context. (89)

Throughout this chapter, but also in Annas's book as a whole, 'ethical theory' tends to be reified, enabling its 'framework' or 'structure', once correctly identified, to serve as the only relevant hermeneutic tool for elucidating her material. I find this strategy a blunt instrument.

But the real interest of this chapter is Annas's vigorous attempt to marginalize the politics of the *Republic*. She traces the origin of the mistaken reading to the Victorians, especially Jowett, who supposedly saw the book as 'Plato's "answer" to the "problem" of democracy' (95). Her attack on the work as 'primarily political' is multi-pronged.

First, she argues that it is 'wholly anachronistic' to suppose that the *Republic* 'was written in the context of, or even as Plato's answer to, contemporary problems of Athenian politics' and to the problem of democracy in particular (73). To assume otherwise rests on various 'extremely questionable' and 'in some cases false' assumptions. These include the suppositions (*a*) that we have any evidence concerning Plato's 'disillusionment with Athenian politics', and (*b*) that Plato's use of terms such as 'democracy' and 'oligarchy' has any 'resemblance to their current political use'. In addition, Annas finds the 'political suggestions' of the *Republic* too 'underdeveloped' and, if taken literally, too 'absurd' to warrant treating the book 'as a contribution to political theory' (82). By contrast Annas invites us to take the *Statesman* and *Laws* to be works that 'we can at least relate to current understanding of political terms' (78).

Readers will be able to decide for themselves what force to attach to these points. What, then, in Annas's view, should we say about the politics of the *Republic*? Rather than seeing the ideal state as the required context for persons to become virtuous, we should see it as no more than 'a model of rational control' for 'the would-be virtuous person to internalize' (81). Hence the 'skimpiness' of Plato's account of the ideal state. Passing over any detailed treatment of the education and politics in books 3–5, Annas proposes that the argumentative structure of the *Republic* as a whole is to prove VSH.

Annas is by no means the first scholar to hold that the politics of the *Republic* is instrumental to Plato's concern with psychic harmony and the virtues of the individual. Yet even Alcinous does not say that Plato wrote this gigantic work simply or primarily to prove VSH. I find this an astonishingly narrow and implausible reduction of the *Republic* so as to fit Annas's specification of eudaimonistic theory. It is controversial, as any reader of Irwin's *Plato's Ethics* can discover by checking the relevant passages, whether Plato implicitly argues for VSH in the *Republic*; and I think it is certain that no passage states that thesis in the dialogue unambiguously. If that is the case, even Annas's marginalization of the dialogue's politics cannot turn the whole work into 'an argument about the sufficiency of virtue for happiness'.

5. What use is the Form of the good?

To this challenging question Annas devotes the chapter that perhaps best displays both the strengths and the shortcomings of her book. Building on her earlier claim that the politics of the *Republic* is simply ancillary to the dialogue's ethical theory, Annas asks what the metaphysics of the central books can contribute to the virtue of the virtuous person (as distinct from asking how it equips philosopher kings to be the best rulers). She excludes the notion that Plato, by now proposing that 'a correct grasp of morality must be based on a correct grasp of metaphysics' (96), has modified the 'content' of the ethics found in the Socratic dialogues. Rather, the 'content' of Platonic ethics remains substantially the same eudaimonistic theory (VSH), with virtue construed as a practical expertise that confers prescriptive authority on those who have it. Although the central books make it very clear that virtue makes an 'impersonal demand' on the virtuous person, 'it is nowhere indicated exactly how the account of Forms is to be taken to produce this understanding' (102). Alcinous treats Plato's metaphysics quite separately from the ethics. In addition:

Since Stoics [like Antipater] can hardly have expressed agreement with an ethical theory which they took essentially to depend on a metaphysical view they rejected, we find that we cannot make sense of the ancient reception of the *Republic* unless we also distinguish the content of its ethical theory from its metaphysical claims, and take the former to be independent of the latter. (103) [19]

Annas considers and rejects the thought that the metaphysics might serve the ethics by providing theoretical support for (pre-existing?) virtuous expertise.

The ethical theory is presented in a perfectly confident way, a way moreover which structures the whole work, whereas the metaphysical theory is hinted at in the broadest and most tentative terms . . . The skimpiness of the presentation undermines any confidence in the connections, as well as in the metaphysical theory itself. (ibid.)

So the Sun, Line, and Cave are irrelevant to Plato's ethics? Not quite. Annas proposes two ways of construing their mutual relationship. First, we may view the *Republic*'s metaphysics as giving us a sketchy macrocosm/microcosm model of cosmic order/human reason such as Plato also advances in the *Gorgias* and *Philebus*, anticipating 'the [Stoic] idea that we should see ourselves, insofar as we are rational, as parts of a rational whole' (107). This, however, stops well short of the 'crude' idea that 'we can derive eudaimonistic concepts from cosmic reason' (108). Secondly, if we follow the MPs, we may fruitfully apply to Plato their (and the Stoics') tripartite division of philosophy into logic, ethics, and physics. Annas favours this model because it is (*a*) non-hierarchical, thus allowing no primacy to any one part, but also (*b*) treats the parts as 'mutually interdependent' (111). In Annas's (highly controversial) interpretation of how the Stoics viewed ethics in relation to cosmology:

We have not been given cosmic premises which mysteriously direct us to act in one way rather than another; rather, we have been given a picture of ourselves as rational beings in a universe where rationality is dominant, and this alters our conception of ourselves by deepening it and putting it in context. (112)

Such a picture in Plato, she observes:

is certainly not explicit as a point of theory. But we have seen how it gives the right picture for what would otherwise be a very puzzling relationship in the dialogue between ethics and metaphysics.

Finally, Annas argues that her account of the relation of physics to metaphysics is confirmed by *Laws* 10.

[19] Note that Chrysippus did not find VSH in Plato (see n. 16 above).

Those who share Annas's presuppositions about 'ethical theory' and the *Republic*'s subordination of politics to ethics may also
share her worries about how the dialogue's higher educational programme can have any direct bearing on the practical expertise of
the virtuous person. Yet, my own response to her observations
(quite apart from those presuppositions) is that they are often remarkably detached from the text of the dialogue. Plato does not say
that Socrates' educational curriculum and its metaphysical content
are being advanced in order specifically to clarify or deepen our
understanding of the moral virtues, but to illuminate the training
and mentality required of philosopher rulers—persons who need
to be lovers of all wisdom as distinct from being lovers of sights
and sounds. The ideal community requires as its guardians persons
who, thanks to their knowledge, 'can establish and preserve what
rules are to obtain here concerning what is fine and just and good'
(484 D). The potential guardians are not simply or only 'virtuous'
persons; they are required to be both completely virtuous and also
to have the temperament and aptitude of someone passionately
committed to all exact knowledge (484 D ff.). Plato, in my opinion,
offers a rather full account of why this combination of virtue and
philosophy equips such persons to be the best rulers. I agree with
Annas that their training and its objects go well beyond anything
we today (or the MPs for that matter) might deem to be relevant
to moral theory, if we are engaging in that study as an autonomous
branch of philosophy, but that does not seem to me to be the context
that Plato has created for the metaphysics of the *Republic*.

I was also puzzled by Annas's treatment of *Laws* 10. According
to her interpretation of the early pages of this book, Plato does
not say that ethical beliefs need to be based upon a philosophical understanding of theology: even those who accept traditional
myths about the gods 'may have nothing wrong with their ethical
beliefs' (114). Such people only need rational theology if their confidence in the gods' existence has been shattered. The point, then,
of the ensuing arguments concerning divine providence is not 'to
justify or ground the ethical beliefs' but to 'stabilize' them in the
case of reflective persons who need arguments to rebut the atheists.

Two points about this. First, I don't find Plato expressing com-
placency about the coexistence of traditional myths with possibly
correct ethical beliefs. The passage cited by Annas, 887 C–888 A,
is heavily ironical. Second, when the philosophical theology is

A. A. Long

launched, the youth to whom it is addressed is told that he has
no hope of understanding how he is situated unless he grasps the
fact that he, as a 'minute part', exists only for the sake of the ex-
cellently organized universe (903 C), and, further, unless he understands what is being said concerning the divine underpinnings of
virtue, vice, and the destiny of souls, 'he will be quite incapable
of giving an account of life in relation to happiness and unhappi-
ness' (905 B). It would be hard to imagine a more explicit statement
about the dependence of ethics on theology or metaphysics.

Plato's anticipations of Stoicism in this passage have long been
noticed by those who think that the Stoics grounded their ethics in
cosmic teleology. Annas has contested that familiar understanding
of Stoicism, which she does not mention here.[20] In her view, then,
contrary to the position I myself uphold, recourse to Stoicism helps
us to see that 'ethics has to be developed on its own' (112), with
physics entering only at the end 'to enable you to see ethics and
human nature in the context of the nature of the cosmos'.

6. Humans and beasts, and elemental pleasures

I turn, much more briefly, to the last two chapters of this book. In
both of these Annas extends her case for a unitarian interpretation
of Platonic ethics, though one that is considerably more qualified
than she advances in her earlier chapters. While moderns generally emphasize the difference between 'Socratic intellectualism' and
Platonic tripartition of the soul, Annas suggests we would do well
to try to

see things from the perspective of Platonists who took it that what appears
to us as 'Socratic intellectualism' is simply an understated view, which is
not trying to abolish parts of the soul other than the rational, but simply
saying nothing about them, and giving us a position which is compatible
with [tripartition]. (121)

In support of this, Annas gives an extended and very interesting
treatment of Alcinous' account of 'perfect' and 'everyday' virtues.
Rather than supposing that Plato has given up the reciprocity of
the virtues to accommodate the tripartite psychology, she finds

[20] Cf. J. Cooper, 'Eudaimonism and the Appeal to Nature in the *Morality of
Happiness*', *Philosophy and Phenomenological Research*, 55 (1995), 587–99, and my
Stoic Studies, 152–5.

'two ways in which Plato regards the divided soul, especially in the *Republic*' (136). One way is the ideal of a 'harmonized and integrated person'; and this fits later Platonic and Stoic thought on the reciprocity of the virtues and the 'Socratic' emphasis on virtue as practical wisdom. The other way is that

in which the person isolates his 'true self' in his reason and then externalizes the parts other than reason as something subhuman, rejected and kept under harsh external control. (136)

Deprecating this model, Annas shows how it attracted some later Platonists, as well as Galen and Posidonius.[21]

In 'Elemental pleasures' Annas proceeds with admirable caution. Her main claim here is that, while we cannot find a 'completely overall view about pleasure and reason in Plato', especially one that incorporates the *Protagoras* (160), the MPs are of some help to us, particularly for our understanding of Plato's views on pleasure in the *Laws* and for comparing Plato with the Stoic position on pleasure. What Annas finds suggestive is the proposal (found in Alcinous and Arius Didymus) that Plato regards pleasure as both a primary and irrational 'emotion' and as something 'supervenient'. Both of these views, as she says, are Stoic formulations, and she shows why they could be thought well suited to characterize Plato's position in the *Laws*:

The desire for pleasure is the most basic motivation that we have, but rational reflection can so educate and train the person that they aim in an appropriately uncompromising way at being virtuous. The person who succeeds in becoming virtuous, and who does not directly aim at pleasure, in fact gets pleasure [superveniently] as a result of his virtue. (146)

Applying this to the *Republic* too, she argues that it enables us to see why VSH (which she takes to be the principal ethical position of both dialogues) is entirely compatible with Plato's holding that happiness includes pleasure.[22] The 'supervenience' concept

[21] My only criticism of this invigorating chapter is Annas's undeveloped claim that Chrysippus was attracted to Plato's account of the tripartite soul. She supports this unusual interpretation by reference to an article by C. Gill that I have not yet had the opportunity to study: 'Did Galen Understand Platonic and Stoic Thinking on Emotions?', in J. Sihvola and T. Engberg-Pedersen (eds.), *Hellenistic Theories of the Emotions* (Dordrecht, 1998), 113–48.

[22] Is VSH really consistent with the fact that Platonic happiness necessarily includes pleasure? VSH says that you are to aim at virtue as the sole requirement of your happiness. But if you also know that virtue must be accompanied by pleasure, is

captures the notion that 'pleasure must accompany the virtuous life but is not the goal of the virtuous person' (146).

I like this idea as a broadly unifying conceptualization of Plato's thinking about the status of pleasure in the good life, but although Annas is careful not to assimilate Plato completely to the Stoics, she goes too far in this direction when she writes:

In both Plato and the Stoics pleasure is natural to us, as the kind of beings we are; this is one major aspect of the fact that desire for pleasure and to avoid pain is characteristically human. (148)

If that were the Stoic view, it would conflict with their opposition to the Epicureans as registered in their concept of primary *oikeiōsis*. On the other hand, Annas could have mentioned, in support of her line, the fact that the Stoics treated *chara*, or rational 'joy', as supervenient on virtue.[23]

7. Concluding comments

Platonic Ethics Old and New is a striking book, vigorous, original, opinionated, suggestive, and provocative. Will it and should it fulfil its author's hopes of showing that 'where Platonic ethics is concerned, we can learn from the old, mainly by seeing how it can contribute more than we might think to the new' and that the MPs are 'best fitted to wake us from our developmental slumbers' (165)? There is no question that our subject needs to be far more attentive than it frequently is to its own historiography, including the interpretations that ancient philosophers themselves gave to their own predecessors. Given our profession, who is better fitted than ourselves to mount an attack on the tyranny of the present and the authority of the merely contemporary?

In order to preserve our material we need to keep it interesting and to show, where we can, that ancient philosophy is perennially excellent *as philosophy*. One of the best ways to do this is to acknowledge the openness of our best material to a range of alternative

it reasonable to suppose that the virtue-seeker can or should completely exclude supervenient pleasure from his motivations? See Irwin, *Plato's Ethics*, 346, on reasons for attributing a 'comprehensive conception of happiness' to Plato.

[23] D.L. 7. 94 (*SVF* iii. 76), and said to be 'not necessary for happiness' (*SVF* iii. 113).

interpretations. Annas's book is clearly designed to contribute to this end, and up to a point it succeeds very well.

My main reservations about her work are these. First, I think that, for all her focus on the old, she is too much guided by the new. What I mean by this is her hypostatization of 'ethical theory' and what strikes me as an anachronistic demand as to what that theory should include or exclude. By construing ethical theory as narrowly as she does in this book, she seems to me often to impose a straitjacket on Plato. Second, and relatedly, I don't think we can achieve an adequate grasp of ancient ethics even as *theory* if we detach it, as this book does, from all considerations of social and political actualities. Third, I am not persuaded by her attempts to defend her general use of the MPs against the obvious objections of anachronism. The MPs had their own agenda and context, just as we have, and before we can use them scientifically we need to be told more about those things than Annas offers us.

Annas could have avoided these objections if she had limited her book to giving an analysis of Middle Platonic accounts of Plato's ethics. But that would almost certainly have been a dull read. Instead, she has put them on the map in a manner that not only brings them to life but also makes them contribute to her own distinctive interpretation of Plato. What people make of that interpretation promises to be matter for discussion over a long time, and it confirms her reputation as one of the most prolific, learned, and versatile scholars of our generation.[24]

University of California, Berkeley

[24] Annas leaves it entirely to her readers to discover that her approach to Plato's ethics and to the *Republic* in particular has changed in the years separating her new book from her composition of *The Morality of Happiness* and *An Introduction to Plato's* Republic. This reticence, though commendable in its modesty, is rather misleading. Even if we can make nothing of Plato's intellectual biography, I wish Annas had said something about how she would like us to regard her own.

Notes for Contributors to Oxford Studies in Ancient Philosophy

1. Articles may be submitted *at any time of year*. They should be typed, on one side of the paper only, and with double line-spacing throughout. Footnotes may at the stage of initial submission be printed at the foot of the page (however, see 4 below). Pages should be A4 or standard American quarto ($8\frac{1}{2} \times 11''$), and ample margins should be left.

2. Two identical copies should be submitted to the editor. Authors are asked to supply an accurate word-count (*a*) for the main text, and (*b*) for the notes.

3. Typescripts of rejected articles will be returned only if self-addressed envelopes with correct postage are provided (in the case of overseas contributors, international reply coupons sufficient for airmail).

4. In the final version submitted for publication, footnotes should be numbered consecutively and located together on separate sheets at the end of the typescript, in double line-spacing. They will be printed at the foot of each page. Wherever possible, references should be built into the text.

5. **Greek should *not* normally be transliterated,** except in the case of words and phrases established in English, e.g. 'psyche', 'polis'. Greek copy must be supplied in a completely legible and accurate form, capable of being reproduced correctly by a typesetter with no knowledge of the language. Greek should be typed and not handwritten.

6. In references to books, the first time the book is referred to give at least the first name or initial of the author, and the place and date of publication; where you are abbreviating the title in subsequent citations, give the abbreviation in square brackets, thus:

> Thomas Brickhouse and Nicholas Smith, *Socrates on Trial* [*Trial*] (Princeton, 1981), 91–4.

The volume-number of a periodical should also be given.

7. Where the same book or article is referred to on subsequent occasions, usually the most convenient style will be an abbreviated reference, thus:

> Brickhouse and Smith, *Trial*, 28–9.

Do *not* use the author-and-date style of reference:

> Brickhouse and Smith 1981: 28–9.

[*The Notes continue overleaf*]

8. Titles of books are always printed in italics and should therefore be underlined in the typescript.

9. Titles of journals will be printed in italics and should be underlined in the typescript. The name of the journal should be given for the first citation, with the abbreviation to be used in subsequent citations given in square brackets:

   Proceedings of the Aristotelian Society [*PAS*], 82 (1982), 97.

   Use the abbreviation suggested in the journal itself for subsequent citations.

10. Full page-extents of articles should be given. Where the reference is to a particular page or pages, specify thus:

    Gregory Vlastos, 'The Unity of the Virtues in the *Protagoras*', in *Platonic Studies*, 2nd edn. (Princeton, 1981), 221–65 at 228.

11. If there are any unusual conventions contributors are encouraged to include a covering note for the copy-editor and/or printer. Please say whether you are using single and double quotation marks for different purposes (otherwise the Press will employ its standard single quotation marks in all contexts). If you specifically require transliteration rather than true Greek, this must be made clear to prevent routine conversion to Greek in the course of editing.

12. Contributors whose contributions are accepted will be asked to send a copy of the final version of their paper on a 3.5″ high density (HD) disk (Macintosh or IBM), indicating on the disk or in an accompanying note the program in which the text is written. **NB. The version on disk must be the *exact* version which produced the hard copy sent in for printing.**